Living in the Lap of the Goddess

· Cynthia Eller ·

Living in the Lap of the Goddess

The Feminist Spirituality Movement in America

CROSSROAD · NEW YORK

1993
The Crossroad Publishing Company
370 Lexington Avenue, New York, NY 10017

Printed in the United States of America

Library of Congress Cataloging-in-Publication Data

Eller, Cynthia.
    Living in the lap of the Goddess : the feminist spirituality
movement in America / Cynthia Eller.
        p. cm.
    Includes bibliographical references and index.
    ISBN 0-8245-1245-6
    1. Women—United States—Religious life. 2. Feminism—Religious
aspects. 3. Goddess religion—United States. 4. Feminist theology—
United States. I. Title.
BL625.7.E45 1993
299′.93—dc20   93-3928
                                                                    CIP

for my sister Sylvia

Contents

Preface

The feminist spirituality movement is one of the most fascinating religious phenomena of the past twenty years. With roots and branches in many places (including neopaganism, political feminism, Jewish and Christian feminism, the New Age, and Native American spiritualities), feminist spirituality has nevertheless emerged as a sociological entity in its own right, too large and too distinct to be adequately understood as a subphenomenon of any other religious or social movement. Feminist spirituality is unique in its determination to remain true to the concerns of women, both politically and spiritually. And it is religiously innovative, always pushing beyond tradition, and often leaving it behind altogether in its search for spiritual resources that will prove powerful and transforming for women.

This introductory road map to the feminist spirituality movement is based on my observation of the movement over the past ten years. I have attended rituals, classes, workshops, and retreats, and have read widely in the literature of the feminist spirituality movement. I have solicited information from spiritual feminist organizations and have conducted extended interviews with spiritual feminists. My goal has been to get inside the lives of the women who make up the feminist spirituality movement, to identify with their concerns, hopes, and experiences, to listen closely to their voices, and to see how they construct their worlds.

The principal basis of this survey is the primary literature of the movement: books, magazines, newsletters, calendars, promotional flyers, song sheets, and so forth. The feminist spirituality movement has produced a tremendous amount of writing by its adherents. Some of this writing is confessional, some theological, some devotional. There are stories, poems, drawings, and songs set side by side with social criticism, analysis of archaeological artifacts, and lively exchanges of letters on topics controversial in the movement. This body of literature provides an intriguing window onto the feminist spirituality movement, and often, into the lives of individual spiritual feminists themselves.

The interview component of the research is purposely small-scale, a quest for depth rather than breadth (since breadth is amply available in literary form and through participant observation). This set of interviews was intended first to be a cross-check against the literary data (to ensure that there are not substantial differences between women who write about their spirituality and those who do not), and second, to allow for firsthand reporting on the beliefs, practices, and motivations of individual participants in the movement. In addition to the formal interviews, I spoke with numerous women at spiritual feminist retreats and workshops, and have occasionally included material from these informal interviews here. Data from interviews is interspersed with that from other sources throughout the book. No effort is made to tell the full stories of the women who were interviewed; rather, their comments on various topics are included when these topics are addressed in the course of the study. (Women interviewed specifically for this study can be distinguished from others through reference to the notes, where the former are cited by last name only).

Interviewees were not selected to form a statistically accurate sampling of spiritual feminists, but rather to ensure variety, particularly in terms of these women's level of participation in the movement. In addition to speaking personally with women for whom feminist spirituality has been an integral part of their lives for many years, I spoke with women who were more peripheral or new to the movement to see how a more nominal identification as a spiritual feminist functioned in their lives. Contacts with interviewees were made mostly by referral from other spiritual feminists whom I met through my research and my participation at spiritual feminist gatherings. My research assistant, Faulkner Fox, interviewed seven of the women in the sample, and interviewed another five together with me. I conducted the remaining interviews myself. All but two interviews took place in the Northeast, owing to financial constraints, but many of the women interviewed have moved around the country extensively, so geographical diversity is thereby included in the sample. The sample is overwhelmingly Caucasian and of the baby boom generation (as is the movement generally). More detailed information about the women interviewed for this study can be found in Appendix A. A copy of the interview guide used in the study can be found in Appendix B. The guide functioned as a skeleton for most interviews, but it was not followed rigorously and no strict quantitative comparisons of women's answers to these questions have been made, since the sample itself is not statistically representative.

Women were given the option to be quoted anonymously or by name. Eleven of the women interviewed requested some degree of anonymity. Many others, though they signed consent forms permitting me to quote them by name, seemed uncertain about doing so and concerned about the possible ramifications of being in a study like this. To spare them any unforseen (and unforseeable) unpleasantness as a consequence of their participation in this study, I have used pseudonyms uniformly. The pseudonyms chosen correspond to the women's ethnicities, insofar as possible, so that some of the flavor of what ethnic diversity as exists within feminist spirituality is maintained. Also, women who have adopted goddess names or given up their patrilineal family names have been given pseudonyms that correspond to these choices. I would like to extend my heartfelt thanks to the women interviewed for this study who so graciously gave of their time and of themselves. I feel honored to have been granted access into their often admirable and always interesting lives, and to spend a season in their magical worlds.

The title *Living in the Lap of the Goddess* was inspired by a comment made to me during an interview with Grete Bjorkman, a spiritual feminist who spoke movingly of her efforts to make her present life and society's future a return to the spirit of prehistory, when, she believes, humanity was living peacefully and securely in the goddess's lap. This image seemed to stand for the dreams of many spiritual feminists, and to represent their deep desire to live in a society that respects and worships "the feminine" and is in easy communion with it.

Throughout the text, I have chosen to capitalize "goddess" and "god" only when it is clear that whoever is speaking is referring to the goddess (singular) of feminist spirituality from within that belief system, or to the god of Judaism or Christianity. It was my feeling that since some spiritual feminists would resist the use of "Goddess" (either because it is singular or because it implies an uncomfortable parallelism to the god of Judaism and Christianity), it would be simplest to use lowercase except in those situations where individual women have indicated an actual belief in or relationship to the deity. Given that many of my sources were verbal rather than written, this has involved a certain amount of guesswork; I apologize in advance for any misreadings of women's preferences in this regard. Similarly, I have not capitalized "witch" or "witchcraft" except when my sources have done so.

A more analytic treatment of several aspects of the feminist spirituality movement raised in this descriptive study will be the focus of a subsequent work, titled *Gender Politics and Feminist Religion*, to be published in 1995. Topics will include the movement's construction and use of gender, its attitude toward men, the legitimacy of its reconstruction of Western history, and its sociological and intellectual relationship to Jewish and Christian feminism, the New Age movement, and the feminist movement as a whole.

Thanks are due to the Henry R. Luce Foundation, which supported the early stages of this study when I was a postdoctoral fellow at Yale Divinity School, and to Professors Margaret Farley and Serene Jones, who encouraged me to undertake this project. I am most grateful to my research assistant, Faulkner Fox, who in addition to conducting a portion of the interviews, was instrumental in developing an interview guide and setting the parameters of the study. I would like to thank her, as well as two other students at Yale, Micol Seigel and Tara Susman, for their personal interest in and investigations of feminist spiri tuality. Their enthusiasm for the subject frequently rekindled my own Teresa Shaw, Sylvia Wolfe, and Robert Spero never tired of telling me that this work was worthwhile, and believe me, I asked them often They were generous with their advice, gave feedback on earlier ver sions of the manuscript, and shared many long distance laughs with me when I needed them most. My gratitude to them is immense. Donald Miller and Robert Ellwood read the entire manuscript, and provided an important perspective with grace and enthusiasm. My editors at Crossroad, Frank Oveis, Michael Leach, and most especially Justus George Lawler, have been a tremendous source of assistance as this project grew from brief proposal to completed work, and I thank them for their continued support. Thanks to Judith Brick Freedman for curing my writer's cramp and to everyone at the Town Hall Deli for keeping the coffee pot full and starting my writing days off with a smile. And finally, my special thanks always to Jonathan Greene, patron of my work and sustainer of my soul.

· 1 ·

Feminists on Spiritual Quest

On a small lake in Maine humming with blackflies and mosquitoes sits a girls' club camp, not yet open for the season. Each cabin is fronted with a rustic sign that has a name artfully burned into it: Bluebird, Gopher, Daisy, and the like. This weekend, each sign is covered over with newsprint, and new inscriptions can be found in magic marker calligraphy: Cerridwen, Kwan Yin, Artemis, Spider-Grandmother. Inside, the wooden walls and plastic windows are covered with epithets: "Janie Grant '86," "Marlee wuz here," "Team #8—softball '77—Champions! Yeah!" But this weekend, the walls are also covered with brightly colored robes and necklaces hung from nails, and several milk crates sit on the floor, topped with velvet cloths, candles, and goddess figurines. Across a grassy slope sits a lodge that has been renamed the "womb room." Xeroxed instructions in the orientation packet explain that this is a "peaceful, sacred space" where participants can spend time alone or with volunteers who are "caring listeners."

But on Saturday night, the cabins have emptied out and the womb room is vacant; the hundred women who have come to the Feminist Spiritual Community's Tenth Anniversary Celebration are all in the dining hall, where tables and chairs have been pushed out of the way to make space for the Crone Ceremony. Three women are being honored tonight for having passed their fifty-sixth birthday, the official age at which they become crones, or wise old women. The ceremony begins with all the women who have already reached cronehood seated on folding chairs in a small circle in the middle of the room. They are surrounded by two large circles of women under 56 years of age who are sitting on the floor. As the younger women listen, the crones talk among themselves about what it's like to be an older woman, how their lives have changed, how other people react to them now.

When their discussion winds down, all the women present break into smaller groups to begin a ritual called The Decades of a Woman's Life. Each group stands in a circle, and when the first decade is called—zero to ten years—all those who have lived for some part of that decade take a step forward, and one by one, each woman gives a single word or phrase to sum up those years of her life. "Confused," "happy," "learning," "abused," "blossoming": a chain of words forms and finishes, and all those who have lived the second decade of their lives step forward and repeat the process. The circle grows first tighter, as all of the women present step together into their twenties, and then gradually smaller and looser, as fewer and fewer women advance into their forties, fifties, and sixties, until finally there is a circle of one, as the lone seventy-year-old sums up her experience of her seventh decade. Adjectives abound, covering a whole spectrum of living. In the decade of the twenties, one woman nearing croning age says, "miserable marriage," to the sound of sympathetic murmuring from the circle. Then the woman next to her, barely into her thirties, says, "*Two* miserable marriages," and the circle breaks into laughter. Later, in the decade of the fifties, one woman triumphantly shouts, "Lesbianism!" casting a fond look across the circle at her partner, and when the next woman giggles and says, "Bisexual," the circle once again erupts in hilarity.

When the decades are done, the group assembles around the crones again, and this time the three women about to be croned are included in the inner circle. Each of the crones describes what she likes about being older: being more at home with herself, not caring what people think of her, having the freedom to love whom she will. Then the official croning begins: Each woman in turn is presented with a "stole," a chain of braided ribbons that the crones in camp have been wearing around their necks as a token of honor off and on throughout the weekend. They are also given a "crone stone" to symbolize the weight and solidity of the wisdom they have gained over the years. The presentations are made by personal friends, who preface the gifts of stole and stone with stories of how they met and what this woman's friendship has meant to them. Several daughters of the new crones are present, and as their mothers receive the symbols of cronehood and acknowledge them, they sit beaming and proud. When all three presentations are made, the larger circle begins to call out to the crones, saying, "I thank you for your wisdom," "I thank you for your strength," "I thank you for your beauty."

The ceremony is closed with singing, as a storm that has been brewing outside finally lets loose with wind and lightning, thunder and rain. But no one is ready to break the mood, and soon a full-fledged party is spilling over onto the patio. Sparklers and bubble soap are passed around, and women bring drums and bells out to play while other women dance. As the storm gradually exhausts itself and the clouds part to reveal a full shining moon, a limbo contest has begun on a patio slick with bubble soap, a new crone and her daughter are singing and dancing the miserlou, and showers of sparks spread out into the night. Inside, volunteer furniture movers are hard at work, getting the dining hall ready for breakfast the next morning. Later, heading back to their cabins are three proud crones, wrapped in their new stoles, and a hundred younger women, glad in the thought that they too will one day reach this age of women's wisdom and power.[1]

This ritual and these women are part of feminist spirituality, a new religious movement begun in the early 1970s that is today growing and flourishing across the United States and Canada, in parts of continental Europe and England, and as far away as Australia. It is a spontaneous, grass-roots movement with no overarching organization, no system of leadership, and no regularized form of membership. It draws on many religious traditions, but answers to none. It has neither institutionalized nor stagnated, and is in constant flux. The primary characteristic of feminist spirituality is variety. For virtually every belief that one woman claims as authentic feminist spirituality, there is another woman who will assert the opposite belief but make the same claim.

Still, it is possible to sketch the movement in terms of the few things that are matters of general (if not total) agreement, and just as importantly, in terms of key areas of tension. The most important agreement is that virtually all practitioners of feminist spirituality view the religion as being uniquely empowering for women: empowerment (sometimes more conservatively termed healing) is both the goal and the reward of feminist spiritual practice. Whatever works to make a woman stronger is valid feminist spirituality. There is also a consistent interest in ritual as a tool of empowerment and a means of communication with the sacred, and in some form of magic, divination, or the cultivation of psychic skills. Nature is almost universally revered, and often personified as a (or the) goddess or as Mother Earth. Women, like nature, are revered, usually for their female biological functions (particularly menstruation and childbirth). However varied the specifics, feminist spirituality always relies on an interest in the feminine, or at least gender, to sustain its system of symbols, beliefs, and practices. Finally, much of the feminist spiritual imagination is given over to speculation about how gender relations have been structured over the history of the human race. This "sacred history" is an ongoing reconstruction of Western history according to which prehistoric societies worshiped

goddesses, and were possibly matriarchal as well, until they were replaced by patriarchal societies, which are today the status quo worldwide. Most spiritual feminists see themselves working to move this
history into its next stage, in which patriarchal societies will be replaced by cultural forms more beneficial to the human race, and especially to women.

Given these areas of agreement, it is not surprising that tensions in
the feminist spirituality movement are mostly collected around varying
perceptions of the nature and importance of gender. The ongoing controversy over the inclusion or exclusion of men in the movement is the
prime example of this tension. In addition, spiritual feminists disagree
over whether women are similar to men, different from men, equal to
men, or superior to men, and in what ways and to what degree. They
disagree over whether differences between men and women are rooted
in biology, cultural experience, or varying combinations of the two.
Nor do they speak with one voice when it comes to describing ancient
matriarchies, the origin and characteristics of the patriarchy, or their
vision of nonpatriarchal societies in the future.[2] Apart from gender
questions, there is dispute over how spiritual feminists should relate
(or not) to traditional religions and how freely women should borrow
from religions not their own. There is also thealogical* debate, though
rarely very heated, over the nature of the goddess: whether she exists,
how she acts or interacts with humans, whether she is metaphor or
personality, one goddess or many goddesses, or all of the above. Questions of morality and the nature of evil also arise, especially in relation
to the practice of magic. And as a movement that simultaneously has
no leaders and too many leaders, there is conflict over how leadership
is to be conceptualized and exercised.

What is perhaps most significant about these agreements and disagreements is that dissension is so easily tolerated, and the urge to
create dogma so readily suppressed. Even the grossest of internal con-
tradictions seem to create very little anxiety among spiritual feminists.
There are a few notable exceptions, but for the most part, spiritual
feminists have agreed to disagree, to overlook differences, to treat com-
peting views as compatible views. There are no factions vying for the
exclusive right to define what feminist spirituality is or can be, and a
"live and let live" policy reigns supreme.

However, there are opinions. And opinions. And more opinions.
While spiritual feminists are willing to let just about anyone station herself under the umbrella of the feminist spirituality movement if that's

---

*Spiritual feminists commonly use the spelling "thealogy" to indicate that they are
reflecting on the divine as feminine, substituting the Greek root *thea*, the feminine form
of the word "god," for the traditional *theos*, which is masculine.

where she wants to be, there is still a great deal of contention about what a really good feminist spirituality looks like, and on the other hand, what are troublesome directions for spiritual feminists to take. Every participant is the acknowledged authority on what works for her, what she knows, what she experiences, what feminist spirituality is *for her.* But this is where authority stops and the free-for-all begins.

For this reason, it is difficult to characterize just what is and is not feminist spirituality. As far as possible, I will function within the participants' worldview, which suggests that there are no sharp boundaries where feminist spirituality ends and something different begins, no place where an individual woman can go so far as to fall off the map of feminist spirituality if it is her intention to be included. Rather than attempting to fix the movement's outer limits, then, I will set myself the task of locating its center. I will be working to trace out a mainstream, to search out its headwaters and its primary direction of flow, but also to find tributaries and eddies, variations upon feminist spirituality's basic themes that may in the future become new centers.

Spiritual feminists, then, are women who say they are spiritual feminists. But this is a definition that begs for greater refinement. What of the woman who worships a goddess, tells everyone who will listen about the matriarchies of prehistoric times, and spends her summer vacations at feminist spirituality retreats, but for whatever reason shies away from the term "spiritual feminist"? (As well she might, for there are an abundance of terms in use to describe this movement or portions of it, and many women feel more comfortable using these other terms with their different shades of meaning.) Is she not to be counted as part of the feminist spirituality movement? There is no one convenient criterion for judging who is part of the movement and who is not. Many participants worship goddesses, but not all do; most find the sacred in nature, but some don't; there are those who meet in spirituality groups with others and those who always practice alone. In short, there are whole constellations of beliefs and practices in feminist spirituality, with no one factor emerging as the universally applicable test of who is a genuine spiritual feminist.

To add to the confusion, much of the social world of feminist spirituality is shared with other spiritually minded individuals. Spiritual feminists can be found alone in their apartments practicing yoga postures, writing in their dream journals, or consulting the *I Ching* for advice on how to run their businesses. They can be found in lecture halls looking at slides of prehistoric religious artifacts or in classrooms taking notes on pagan holidays and the sacred tools of witches. They can be found patronizing masseuses, herbal healers, and psychics in the marketplace of a New Age fair, or standing in circles under the stars at a neopagan festival, chanting the many names of the goddess.

They can be found at Native American sweat lodges, in Buddhist meditation halls, in 12-step groups, and at academic conferences.

Feminist spirituality intermingles with all these religions and spiritualities. Furthermore, it overlaps extensively with two specific alternative religions, both larger than itself, making it even more difficult to isolate feminist spirituality. Feminist spirituality's first burst of religious zeal took the form of neopagnism or witchcraft, a religious movement that predated feminist spirituality and that was based on the recovery of pre-Christian European religions. Many early spiritual feminists thought of themselves as neopagans or witches who were advancing a particular *type* of neopaganism—feminist witchcraft or Dianic witchcraft—but not a new religion of their own. It is still common to hear spiritual feminists define themselves as "witches," "pagans," or "feminist witches," and many spiritual feminists participate in neopagan groups or gatherings. Feminist spirituality also overlaps with the New Age movement, and the two borrow so heavily from one another that some commentators say they are coextensive.[3] Yet feminist spirituality is a distinguishable phenomenon, one not limited to or contained by either neopaganism or the New Age movement. All feminist spirituality, whether it claims to be neopagan or not, has features that set it apart from mainstream neopaganism. The same can be said of the New Age movement. In places where feminist spirituality is practiced in its purest form, mainstream neopagans and New Agers with their differing agendas would not necessarily feel comfortable, nor in some cases would they even be welcome.

I believe it is most helpful to think of feminist spirituality as a cluster of characteristics, and that any woman revealing some proportion of those characteristics counts as a spiritual feminist. It is therefore possible to have two women who share little in common, but who have enough of the attributes of feminist spirituality that both are rightly considered spiritual feminists.[4] In deference to the movement's self-understanding, I will count as a spiritual feminist any woman who sincerely believes herself to be one, whatever she may believe or practice. But I will also count women who shun the identification, but adhere to at least three of the five major characteristics of feminist spirituality discussed above: valuing women's empowerment, practicing ritual and/or magic, revering nature, using the feminine or gender as a primary mode of religious analysis, and espousing the revisionist version of Western history favored by the movement.[5]

Locating Feminist Spirituality

This description of who spiritual feminists are derives from the characteristics of a particular population of women, those who occupy what

I would consider to be the heart of the feminist spirituality movement. These are women who inhabit that social world which defines itself first as feminist spirituality, and only secondarily, if at all, as neopagan, New Age, or something else. It is this world that is the hub from which individual women radiate out to immerse themselves in the broader alternative religious culture as spiritual feminists.

This core of feminist spirituality can be situated sociologically in a number of ways. First of all, the movement is separatist, in the sense that it is focused on women. Whether men can or should be included in feminist spirituality is a live debate, and in fact, there are men who participate in feminist spirituality rituals and who identify themselves as being a part of this movement. But it is women who hold the center, and many groups and retreats exclude men (and even baby boys) altogether. Even when men are included, they are never more than honorary members, for they never have the same right accorded to them that is automatically granted to every woman in the movement: that is, to define what the movement is *for her* (or in this case, for him). Women are given at least a token respect, however wild and ridiculous their ideas may seem to the majority of their sisters. Men who cannot defer to the authority of women to define what feminist spirituality is and will be are simply excluded.[6]

Second, the movement is centered outside traditional religions, and can be seen most accurately to be a part of an alternative religious milieu. There are Christian and Jewish feminists who consider themselves a part of feminist spirituality, and there is no effort made to exclude such women. But though feminist spirituality reaches into synagogues and churches, and parallel movements are happening there, the center is firmly outside, and indeed, sets itself in opposition to traditional religions. This is revealed in the terminology used: when feminist spirituality happens inside traditional religious institutions it is almost always qualified as "Christian feminist spirituality" or "Jewish feminist spirituality." Unqualified feminist spirituality typically occurs far from the terrain of traditional religions, and only sporadically includes Jewish or Christian symbols, more often rejecting them outright.

Third, the movement is feminist, broadly defined. The women who occupy the center of feminist spirituality see themselves operating out of some sort of feminist consciousness, believing that either women's condition or the general state of gender roles in society as we now find them are unsatisfactory and need to be changed. The overlap between political feminism and feminist spirituality occurs throughout the movement, in the center as well as on the margins.

Finally, feminist spirituality is centered on the English-speaking world, and particularly the United States and Canada, although it has found its way to other spots on the globe. Ursula King, a British feminist and the author of *Women and Spirituality*, notes the presence of feminist spirituality in Britain, but adds, "In the USA the interest [in feminist spirituality] is much greater still and began much earlier."[7] For this reason, this study is restricted to feminist spirituality in the United States (though there will be occasional mention of similar movements elsewhere).

The most intensive centering of self-described feminist spirituality is the utopian commune, where groups of women willing to dedicate themselves full-time to their spiritual feminist ideals gather together to live and work. Successful communes mark the innermost core of feminist spirituality, but at this point they are more experimental than established, and are neither numerous nor long-lived enough to provide a solid base for the movement.[8] Besides, as in most religions, the monastery is the ideal for the few rather than the many, and most women who are spiritual feminists seek to live out their spirituality in a wider world. The ideal for these women is more likely to be the "coven" or other small group where spiritual feminists come together on a regular basis to do ritual and to celebrate, to heal and support one another, and to share their spiritual learnings. Such groups do exist, and some of them provide vibrant communities that sustain and nourish their members. Some women I spoke with reported being active in groups that—with or without them—had been meeting for as long as six or eight years. More commonly, I heard of groups that had been meeting for less than a year, or of groups that met successfully for a year or two and eventually disbanded as their members moved on to other locations or other pursuits. Other women told me they belonged to loose communities of women, and sometimes men as well, who met on a sporadic basis for special holiday rituals.[9] However evanescent, these groups have often been very important for the women who have participated in them. Women who have not yet had a satisfying experience with a group or who are temporarily without one talk of their hope that they may some day find a congenial community with which they can share their spirituality.

Part of the problem in effective organization has to do with the rugged individualism of feminist spirituality. Because each woman is breaking her own spiritual path, being able to travel together with other spiritual feminists is fortuitous, but often only temporary. Given this failure to reliably organize at a local level, spiritual feminists have made a number of efforts to provide a larger structure under which small groups can function. One very loose structure is offered by the Re-formed Congregation of the Goddess (RCG). The RCG exists primarily to give tax-exempt status to itself and other spiritual feminist enterprises, and to allow spiritual feminists to act as clergy for legal purposes (e.g., weddings). But the RCG also encourages networking and communication between spiritual feminist groups, and through its publications, helps women interested in forming groups find one another. A somewhat more rigid structure for feminist spirituality is offered by Women in Constant Creative Action (WICCA), an organization based in Eugene, Oregon. Their form of operation is to sponsor small groups called "wings" (and individuals, called "feathers"), and to provide these groups with tapes and other curricular materials on a regular basis.[10]

The feminist spirituality movement is also found in the context of classes, training programs, and workshops, where some women act as teachers and others as students, usually with money changing hands. This is one of the most common settings in which spiritual feminists congregate, and has the advantage of providing the sort of environment where women can feel that they are not compromising their own spiritual paths, but are taking the opportunity to learn from others more experienced or knowledgeable in certain areas than they. There are many classes available through adult schools or alternative learning centers, and schools or libraries will sometimes sponsor guest lectures on spiritual feminist topics. For example, in the spring of 1991, the Open Center in New York (which describes itself as "a nonprofit holistic learning center") offered lectures and workshops titled "Women's Stories: Women's Healing," "The Goddess Within: Discovering the Qualities of the Inner Feminine," "The Re-Emergence of the Goddess: A Major Paradigm Shift," "The Sacred Prostitute: Eternal Aspects of the Feminine," "Woman, Rhythm, and the Frame Drum: Returning to the Goddess," "The Woman in the Tower: Freeing Our Imprisoned Feminine Nature," and "The Once and Future Goddess: Her Re-Emergence in Our Cultural Mythology." Most were led by women who are well-known authors and speakers in the feminist spirituality movement.[11]

There are also summer camps and weekend retreats for spiritual feminists, such as "Her Voice, Our Voices," the Women's Alliance Summer Camp, offered in Nevada City, California; the annual Womyn and Witchcraft Conference held in Wisconsin under the auspices of the RCG; and Womongathering, a large festival held annually in eastern Pennsylvania. These camps and retreats usually offer a smorgasbord of workshops to the women who attend. Other retreat centers have individual workshops on more focused topics. For instance, the Wise Woman Center in Woodstock, New York, offers workshops on everything from "Faerie Songs and Goddess Chants" to "Sacred Sex" and "Talking With Plants."[12]

One relatively new phenomenon is the training school, which consists of one or more intensive retreats designed to provide the basis for an ongoing spiritual practice and to give spiritual training to women who can then spread their knowledge and experience to others in their home communities. One example of this is "Keepers of the Flame: A Sacred Mystery School for Women," sponsored by Full Circle Workshops in Amherst, Massachusetts, whose two main instructors lead six weekend retreats over the course of ten months for a small group of women. Another example is "The Way of the Mother: Women's School of Mystical Awareness," run by an organization in the Baltimore area called the Sisterhood of the Lavender Dawn, which meets for six weekends over the course of six months.[13]

All of the above settings for the feminist spirituality movement are characterized by face-to-face interactions, but much—perhaps the majority—of feminist spirituality is transmitted via the print media. The most structured versions of print interactions are mail-order courses offered by enterprising spiritual feminists. The RCG, for example, offers the Thealogical Institute Cella Training Program, described as "a course of study for ♀ witches." Students are asked to sign two affirmations (an "affirmation of ♀ spirituality" and a "consecration affirmation"), and are then asked to choose a focus (Creatrix, Earthwalker, Scholar/Teacher, Ritualist, Healer, or Organizer) and begin independent study that is to last for three "cycles" (years). Other examples of mail-order courses are Jeannine Parvati Baker's Hygieia College of holistic health care and midwifery, Marah's Wicca Way Course on divination and the goddess, and Shekhinah Mountainwater's "The Mysteries of the Goddess: A Study in the Lore and Craft of Woman."[14]

Feminist spirituality is also available via mail through Nan Hawthorne's Circles of Exchange, which is a network of active spiritual feminists rather than a structured course of study. Women who participate in Circles of Exchange are put into five-women groups who circulate a round-robin letter on a spiritual topic of special interest to them, such as astrology, dreams, crystals, farming and gardening, healing, herbs, mythology, ritual, tarot, herstory, journal writing, Native American tradition, yoga, and so on. A newsletter, *Mooncircles*, serves to disseminate general information and to locate lost packets of letters.[15]

As much as anything else though, feminist spirituality is spread by the vast quantity of books, newsletters, magazines, and journals that it publishes. Serial publications, ranging from slick monthly magazines to the humblest of xeroxed newsletters, help spiritual feminists enlarge their spiritual lives and keep abreast of happenings in the movement. In addition, a great many books on various aspects of feminist spirituality have been published, and judging from personal testimonies, they have been responsible for introducing many women to the movement.[16] One good place to find spiritual feminists, then, is in women's bookstores or occult supply stores, standing in front of the spirituality rack.

This world of communes, small groups, makeshift organizations, workshops, retreats, training schools, and mail-order courses is the social turf that feminist spirituality claims as its own. This is not where feminist spirituality stops, for most spiritual feminists move off from this turf to seek spiritual sustenance in a broader world of alternative religions. But it is here that feminist spirituality is found in its purest form, and where women's interest in empowerment, ritual, magic, nature, the feminine, and sacred history emerges in full force.

· 2 ·

The Women of the Feminist Spirituality Movement

Suzanne Courveline is a witch. She lives with her brother and her son in a fifth-floor apartment in Manhattan, where the glitz of the Upper East Side gives way to the spreading poverty of the south end of East Harlem. Encased in a world of concrete, Suzanne is a worshiper of nature and a friend to animals. Her small apartment is crowded with cats and dogs, many of whom she is nursing through various stages of recovery from disease or injury. Against every wall leans a painting or two or three, the fruit of Suzanne's morning labors when she has the apartment to herself. The canvases are covered with people: large, moody figures of men and women, in dramatic blocks of color, laid geometrically against abstract backgrounds. Though a painter by morning, in the afternoon Suzanne picks up her son from school and lives the life of an urban single parent, caring for the people who live in her small corner of the world.

Some nights Suzanne pushes the furniture back against the walls, turns off the lights, and sets up four altars, one for each of the four cardinal directions. She marks each direction with a white point candle. In the east, she also places incense on the altar; in the south, a red candle; in the west, a chalice filled with salt water; and in the north, a dish of salt. She adds flowers, feathers, crystals, silk, goddess figurines—whatever the occasion and the mood seem to require. Sometimes she works alone, sometimes with her family, sometimes with another witch. In the flickering candlelight, she calls on the goddesses and gods who govern those areas of life in which she needs help or wishes to give thanks. She prepares charms, beseeching the goddess and trying to delight her with ritual offerings. Psychically moving the energetic forces of the universe, she enters a trance state and opens herself up to communion with unseen forces that drive her life, your life, my life, the life of the world. And sometimes, in small ways—in gradually larger ways—she makes a difference. Her home becomes more peaceful, her brother wins a court case, her painting develops in skill and substance. She spreads the message by penning graffiti over sexist advertisements on the city buses, writing in the voice of the goddess: "All acts of love and pleasure are my rituals." Her life takes on color. It takes on meaning.

Suzanne joined her first coven after hearing a lecture by Starhawk, one of the most prominent thinkers and writers in the feminist spirituality movement. Suzanne met some other women at the lecture, they exchanged names and phone numbers, and began meeting together to teach themselves and each other the ancient—and thoroughly modern—art of witchcraft. She was forty years old then. Now she is forty-three, and has been a practicing witch for three years—that is, if you don't count the first forty years of her life. She was a witch then too. She tried to deny it, to bury it. She immersed herself in born-again Christianity—once, twice, three, even four times—but always abandoned it in depression and frustration. Finally, atheism became her religion, giving her a solace and comfort she never found in Christianity. She took a rest from the demands of the other side, from spirits, psychic forces, heaven, hell: the whole panorama of the nonmaterial.

Suzanne had been a feminist as long as she had been a witch—forever—but now she was a very angry feminist. Too angry, she says. This is in part what attracted her to feminist witchcraft. Suzanne was trying to resolve a conflict between her intense anger at men and her love for her own male child. As she sat listening to Starhawk lecture, she began to see a way out. But she also began to see a way in, a way back into the magic of her childhood, of her adolesence, of all those times in her life when she had felt most fully alive, most fully herself, least under the thumb of patriarchal gods and patriarchal society.

Suzanne was born in Washington, D.C., but grew up in Illinois and Tennessee. She describes herself as having been an intuitive, psychic child: she had prophetic dreams, she experienced precognition, she had instincts about people. Once while she and her mother were visiting her grandmother's house in the country, a god came to her in a dream. She was in bed with her mother, sleeping, and her mother had been reading a book, but had fallen asleep too. As Suzanne dreamt, the god spoke to her, and he said: "You can't be frightened, you need to do something, and you shouldn't be frightened. This is what you're going to see: there's a great rat down there, it's about to bite your mother's feet. But don't be afraid, because I'm telling you in advance.

What you have to do is wake up, very quietly, wake your mother very quietly, and that's all you have to do. Then you can go back to sleep. OK, I'm going to wake you up." The god woke her, and she saw just what she had seen in the dream. She woke her mother, as the god had told her to do. Her mother screamed, and she and Suzanne's grandmother chased the rat into the pantry and killed it with a piece of poisoned potato.

Suzanne's mother was a Methodist, and this was the church Suzanne attended as a child. Her father died when she was ten years old, and the family settled in Tennessee. It was there that she had her first experience with born-again Christianity, through the auspices of a "child evangelism" class at the local Methodist church. The class horrified Suzanne: she was told that psychic experiences—such as those she had had—were of the devil. She began to think of herself as possessed of some hidden evil. At night, she dreamed of crucifixions, certain in the knowledge that she could never be good enough for Jesus. After several months of living hell, she came to the conclusion that she would just have to give up this brand of religion and think for herself.

And think for herself she did. One of the things she thought about was how unfair it was that girls were treated so differently from boys. She remembers asking her mother: "Why do you always, if you're talking about people in general, why do you say he or his? Why do you say man? Why don't you say her or woman or girl?" Her mother answered, "Well, you have to say one or the other, and they picked he." Suzanne asked why, but she got no answer. She remembers bitterly how girls who excelled in elementary and junior high school suddenly stopped acting intelligent when they reached high school. She remembers signing up to take machine shop classes, because she knew she wanted to go to art school and do sculpture, and she needed to know how to use power tools. She was automatically transferred into home economics.

So when in her late teens Suzanne found a copy of Simone de Beauvoir's *The Second Sex*, it was food to her hungry soul. She discovered the National Organization for Women (NOW) and immediately asked to be put on their mailing list. Meanwhile she continued to have prophetic dreams and precognitive experiences, and started to channel voices from outside herself, either in writing or in speech. She also began "to poke around in the dusty stacks at Vanderbilt University looking for old treatises on witchcraft, because I hoped they would be able to give me some spells that I could try." Gradually, she came to some important religious insights:

I began to read cards, not tarot cards, and I didn't know from the card, but I just knew that the cards were like a coat hanger to hang the mind on. . . . I began to realize that in my dreams and also in the world, there was a certain iconography, things that appealed to me, and symbols to which I responded, and things that seemed to relate to one another and be connected, but there was no apparent connection.

The nature of the connection finally became clear to Suzanne when she discovered the work of Robert Graves (author of *The White Goddess*, an early work on goddess worship) in the public library. Her internal symbol system made sense in light of what she calls "this wonderful lost tradition." As she says: "I thought it was the most exciting thing I had ever read in my life. It was just a very creative time."

The combination of feminism and witchcraft was a powerful tonic, and Suzanne drank it down with gusto. She recalls:

Of course, it was during the sexual revolution, and it was wonderful for me, because I have a mother, you understand, that told me to be sure to be a virgin when I married, and not to give away "the only thing I had." That is a direct quote, right? But suddenly, I had the NOW newsletter, suddenly I was doing my own witchcraft thing, and suddenly I started sleeping with anybody I wanted to sleep with. And I discovered that I mattered a lot more to them than they mattered to me. And that they needed me a lot more than I needed them. And that when I was able to live, in a tiny way, like I think women used to live, I was sane, and the world was sane, and I was *much* happier. So I had a sexuality, and I had an identity, and it was very, very rich.

Such happiness was not destined to last. Suzanne had befriended some fundamentalist Christians and participated in their activities for awhile, but she eventually quit. Her friends did not approve of her new life-style, and one day some of them dropped by her house and asked her if she would like to go for a ride in the country. She said sure, got in the car, and asked, "Where are we going?" Her friends smiled, but didn't answer. They drove her out into the country, where some people from the church were waiting for her. They had decided she was possessed by demons, and they took it upon themselves to exorcise her. The exorcists had come equipped with a roll of paper towels, since they expected her to vomit up some demons, but she did not oblige them. They misquoted the Bible to her, and she corrected them, and finally they came to the conclusion that they were not going to get anything evil out of her, so they drove her home. But a few days later they came to her house, pulled all of her books on feminism off her shelves, and burned them in her front yard, even threatening to burn her drawings along with her books. Suzanne called the sheriff to complain. He told her that her friends meant well, and left it at that.

Around this time, Suzanne lived in a log cabin in the country, where she says she felt very close to nature. Some hornets built their nest on her back porch, and not wanting to disturb them, she decided instead to give them some simple instructions: she told them that they were not to bother her or sting her dogs, and in return, she would leave them in peace. Unfortunately, her boyfriend had not been included in the bargain, and one day when he came to visit, the hornets buzzed out of their nest and began chasing him around the house. He ran around and around the house, screaming, "Help me! help me! help me!" After about three circuits, Suzanne took pity on him and went out and addressed the hornets. She raised her hands in the air and said, "Go back!" and they turned around and returned to their nest.

In her early twenties, Suzanne left Tennessee for New York to study painting, and also "to see if I could find any people who were at all like me." After another unsatisfying bout with born-again Christianity, she returned to a deepened interest in witchcraft. As she explains: "The experiences that I had that I would now call witchcraft experiences were so much stronger than these other things . . . it felt like being in a stream. What I was going to do was listen to myself. And I began to do that. And when I did that, my life began to take shape in a way that I recognize now was very, very pagan. . . . And I lived like that for a couple of years, sort of finding my own way and mapping out my own territory." Again, it did not last, because the born-again Christians came knocking on her door. They hooked her back into fundamentalist Christianity in two ways: First, they asked someone she loved to call her up and tell her how important Christianity was to them. This time it was her brother, and when she told him that the religion hadn't worked for her, he began to cry and say: "This is the most wonderful thing in my life, and you just spat on it. It's like you spat on me." Second, they told her that she hadn't given one hundred percent of herself in her previous involvements with born-again Christianity, and she felt guilty, because she knew it was true. In Christianity, she found, there was always more to give.

After freeing herself from fundmentalist Christianity this last time, Suzanne became an atheist, describing it as "a great relief." As she tells it: "I shut down everything. I shut down all the doors." Her anger at Christianity oozed into a feminist anger at the narrow roles fundamentalists asked women to play, and she did her best to set her psychic experiences aside as something she couldn't ultimately explain, but no longer wished to dwell upon. The world of religion had let her down too many times, and she wanted no part of it. Instead of reading cards or speaking in tongues, she took up karate at a women's karate school.

When she reintroduced spirituality into her life, Suzanne did it gradually this time. As reluctant as she was to get involved in anything religious, she continued to be drawn by the same symbols and images that had always fascinated her. Living in the midst of the feminist art world, goddess images were unavoidable and very attractive to her. Suzanne remembers telling a friend at the time, "You know, sometimes I would really like to pretend that there's actually something to this, but of course I won't do that." So she dabbled around the edges, and went to hear Starhawk speak in hopes of seeing a slide show of goddess figures. But after hearing Starhawk's lecture, she decided to plunge in again, this time with the backing of a solid group of those who shared her ideas and experiences. Where before she had always worked out her spirituality very much on her own, she now had companions for her journey.

Suzanne credits feminist spirituality with restoring to women the right to be sexual, not only as young women, but as older women. She believes it gives her balance and integrity in her personal life, and hopes that feminist witchcraft will yet save the world from destruction. The earth, according to Suzanne, is a living manifestation of the goddess that is in grave danger of being destroyed, having refused to accept any more abuse. People all over the world, connected via some form of telepathy, are responding to this crisis with the witchcraft that may save this creation from destruction. In this cosmic contest, Suzanne has defected from the patriarchy and signed on with the forces of the goddess. Having had intimate contact with patriarchal religion, and well knowing its strength (even over rebellious people such as herself), Suzanne is not optimistic about the outcome. But at last she has grounds for hope. Meanwhile, an alienated identity she has long struggled with is crystallizing into one she can be proud of, one that a whole community of people recognizes as valid. The spirituality that has surfaced at the best, least clouded periods of her life has turned out to be the spirituality of a movement: a movement that respects her, accepts her, and does not regard her as inferior because she is female.[1]

Suzanne's story is not the story of every woman in the feminist spirituality movement, but if it is not typical in every detail, neither is it unfamiliar as a whole. The feminist spirituality movement is filled with women like Suzanne, and also with women who resemble her only remotely. In getting to know the women of the feminist spirituality movement, it is helpful to look at these women on two levels: the sociological and the psychological. In the first case, we can get a better feel for what races, social classes, professions, religious backgrounds, and sexual preferences these women represent, and in what proportions. In the second, we can find what brought these women in contact with feminist spirituality and predisposed them favorably toward it.

A Sociological Profile of the Feminist Spirituality Movement

The sociological profile of the feminist spirituality movement can be summed up like this: white, of middle-class origins, fairly well educated (beyond high school), of Jewish or Christian background (usually, though not always, having had a significant amount of religious training), in their thirties or forties, and disproportionately lesbian. There are many women who are exceptions to one or more (or all) of these rules, but most approximate this profile.[2]

To expand on the profile, in terms of age distribution, most spiritual feminists are members of the baby boom generation, meaning that they are now in their late twenties to mid-forties. If feminist spirituality were equally attractive to women aged zero to one hundred, there would still be a disproportionate number of women in their thirties and forties, because there are more women in this age group in the general population. However, at both large festivals and smaller rituals it is impressive to note how few women there are below thirty, and how many there are who are fifty and older. There are women in their teens and twenties, but not many. But lest feminist spirituality be interpreted strictly as a baby boom phenomenon, there is the presence of a healthy number of older women to indicate otherwise. It is a religion of adults past adolesence, most of whom participate strictly as individuals and not as parts of family units.

There is a great deal more variation in age than there is in race. In all my travels through the feminist spirituality movement, I believe I can still count on my fingers and toes the total number of women I have seen who are not obviously Caucasian. There are women of color in the feminist spirituality movement, and certainly one finds their writings included in the movement's journals. However, judging from the amount of concern voiced in feminist spirituality publications about the lack of women of color in the movement, and the quest for ways to bring them in, it is clear that the overwhelming whiteness of the movement is not in serious question. If anything, observation suggests that black, Asian, Hispanic, and Native American spiritual feminists are either not very numerous or are sharing their spirituality together without white company.

This is not a fact about which white spiritual feminists are very happy. It is at odds with their dream of a feminist spirituality that brings together women of every race and nationality. Most spiritual feminists understand themselves to be first women (or sometimes lesbians), and only later, far down the line, as people with red hair or from a Catholic background, as New Englanders or pet store owners, as tall people or fat people or libertarians or Democrats. This primary identification as female is key to the very existence of the feminist spirituality movement, a religion for women. Because they are mainly white, spiritual feminists' racial identity is not problematic for them: it is the norm in American society, and is easily regarded as peripheral to their central identity as women. It saddens them that women of color are not equally enthusiastic about celebrating shared femaleness. It is not that the white women of feminist spirituality do not want to recognize the existence of race; they are eager to acclaim the diversity of womankind, and want to see their rituals filled with women of all colors and from all cultures. They have no desire to insist that African-American or Hispanic-American women give up their racial or cultural particularity. On the contrary, they hope that the movement will be enriched by the music, ritual, foods, and folklore of participants from many cultures and subcultures. They are interested in learning what they can do to better communicate with women of other races and to join in the fight to overcome racism. But they wish to do so with the implicit understanding that though women come in many colors, black skin is ultimately no more significant than red hair in light of the larger fact of a common female physicality and the experience of being women in this world.

Some women of color can feel comfortable with the assumption of a primary shared femaleness with women of all races. They see themselves as plagued by sexism and blessed by their feminine natures and female experiences, and they feel that anyone else who shares these things with them, whatever their race, is someone with whom they can work in solidarity. Luisah Teish has discovered this to be true in her own life. Her work with African-American spirituality and voodoo was much envied by women in the feminist spirituality movement, and as Teish began to share with them, she says: "Much to my surprise I found that many women out there were kin to me. Black women and white women. Women yellow, red, and brown." She sees feminist spirituality at its best as a way of mending racism.[3] But other women of color don't see shared femaleness as an adequate reason for trusting white women with their religious lives. Even though they may be interested in spirituality, they do not feel at ease exploring it with a group of mainly white women. Nor do they necessarily feel that their cultural gifts are adequately appreciated, fearing instead that they are merely being co-opted.

And so the movement remains predominantly white, while the dream of a multiracial women's spirituality lives on. So dear is this dream that many women confuse it with the reality. Jean Mountaingrove, one of the founders of *Womanspirit* magazine, remembers its readership as being composed of every race, religious background, sexual preference, and economic class imaginable (which, though true insofar as there may have been at least one representative of each category, neglects their relative presence in the movement). Descriptions of rituals found in spiritual feminist literature often rhapsodize about circles filled with women of "all ages, sizes, colors, abilities." This tendency to wish a greater diversity for feminist spirituality than actually exists became particularly clear in an interview with Renee Landau, a spiritual feminist who has been participating in a multiweekend women's mystery school. When asked about the ethnic composition of this group, she responded enthusiastically, "Oh, we've got everything!" But then followed up: "No, I'm sorry, I have to take that back. It's all Caucasian. But within Caucasian, we have Protestant, Catholic, Jewish, and a wide diversity of ethnic groups, as far as I can tell." Still later, she apologized, "Unfortunately, our group is very definitely middle-class and white. We have a couple that would be a little bit lower than middle class maybe. That's an issue that we've talked about."[4]

There is a higher level of racial integration among lesbians in the movement. It is at the festivals sponsored by lesbian organizations that one is most likely to find women of color represented in numbers that are anywhere close to their representation in the general population. Apparently, the existence of an additional outsider identity (female homosexuality)—and a socially stigmatized one at that—takes some of the edge off of racial outsider identities. In view of their common sexual persuasion, racial differentness seems less divisive. It is also within the lesbian community that one finds the greatest concentration of spiritual feminists. If some form of watered-down biblical religion may be called the civil religion of mainstream America, it is fair to say that feminist spirituality (also in a lukewarm version) is now the civil religion of the lesbian feminist community. Certainly not all lesbians, nor even all radical feminist lesbians, are practitioners of feminist spirituality. But the religion is very much present as a backdrop in the lesbian feminist community. In recent years, the annual Michigan Womyn's Music Festival, attended by as many as ten thousand lesbians, has included rituals and workshops on many aspects of feminist spirituality in addition to its traditional musical offerings. Zsuzsanna Budapest (often called "Z"), one of the earliest pioneers of the feminist spirituality movement, has attended in years past and presided as priestess over lesbian marriages. She and others have offered blessings and invocations for the gathering, which no doubt operate for the nonspiritual among lesbian feminists in much the same way that loosely Judeo-Christian prayers offered at governmental functions work for the secular members of the audience. They are *pro forma* recitations, token acknowledgments of something higher, and a recognition of a clergy empowered to fulfill certain legal functions. With this kind of visibility in their communities, it is no wonder that many lesbians with religious inclinations find their way into feminist spirituality in greater percentages than do heterosexual women.

Still, probably the majority of spiritual feminists consider themselves heterosexual, as do most women in society generally. In spite of this, lesbianism or at least bisexuality is something of a norm in feminist spirituality, and heterosexuality is regarded as a deviation—at times a wholly unacceptable one. The distinction might best be captured by saying that lesbian sexuality is celebrated while heterosexual sexuality is (sometimes) tolerated. At most feminist spirituality retreats, it is fine for a woman to talk about her experience of her own sexuality, about her "female" sexuality. And if her partners are women, she can talk about their shared sexuality. But if her partners are men, she would be risking social censure to talk too long or loudly about her lovers or about male sexuality or about the sexuality that they share together. *Her* sexuality is an acceptable topic of conversation, but only if she can abstract the man out of the picture.

Spiritual feminists are, relatively speaking, a highly educated group of women. Of the many women with whom I have spoken in greater depth, I have met only one high school dropout; most have taken at least some college, and many have professional degrees as well. Even those women who have not had much formal higher education often talk about the classes they have taken in night school, the lecture series they have attended, and so on, which is in keeping with the general literary/artistic nature of the movement.

All of this education does not necessarily translate into sterling careers and upward mobility for spiritual feminists, at least not in mainstream terms. There are spiritual feminists who are lawyers, doctors, professors, psychologists, social workers, librarians, administrators, architects, and so forth, and many are very successful. There are also a lot of struggling artists in the movement, and clerical workers, house cleaners, professional psychics, waitresses, and so on, who are often hard pressed to stay afloat financially with whatever temporary or part-time work they can find. For some this is a choice dictated by their pursuit of spirituality. A number of spiritual feminists interviewed for this study have given up professional careers or careers-in-the-making in order to free up time for their spirituality. Helen Littlefield left a financially lucrative career in banking to study psychology, and is now cleaning houses to pay her bills while she experiments with alternative forms of healing. Renee Landau, a professional consultant who was climbing the mainstream ladder of success, stepped down many rungs to train as a carpenter's assistant and investigate macrobiotics. Nancy Robison earned a doctorate in education and worked as an administrator for both colleges and Fortune 500 companies before leaving it all to spend several years traveling around the world attending Buddhist retreats and transformational psychology seminars. And after training and working as a city planner, Carol Schulman quit her demanding job to substitute teach in public elementary schools so that she would have more time to enjoy life and follow out her spiritual quest.[5]

While these women have chosen their downward mobility and their vagabond economic life-style, others have from the beginning chosen careers that entail great sacrifice and little hope of financial reward or stability (art, music, and the like). Still others have been victims of economic hard times and women's compromised earning potential in America. In addition, many spiritual feminists are single or are single parents, with the additional financial challenges that entails. Because there are so many working-class and lower-class spiritual feminists, it does not seem accurate to describe the feminist spirituality movement as a middle-class movement (as many people do). However, it is true that the vast majority of spiritual feminists were either raised in middle-class homes or have since entered the middle class as adults. There are exceptions of course, but very few spiritual feminists were born into poverty and have remained there or were born into wealth and have prospered. The feminist spirituality movement has not grown out of financial hardship, nor has it come out of a moneyed leisure class, and in this sense the movement bears the stamp of middle-class origins.

Spiritual feminists come from all sorts of religious backgrounds. They have been raised as Catholics, Episcopalians, Presbyterians, Methodists, Reform Jews, Lutherans, Orthodox Christians, Orthodox Jews, Baptists, Unitarians—almost any American religion you would care to name. And again, though there are exceptions, most of them attended church or synagogue as children, and had an in-depth exposure to their religion of birth. There is a popular conception that there are more former Catholics and Jews in feminist spirituality than there are former Protestants. Angela Price and Corrine Foster, both of whom have taught feminist spirituality classes and workshops, say that they meet more Catholic and Jewish women in the course of this work. Both suggest that the reason for the presence of more Catholic and Jewish women is because they have a familiarity with ritual and the use of religious symbols, and so they have a natural attraction to feminist spirituality. They suggest that for Protestant women feminist spirituality is more of a stretch.[6]

Certainly I have met many former Jews and Catholics, but also many former Protestants, and I would hesitate to say that any one of these classes of women is disproportionately represented in the feminist spirituality movement. However, it is interesting to note that a number of former nuns have become involved in feminist spirituality. I have met several, and twelve of the seventeen nuns contributing to *Lesbian Nuns: Breaking Silence* have left their orders and are now exploring "astrology, Goddess, imagery, Tarot, dreamwork, *I Ching,* herbal healing, meditation, massage and body . . . psychic work . . . communal rituals for solstices, equinoxes, and full moons"—in other words, feminist spirituality.[7] This phenomenon may be partially explained by the resistance of the Catholic hierarchy to placing women in leadership roles. While most Protestant and Jewish denominations have opened up their clergy to women in recent years, the Catholic church has not, and proclamations from the church insisting that women cannot act in a sacramental capacity because their genitals do not resemble Jesus's indicate that it may be some time before Catholic women win the right to be ordained.[8] The Catholic woman who feels she has a true calling to religious leadership has fewer options than her Protestant and Jewish sisters, whose continued activity in their churches and synagogues requires fewer compromises, and so she may be more open to feminist spirituality's appeal.

Converting to Feminist Spirituality

This sociological profile of the feminist spirituality movement gives some picture of who spiritual feminists are, at least in terms of relatively easily observable characteristics. But if spiritual feminists tend to fall into certain social categories, it is nevertheless true that not all people in these categories become spiritual feminists. Something more is required to make a woman a spiritual feminist, something less tangible and more amorphous than a laundry list of sociological characteristics. Why do some women convert to feminist spirituality when others do not? At least two things are required: first, a woman must be receptive to that which feminist spirituality has to offer; second, she must be exposed to the movement in a way that she finds inviting.

Conversion can be described as that time when one's old religious identity is sloughed off, and a new identity coalesces. For many spiritual feminists, their conversion experience is also their entry into feminist spirituality. But for others it is not. These women convert to a new religious identity before being exposed to feminist spirituality. When they find feminist spirituality, they refine their religious identity, but they do not experience a real conversion. In ways, the word "conversion" is misleading: it seems to suggest a sudden, total change, a 180-degree turn from an old life into a new one. For some women, their conversion is just that. But far more often, there is tremendous continuity between a woman's former life and her conversion to feminist spirituality (as there was in Suzanne Courveline's story of early psychic experiences, occult experiments, and protofeminist instincts, and later identification as a feminist witch). Margot Adler has suggested that most neopagans do not experience conversion so much as return. She writes: "In most cases, word of mouth, a discussion between friends, a lecture, a book, or an article provides the entry point [to neopaganism]. But these events merely confirm some original, private experience. . . ." A practicing neopagan herself, Adler says: "I never adopted any new beliefs. I simply accepted, reaffirmed, and extended a very old experience. I allowed certain kinds of feelings and ways of being back into my life."[9] Spiritual feminists are very like mainstream neopagans in this regard. Not only do many women report that feminist spirituality echoes and affirms their older beliefs, but this sense of returning to things previously known is the accepted model for conversion in the feminist spirituality movement. It is the way conversion is supposed to happen.

It is important to stress that not all religions regard conversion in this light. Christian fundamentalist sects, for example, often specialize in conversion stories whose model is the 180-degree turn. If one cannot stand up and tell a good story with the basic form, "I started out bad, tainted with sin; I got worse, I wallowed in sin; just when I hit bottom, drowning in sin, Jesus saved me," then the authenticity of one's conversion is in doubt. In contrast, spiritual feminist conversions have this form: "I started out different, special, keenly aware of truths that the people around me neglected or denied; I tried traditional religions but rejected them as sexist; I explored different spiritual practices trying to quench my spiritual thirst; I finally found feminist spirituality, and I knew I had come home, I knew I had found something big enough to encompass everything I need." If the metaphors for fundamentalist Christians are "being saved" and "being filled with the love of the Lord," the metaphors for spiritual feminists are "coming home" and "finding myself." For these women, the language of feminist spirituality may be new, but the experiences are old and familiar. Time and again, one hears comments like this: "It was like relearning a language I had forgotten"; "I felt their religion put a name on experience I had already had"; "I started reading [*The Spiral Dance,* a book by Starhawk], and everything just hit me as, 'yeah, yeah, that's exactly what I think.'" Susun Weed, an herbalist and healer, says that what she enjoys most in her work is when women say to her, "You know, Susun, I always knew what you had to say about this tradition of wise women, but I needed someone to say it for me in order to remember it."[10]

Religious Experiences in Childhood

A prominent theme in spiritual feminist conversion stories is the way that feminist spirituality provides a link to childhood religious experiences. What spiritual feminists come home to is a spirituality they knew as children, one which was disparaged by traditional religions and then stripped away by years in the adult world. Though it has its own unique characteristics, Joan Maddox's story could serve as the prototype for conversion to feminist spirituality:

> I remember coming out [as a lesbian] and starting to think about my spirituality—for want of a word that would do it for me. I felt like a direct line had jumped over all the garbage in the middle that was destroying my spirit. That somewhere back there I was born with a certain kind of spirit, and that I had it for awhile as a young child, and it was more present to me, or me to it, or whatever. And then all the socialization of being female destroyed it, or tried to destroy it. And I remember going through this and thinking all along, I know I deserve something better than what I have here. I know there's something there that gives me joy. It's magic, it's joy, I don't know what the word is for it, but it was there and it still is there, and I had to get to be a lesbian separatist to have some access to it. It is all about all that stuff that was laid on me and is laid on every single woman all her growing-up years that takes her from herself.[11]

Not all women stress the evil effects of female socialization, but there is always some sense in spiritual feminist conversion stories of childhood persecution, of being misunderstood, of having what is best in oneself sneered at by an ignorant world.

Women who grew up to become spiritual feminists were most often girls who experienced a deep spiritual sense in themselves, and felt like misfits in traditional religions and in the secular world. They did not grow up feeling happily atheistic, unconcerned with matters unseen and loving their quotidian lives. Feminist spirituality is for most women the oasis at the end of a long, hot, dry, lonely journey through a patriarchal desert, where the only thing that has sustained the pilgrim is her inner self and her vision of who she was meant to be. Long before these women encountered feminist spirituality, they had experienced or established some kind of outsider identity, some sense that society as it was made was not made for them.

Marguerite Keane remembers her growing awareness as a young girl that she had been consigned by gender to a narrow life, an insight that weighed heavily upon her. She says, "I was acutely aware that there were absolutely no role models for women of women who were powerful or who did anything. I mean, I was aware of that at an extremely young age. I saw women as movie stars or as sort of housewives, really." Several women told me how they came to see very early that the cards were stacked against them as girls. Often any feeling of outsiderness these girls had was doubled or trebled by being female. There was simply no way for them to integrate the identity a male-dominated society handed them with the one they felt inside. Diane Turcott, who grew up being sexually abused by her stepfather, understood that being a girl had its drawbacks, to put it mildly. But the depth of this male conspiracy was driven home to her when she finally forced her mother to leave her stepfather by threatening to kill him if she did not. After they escaped, the government tracked down Diane's mother and told her that she either had to go back to her husband, or send their son (Diane's half-brother) to live with his father. With only these choices, they packed their things and moved back in with Diane's stepfather, where the abuse began afresh. To Diane, the world certainly seemed an unfriendly, dangerous place for women and girls.[12]

But if being female aggravated the situation, most spiritual feminists do not suggest that it was the sole cause of their sense of outsiderness. They felt themselves to be internally different, to have experiences that were not accepted or even acknowledged as real by mainstream society. Larissa Vilenskaya, a psychic researcher from Russia now living in the United States, captures this feeling of set-apartness: "In high school, I was a bit of an oddball—other girls with their interests in boys, fashionable clothes, and dancing seemed to me very superficial and often boring." For most, this feeling arose much earlier than high school. Lynn Andrews, a popular author of works on Native American spirituality, remembers that as a young girl "I was lonely . . . but I sensed some kind of destiny, although I didn't have a clue of what that was." Petey Stevens, owner of a psychic school called Heartsong, recalls: "From the time I was a very little girl I had always thought about healing the world."[13]

These vague yearnings frequently caused spiritual feminists-in-the-making to gravitate toward traditional religions, where experiences of meaning and connection to a spiritual world were culturally sanctioned. Many women interviewed said they were extremely devout as children. Sal Frankel went to church six days a week between the ages of five and thirteen; she attended Mass on Sunday, and went to church the other five days to sit and talk with Mary and Jesus. As a child, Esther Hoffman rode the bus five miles into town to go to church on those days she was not attending parochial school. She says: "I would pray on my knees so long I'd see the Virgin Mary move. I used to sing in the choir every day. I'd go to Mass and Communion every day during Lent. I was just fanatical." It was not that these women came from extremely religious homes. Some did. But even those who did not come from religious homes developed an independent interest in religion. During her childhood, Jeannie Garawitz's family was trying to assimilate to a dominantly Christian culture, and they downplayed their Judaism. But after going to Jewish summer camp, Jeannie came home and began to ask her mother, "Why don't we keep the Sabbath? Why don't we do this, why don't we do that?" Karen Whiting remarks of her United Church of Christ background: "It wasn't important to my family at all. To me it was very important. . . . I think the search for a god and a connection with a god was very important to me, especially from about age twelve on. . . . But even when I was younger, I was always curious about God and, you know, raising big questions, and thinking very strange things."[14]

If spiritual feminists were attracted to religion as children, they did not accept it uncritically. They describe themselves as children who could never settle for easy answers, who always wanted to know more, to have things explained more completely. Sara Copeland, who had no formal religious education, was a teenager when she first asked her parents, "What religion are we anyway?" and was told that they were Protestant. But even without an involvement in organized religion, Sara was pursuing religious questions. She remembers:

> I would ask questions like "Where is God?" My mother would tell me, "Everywhere." So then I would picture this man who was like everywhere at once. . . . I was very interested in what happened to people when they died, and I made up my own little prayers that I would say before I went to bed every night. I would repeat the alphabet a few times, and the idea was to give people, dead people, the ability to talk by giving them these letters, so they could communicate.[15]

However devout and earnest they were as children, spiritual feminists say they had a rough time with traditional religions, and found that their inner spiritual self did not ultimately fit in there any better than in the outside world. Again, one reason for the lack of fit was their gender. Corinne Foster, raised as a Catholic, says: "I remember as a little kid loving to march down the aisle, kissing the little flowers, you know, 'I love you Jesus.' Sort of very powerful moments and memories. But also feeling like somehow I was detached from it, because the most I could be was a nun. . . . Nun is none, that's it, what do you have? So it was sort of like a dead end after awhile."[16] In Luisah Teish's case, the fit was bad with traditional religions not only because of her gender, but because of her race as well. She explains:

> As a child I had serious problems with the Christian God. First of all he was a white man. I grew up in the pre-integrated black South. When I looked around me—you know—hey! This is cracker time! I'm supposed to spend my time on my knees praying to a cracker?! Give me a break! He was this great bearded dude in the sky who didn't hear people's petitions, who had cast me into slavery because I was black, and who had me inferior because I was a woman. Right?![17]

But the lack of fit was broader than gender and race, and traditional religions left budding spiritual feminists confused and hungry for something different. Sharon Logan was thirteen years old when she became involved with a fundamentalist organization called The Word of Life:

> It was this intense fundamentalist scene, where you'd go to one of these meetings, and at one point they'd have you close your eyes, and they'd ask everybody that's not saved to raise their hand. So anybody that raised their hand, then the adults would be assigned to them, and they'd get you in these corners afterwards and tell you the horrible things that were going to happen to you because Christ was coming back at any minute. In the twinkle of an eye, he was gonna return. And if you hadn't been saved, everybody that was saved was gonna disappear, and you were gonna be left with all these horrible monstrosities on the face of the earth, and you would never get a chance again, you were in hell forever.
>
> So all you had to do to avoid this terrible fate was to open your heart to Christ and ask him to come in, because he's there knocking on your heart door. Well, I convinced them that I was saved, so they let me out of the corner. And I went home, and I like fearfully pleaded with him to come into my heart. But nothing happened, nothing happened. So for a year I lived this life of this fraudulent person, because nothing happened. I would pray, and nothing happened. . . . I was petrified, because I knew that he might come back any minute, and he hadn't come into my heart.[18]

Rosemary Sackner reached her first crisis with traditional religion as a twelve-year-old acolyte in the Episcopal church. One Sunday before the service, Rosemary was lighting the candles. She accidentally lit the flowers that were beside the candles, and they started to burn. The minister rushed over and yelled, "God saw you burn the flowers in his house!" Rosemary says: "It totally freaked me out. I went into this whole 'oh my God, I'm going to go to hell' thing for awhile, for about three weeks. And then I just woke up. It was like 'bullshit, that man's crazy, and this is not what religion's supposed to be about.'"[19]

If spiritual feminists struggled as children to fit into the religious forms of their society, the fact remains that most of the spiritual experiences they regarded as deeply significant happened outside traditional religions altogether. It is these experiences that most often move them to say that feminist spirituality was a return to their original childhood spirituality. This original spirituality, according to some women, included many if not all of the elements of their later feminist religion: self-designed ritual, goddess worship, nature worship, psychic experiences, and even a protowitchcraft. This is, of course, in keeping with the model for spiritual feminist conversion stories, and it is undoubtedly partly a function of hindsight: certain childhood experiences, unremarkable at the time, are elevated in later tellings to stand as foreshadowings of an adult spirituality. Still, it is impressive to hear of the spiritual precocity of these women. Their sense of spiritual differentness came early and was subdued only with great effort, if at all.

Diane Turcott traces her special spiritual nature all the way back to her birth. She was born on her mother's living room sofa in Mississippi, and claims to remember the event, having received psychic messages at the time from her great-grandmother who was present in the room. Zsuzsanna Budapest had her first precognitive experience at the age of three, when her grandmother came to visit her in her astral body and told her that she was dying, but that she would always look after Zsuzsanna from her vantage point in the spiritual world. Luisah Teish had visions as a child that she could neither explain nor interpret in which a toothless little girl on a balcony across the street would smile at her and then dive headfirst over the railing, disappearing just as her head hit the sidewalk. Helen Littlefield describes herself as having been "a very psychic child, a real porous child." Petey Stevens also talks about having been psychic as a child, saying, "There are many degrees of sensitivity and mine was acute and intense."[20] Spiritual feminists are proud of their special skills, but they also see them as having been sources of pain in the years before they found any social support for their identity. It was difficult to live with fuzzy boundaries between self and outside world, between past, present, and future; and moreover, to do so in the face of others thinking them crazy.

Early spiritual experiences did not always involve psychic skills, but they were experiences that mainstream religions did not credit to a valid spiritual source. Some were experiences with nature. Starhawk says that as a teenager, she had powerful experiences in nature that seemed to her mystical and spiritual, but that "didn't seem to fall in the framework of Judaism—or at least not what I had been taught about it, or had learned about it." Sal Frankel made up her own rituals to act out her experience of nature, and vividly remembers singing to the sea as a child.[21] For some, what did not fit easily into traditional religions was a direct experience of the divine as female. In her childhood Catholicism, Lady Miw was very attached to Mary. She says she prayed to Jesus and to the saints, but "always went running back to her." In an effort to find something feminine in the trinity, Lady Miw decided that the Holy Ghost "must be the mama part." Jonnie Vance was not consciously aware of a goddess or the divine feminine, but says that when she began reading books in feminist spirituality, she felt "a physical pain of surprise—surprise that I have always known Her."[22]

A few women relate childhood spiritual experiences that could be lifted right from the pages of any current work on feminist witchcraft or spirituality. Barbara Walker, author of numerous books on feminist spirituality, tells a fascinating story of a vision she had when she was thirteen years old, one that included many themes that have since found their way into spiritual feminist thealogy. While walking in the woods with her dog, she found a snakeskin and a white flower lying on the ground. When she looked up, she saw a tree that before her eyes turned into a woman with three faces: one young, one adult, and one old. She remembers:

> It wasn't just a tree that resembled a woman; it was the woman herself. She was a hefty, hippy, bosomy, naked green woman with three heads and huge, powerful legs planted in the earth like a strange new version of the Jolly Green Giant. . . . Out of the dark triangle of the giant woman's crotch, between her massive thighs, poured an endless stream of living things. All species of plants and animals were mingled in a mass flowing like the waters of a river. Within the mass I distinguished sheep, goats, horses, deer, rhododendron bushes, cacti, bears, birds, cattle, fish, vines, seaweeds, foodstuffs, and people.[23]

Walker reflects: "I had never heard of the Triple Goddess with her Virgin, Mother, and Crone forms. More than two decades would pass before I saw a picture of the Willendorf Venus, whose body resembled that of my tree woman. I knew nothing about Earth Mothers, sacred groves, fertility symbols, pagan religions, or tree worship."[24]

Having had three-dimensional visions of goddesses or even inner experiences of them as children is not the norm for spiritual feminists. But on a somewhat tamer level, many women say that they were fascinated with what goddesses there were in modern Western culture, namely the goddesses of Greek and Norse mythology. Margot Adler, author of *Drawing Down the Moon,* says that as a child she was very drawn to the Greek pantheon, and made up her own fantasy games involving them. Karen Whiting remembers a period of her life in which she wrote poems to Aphrodite, and kept a rose in her room as a symbol of this goddess. Poet and novelist Erica Jong was similarly taken with Greek mythology, and remembers being "passionate about the Persephone myth. It spoke very, very deeply to me."[25]

The "Wandering Years"

What happened to these women as they grew up? Did they keep singing to the sea and writing poems to Aphrodite? Did they keep trying to find their way in traditional religions? Or did they give up on religion altogether? The answers are of course individual; different women made different choices. But in general, most women who later became spiritual feminists left traditional religions if they had been in them; and whether they had been in traditional religions or not, they experimented with alternatives. This is the all-important bridge in the spiritual feminist conversion story: the time that passed between an original childhood spirituality and the establishment of a new religious identity as a spiritual feminist.

More often than not, the signpost that marked the end of involvement with traditional religions was feminism. Rosita Veracruz, for example, had always been critical of Catholicism, even though she was very attracted to religion. She remembers writing her senior essay in high school on "The Rise and Fall of the Catholic Church" (only after rejecting an essay titled "Was Mary a Virgin?" for fear of being too controversial). But in spite of her misgivings, Rosita became involved with Catholic social justice movements in college, and when she graduated, she took a job as a religious education coordinator for several parishes. She was able to compromise with the church at the time because there was a real effort under way to include different perspectives within the church, and to open up leadership opportunities to more people. Women's ordination seemed a natural and inevitable step in this process to Rosita, and she enrolled in seminary in the anticipation that she would one day be ordained as a Catholic priest. Her disillusionment was gradual, but she remembers recognizing at one point, "Wait a minute, everybody who's in a position of authority or divinity here wears a penis." She began watering the seeds of her feminist consciousness, and what germinated was a realization that male domination in the Catholic church was not simply a matter of men in priests' robes, but of a theology that had no conceivable place for women apart from their traditional roles as devout drones. Rosita finally concluded: "They're not gonna ordain women in my lifetime and I'm not gonna waste my time banging my head against the wall and talking to a bunch of boys in skirts about, 'oh, please, consider me worthy.' I'll do my spiritual work through psychotherapy." And Rosita set religion aside. Rosita Veracruz was not the only woman who sought out a leadership position in the church, only to decide that the glass ceiling on her career ladder was too low, and the church too irrefragably patriarchal. Several women interviewed either attended seminary or thought about it.[26]

Others gave up on traditional religions at a younger age, virtually as soon as they developed any feminist consciousness. Melanie Engler, who was an enthusiastic Baptist throughout her childhood, discovered feminism in her first year at a Christian college. With virtually one stroke, she severed her ties to Christianity and gave up on organized religion. Like Rosita Veracruz, Rosemary Sackner wrote her first essay damning the Christian church during her senior year in high school. She attended an Episcopal boarding school, and was impressed by how hypocritical the religious life was there. Students attended chapel regularly, but rebelled in ways that Rosemary found ridiculous, such as having sex on the altar. She began to associate religion with being rich and fulfilling some sense of social duty, but not with what she considered religion's real purposes. And though she says her feminism was rather inarticulate at that point, she remembers the atmosphere at school as being "totally patriarchal," and that that was religiously reinforced. So Rosemary put religion on the back burner during her college years. Nancy Robison also left organized religion in college, breaking with it for feminist reasons. As a child, she wanted to be a nun; as a college student, she wanted to be a social activist and a career woman. She gave up Catholicism as male-dominated and money-grubbing, and looked for a Jewish or Protestant replacement. But in her search for replacements she finally came up empty-handed, and so she abandoned the search and spent nearly fifteen years in what she calls her "gung ho, career woman, gonna change the world phase."[27]

For some women, leaving traditional religions spelled freedom to roam at will through the world of alternative religions, while for others it meant sealing off access to spirituality. Those who walled off religion as overpatriarchal often made feminist spirituality the next stop on their spiritual journey. Those who dabbled more enthusiastically had serial or multiple involvements with other alternative religions (what one woman calls "shopping mall spirituality"[28]) before incorporating their practice under the broad heading of feminist spirituality. Prior to focusing on feminist spirituality, various women tried hatha yoga, transcendental meditation, chakra cleansing, ritualistic performance art, Haitian voodoo dance, Zen body dynamics, Baha'i, Church of the Science of Mind, Egyptian sun worship, taiji, Vipassana Buddhist meditation, Sufism, and many types of therapy, both traditional and nontraditional.[29] In the course of their religious odyssey, the most important thing most spiritual feminists found was that they could not walk away from religion, that it was a hunger that could not be starved out of existence. Those who spent some years in a state of irreligion talked about feeling that there was a hole in their lives where their religion used to be,[30] and those who experimented with many religions still felt a lack, still felt that their deepest religious instincts had found no adequate home. For both, what was lacking was a religion that bore no stain of patriarchy. And having become highly sensitized to any hint of sexism, it would not do to simply ignore gender; nothing would suffice but to glory in femaleness, to proclaim the spiritual potential inherent in womanhood, to take the "weak vessel" of Christianity and make her the holy chalice of the great goddess. This is what these women found in feminist spirituality.

Discovering Feminist Spirituality

Many women have no difficulty recalling the moment when they were set on the path of feminist spirituality. Something clicked in their minds, and they knew they were where they wanted to be, needed to be, were destined to be. Others recount a progression of events, each adding to those before. Some have no clear conception of how it all started: there was something in the air, and something in their hearts, and the two came together very gradually. Still others can tell of an experience that got them started in some other alternative religion, one that eventually led them into feminist spirituality.

The most common entrée into feminist spirituality was through books. On the recommendation of friends or just by browsing in a bookstore, many women came upon a book that brought a new and welcome light to bear upon their spiritual lives. Some women can name a single book that began their spiritual feminist quest, and even remember the details of how the book came to fall into their hands. For Rachel Laura, the book that captured her interest was an early one by Zsuzsanna Budapest. As she says: "When I became a feminist and a lesbian, one of my lovers was very into tarot and *I Ching* and all that kind of stuff, and I thought that was all sort of weird, but I was certainly interested in humoring her. Until I came across Z Budapest's original *Feminist Book of Lights and Shadows*. And that really excited me.

I really felt that here was a woman who was real." She went out the next day and bought a deck of tarot cards. Diane Turcott discovered feminist spirituality when a friend loaned her a copy of *The Spiral Dance:* she remembers copying passages from it by hand. Others mentioned Vicki Noble's *Motherpeace,* a guide to a feminist tarot deck designed by Noble and Karen Vogel; *Dreaming the Dark* by Starhawk; Mary Daly's *Gyn/Ecology;* Merlin Stone's *When God Was a Woman;* a special issue of the feminist art journal *Heresies* on the great goddess; Margot Adler's *Drawing Down the Moon;* books by Barbara Walker and Kim Chernin, and many more. One woman I met when she was attending her first feminist spirituality meeting had just finished reading Marion Zimmer Bradley's novel *The Mists of Avalon,* and was so inspired by it that she immediately sought out this group to learn more. Bradley's best-selling novel, a mammoth retelling of the Arthurian legend from the point of view of the women involved, interprets the story as a struggle between a preexisting paganism and a Christianity in the moment of taking total power. In one workshop I attended on feminist wicca, the leader asked if anyone among the approximately twenty women present had read *The Mists of Avalon.* At least eighteen women raised their hands.[31]

Some women discovered feminist spirituality only after having been involved in some other alternative religion or in therapeutic movements. Renee Landau encountered feminist spirituality in the course of a spiritual adventure that began when she picked up a copy of *Vegetarian Times* in the waiting room of her chiropractor's office. She read about macrobiotics, contacted the organization, and eventually went to the Kushi Institute to study several levels of macrobiotic lore. This interest led her into a New Age bookstore, and it was there that she found a flyer about healing circles and became interested in crystals. When she dropped in on a healing circle, she learned that they were doing healing and meditation to prepare for the 1987 "harmonic convergence," a gathering of thousands from the alternative religious community held at 350 different "sacred sites" across the country.[32] She attended the harmonic convergence, and met some women who invited her to participate in a sweat lodge in Vermont. Later, in her naturopath's office, she saw a catalog for a local alternative education center, which advertised a "woman's circle." Having found through the sweat lodge that she enjoyed working in groups with women, she signed up for the workshop. She has been pursuing feminist spirituality ever since.[33]

Landau's odyssey is not at all unusual. Women like her bumped into feminist spirituality through 12-step groups, Native American religions, and earth spirituality.[34] Others stepped into feminist spirituality from the lesbian community. Debra Fleming drifted into a feminist witchcraft coven when she was living in Northampton, Massachusetts, and was part of the lesbian community there. As she tells it:

> I don't think it's anything I ever sought out. I think it's more a matter of that I knew women who were interested in certain things, who did certain things, and I became curious about what they were doing. I don't think that any of the structured parts of what is considered feminist spirituality have ever appealed to me very much. It just never did it for me. The little rituals, and the little charm bags . . . it just never did it for me. So I think it was more a matter of circumstance that I got interested in it. I was around women who were doing this sort of thing. But I never really initiated anything in that direction. I was intrigued and curious about what women thought about it simply because it was different and it was something women were doing that seemed very anti-Christian, so in that sense it was intriguing to me.[35]

Jade, a more zealous religious seeker, heard of feminist witchcraft through the lesbian feminist community in Louisville, Kentucky. Thrilled with the prospect of developing her psychic skills, she and a few others went to Columbus, Ohio, for a Witches and Amazons conference. Zsuzsanna Budapest spoke there, and Jade was so moved by her presentation that on the way home she told one of the women who was with her that if she only had some money, she would organize for the goddess. Jade says: "At the time I thought this was a pretty far-fetched idea, but when I returned home, the phone was ringing. It was my mother calling to tell me that my Grandmother had died and left me a small inheritance. With this I began my work organizing in the women's spiritual community."[36]

Some spiritual feminists got their start in groups that were not originally intended to be feminist spirituality groups at all. I have met several women who discovered feminist spirituality in their local Unitarian churches through their participation in the Cakes for the Queen of Heaven curriculum, which discusses ancient goddess worship and female images in Judaism and Christianity. Evelyn Hart also became involved with feminist spirituality—indirectly—through the church, in this case the Metropolitan Community Church. Some people from her local congregation formed a study group on patriarchy in the church. They found so much patriarchal influence in Christianity that they ultimately decided they had to leave the church and become a neopagan group. Evelyn heard of the transition, and joined. Oceana Woods wended her way into the feminist spirituality movement through her first pregnancy, and her decision to have a home birth. She found a midwife to deliver her child at home, and it was her midwife who connected her to a group of new mothers who had also had home births. They met together for over a year, until one day a woman asked, "Has anyone done any work with spirituality or ritual and magic?" By the end of the meeting, their mothers' support group had become a spirituality group.[37]

For Carol Schulman, the impetus to track down spiritual feminists came from a vision she had one day in the dentist's chair:

> I was at my dentist, I had not had any drugs . . . I was lying in back in the dentist's chair kind of falling asleep, very relaxed, and I had this vision of this woman of light coming up behind me, and she touched me on the back of the neck. And I got this little jolt of energy. Technically I think they call it hypnagogic imagery or something, when you have these very, very vivid dreams when you're just falling asleep, something like that. It was really interesting though, because she was behind me, but I could see her, so I really was out of my body. And she wasn't wearing clothes, she was just kind of luminous and radiant. It felt very good. And I sort of took this as a sign that I was supposed to start working with women.[38]

Barbara Otto was also drawn into feminist spirituality through a spontaneous vision. Barbara, an artist, was at the time making a series of sculptures involving webs. A friend sent her some silver veils she had discovered in the attic of her new home, which had been abandoned for many years. When Barbara received the veils, she put one on her face and walked to the mirror. As she describes it: "It's hard to explain, a vision is not the right word—epiphany maybe is a better word. It wasn't really a visual experience. . . . It was like in this flash, I understood how everything in the universe is interconnected. And I saw the universe as a web. And I said out loud, 'Spider woman.'" Later she learned that Spider Woman is a Native American deity said to be responsible for the creation of the entire world. Soon Barbara found herself organizing solstice rituals and joining a collective responsible for producing a special issue of the feminist journal *Heresies* on "The Great Goddess."[39]

Others came into feminist spirituality through a real crisis in their lives. Diane Turcott's crisis was one she had been building up to for a very long time. Her alcoholic stepfather beat her and raped her routinely for many years, with her mother's apparent approval. In her desperation to get out of the house, she got pregnant at age sixteen and married the father of her child. After bearing three children before the age of twenty-one, she left her husband, and her children were taken away from her and put into a Catholic orphanage. She tried to keep a legitimate day job so she could convince the courts that she was a fit mother, but at night she was turning tricks to earn enough money to get out to the orphanage to see her children. Diane had no success in winning her children back. Instead, she rose to the top of her profession and became a madam, running her own high-class prostitution ring out of her penthouse apartment in New York. After sixteen years in the life, she began to realize that she had never been happy. She remembers one poignant evening alone, looking at pictures of herself in beautiful clothes with famous people, and noticing that in every picture, she wore the same frozen smile. Feeling utterly out of touch with who she was, Diane sold everything and moved to the country to begin to reclaim herself. It was then that she read about feminist spirituality and molded it to fit her needs and her life.[40]

Of course, not all women's initiations into feminist spirituality were so dramatic. Some happened very gradually indeed. Karen Whiting, a Jungian therapist, put together a slide show of goddess images twelve years ago that she displayed for various women's groups. She was interested in symbols of women's power, but as she says, "I didn't make a personal spiritual connection." She even addressed the topic of goddesses as they surfaced in the dreams and thoughts of women who were seeing her for therapy. It was only after many years of intellectual interest in the goddess that Karen finally recognized a presence within herself, "a sense of power or being that I recognized as feminine." It was then that she realized that her academic interest had become quite personal, and quite spiritual.[41] She had finally found her religious home.

Most of the women who are involved with the feminist spirituality movement today had something to come home to: a religion that had a wealth of written materials and spiritual organizations. When these women first met with feminist spirituality, it was a dynamic, young religion, at most a couple decades old, but it had already begun the process of building its liturgy, mythology, and thealogy, and it was swinging wide the doors for newcomers. Earlier women of similar temperament and experience, however, had nothing to come home to: no religion—certainly not traditional ones—offered them what they sought. And so they were driven to create a new religion, a religion for women, out of the usable shreds of whatever religions they could find.

· 3 ·

The Birth of a New Religion

For those who grew up spending Sunday mornings in classrooms decorated with clay models of the temple in Jerusalem and poster-sized maps of "Bible lands," religions often appear to be quite fixed and unchanging. Of course, sometime long ago they had a birthday: Muhammad made a pilgrimage to Mecca, Jesus was born in a stable in Bethlehem, Abraham made a covenant with God. They even had a childhood, where for a few years (or a few hundred years) things weren't entirely settled. People had to decide just what these encounters with the divine portended and how they were to be interpreted. Knowledge of the new events had to be spread, and people had to be persuaded to give up their old religious ways. But by now these religions possess strength and substance, they are themselves, and they are addressed by their proper names: Islam, Christianity, Judaism. One has to advance relatively far into the world of religious education to be told that Christianity includes elements of prophetic Judaism and Greco-Roman culture, or that Islam is a creative mixture of Christianity, Judaism, and Arabic tribal religions. For most people, most of the time, traditional religions are monolithic, unassailable fortresses of preserved religious wisdom. Their teachings, their stories, their rituals are all their own: not borrowed, not retreads, but patented originals.

In contrast, something like the feminist spirituality movement looks like a hopeless junk heap of borrowed (or stolen) bits of religious detritus. Its birthday is not shrouded in the mists of time, but lives in recent memory, and everything it tries to claim as its own is trailing sod-covered roots behind it. Far from having a tradition to transmit, it has only various assemblages over which to argue. It hardly seems to have earned its own name: it is not itself, feminist spirituality, but an admixture of Jungianism, ecology, Native American religions, political feminism, paganism, Buddhism, Theosophy, and just about anything else you would care to list. And unlike Islam, Christianity, and Judaism, which proudly bear the moniker "religion," many spiritual feminists resist that label, insisting that they are not in the business of creating a religion at all, but are only exploring their female spirituality.[1]

Yet I would submit that spiritual feminists *are* creating a new religion, and doing so in the time-honored fashion of all religions—and particularly those religions in the United States that have surfaced as alternatives to the mainstream. Spiritual feminists steer clear of the term "religion" because for them it is inseparably bound up with restrictive social institutions and the demand to swallow dogma whole. Religion is for them established religion, and they have been chafing against it too long to give their new project the same family name. But I am using the term religion in a different way, drawing upon the definition offered by Joachim Wach. In his classic *Sociology of Religion*, Wach says that religion involves relation to a numinous or sacred reality, and further, that it expresses this relation in three ways: the theoretical, the practical, and the sociological. Religions are characterized by the simultaneous presence of ideas and stories about the numinous; practices such as meditation, ritual, or prayer; and the presence of groups of individuals who join to share their experiences of the sacred.[2] Spiritual feminists, with their devotion to nature or goddess and their stories of ancient matriarchies, their practice of ritual and magic, and their many groups, workshops, and retreats, are clearly practicing religion by this definition. In shuffling an old deck of religious elements with a feminist hand and slipping in a few new cards, spiritual feminists are creating a new religion in our own time.

All religions, however established and illustrious they are, were once similarly constructed from older elements. Creating a religion is always a matter of rearranging existing religious forms, taking a new slant on old practices, perhaps introducing a new element or two from outside the common cultural storehouse. Religions that survive and thrive continue this process of borrowing and refining throughout their histories, adjusting their doctrine and practices to suit new cultural and scientific insights, or to adapt and intermingle with other cultures and religions that they encounter. Still, there are differences between how religions like Christianity and Judaism and movements like feminist spirituality go about the process of religious change. The key factor that separates the two is that of social status. Established churches are, in a word, established: they are given a nodding respect and command roles as the default religions of their cultures. This does not mean that established religions cannot change, because they can and do change very quickly at times. But when they change, they do so in reference to a tradition that must at least in part be conserved, and with the presumption that where they go, the bulk of society will follow. New insights are melded with old ones, and today's wisdom is interpreted in the light of yesterday's.

This process is entirely satisfactory for many people. Some do not see religion as relevant to their lives, and are content to be nominally included in established religions while making no effort to belong. Some find all the religious answers they need right at home, in the tradition of their ancestors. Some, tormented by questions their tradition does not adequately answer, or impressed by insights that seem out of place, are able to work for religious change, adapting their experiences to the established religions in which they find themselves or adapting these religions to take account of their experiences. Others, however, find the disjuncture between experience and tradition simply too painful or religious change too slow, and they set up shop in spiritual havens far afield from their local church or temple. They may include elements from traditional religions, or even consider themselves to be a part of an established religion, but they have gone beyond the bounds of what the established religion considers acceptable deviation.

In this world of alternative religions, novelty is positively valued and tradition is not the measuring stick for change. The order of the day is not conservation, but improvisation. When established religions undergo change, they stress connection to earlier tradition. But when alternative religions dress up old ideas in new clothes, they are likely to herald the change with a new name and declare themselves a new religion.

But this is only half the story, for the central beliefs and practices of these religions, however recently reconceptualized, are believed to be very ancient. Robert Ellwood, author of *Alternative Altars*, explains:

> If anything unites the subjective experience of these [alternative religious] groups, it is conviction that what they are participating in is not rightly understood by emphasizing the smallness, recentness, and marginality of the group. . . . They will . . . insist that their group is older and deeper than the more visible churches. Thus Spiritualism, not unaware of its parallels with paleolithic shamanism, calls itself "the oldest religion in the world." Theosophy speaks of its lore as "the Ancient Wisdom." Zen claims to be the essential but unspoken message of the Buddha, if not something even older than the Enlightened One.[3]

And indeed, in this world of alternative religions, at least as it is found in the United States, there are commonalities that make of these religions another tradition, apart from and often in opposition to that of the established religions. Ellwood refers to this world of alternative religions as "the emergent tradition," indicating that it continually emerges in new forms, but is nevertheless a tradition in which certain religious symbols and patterns of individual and group identity are perpetuated over time.[4] This tradition flows alongside the established tradition, sometimes coaxing it into new territory, sometimes providing an extreme against which the establishment can situate itself. And though both establishment and emergent traditions work to separate themselves from each other and to stake out their own social space, there is still a great deal of commerce between them, with people and ideas constantly crisscrossing the boundaries.

Feminist spirituality has made its nesting grounds in the emergent religious tradition, where it has been permitted the freedom necessary to hatch a new women's religion unhampered by biblical and ecclesiastical authority. But obviously spiritual feminists did not immigrate to an unpopulated land, and the form their religion has taken is profoundly influenced by their adopted environment and their new neighbors. Spiritual feminists have created their religion out of the elements at hand, scavenging a twig here and a thread there, which along with the wares they carried from their previous homes, have formed the unique combination of elements that is feminist spirituality.

Sources of Feminist Interest in Religion

That feminists interested in creating their own religion should gravitate toward the emergent tradition is only sensible. After all, this is where the creation of alternative religions is encouraged. But it still remains to be asked why feminists would develop an interest in religion in the first place. Why not stick to getting women into public office, securing abortion rights, and interesting men in housework and typing? Looking to the early development of feminist spirituality, it seems that there were two basic motivations for the move into the emergent religious tradition: First, secular feminism gave rise to concerns with religion and spirituality for some women whose experiences with feminism were particularly all-encompassing. Second, Jewish and Christian feminism went so far beyond the bounds of orthodoxy in some quarters that a new spirituality became necessary. These two social trends came from outside the domain of alternative religions where feminist spirituality would eventually make its home. Fortunately, there was already a female, protofeminist presence in the emergent religious tradition, women who were there to welcome the influx of sisters in search of a feminist spirituality and teach them the lay of the land.

Those most important to the developing feminist spirituality movement were women practicing neopagan religions.

Secular Feminism

The journey some women took from secular feminism to feminist spirituality was direct and simple: feminism precipitated such deep and
comprehensive changes in consciousness that it already functioned as
spirituality. A sufficient change in the quantity and scope of secular
feminism became a qualitative change to religious feminism. Emily
Culpepper, a scholar of religion, observes that "as women seek tc
articulate the wholistic, primal level of change that radical feminisrr
means in their lives, reference is increasingly made to spiritual depths
of truth and knowledge." She includes herself as one of those who is
"exploring a philosophy of feminist consciousness that has inherent
spiritual dimensions." This pattern of entry into spirituality through
radical feminism was particularly marked in the lesbian community,
where for many women religion came as an unexpected but natural
outgrowth of their experiments in radical feminism. In a 1991 issue of
the *Medusan Update*, a newsletter on lesbian feminist spirituality, Billie
Potts reflects on the lesbian separatism of the 1970s, calling it "an
experiment in the politics of reversal, taking hold of our situation as
outlaw-pariah-outcast-non-conformist dykes and saying this gives us
perspective and strength, insight and freedom." One of these experiments of the 1970s was *Womanspirit*, a magazine published by a small
collective in Oregon from 1974 to 1984 that served as a weathervane
for the early feminist spirituality movement. Though not limited to
lesbian separatists, it was from the lesbian community that the greatest
energy for *Womanspirit* came. That spirituality was for these women
an acquired language rather than a mother tongue is perhaps evident
in the fact that, according to Carol Christ, early contributors to
Womanspirit hesitated to speak of goddess.[5] Apparently, the concept of
a deity smacked too much of established religion, and provoked anxiety on the part of those who were just trying to get their sea legs
underneath them for the journey into alternative spirituality.

For other women, feminism was not tantamount to a religious conversion experience, and did not naturally present itself as having spiritual depths. But a feminist perspective that began by asking why little
girls had to wear pink and big girls had to wear high heels segued
naturally into one that asked why God was a man and women's religious experiences went unnoticed. Jean Mountaingrove, one of the
founders of *Womanspirit*, describes the process in this way:

Feminism tells us to trust ourselves. So feminists began experiencing something. We began to believe that, yes indeed, we *were* discriminated against on the job; we began to see that motherhood was not all it was advertised to be. We began to trust our own feelings, we began to believe in our own orgasms. These were the first things. Now we are beginning to have spiritual experiences and, for the first time in thousands of years, we trust it.[6]

As one spiritual feminist, Rosita Veracruz, explains, once Betty Friedan's *The Feminine Mystique* prompted women to ask, "What's wrong with this picture?" the urge to question bigger and bigger pictures was set in motion, ending where questions of universal import tend to, in the world of religion.[7]

This belief that feminist spirituality is the natural outcome of feminist questioning has been reified into what might be called the movement's "myth of origins." For when spiritual feminists turn to the topic of the movement's beginnings, they are inclined to talk about consciousness-raising as the seedbed from which feminist spirituality sprang. Consciousness-raising (CR) groups were active in the late 1960s and early 1970s, and were a place where many women first began to think through what being a woman in American culture entailed. The intention, captured in the phrase "consciousness-raising," was to wake women up to an appreciation of their oppression as women and to recruit them for the feminist movement.* Early CR groups came together spontaneously, and were first called "rap sessions" or "bitch sessions," only later (around 1970) defining themselves as consciousness-raising groups. By 1972, the National Organization for Women (NOW) along with CR's pioneers, the New York Radical Feminists, took a hand in CR, helping groups to organize, providing a prepared list of discussion topics, and introducing new groups to the CR format. In 1973, probably the height of CR, 100,000 women in the United States belonged to CR groups.[8]

The basic format of CR was to select a discussion topic for the evening, and with all the women present sitting in a circle (usually from five to fifteen women), each would take turns speaking about the topic. Each woman was to be allowed to talk without interruption, and without criticism or praise from the other women, in an effort to ensure that all felt free to say whatever was on their minds. Oftentimes women discovered that experiences they had believed to be unique to them were shared by many other women, and together they began to explore

---

*It often had that effect, but there were also women who entered and exited CR without any commitment to feminism, using CR more as a way to socialize with other women or as a form of group therapy.

the reasons why. Some of the experiences women related were spiritual experiences, and one arena that came to be seen as male-defined was established religion.

It is surely true that some women began a process of questioning in CR whose end result was a denunciation of established religions and an attempt to create a religion for women. Yet the place of CR in feminist spirituality's self-understanding has become greater than the experiences of these few women (who do not make up the majority of women in the feminist spirituality movement). Now when spiritual feminists refer to CR, they see it not just as a type of discussion group, but as a ritual group, the natural predecessor of today's feminist spirituality groups. For example, Grace Shinnell, in her article "Women's Collective Spirit," writes: "Ten years ago political women began a movement from a circle. . . . We did consciousness-raising as a political/spiritual process." Or as Carol Christ puts it in *Diving Deep and Surfacing:* "Ritual forms are spontaneously emerging in every area of women's culture, not just from those whose special interest is spirituality. . . . consciousness raising can be seen as a ritual in which stories are shared and sisterhood is affirmed." The tendency to enshrine CR as the birthplace of feminist spirituality reaches its apogee in a casual reference made by Jade in *To Know: A Guide to Women's Magic and Spirituality.* In a discussion of women's exploration of the history of medieval witchcraft, she remarks, "Back in the consciousness-raising groups, which by now had turned into spirituality groups . . . ,"[9] seeming to indicate that the transition from CR to feminist spirituality was smooth, uncontested, and complete.

It can be shown fairly conclusively that there was no such comprehensive switch from CR to feminist spirituality,[10] but there is an obvious affinity between the two, as well as a real historical progression from one to the other. That spiritual feminists should hearken back to CR as their birthplace reveals much about how they perceive themselves and their movement. They could have seized upon a different homeland—for instance, feminist political demonstrations or the countercultural movements of the 1960s—but they did not, and their choice of CR is significant. CR was a place where women looked into themselves, into their personal lives, feelings, and reactions, to discover important truths about the status of women generally and the nature of a society that worked to exclude and belittle them. The move was inward, particularistic, but the discoveries were broad, even universal. In choosing CR to encapsulate a myth of their origins, spiritual feminists are seeing in CR a pattern that is essentially that of the religious quest: an inner journey, shared with other seekers, that reveals insights of cosmic importance reaching far beyond the bounds of any one individual's experience.

One final path secular feminists took into feminist religion was somewhat less direct, though it brought them to a similar place as those women who found feminism itself to be a religion, or at least a frame of reference that eventually led to matters of religious importance. This group of women took an excursion through political feminism that proved unsatisfying to them, and they turned to spiritual feminism in the hope of finding something better. Their primary disappointment with political feminism was that it did not seem to provide a position from which they could make broader criticisms of male-dominated society or from which they could create real alternatives. Political feminism sought to give women equality with men, but for many feminists this was simply not enough. They did not just want the freedom to do what men had always done (though they generally wanted that too); they also wanted the freedom to do what women had always done, but to see it valued differently. Further, they wanted to use not just traditional political means for reaching these ends, but to utilize the full range of their capabilities to live in new, self-realized ways as women, and to offer other women the cultural space to do the same.

This branch of the women's movement is sometimes called "cultural feminism," and though the term has taken on pejorative meaning for many, it remains a useful term for distinguishing the quest for political equality and gender-blindness from the effort to incorporate traditionally female values into our common life.[11] These two patterns of feminism are not mutually exclusive, but feminist spirituality encourages attention to the latter, and is frequently less interested in the former, even though it may share these goals as well. The Feminist Spiritual Community's statement of purpose provides an instructive example. In a brochure describing their feminist ideals, they list (among others): "valuing women as full human beings with all power, rights and responsibilities thereof; valuing women's contribution to the human story; valuing the roles and responsibilities traditionally delegated to women."[12] The first of these implicitly promotes gender-blindness: women are to be categorized as "full human beings," who, presumably along with men, have certain natural rights. But the second two wish to affirm values that have at least historically been the province of women, and to reclaim these as important cultural resources (contributions "to the human story") for both sexes.

Some spiritual feminists began with a commitment to gender-blindness, but eventually traded that in for an interest in women's traditional roles and quintessentially female experience. One spiritual feminist,

Rosemary Sackner, describes what she perceives as an overall shift in the feminist movement that paved the way for feminist spirituality:

> Women for a long time tried to say, "OK, we can do everything that men can do, and that's the way we're gonna get respect." And then they sort of realized in the second phase, like, "Why should we want to do everything that they do? They're assholes." But they needed to prove that first. But then to sort of go on and say, "Well, what do we want to do?" And it necessarily took itself out into different directions which men don't deal with. It was an outgrowth of the feminist movement of the sixties and seventies, but it was also a frustration in the sense that that movement didn't go far enough.[13]

Sackner's criticism is not only that the early feminist movement restricted itself to seeking political equality, but that its toolbox for effecting change was too small, and finally inadequate for the sort of sweeping social transformations she and other feminists desire. In her critique of early political feminism, Sackner goes on to say, "It did not deal with enough extrarational kinds of solutions, and sort of subversions on all levels."[14] Here spirituality is not the logical extension of political feminism, but something new: it is because political feminism cannot go far enough that these women found themselves sailing for the shores of emergent religion.

Jewish and Christian Feminism
Some women did not need to be led or driven to religious concerns by the strength of their feminism; their first language was religious, and they were already enmeshed in a religious world. These women were active in established religions when the feminist movement came along, and noticing and criticizing the male slant of these religions was an obvious focus for them. They were merely discovering the sexism in their own backyard—which is where secular feminism was encouraging them to look for it anyway. The first wave of feminism had provided important critiques of male-dominated religion, so religious feminists had foresisters to whom they could appeal. Elizabeth Cady Stanton and friends wrote a feminist exegesis of the Bible in the late 1890s under the title *The Woman's Bible;* in 1893, Matilda Joslyn Gage's *Woman, Church, and State* provided an analysis of how Judaism and Christianity worked to oppress women.[15] Infused with the vitality of a growing women's movement, feminists in traditional religions updated and expanded on this work, and their attacks on sexism gradually gained force and momentum.

Initial feminist onslaughts against established religions demanded specific reforms: women should be admitted into the rabbinate, priesthood, or ministry; hymns and prayer books should use language that included women. But increasingly, larger targets emerged: biblical texts were found to be sexist, religious ethics were seen to fit men's experience and men's interests and not those of women. Eventually, feminists in established religions took on the Big Man himself, the God who was described and invoked in almost exclusively male terms, in spite of theological apologetics that insisted on his ultimate lack of gender. Many feminists felt a sufficiently deep attachment to established religions that they remained within them to work for change. Others came to believe that traditional religions were so laced with patriarchal ideology that the surgery necessary to remove it would end up killing the patient, and, as Mary Daly puts it, they "graduated" from Christianity and religious Judaism.[16]

Mary Daly, a brilliant Catholic theologian and an ardent feminist, led the way for many women to matriculate into feminist spirituality after long years as the perennial freshmen of the established religions. In 1971, Daly was invited to be the first woman preacher in Harvard Memorial Church. Her sermon topic was "The Women's Movement: An Exodus Community." She ended her sermon by walking out of the church in protest against it, and inviting the other women present to do likewise. She defended this exodus in her sermon, saying: "We cannot really belong to institutional religion as it exists. It isn't good enough to be token preachers. . . . Singing sexist hymns, praying to a male god breaks our spirit, makes us less than human. The crushing weight of this tradition, of this power structure, tells us that *we do not even exist.*" In an article published in *Commonweal* that same year, Daly advised: "The women's movement will present a growing threat to patriarchal religion less by attacking it than by simply leaving it behind. Few of the leaders in the [women's] movement evince an interest in institutional religion, having recognized it as an instrument of their betrayal."[17]

This feminist rejection of established religions saw women's oppression in patriarchal religion occurring along many axes—theological, biblical, institutional, and so on—and all of these came in for feminist criticism. But the entire interlocking system of oppressions was finally summed up in a single metaphor: the maleness of God. Simply put, a religion with a male god is no religion for women. Mary Daly explains: "If God in 'his' heaven is a father ruling 'his' people, then it is in the 'nature' of things and according to divine plan and the order of the universe that society be male-dominated." Male gods were first condemned close to home, in Judaism and Christianity. But soon spiritual feminists were noticing male deities heading up patriarchal religions that served patriarchal societies all over the world. In *The Skeptical*

Feminist, Barbara Walker remarks: "All patriarchal societies place a father-god at the top of their inevitable hierarchy and use him as the ultimate prop for gender inequities." Or as Charlene Spretnak asserts in her essay "The Politics of Women's Spirituality": "The underlying rationale for patriarchal societies is patriarchal religion. Christianity, Judaism, Islam, and Hinduism all combine male godheads with pro-scriptions against woman as temptress, as unclean, as evil."[18]

It was a matter of some consensus among religious feminists that exclusively male language for God was not in the best interests of women. But those feminists who came to believe that the maleness of God mandated the subordination of women took this one step further. In pointing the finger back at the god of established religions, these feminists said that he was not *a* cause of women's oppression, but *the* cause: the "ultimate prop," the "underlying rationale." This is in part a social analysis of how the patriarchy operates, but for most of these women, it was also a larger comment on how the world operates. It was not only that a male god happens to be the linchpin of a patriarchal social system, but that religion is always and inevitably the distilled essence of what a culture holds valuable. Starhawk defines religion as "the soil of culture, in which belief systems, the stories, the thought-forms upon which all other institutions are based are consciously or unconsciously grown." Religion and culture are in intimate communion, with religion playing the leading role. Patriarchal religions publish the blueprint for patriarchal societies, and act as prime indoctrinator and enforcer as well.[19] The end conclusion of this line of thought is that men are able to obtain and hold control of society because they invent religions in which God is male.

This being the case, what is a feminist to do? Well, if male gods support male power, women must stop worshiping male gods. If the patriarchy is built on the foundation of patriarchal religion, male dominance will not be eroded until the foundation is razed. But more than this, a nonpatriarchal society cannot exist until a foundation has been prepared for it, a foundation that must of necessity be religious. This is the true source of the surge of religious feminists into the feminist spirituality movement. Some feminists gave up on traditional religions when they decided they were too sexist to be tolerated or reformed, but were not inspired to sashay into the world of alternative religions. They were just tired of religion altogether. But for women who came to believe that religion is necessarily a culture's building blocks, the repertoire on which it can play variations but no new themes, religion could not be abandoned. It had to be transformed.

Some religious feminists stayed within established religions and pushed for gender-neutral language for God. The women who left established religions for emergent ones felt that this reform did not go far enough. After thousands of years of masculine god language, they argued, the maleness could not be extracted from God just by changing his name. The maleness went deeper, and infected not only language, but also theology, and the images stored deep in the subconsciousness of believers. Mary Daly, after an earnest attempt to degender God, finally gave up with the publication of *Gyn/Ecology* in 1978, saying in the preface to that book: "There is no way to remove male/masculine imagery from *God*. Thus, when writing/speaking 'anthropomorphically' of ultimate reality, of the divine spark of be-ing, I now choose to write/speak gynomorphically. I do so because *God* represents the necrophilia of patriarchy, whereas *Goddess* affirms the life-loving be-ing of women and nature."[20]

If in his maleness God sanctions a patriarchal social structure, it would seem that there is none better than a goddess to remedy the situation. In her adult education curriculum *Cakes for the Queen of Heaven* Unitarian Universalist minister Shirley Ann Ranck asks wistfully, "What would it have been like to grow up in a world where God was a woman?"[21] It is a question that provokes endless fascination for spiritual feminists, and though the answer is not univocal in its particulars, all respondents seem to agree this far: it would have been very, very different.

Religious feminists, with their fluency in the language of religion, contributed much to the growing feminist spirituality movement, and particularly to the primarily secular feminists who were pulled into the orbit of the movement through the strength and urgency of their feminist concerns. But both of these groups of women entered unfamiliar territory when they came to build a new home in the emergent religious tradition. Fortunately, other women were there already, sharing many of the same concerns by virtue of their own contacts with the feminist movement.

Neopaganism and Feminism

When feminists arrived on the shores of the emergent religious tradition, the initial point of contact was with neopaganism or witchcraft. Spiritual feminists eventually spread out into most corners of the alternative religious landscape, but feminist spirituality's most important base is still pagan. This continuing contact with neopaganism has left its mark on every aspect of feminist spirituality: its thealogy, ritual, and social organization. Indeed, many spiritual feminists happily call themselves neopagans or witches, though their particular feminist adaptations of neopaganism set them apart from the mainstream of that religion. Feminist spirituality and mainstream neopaganism coexist and overlap, usually (but not always) quite happily, but they are not the same thing.

Neopaganism in America is a movement organized (or not) in much the same way as feminist spirituality. Small groups of practitioners join together on a regular basis, though probably as many practice alone. There are large festivals and retreats, magazines and newsletters, bookstores and occult supply shops, and one effort at an umbrella organization (the Covenant of the Goddess) that serves as a clearinghouse of information and a badge of respectability (and tax-exempt status) for the neopagan community. As with feminist spirituality, variety is the order of the day, and there are numerous schools of thought and types of practice available for the interested seeker, and plenty of interaction between neopaganism and other types of alternative spirituality. The number of people who are affiliated with neopaganism is difficult to estimate, since there is nothing remotely like an official membership roll. However, in a recent attempt to quantify the movement, Aidan Kelly has extrapolated from book sales, mailing lists, and festival attendance to come up with a figure of somewhere from 50,000 to 100,000 "serious adherents" of neopaganism.[22]

Neopagans believe they are reviving (and sometimes creating anew) ancient nature religions. They usually trace their genealogy to Europe, and sometimes even more narrowly to Britain. Many call their religion "witchcraft" as well as paganism, since they believe that when paganism was forced underground by the Christian church, it was passed in secret from parent to child (or believer to believer) as witchcraft. Unfortunately, witchcraft was only temporarily and intermittently tolerated by the Christian church, and eventually witches became the object of a virtual genocide in the Middle Ages. The church portrayed witches in terms similar to those that Senator Jesse Helms used in the mid-1980s in his proposed congressional legislation against witchcraft: "the use of powers derived from evil spirits, the use of sorcery, or the use of supernatural powers with malicious intent." Contemporary neopagans give quite a different definition for witchcraft, saying that the word derives from the Anglo-Saxon root *wic* meaning to bend or shape, and that wiccans (or witches) are those who can bend unseen forces to their will. Far from having malicious intent, modern witches say that they—like their persecuted predecessors—are bending unseen forces for the good of all. Time and again they stress that they are not Satanists, and have no interest in or use for the Christian devil, since their religion dates from long before Christianity. Though some neopagans have given up on the word "witch" as too laden with negative connotations, others attempt to reclaim it as a word that rightfully describes a "healer, minister, and wise person."[23]

In spite of its insistence that it dates to ancient times, neopaganism also has a more recent history, dating to 1954, when Gerald Gardner published *Witchcraft Today*. Gardner was a British folklorist, nudist, and occultist, who after his retirement in 1936 joined an occult society with connections to the Rosicrucians and Theosophists. He says that he was initiated into wicca (or witchcraft) by an old woman in 1939, a woman who had herself been initiated by someone else in a line reaching back, presumably, to the Middle Ages if not further. Gardner wrote one book on witchcraft under a pen name, and after the last of the Witchcraft Acts were repealed in Britain in 1951, he wrote two more books in his own name, *Witchcraft Today* and *The Meaning of Witchcraft*. The witchcraft he described included the worship of a goddess and a god, the officiation of a priestess, and communal rituals involving dancing, nudity, chanting, and meditation that took place on the solstices, equinoxes, and the four cross-quarter days that fall between them.[24] All these forms are still common among neopagans today. Gardner himself initiated many individuals into a neopagan practice that came to be called "Gardnerian witchcraft" after him. Some of Gardner's apprentices split from him to create different witchcraft "traditions," and other sects of witchcraft sprang up with little connection to Gardner, giving rise to the tremendous variety found in modern neopaganism.

Gardner is what many neopagans would call "a hereditary witch," claiming to have fallen heir to a tradition of witchcraft that existed prior to the twentieth century. Those who say they are hereditary witches are rare; some practitioners note that their families passed along interesting bits of folklore, but nothing akin to the comprehensive religion that Gardnerian witchcraft purports to be. But especially in its early years, hereditary witchcraft was very important to neopagans as proof that the religion they practiced had a real tradition behind it. Notebooks of charms and rituals called "books of shadows" were circulated as remnants of an earlier European witchcraft, but none were ever authenticated as such. One invocation, "The Charge of the Goddess," was used in the neopagan community for many years as a bit of "traditional" wiccan lore, but it was revealed in the late 1980s that it was the work of Doreen Valiente, a student and colleague of Gerald Gardner, who wrote it within the last forty years.[25]

Wiccan lineages and ancient practices are of less and less importance nowadays, as neopagans feel more secure in the religions they have created (or maybe only more certain that their hereditary claims will be disproved). Modern witches accept, sometimes even revel in the novelty of what they create. Still, the lure of the ancient calls to them. Gwydion Pendderwen does an excellent job of summing up how most neopagans feel about the newness of their religion: "What has come down [from the Old Religion, or paganism] is so minimal, it could be thrown out without missing it. Many groups have received nothing through apostolic succession and do not miss it. Objectively, there's very little that has gone from ancient to modern in direct succession. But subjectively, an awful lot is ancient. It is drawn from ancient materials. It represents archetypal patterns."[26]

Neopagans (who sometimes refer to themselves simply as pagans) agree on little, and count it as one of the advantages of their chosen religion that they do not have to agree. Still, many neopagans have tried to define just what holds them together, and the thing they mention most consistently is nature worship. Selena Fox, a priestess who heads up Circle Sanctuary, a pagan retreat center in rural Wisconsin, offers this description of wicca: "The Wiccan religion is a nature religion with roots that go back to pre-Christian Europe. It's a religion that focuses on communing with the divine through nature. . . . Wiccans worship the 'life force' in all people and animals, revere nature and harm no one. We believe that all of life is sacred and we see ourselves as part of a community of life forms on the planet."[27] What Fox doesn't mention is that most neopagans also worship a goddess. This is often coupled with worship of a god, and their gender polarity is frequently seen as expressing an important truth about the cosmos. But following Gardner, the goddess is usually given some kind of primacy,* and in some neopagan circles women's presence is required for rituals to occur.

The appeal of neopaganism to feminists newly arrived in the emergent religious tradition must have been tremendous: here were people already worshiping a goddess, naming women as priestesses, and talking about "the feminine." There were no elaborate rites of entry, if one wished to avoid them; groups were small and intimate, leaving ample space for individual experience; and in a religion with no central headquarters, religious hierarchies were unlikely to get in the way. For a radio show titled "The Return of the Goddess," a woman named Antiga describes her discovery of witchcraft like this:

> As I studied witchcraft, in spite of the bad name it always had, I thought it makes perfect sense for any woman to be a witch, because of the way patriarchy has treated and defined women. Any religion

---

*Some neopagans worship no deities or a goddess alone, but I have never encountered any who worship only a male god.

that gives us a female divinity, that gives us a goddess, that gives us respect for women, it just made sense to me. I still didn't think that I might ever be a witch, or that I was in fact already practicing what some other people called witchcraft, but I went on with a new moon group. The question it was based on was, what would spirituality be like if it were based on women's experience? We did what felt right to us, and a lot of what felt right to us, I later learned, were the things that witches do. One of the things was telling our story in an environment where whatever we said would be OK. Another was invoking the goddess, the female divinity, who is both inside and around us. Chanting, using candles, using incense: a lot of these things that engaged our other senses too just felt really, really good to me.[28]

Feminism and witchcraft seemed a natural match.

But well before feminists discovered neopaganism en masse, the word witch entered the feminist vocabulary in other, highly politicized terms. In New York on Halloween of 1968, a collective of women named themselves WITCH, an acronym standing for "Women's International Terrorist Conspiracy from Hell." This first group was followed by others across the United States, all of whom used the same acronym, but different names to indicate the targets of their rage: "Women Infuriated at Taking Care of Hoodlums," "Women Incensed at Telephone Company Harrassment," "Women Indentured to Traveler's [insurance company] Corporate Hell," and so on. These first feminist witches did not gather to worship nature, but to crush the patriarchy, and to do so in witty, flamboyant, and theatrical ways. They engineered various political actions, drawing on the witch theme. Robin Morgan, a principal in the WITCH movement, describes one such action dating from 1968: "At Max's Kansas City (an 'in' restaurant with The Would-Be-Beautiful People), the Coven distributed garlic cloves and cards reading: We Are Witch We Are Women We Are Liberation We Are We, chanted 'Nine Million Women, Burned as Witches' (historical fact), and questioned women customers about selling themselves like pieces of meat for the price of a dinner." The Chicago WITCH group visited the sociology department of the University of Chicago, and showered it with hair cuttings and nail clippings to protest the firing of a radical feminist professor.[29] The original WITCH manifesto reads:

WITCH is an all-women Everything. It's theater, revolution, magic, terror, joy, garlic flowers, spells. It's an awareness that witches and gypsies were the original guerrillas and resistance fighters against oppression—particularly the oppression of women—down through the ages. Witches have always been women who dared to be: groovy, courageous, aggressive, intelligent, nonconformist, explorative, curious, independent, sexually liberated, revolutionary. (This possibly explains why nine million of them have been burned.) Witches were the first Friendly Heads and Dealers, the first birth-control practitioners and abortionists, the first alchemists (turn dross into gold and you devalue the whole idea of money!). They bowed to no man, being the living remnants of the oldest culture of all—one in which men and women were equal sharers in a truly cooperative society, before the death-dealing sexual, economic, and spiritual repression of the Imperialist Phallic Society took over and began to destroy nature and human society.

WITCH lives and laughs in every woman. She is the free part of each of us, beneath the shy smiles, the acquiescence to absurd male domination, the make-up or flesh-suffocating clothing our sick society demands. There is no "joining" WITCH. If you are a woman and dare to look within yourself, you are a Witch. You make your own rules. You are free and beautiful. You can be invisible or evident in how you choose to make your witch-self known. You can form your own Coven of sister Witches (thirteen is a cozy number for a group) and do your own actions.

Whatever is repressive, solely male-oriented, greedy, puritanical, authoritarian—those are your targets. Your weapons are theater, satire, explosions, magic, herbs, music, costumes, cameras, masks, chants, stickers, stencils and paint, films, tambourines, bricks, brooms, guns, voodoo dolls, cats, candles, bells, chalk, nail clippings, hand grenades, poison rings, fuses, tape recorders, incense— your own boundless beautiful imagination. Your power comes from your own self as a woman, and it is activated by working in concert with your sisters. The power of the Coven is more than the sum of its individual members, because it is *together.*

You are pledged to free our brothers from oppression and stereotyped sexual roles (whether they like it or not) as well as ourselves. You are a Witch by saying aloud, "I am a Witch" three times, and *thinking about that.* You are a Witch by being female, untamed, angry, joyous, and immortal.[30]

Though never pretending to be a spiritual group, and probably unaware of the neopagan revival in America, WITCH anticipated several of the motifs of the feminist spirituality movement that was to follow upon the meeting of feminism and neopaganism. WITCH justified its existence by citing its political mission ("witches and gypsies were the original guerrillas and resistance fighters against oppression"); it posited a long-dead golden age ("the oldest culture of all . . . a truly cooperative society"); named nature as one of the patriarchy's primary victims (along with human society); and rested its social analysis on the single cornerstone of male domination ("the Imperialist Phallic

Society"). It advocated creativity and independence, and exulted in the innovative use of all manner of media to communicate personal and political views. But the most significant aspect of WITCH was its choice of central symbol: the witch. By choosing this symbol, feminists were identifying themselves with everything women were taught not to be: ugly, aggressive, independent, and malicious. Feminists took this symbol and molded it—not into the fairy tale "good witch," but into a symbol of female power, knowledge, independence, and martyrdom.

This latter association with witchcraft, that of martyrdom, was particularly important to early feminists. Mary Daly in her 1973 book *Beyond God the Father*, and Andrea Dworkin in 1974 with *Woman Hating*, laid the groundwork for a feminist martyrology by researching the witch persecutions of the Middle Ages and labeling them "gynocide," the purposeful murder of women. This theme was further developed in Daly's 1978 work *Gyn/Ecology*, in which the witch burnings were portrayed as an instance of the patriarchal "Sado-Ritual Syndrome," a pattern of the abuse of women that Daly locates cross-culturally and trans-historically. For Daly and those who followed her, words like "witch," "hag," "crone," and "spinster" became titles of honor, capturing the proud spirit of those women who remained true to themselves and their sisters even in the face of persecution.[31] This identification of women with witchcraft was not an explicitly religious one. Women were not named witches because they worshiped a goddess in circles in the woods or because they made herbal charms to encourage prophetic dreaming. Women were named witches because they refused to submit to demeaning and limiting roles, even knowing that this rebellion might literally cost them their lives.

Witchcraft was fast becoming a feminist symbol, even a religiously charged one, dealing as it did with ultimate commitment and ultimate value. But it was a symbol without a practice. It still remained for someone to lower the drawbridge and let religious neopaganism out and feminists in. The first to take on this task was Zsuzsanna Budapest, the closest thing feminist spirituality has to a founder. Budapest grew up in Hungary and took her city's name as her own when as a teenager she left for the West to escape the failing Hungarian revolution. Later, after immigrating to the United States and leaving her marriage, she moved to Los Angeles and became very active in the women's movement: organizing protests, attending meetings, helping to form an antirape squad. But, like others, she came to believe that the women's movement needed a women's religion, and she proposed to give it one. In this, Budapest did not come without resources: she claimed to be the heir of a witchcraft tradition at least eight hundred years old, inherited from her mother, Masika Szilagyi. According to

Budapest, Masika was initiated into witchcraft by Victoria, a household servant, who in addition to teaching Masika psychic skills, took her into the woods at night to meet with groups of witches who invoked the goddess, sang of ancient shamans, and spat into the fire. Masika communed with the dead in her dreams, and could speak ancient Egyptian while in a trance, a talent Budapest attributes to Masika's previous incarnation as a priestess of Hathor in ancient Egypt. In her *Holy Book of Women's Mysteries*, Budapest includes materials she received from her mother, including her "book of superstitions," "book of dreams," "book of cures," and "book of sorrows." They are a treasure trove of Eastern European folk wisdom, including such gems as: "If a bird shits on you, you will have good luck all that day if you don't wipe it off until the following day"; "If you bang your elbow into a corner, an unexpected visitor will soon arrive"; and "If you are chased by wild animals in your dreams, it simply means you ate too much dinner."[32]

If these provided the seeds for Budapest's women's religion, the sprouting and blossoming were strictly her doing, and that of her feminist sisters. Budapest's experiments in feminist witchcraft began in 1971, when she and a few friends celebrated the winter solstice together. They named themselves the Susan B. Anthony Coven No. 1, to stress their commitment to feminism—and, it would seem, to express their hope that others would follow in their footsteps, adding covens numbers 2, 3, 4, et seq. And others did follow, though with names of their own: the Amelia Earhart Coven in New York, the Elizabeth Gould Davis Coven in Florida, the Sojourner Truth Coven in the Catskills, the Jane Addams Coven in Chicago, and the Elizabeth Cady Stanton Coven in Orange County, California. The Susan B. Anthony Coven itself grew rapidly, by its founders' reports, from the six women who met at the 1971 winter solstice, to seven hundred initiated members just nine years later.[33] Women came and went, and there were never seven hundred women meeting at one time, but it is reported that Budapest led rituals in the 1970s where attendance was well over one hundred.

The original intentions of the Susan B. Anthony Coven No. 1 are made clear in their manifesto:

> We believe that Feminist witches are wimmin* who search within themselves for the female principle of the universe and who relate as daughters to the Creatrix.

*Alternative spellings of "woman" (womon), "women" (wimmin, womyn), and "human" (hummin), are used by some feminists to avoid the inclusion of the root words "man" and "men" in language referring to women alone or to people in general.

We believe that just as it is time to fight for the right to control our bodies, it is also time to fight for our sweet womon souls.

We believe that in order to fight and win a revolution that will stretch for generations into the future, we must find reliable ways to replenish our energies. We believe that without a secure grounding in womon's spiritual strength there will be no victory for us.

We believe that we are part of a changing universal consciousness that has long been feared and prophesized by the patriarchs.

We believe that Goddess-consciousness gave humanity a workable, long-lasting, peaceful period during which the Earth was treated as Mother and wimmin were treated as Her priestesses. This was the mythical Golden Age of Matriarchy.

We believe that wimmin lost supremacy through the aggressions of males who were exiled from the matriarchies and formed the patriarchal hordes responsible for the invention of rape and the subjugation of wimmin.

We believe that female control of the death (male) principle yields hummin evolution.

We are committed to living life lovingly towards ourselves and our sisters. We are committed to joy, self-love, and life-affirmation.

We are committed to winning, to surviving, to struggling against patriarchal oppression.

We are committed to defending our interests and those of our sisters through the knowledge of witchcraft: to blessing, to cursing, to healing, and to binding with power rooted in womon-identified wisdom.

We are opposed to attacking the innocent.

We are equally committed to political, communal, and personal solutions.

We are committed to teaching wimmin how to organize themselves as witches and to sharing our traditions with wimmin.

We are opposed to teaching our magic and our craft to men until equality of the sexes is reality.

Our immediate goal is to congregate with each other according to our ancient womon-made laws and to remember our past, renew our powers and affirm our Goddess of the Ten-thousand Names.[34]

The Susan B. Anthony Coven manifesto provides an interesting counterpoint to the WITCH manifesto. It is more unabashedly religious in scope than the WITCH manifesto (which never mentions goddess or indeed any transcendent principle). Its worldview is more apocalyptic, stating with certainty that women in general and witches in particular must lead the revolution that ushers in a new age. Finally, it assumes that there is a "magic" and a "craft" that can be learned, a body of knowledge both desirable and powerful. WITCH's magic, in contrast, is available to any woman who chooses to invent it. The difference between the two manifestos is indicative of the progression from radical feminism to feminist religion.

Though Zsuzsanna Budapest was a ground-breaking figure in the feminist move to neopaganism, she was not alone. In addition to the women working with her, there were other women across the country building bridges between feminism and paganism: some by reaching out to existing wicca groups in their areas, some by radicalizing the covens of which they were already members, some by creating new groups with new traditions. By the mid-1970s, resources were beginning to become available in the women's community, and feminists were able to invent their religion secure in the knowledge that there was a groundswell of feminist energy behind them. Interest in witchcraft as women's persecution history broadened into inquiry into ancient goddess worship. The publication of Merlin Stone's *When God Was a Woman* in 1976, a study of representations of prehistoric goddesses woven together with a story of their overthrow in historical times, gave the feminist wicca movement credibility in new quarters, and inspired more women to search out the supposed surviving remnants of ancient goddess worship in neopaganism.[35] Feminist imagery and politics was rapidly becoming feminist spirituality, as women went beyond talking about witches and goddesses as symbols of female power, and started to become them and worship them.

Yet the meeting of feminists and neopagans was not one big happy family reunion, with everyone rushing deliriously into each other's arms. The neopagan movement was small, and feminists entered in numbers large enough to make a real impact. Moreover, they did not usually enter humbly and meekly, asking if they might please be initiated into the wise ways of the witches. Quite the contrary, they flung open the doors, squared their shoulders, and swaggered in, ready to rearrange the furniture. And in spite of substantial areas of shared interest, there were real differences between the newly anointed feminist witches and neopagans of older vintage.

The first point of conflict was that feminists by and large had no interest in sharing their circles with men, and precious little interest in worshiping a god of any sort. With their palate not yet conditioned to savor the new tastes of the emergent religious tradition, they often were impatient with the measured pageantry and role-playing that characterized some neopagan rituals or for the encyclopedic lists of greater and lesser divinities and spirits. They wanted to worship a goddess—a big one, bigger than the god of patriarchy—and they wanted to worship themselves through her. For many traditional neopagans, this was anathema. Polytheism and gender duality were considered essential parts of witchcraft: if true magic were to happen, both male and female deities had to be invoked, and according to some, both women and men had to be present, fulfilling their gender-prescribed tasks. A further conflict was that most neopagans valued secrecy, partly out of fear of persecution, but also out of a love of the concept of hidden lore, of mystical truths that could only be revealed to the initiated few. Feminist witches, in contrast, tended to be more evangelical, wanting to get the good word out to their sisters. Far from insisting on long periods of training and gradual initiation into higher mysteries, feminist witches hearkened back to a phrase from the WITCH manifesto: "You are a Witch by being female . . . " They encouraged one another to form covens of the utterly inexperienced, to make things up as they went along, and to publish accounts of what worked for them so that others could draw on their experience.[36]

Another complicating factor was that a number of practicing mainstream neopagans were sexist, a rude surprise to feminists who thought they had left all that behind in established religions. Oceana Woods, an active spiritual feminist, reports her disappointment with the world of witchcraft: "The first ritual of a witchcraft coven that I ever went to, there was a man there who was a witch, who worshiped the Goddess, who owned a bookstore that sold pornography. Now I have a problem with this. I have a real problem with this. . . . While that is witchcraft, and that is a coven, I don't feel that that . . . truly would be considered feminist spirituality."[37] Even women who entered the world of witchcraft before it was in feminist vogue voiced complaints about the sexism of modern neopaganism, complaints more likely to receive a hearing once feminists involved themselves in that world in significant numbers. Lady Miw, owner of a magic and occult supply store in New York, remembers:

> When I got into Gardnerian wicca—which I adore, I am Gardnerian, proud to be Gardnerian—I couldn't understand why just because I was a woman, why I couldn't draw down the moon into another woman. The men didn't like this at all. I thought, well if we're witches, and we're spiritual, and this is a spiritual thing here, then I'm not female and I'm not male. I'm female *and* male. And everybody in this circle is female and male. So does it really matter on a physical plane of consciousness if I sit next to a man or a woman? . . . if I'm male and female, and the guy is male and female, the same thing, isn't that sort of like really Baby Wicca 101?[38]

The downside of the feminist/neopagan combination notwithstanding, overall the combination has proved to be a productive one. The success of the relationship owes much to Starhawk, a witch, feminist, and widely read pagan author. Starhawk found witchcraft and feminism around the same time, and though she saw them as having a real compatibility, she was not specifically drawn into one as the result of her interest in the other, as many women were. Having already been exposed to neopaganism, she was introduced to feminist witchcraft in the early 1970s by Zsuzsanna Budapest.[39] Starhawk's covens are not all separatist (men are allowed to participate and be initiated), but her writings are insistently feminist, and it is clear that she regards witch-craft's attitude toward women and the female to be among its greatest strengths. In many ways, Starhawk has served as a translator and mediator between feminists and neopaganism: she has worked with gender polarity, but evolved away from it; she has developed convinc-ing thealogical justifications for conceiving of goddess as both mono-theistic and polytheistic; she has carved out a central, indisputable place for women without excluding men; and she has praised flexibility and creativity while upholding the value of things taken to be tradition-ally pagan.

Today there is considerably less friction between feminist witchcraft and the broader neopagan movement than there was initially. There are several reasons for this, one of which is that over the past twenty years of cohabitation, feminist witches have become acculturated to the neopagan world. Things that they initially found odd or off-putting—ceremonial tools and language, polytheism, male deities—have become familiar, even beloved to them, and in some cases have been incorpo-rated into their practice. And for neopagans, feminists are no longer angry alien infiltrators in a settled world of happy, naked, dancing nature-worshipers; they have become a part of the scenery. Finally, controversy between the two parties has lessened in part because the feminists won their right to the goddess. By sheer force of numbers and enthusiasm, their success drowned out all but the most hardened opposition. Neopaganism flourishes today, perhaps more feminist and less hierarchical in flavor than it was before, and feminist witchcraft flourishes alongside and to some extent within it. The most deter-minedly feminist witches are sometimes called "Dianic," and they often prefer their own company to that of the broader neopagan com-munity. Zsuzsanna Budapest originally called her witchcraft Dianic, and the term has been taken over particularly by lesbian witches, but also by women, heterosexual or lesbian, who are separatist in their practice.[40]

In the wider world of feminist spirituality, however, Dianic witches are in the minority, and neopaganism is more of a subtext than a centrally defining feature. The symbol of the witch still plays a role in spiritual feminist circles, if a somewhat less dramatic one than it used to. In an interesting echo of the WITCH movement, another acronym has made its way onto T-shirts and the letterhead of at least one spiritual feminist group: "Wild Independent-Thinking Crones and Hags." A token use of the symbol of the witch can also be seen in some of the songs that are popular in the feminist spirituality movement; for instance, one very bouncy, upbeat tune with these lyrics:

> Who are the witches, where do they come from?
> Maybe your great-great grandmother was one.
> Witches are wise, wise women they say;
> There's a lot of witch in every woman today.[41]

But many women find it too difficult to rehabilitate the word "witch" from its negative connotations, and finally pointless. They feel that they can better communicate their identity to others in different words, or are reluctant to label themselves at all. Recently it has become more common to think of the word witch as denoting a practitioner of wicca, and many women avoid applying the term to themselves simply because they perceive their spirituality as being broader in scope. Other women do not call themselves witches because they see witchcraft as a religion that is wholly derived from European roots. (Luisah Teish, for example, explains that spiritual women in the African traditions prefer to call themselves "root woman," "ju-ju woman," or "two-headed woman" rather than "witch.")

In the feminist spirituality movement today, there is a subtle trend away from identifying oneself as a witch. Partly this is a transition into a more free-form type of spirituality precipitated by a growing conviction on the part of feminists that what they are doing counts as religion in its own right, without the added status conferred by an affiliation with neopaganism. As Anne Carson notes in the preface to her bibliography on feminist spirituality, "As the 1980s progress there seems to be less of an interest in witchcraft per se among feminists, at least in terms of ritual practice, as we begin to leave behind one traditional structure in order to create our own visions and philosophies." Dianic witchcraft has acted as a launching pad for a spiritual movement that is now far more diverse, reaching far beyond neopaganism, into Native American religions, other world religions, New Age practices, and even—sporadically—Jewish and Christian feminism.[42]

· 4 ·

Affinities and Appropriations

With some feminists having established a beachhead in the neopagan community in the early 1970s, women felt increasingly free to fan out into the alternative religious tradition in their quest for a truly feminist spirituality. The alliances they formed there greatly expanded feminist spirituality's religious repertoire, setting the stage for the religious diversity that characterizes feminist spirituality today.

The influx of feminists into alternative religions in the early 1970s was not entirely without precedent. The emergent religious tradition has long been sympathetic toward women, and to at least a variant of feminist politics, in ways that the established tradition has not. One of the main symbols of alternative religion that Robert Ellwood notes appearing throughout American religious history is that of women's leadership and "feminine identity in the divine."[1] In this sense, feminist spirituality is not radically, but only relatively new. The alternative religious tradition has long provided a refuge for women (and men) to incorporate femaleness into divinity, to experience gender religiously, and to offer women special religious roles. But the emergent religious tradition feminist spirituality entered in the early 1970s was in a state of great agitation and flux. While it had not disavowed any of its traditional openness toward women and the female, it had been revivified, expanded, and seen its foci shift into new territories through the agency of the countercultural movements of the 1960s. There was considerable overlap between feminist interests and countercultural ones, in part because many of the individuals who made up the developing feminist spirituality movement already had a charter membership in the counterculture. Some of the key elements of the counterculture were taken up by women and given a feminist spin: The alternative forms of healing that the counterculture advocated resonated with the feminist desire to take women's bodies out from under the control of a patriarchal medical establishment. The back-to-nature movement and concerns with ecology became in feminist hands an analysis of the similarities between the patriarchy's treatment of nature and its treatment of women, and a demand for new models. Countercultural enthusiasm for bodily pleasure translated into the rescue of women from the constrictive sexual options of madonna and whore, and a potential sanctification of women's sexuality.

With common ground like this, the path to a feminist spirituality was greatly smoothed. Spiritual feminists came into contention with certain aspects of the counterculture (and the emergent religious tradition of which it was a part), but in the main they were given a forum in which they had sufficient freedom to meld their feminist insights with religious practices. With a whole religious world at their fingertips and the permission to pick and choose, feminists set about claiming religious images and practices that enhanced women's power. In 1975, Susan Rennie and Kirsten Grimstad reported that this process of feminist religious syncretism was already well underway. Rennie and Grimstad traveled throughout the United States acquiring material for *The New Woman's Survival Catalog*, and this is what they found:

> Wherever there are feminist communities, women are exploring psychic and non-material phenomena; reinterpreting astrology; creating and celebrating feminist rituals around birth, death, menstruation; reading the Tarot; studying pre-patriarchal forms of religion, reviving and exploring esoteric goddess-centered philosophies such as Wicce; developing and cultivating dream-analysis, ESP, astral projection, precognition; learning psychic and homeopathic healing; rescuing the wholistic perspective of the right hemisphere of the brain from the contempt of left-brained linear-mindedness; practising meditation and yoga; rewriting the *I Ching*; revolutionizing our food and natural resource consciousness of our connectedness with the rest of the biosphere.[2]

From the length of this list, it would seem that when feminists turned themselves loose in the world of alternative religions to choose religious practices empowering for women, they decided to pick everything. There is a lot of truth to this observation. For almost every religious artifact in the emergent religious tradition today, there is a feminist counterpart: there are many books on astrology, and a few on feminist astrology; many guides to homeopathic healing, and a few on women's homeopathic healing; many Buddhist sanghas (communities), and a few for women exclusively; and so on. Feminist spirituality cuts across the emergent religious milieu, giving a feminist echo for every shout, and sometimes shouting loud enough itself to provoke the rest of the alternative religious tradition to echo with new ideas.

Affinities

The New Age Movement

Apart from neopaganism, the most significant source for spiritual feminist ideas and practices has been the New Age movement. An obvious reason for this is not only the prominence of the New Age movement in the past ten to twenty years, but its breadth. In a sense, "New Age" has taken over where "counterculture" left off, setting a name to the impulse to explore non-Western religions, occult practices, and innovative forms of psychotherapy freely and indiscriminately, apart from any commitment to a single religious institution. In a journalistic account of the New Age movement, Russell Chandler, religion writer for the *Los Angeles Times*, traces the movement's roots to sources as various as Hinduism, Buddhism, Western occultism, the oracles of ancient Greece and Egypt, Abraham Maslow's theory of self-actualization, transcendental meditation, and Werner Erhard's "est" seminars. The subjects he chooses to treat as properly New Age include crystals and pyramids, Native Americans and shamans, goddesses and neopagans, holistic health and healing, and general principles of mind over matter. He cites J. Gordon Melton as dating the movement's beginnings to 1971, when the *East-West Journal* was first published and when Baba Ram Dass (formerly Richard Alpert) released his first book.[3] "New Age" in this account begins to sound like the counterculture with less drugs, less music, and more religion.

The attentive reader will have noticed that Chandler includes "goddesses and neopagans" among those things he calls New Age, and he specifically mentions feminist spirituality as belonging in this category. Certainly the feminist spirituality movement and the New Age movement rub up against one another frequently enough. Classes and workshops in feminist spirituality are offered through New Age centers; spiritual feminists patronize New Age shops in their area to purchase incense, jewelry, and books; articles on women's spirituality make their way into New Age journals.[4] Because there is so much overlap between the two movements—and because the New Age is the larger of the two—it sometimes seems as though feminist spirituality is merely the women's auxiliary of the New Age movement, occupying a position similar to that held by the women's mission society or ladies' prayer breakfast in a Protestant church. This implies that the New Age movement came first, and that feminist spirituality sent branches off of it when there were a sufficient number of women interested in developing their New Age spirituality in a particularly feminist or female way. It is true that many women first involved themselves in countercultural or New Age spiritualities, and only later came to experience them as feminist, but there is also a contingent of women who came into these spiritualities for specifically feminist reasons. Also, it is important to remember that if the dating system Melton advocates is accepted, the New Age movement and feminist spirituality were started at essentially the same time. It would seem more reasonable then to think of feminist spirituality and the New Age movement as following related, but not identical paths.

Nevertheless, it is also impressive to note the influence of the New Age on feminist spirituality, because it is ubiquitous. Throughout spiritual feminist literature, there is discussion of crystals, chakras, channeling, past life regressions, astrology, and other topics usually taken to be New Age in provenance. (There are also interesting echos of earlier alternative religions: references to astral bodies and etheric doubles that are reminiscent of Theosophy.) Spiritual feminists report having their astrological charts analyzed, going to rebirthing seminars, consulting with healers, and so forth, sometimes through other spiritual feminists who are taking a feminist approach to these activities, but often through the broader New Age network.[5]

Therapy as Religion
Feminist spirituality has also been influenced by the presence of therapeutic groups in the emergent religious tradition, particularly by the 12-step programs first developed through Alcholics Anonymous. Some of the rhetoric of these programs ("Higher Power," "working the steps") is heard at spiritual feminist retreats, and meetings and workshops with therapeutic foci are offered for those who wish to attend. For example, at the 1990 Womongathering retreat, a workshop titled "Bodywork for Adult Children of Alcoholics" was on the program, and the description of the workshop made no mention of feminism, women's experience, goddesses, or anything else that made a direct tie back to the feminist spirituality movement. There is also a move afoot to take the 12-step programs many women have found helpful and interpret them in a manner more in accord with feminist spirituality's thealogy.[6]

Vicki Noble, known among spiritual feminists for her design of a new feminist tarot deck, describes women's involvement in therapeutic programs:

> All over the United States, women are in "recovery." We are seeing private therapists and joining groups to talk about our pain and

helplessness around incest, rape, pregnancy, "loving too much," over-eating, being abused by our husbands, and all the addictions to the various substances our culture offers for the dulling of pain and awareness, and the escape into denial that has characterized our lives. It is time we name this "recovery movement" and see it in the broadest sense possible, so that we include all the women who are choosing to get well. Women are choosing to heal ourselves from the world illness of Patriarchy.[7]

Noble here works to claim all types of therapy, traditional and alternative, individual and collective, as part of a spiritual feminist project. Indeed, concerns that are generally labeled therapeutic—recovering from childhood trauma, for example—are a common focus of spiritual feminist thought and ritual action.

Jungianism

Another resource for feminist spirituality, one that emerged early in the history of the movement, is Jungianism. For a movement interested in experimenting with different images of women, Jung had much to offer. Not only did he elevate femaleness and female power to a degree that mainstream society did not, he also gave spiritual feminists a theoretical structure through which they could validate their personal experiences of goddesses as legitimate knowledge. Through the theory of archetypes and the collective unconscious, women could conceive of goddess images as something more than merely modern inventions (an important contribution to the movement in the days before archaeological evidence of alleged ancient goddess worship had been widely disseminated). Spiritual feminists often employ the theory of archetypes in their spirituality, whether they mention Jung explicitly or not. As one woman explains in the spiritual feminist newsletter *Of a Like Mind*: "These [goddess-inspired] images represent archetypes that dwell, slumbering, in the deepest parts of our souls. Awaken their presence in your life through meditation, visualization, and interior dialogue. . . . The Goddesses have much to say to us if we can be still and . . . listen."[8]

What the New Age movement, therapeutic programs, and Jungianism have in common is that they are all European-American and modern in orientation and thus draw on the "home" tradition of the predominantly white adherents of feminist spirituality. But much of feminist spirituality's borrowing is from other cultural and religious traditions—including Eastern, ancient Greek, Native American, and African religions—and these materials must be appropriated.

Appropriations

Ancient Religions
Probably the greatest area of feminist borrowing is from ancient cultures. It is not the intent of spiritual feminists to reconstruct and replicate ancient goddess worship, but to find images and myths they can use today in their own feminist way. Carol Christ describes this relationship of spiritual feminists to ancient goddess symbols in her book *Laughter of Aphrodite: Reflections on a Journey to the Goddess:*

> Though nourished by ancient symbols of Goddesses from around the world, women's imagination is by no means subject to the authority of the past. Instead, modern women joyfully discover what is useful to us in the past and reject what is not. We understand that many symbols of the Goddess have come down to us from patriarchal cultures, and, using feminism as a principle of selection, we reject those aspects of ancient mythologies that picture Goddesses as legitimizers of the power of men.[9]

Myths featuring goddesses that come down to us from cultures all over the globe are lovingly retold—sometimes reinterpreted—by spiritual feminists. They are often a part of ritual, and certainly a favorite reading subject. Artistic reproductions of female statuettes recovered from archaeological sites (particularly European and Middle Eastern ones) are printed in books and calendars, placed on altars, or worn in the form of jewelry. Such images are often the subject of meditation or group discussion, and they play an important role in the movement's reconstruction of Western history.

Eastern Religions
Another fertile field spiritual feminists harvest is that of Eastern religions (here taken to mean religions found east of Europe and south of Russia). Spiritual feminists have encountered Eastern religions mostly in the context of their presence within the emergent religious tradition in the United States,[10] though occasionally through individual pilgrimage to Eastern centers of religious practice and learning. They have found much to like about Eastern religions, including meditation and chanting rituals as taught by Buddhists and Hindus of all stripes; alternative forms of healing such as acupuncture; dietary programs like macrobiotics; and movement traditions such as hatha yoga, taiji, sufi dancing, traditional Indian dance, and Soaring Crane Qigong. In addition to adopting specific practices, many spiritual feminists have been

drawn toward the East for more general qualities they find in Eastern religions. They condemn Western religions and Western gods as punitive and guilt-producing, while praising Eastern religions as spiritualities of growth, holism, and integration that allow the believer to pursue spiritual growth over many lifetimes.[11]

But of the many things that spiritual feminists find to love in Eastern religions, it is above all their goddesses that attract the attention of spiritual feminists. In Eastern religions spiritual feminists discover the living remnants of what they believe was once a worldwide phenomenon of goddess worship. Where Western cultures have virtually rubbed out any female presence in the divinity, they argue, Eastern cultures have retained it. As Sharon Logan asserts, "the real lineages are still Eastern religions: Hinduism, Tibetan Buddhism, and Tantra." Even women whose natural inclination is not toward the East have nevertheless been moved to embrace its goddesses. Luisah Teish, who in the late 1960s and early 1970s rejected Eastern religions as distractions from Western politics, has since become interested in Eastern goddesses. She explains, "It was feminism that made me cast my eyes eastward. The Eastern Goddesses Sarasvati, Quan Yin, and the Green Tara took their places on my altars." Some Eastern goddesses have been so thoroughly incorporated into feminist spirituality that their specific origins have been lost altogether. For example, one spiritual feminist listed her favorite goddesses for me: Kali, Tara, Artemis, Aphrodite, Isis. She keeps a statue of Tara on her altar, and uses this image in her meditation practice. However, when I asked her what tradition Tara came from, she was unsure, saying it was either Hindu or Buddhist; something Eastern at any rate.[12]

Overall, spiritual feminists are enthusiastic about the adoption of the goddesses of Eastern religions, but there are some dissenting, or at least uncertain voices. Spiritual feminists who actively dissent from the consensus excoriate Eastern religions for their demand that women sacrifice their egos—which are poorly enough developed as it is—and for their hostility toward life in the body and in the world. Monica Sjöö and Barbara Mor, in a comprehensive work titled *The Great Cosmic Mother,* castigate Buddhism in this way: "The sexual misers and misogynists of Buddhism, practicing a secret and dangerous self-indulgence in the form of spiritual nihilism, leading to institutionalized sadism, neglect, and hatred of their fellow creatures, are very similar to the patriarchal monastic Christian world of the European Middle Ages." Several women interviewed were more moderate in their criticisms, saying they were happy to bring Eastern goddesses into feminist spiritual practice, but disturbed by the patriarchal nature of the religions and cultures from which these goddesses have been taken. They note an uncomfortable discrepancy between the powerful goddess images of these cultures and the treatment of women in the same cultures, and conclude, as does Rosemary Sackner, "You can pull stuff out of [the religions of India, China, and Japan], but you can't just accept the whole thing any more than you could Christianity." Marguerite Keane, who is herself involved with Hindu and Buddhist meditation in addition to and as part of her feminist spiritual practice, remarks, "Everything has the overlay, the accretion of patriarchy."[13]

Others feel a real affection for Eastern religions, and want to continue to practice them in some form, but have experienced despair in the course of their efforts to relate to the organized manifestations of these religions in the United States. They say that they have been disappointed by the hierarchical nature of their leadership, by some of the traditional texts and liturgies that are antifemale, and especially by the sexual improprieties of male leaders, gurus, and masters. Such experiences have, in a backward way, strengthened feminist spirituality: Women who might otherwise have stuck to an early, exclusive commitment to a particular Eastern tradition have been cast back on their feminist sisters for a sense of community. They have begun to search out other, non-Eastern religious traditions to complement and "feminize" their Buddhist or Hindu practice.[14] Though such women may still describe themselves first as Buddhist or Hindu, the combination of their syncretistic mood and their feminist hermeneutic brings them closely into the orbit of the feminist spirituality movement.

Native American Religions
The most popular source for feminist religious borrowing over the last decade has been Native American religions. These days at feminist spirituality workshops and retreats, one is as likely to run across the symbols and rituals of Native American religions as those of wicca. (This dissemination of Native American spirituality is not limited to feminist spirituality, but is permeating the entire emergent religious culture.) A key figure in the growing connection between women and Native American religions is Lynn Andrews. In 1981, Andrews adopted a Native American mentor and began a series of books lauding Native American connection to nature. These books also revealed the existence of a secret sorority of spiritual women from tribal cultures, adding gender to the old brew of vision quests and medicine bundles.[15] Like Carlos Castaneda before her, Andrews is widely suspected of creating her Native American mentors and their marvelous experiences in the privacy of her own home, though she has always insisted that her books and the characters in them are not fictional. Lynn Andrews is rarely praised very highly by spiritual feminists, but

some say they have enjoyed her books; it is certainly true that she has been largely responsible for precipitating and feeding an interest in Native American spirituality among white women.

The title "medicine woman," like "witch" before it, has now found its way into the spiritual feminist vocabulary (though it lacks the common currency in the feminist movement as a whole that "witch" has enjoyed). In her flyer "The Modern Medicine Woman," Shirley Schnirel of Rising Signs, an organization in Utah, reassures women that "either you already are, or have the potential to be, a modern Medicine Woman," regardless of ethnic ancestry. She describes a medicine woman as "a woman who works with natural healing energies of her own mind and hands, a teacher, a listener, a caretaker of the earth (including water and air), and a protector of earth's children, including the two-footed, the four-footed, the winged, and the water creatures." The annual Medicine Woman Retreat offered by Rising Signs with the multiple subtitles "Exploring Your Shamanic Path, Reconnecting with the Ancient Mother, Meeting Your Personal Power Animal, Creating a Sacred Sisterhood" is a potpourri of what happens when feminist spirituality meets Native American religions.[16]

Those spiritual feminists who adopt Native American religions (or pieces of them) are mostly European-American women, but there is a core of Native American women who act as teachers and leaders and grant a certain legitimacy to the project. Among the most prominent of these Native American teachers are Brooke Medicine Eagle and Dhyani Ywahoo. They and others like them say that they have been instructed by their elders or spirit guides to release formerly secret teachings to outsiders so that they may be of use in the present perilous age. Though their teachings are predominantly Native American, they are also eclectic: Dhyani Ywahoo is the director of the Sunray Meditation Society in Vermont, which combines Native American spirituality with Tibetan Buddhism; Brooke Medicine Eagle receives guidance from "the Masters of Light" (her Native spiritual guides), but also draws on Feldenkrais practice and Neurolinguistic Programming.[17]

Spiritual feminist interest is focused less on living Native American cultures and more on what is reported about preconquest Native American cultures. A seminal work in this area is *Daughters of Copper Woman*, by Anne Cameron, in which a series of origin tales—all of them featuring strong female characters—are transcribed from the oral tradition of the Native Americans of Vancouver Island. In addition, Cameron includes stories of the coming of Europeans to the island, and the dreadful events that ensued, not the least of which was the subjection of women. Cameron asserts that these tales come from women "who are members of a secret society whose roots go back

beyond recorded history to the dawn of Time itself. . . . A few dedi-
cated women [who] belong to a matriarchal, matrilineal society." Just
as spiritual feminists are drawn to Eastern goddesses as remnants of
an earlier matriarchal, goddess-worshiping culture, they are drawn to
Native American mythology and culture (and Native American women
themselves, as mythic stand-ins) as remnants of a more recent matriarchy. In a workshop titled "Sharing the Medicine Bundle: A Giveaway
from the Grandmothers," the leader, Amy Lee, made casual reference
to her heritage in "the Iroquois matriarchy"; in an article titled "Cultural Robbery: Imperialism, Voices of Native Women," Jeanette C.
Armstrong explains that in her own Okanogan culture—precontact—
there was no rape, the dignity of women was protected, and their
language contained nothing corresponding to male and female pronouns.[18] Native American culture is further admired for the institution
of the menstrual hut in which women were secluded each month during their menstruation.* As Paula Gunn Allen explains in her article
"Grandmother of the Sun":

> The water of life, menstrual or postpartum blood, was held sacred
> [in preconquest American Indian culture]. Sacred often means taboo;
> that is, what is empowered in a ritual sense is not to be touched or
> approached by any who are weaker than the power itself, lest they
> suffer negative consequences from contact. The blood of woman was
> in and of itself infused with the power of Supreme Mind, and so
> women were held in awe and respect.[19]

Other Native Americans and spiritual feminists stress that in addition to the prominent place given to women in Native American religions and cultures, it is also important to recognize that these religions
developed on American soil, and were not imported from other lands
as were Christianity, Judaism, Buddhism, Islam, and even witchcraft,
whose roots are European. They argue that there is something special
about this relationship between spirituality and land, and that if
Americans are to restore a sense of sacredness to the earth, they need
to take their cues from Native Americans who are already expert in
relating to the "energies" of this continent. Carol Lee Sanchez recommends that "non-Tribal Americans . . . acknowledge their own connections to *this* land (through birth or adoption) and to revere this land
base more than they revere an abstract notion of freedom symbolized
by their Declaration of Independence, their Constitution, and the flag

---

*This is somewhat ironic, given that early feminists used this same institution as a
particularly heinous example of the subordination of women.

that flew over their conquest and disenfranchisement of approximately forty million native peoples."[20]

The spiritual feminist reverence toward and appropriation of Native American religions is frequently extended to encompass all indigenous or tribal religions in whatever part of the world. Though these are not specially connected to the North American continent, tribal religions generally are beloved by spiritual feminists for the same reasons that Native American religions are. They "live close to the land," they respect women and women's special powers, and are held to be the living fragments of a global culture that was nonsexist. Fascination with tribal cultures is often captured in the term "shamanism." Shamanism is very au courant, occupying a place in the emergent religious tradition that witchcraft and paganism only approach. It has succeeded in making great inroads in the feminist spirituality population as well, where many women aspire to being "shamans" (or less often, "shamanesses"), instead of "wise women," "witches," "pagans," "crones," "medicine women," or any of the other honorifics available to them. The shaman is described as one who can transform both the seen and the unseen, who can journey to other realms, who experiences trances and visions and can predict the future, and who can move between this world and a less substantial—though ultimately more "real"—world for the benefit of others as well as herself. It is not a description that is markedly different from that of the nineteenth-century spiritualists, but it conjures up a different set of associations, ones that exert a greater appeal to late twentieth-century feminists. Rather than associating to crystal balls, gypsies, and darkened rooms, as does spiritualism, shamanism associates to ritual masks, tribal peoples, and ecstatic dancing under the open sky.

African Religions

Spiritual feminists are also interested in African religions for some of the same reasons they find Native American religions attractive. Again, there is a population of women who are African-American, and who explore African religions in search of their distant heritage, or as the proper lineage of the voodoo practices or black folk Catholicism they learned as children. Much larger is the group of European-American fellow travelers in search of feminine symbols, "authentic" spirituality, and a form of religion that makes room for women. Study and practice of African religions is usually limited to West Africa, to the ancestral homelands of those who were taken to the Americas during the slave trade. Use of African symbols and goddesses was not common in the early days of feminist spirituality, but is more so now, mostly owing to the efforts of black spiritual feminists. In 1982, Sabrina Sojourner complained: "The lack of information about black Goddesses in most works on Goddess worship might lead one to believe that such information does not exist. That simply is not so! We of African descent have a rich Goddess and matrifocal heritage." In 1985, with the publication of *Jambalaya* by voodoo priestess Luisah Teish, African religions were made more available to the general feminist spirituality movement. Teish claims that voodoo has much to offer women: as the "child of matristic tradition, it recognizes spiritual kinship; encourages personal growth; respects the earth; and utilizes the power of sexuality and women's menstrual blood."[21]

Interest in African religions among white women is largely due to the fact that African religions have goddesses, and spiritual feminists are always eager to discover new goddess images and new goddess names. But there is also interest in African or African-influenced religions because they have had several hundred years in the Americas to develop into an alternative tradition, and thus have a more visible history behind them than has European witchcraft, for example. Also, there is some sentiment among spiritual feminists that Africa is the motherland, the cradle of humanity, and thus the source of the earliest goddess-worship humanity has known. Finally, from the beginning, an important policy of spiritual feminists has been to locate the most negative images of women available and to find in them instead the very best of what the human race has to offer. Just as "woman" and "witch," "dyke" and "crone" are rescued from patriarchal disapprobation, so is blackness. Liturgically, spiritual feminists often talk about "going into the dark," "going underground," "entering the night," as a pointed contrast to the New Age or Eastern call for "enlightenment." Adopting African religions and black goddesses is another way of reversing traditional symbol structures, siding with the oppressed and making them the real heroines of spiritual feminist culture. For example, Monica Sjöö and Barbara Mor, in *The Great Cosmic Mother*, construct the spiritual feminist role model like this: "The original witch was undoubtedly black, bisexual, a warrior, a wise and strong woman, also a midwife, also a leader of her tribe."[22]

Judaism and Christianity

In the main, feminist spirituality has been little interested in adopting images or practices from the dominant established religions of America. However, there have been some small-scale incorporations of Jewish and Christian elements into feminist spirituality. These mostly occur in individual rather than group practice, except in those cases where a group of women is meeting specifically to experiment with linking feminist spirituality and traditional religions. When aspects of Judaism and Christianity become a part of feminist spirituality, they usually change so drastically (in context, if nothing else) that they would not be recognized by practitioners of these traditional religions. Judaism and Christianity, though native to most spiritual feminists, have had to be appropriated for spiritual feminist use.

Feminist spirituality, particularly in its early days, spoke of the Shekhinah of Judaism as another in its list of goddesses, and it interpreted some women of the Hebrew Bible to be early feminist role models. Joan Maddox, for example, hails Judith as a woman "you can want to be like in terms of how you live your life with integrity, how you kill some fucker who's gonna destroy your tribe; you know, if you can do it, you go and do it." I have also heard of a few spiritual feminist groups, composed mainly of women of Christian extraction, that have experimented with holding greatly modified Passover seders, and I attended one ritual that included the Hebrew blessings over wine and bread (immediately after an invocation to "the grandmothers of Turtle Island" [a Native American term for the North American continent]).[23]

The use of Christian images in feminist spirituality has been slower in coming, and is still practically invisible. A few women interviewed mentioned that they include female Christian figures in their spiritual practice, but they justify this inclusion by stressing these figures' pagan roots. For example, Barbara Otto has an extensive collection of icons and photographs of Our Lady of Guadalupe, and has made several trips to Mexico to visit her sacred sites. She explains: "[Guadalupe] is the old Aztec moon goddess, really. Now, of course, the Church has taken her over. . . . But she is God, she is God in Mexico. . . . You go into Catholic churches and there's no Jesus and there's no crucifix. She's right there on the altar."[24] More rare is adoption of Christian symbols or personages without any such appeal to pagan roots, as seen in Helen Littlefield's desire to include Jesus in her spirituality:

> For the first time in my life, over the last couple months, it's occurred to me that I might be able to develop some sort of relationship with Christ. . . . Now I'm not saying I'm interested in developing this relationship with Christ exclusive of any other relationship. I'm not exclusive. But I've had some very interesting experiences over the last couple of months that lead me to believe that that might be possible.[25]

Littlefield's hopes for her own spiritual life notwithstanding, Jewish and Christian elements are still handled very gingerly in feminist spirituality, if at all.

The Ethics of Cross-Cultural Borrowing

The joy of feminist religious syncretism is marred somewhat by the fact that when one borrows religiously, one is borrowing *from* someone (or some culture), and often without their permission. This is a problem that has troubled spiritual feminists, though not ultimately prevented them from lifting myths and images that suit their purposes from almost any place they can be found. Still, there is a tremendous variety of opinion among spiritual feminists as they try to decide what entitles them to borrow elements from other cultures and just what they are permitted to take. At one end of the spectrum, women feel comfortable taking anything they like from wherever they find it, while at the other end, women agonize over how to be ever more circumspect in sticking to those things that are uncontestably theirs by birthright.

Those who love to dabble in other religions and see no reason not to, often speak in glowing terms about the family of humankind or the global community. That vastly different cultures separated in time and space have come up with similar religious elements is in itself an epiphany for them. Spiritual truth is more likely to be true, they reason, if it surfaces repeatedly over the course of history and across the face of the earth. Barbara Otto likes to put together rituals that draw on many different religious traditions as a way of focusing on what is most universally human. Oceana Woods calls herself a "rainbow witch," because she feels that in a global age, it's important to include materials from all over the world. Even Zsuzsanna Budapest, who is usually quite adamant about sticking to her own European tradition, says in the preface to *The Grandmother of Time:* "The focus of this book is the lost traditions and holydays of the ancient Europeans before they were Christianized by force, but I could not resist the rich culture of Asia, Africa, and North and South America to show the unity of spirit."[26]

Women enamored of the grab-bag approach to feminist spirituality have little patience for those who wring their hands when a spiritual feast is laid before them. At one retreat I attended, there was quite a lot of informal (and some formal) discussion of the problems associated with religious borrowing. Several women were clearly annoyed that the matter even came up, saying that if they chose to use another culture's spirituality, they were paying them a compliment, and it should be taken as such.[27] But some women aren't receiving the compliment; they are taking it as more of an insult. At the National Women's Studies Association meeting in 1990, Andrea Smith circulated a paper titled "Indian Spiritual Abuse" to encourage women to boycott workshops, retreats, books, and records about Native American spirituality that were led or authored by white women. Smith states:

> The New Age movement has sparked a new interest in Native American traditional spirituality among white feminists. . . . Not surprisingly, many white "feminists" see the opportunity to make a great

profit from this new craze. They sell sweat lodges or sacred pipe ceremonies which promise to bring individual and global healing. Or, they sell books and records which supposedly describe Indian traditional practices so that you, too, can be Indian. . . . While it may appear that this new craze is based on a respect for Indian spirituality, in reality, these white feminists are continuing the same exploitative and genocidal practices of their forefathers/mothers. Despite the fact that there does not seem to be any desire amongst these writers to really understand Indian spirituality on its own terms and to respect its integrity, these white so-called feminists, unwilling to give up their romanticized view of Indians, and despite the protestations from the Indian community, continue to buy what they see as Indian spirituality.[28]

The only "white New Age feminist" Smith accuses by name is Lynn Andrews, and the accusation is understandable. For if Andrews is a contemporary Carlos Castaneda, it is with a heavy dose of Jackie Collins: in her early books particularly, she portrays herself as a fashionable, wealthy Beverly Hills socialite who through her naive interest in Native American art finds herself off on an adventure she is ill-equipped to handle. In her first book, *Medicine Woman*, she peppers her prose with references to her "Jaguar sedan," "Gucci bag," and "Sassoon jeans"; she eats out at La Famiglia, where she is a regular customer who is allowed "long hours for talk over dinner." When her Native American quest leaves her frustrated, she drops in on dinner parties at the homes of her famous producer friends. Among the tragedies that befall her when she is in Manitoba, where her mentor Agnes Whistling Elk is waiting for her, are a flat tire, a broken fingernail, and the forced purchase of three packages of Twinkies. In an especially comical passage, she relates her frustration over being unable to find a photograph of a Native American marriage basket that she is sure she has seen at a gallery showing. She concludes: "I needed a dose of reality. I decided to go to Elizabeth Arden's and have a pedicure."[29] By 1987, in her fifth book, *Crystal Woman*, Lynn Andrews is no longer from Beverly Hills: she now hails from Los Angeles. There are no more references to Elizabeth Arden or Gucci, and she is now no spoiled socialite, but an earnest apprentice questing after spiritual truth under the tutelage of her faithful Indian guides.

Although Andrews has adopted a new image for herself, she has retained the same image of her Native American mentors and sisters: they are "ancient" and "primitive" women who lack all ordinary signs of intelligence or civilized values, but who nevertheless exude an inner wisdom and almost surreal nobility. As Andrews says of Agnes Whistling Elk, she "had difficulty expressing the simplest thoughts in English" but "she was as erudite as anyone I have ever known, and she had great dignity." Andrews's native guides are living icons of what Andrews and other spiritual feminists celebrate spiritually. She describes one of her guides, an Australian aboriginal woman, in these words: "Her elderly dark face was creased and withered like the crusty earth from which she was born." The portrait is consistent with a general romanticism in feminist spirituality toward "primal peoples," "aboriginal peoples," or "Third World peoples," who are felt, despite all their cultural and religious differences, to share spiritual insights that are undisclosed to First World peoples.[30] Some Native Americans object to being white women's icons, and resent the implication that all Native American cultures (or all aboriginal cultures) are the same, that anything like a generic Native American spirituality exists.[31]

Similar complaints have come from African-American women. This fragment from Lorraine Bethel's poem "What Chou Mean *We*, White Girl" puts a fine point on their anger:

> So this is an open letter to movement white girls:
> Dear Ms Ann Glad Cosmic Womoon,
> We're not doing that kind of work anymore
> educating white women
> teaching Colored Herstory 101.[32]

These are probably the sorest points in the feminist spirituality community. Though women occasionally fret over worshiping a Buddhist goddess, this is rare. The people spiritual feminists worry about offending are the people that white culture has already offended very deeply: Native Americans and African-Americans. The concern is that European-Americans have destroyed or appropriated nearly everything about these oppressed cultures, and are now scouring around to collect the last shred of precious spirituality they have left. In her article "New Age or Armageddon?" Monica Sjöö launches this blistering attack: "New Age shamanism is left out of the context of tribal life and the struggle for survival and sacred communication with the Earth and Cosmos, and is used by wealthy privileged white people. White culture rips off a people's land and leaves them dying in poverty, and enriches itself on their spiritual teachings."[33] European-Americans are accused of practicing what Renato Rosaldo calls an "imperialist nostalgia," initiating the imperialist culture contact that leads to the destruction of whole cultures, and then mourning over the loss of these same cultures, and hungrily collecting their myths, rituals, and traditional crafts for use or preservation.[34]

Navigating in these rough seas is a challenge for all those spiritual feminists who are eager to have a female-oriented spirituality that their own mainstream culture does not offer them but are reluctant to trample over other people's "property" to get it. Compromises and rationalizations scatter all across the spectrum. Those of the Jungian persuasion are inclined to believe that if they see a goddess from another culture in a dream or a vision, it is as much their property as anyone else's, having arisen from the collective unconscious.[35] Others suggest that if one is careful to say that what one is practicing is not the religion itself, but simply some element from it, it is permissible to borrow. So, for example, it is all right for white women to smudge with cedar and sage as Native American peoples have, if the proper source is credited and participants are clear about the fact that they are not practicing a Native American religion—because they are not, by virtue of ethnic identity, qualified to define what Native American religion is.[36]

Still others stress the importance of borrowing judiciously and with respect, avoiding the temptation to, as Angela Price says, "feel that we are entitled to the cream off the top once again."[37] Portia Cornell, who has participated in a number of sweat lodges with other white women in Connecticut, attempts to embody this type of respect:

> We have been asked how we feel about borrowing from a ceremony that is sacred to Native Americans. We have respect and gratitude to Native Americans for showing us a form that works so well. We feel drawn to using the sacred rites of Turtle Island to heal her of the havoc she is wreaking worldwide. We hope it offends no one that we use this form to empower us to continue our work of healing the Earth Mother.[38]

In part though, spiritual feminists advise respect not in consideration of those they are borrowing from, but in a concern for the integrity of their own spiritual practice. They describe the spiritual pastiche approach as "dangerous" and "flaky," and caution that one may accidentally invoke energies or powers that can't be readily controlled by the uninitiated.[39]

A number of white spiritual feminists seek to avoid the whole issue by staying within that spirituality that they believe is properly theirs. They speak of the need for religions to come organically out of cultures if they are to have power and meaning. Sal Frankel notes a tendency on the part of Americans, "because we're such a polyglot society," to "think everything's much more interesting than our own culture." She recommends looking at other cultures but remembering to come back home. Those who have centered their practice on feminist witchcraft are most outspoken about this position, saying, "Let's not overlook the rich tradition which exists in our own backyard," and "Let's look at our own heritage." Zsuzsanna Budapest enthuses (to what she assumes is an exclusively white audience): "We know more about Native American shamanism than our own. We have honorable spiritual roots, so let's reclaim them! White people worshiped Life and the elements of nature; they prophesied by the birds and the winds; they practiced rune magic. Most significantly, they used song and dance as magical tools."[40] Angela Price similarly finds a real strength and redemption from white liberal guilt by practicing a European-American spirituality:

> We need to look at what there is that's positive in the white Anglo-Saxon tradition. We hate ourselves so much, we hate our whiteness in ourselves as a result of the cumulative guilt so much that there really is something to be said for looking at what in our own tradition is real positive. . . . European Witchcraft is a white, Anglo-Saxon tradition, and for somebody who is a white Anglo-Saxon person, there's something to be said about owning that.[41]

But some white spiritual feminists, however anxious they are not to offend, just cannot walk away from religious traditions not their own. These traditions speak to them too powerfully. Such women offer a variety of rationalizations for their decision to continue to use what works for them. Those who practice feminist versions of Native American religions will refer to the fact that Native American teachers have been instructed by elders or spirit guides to reveal this spiritual information to white women. Others say that though they may not be entitled by blood to use Native American religions, they are entitled by residence upon this continent. Some employ the doctrine of reincarnation, suggesting that they have had former lives as indigenous persons. Lynn Andrews, for example, says that according to her mentors, she has "walked the moccasin path as a shamaness in previous lifetimes." Helen Littlefield assured me that her friends say her aura is Native American.[42]

Another way spiritual feminists justify interest in the religions of other cultures is to expand the territory of what they consider to be their own tradition. Rosemary Sackner, who after exploring wicca for several years returned to a previous love for voodoo, tells her story like this:

> I feel like for a long time I tried to force myself into this Anglo-Saxon thing, because I felt like I'm white and this is my tradition, or whatever. But I guess recently the way I've sort of come to think is that that's not exactly true. Because I grew up in the South, and I

just feel like the South is profoundly African in this kind of way that I'd say about ninety percent of white people would not acknowledge because of racism. So I grew up in a culture that is African in a lot of ways, so that it does feel familiar to me, it does feel like it's some part of my culture.[43]

One final solution to the problem of religious borrowing suggested by some spiritual feminists is that it is permissible to borrow from another culture, but only if one contributes something back to that culture in return. In *The Heart of the Goddess*, Hallie Iglehart Austen instructs her readers: "If you receive great inspiration from the Goddess Tara, send aid to Tibetan refugees and/or write letters to world leaders in support of human rights in Tibet. If you experience Spider Grandmother guiding you, work for Native Americans' rights to regain and keep their lands."[44]

The problematics of cross-cultural borrowing have deeply impacted the feminist spirituality movement. If a spiritual feminist feels she has been born into a religiously impoverished culture, is she doomed to remain there the rest of her life in deference to the sanctity of ethnic and cultural borders? If feminist wicca is a terrific way to experience one's whiteness positively, does this mean that black women are not welcome? If they are, then are there reasons why white women should not study and worship African goddesses? These questions continue to be debated, and even before they are answered, they tend to sway the movement in certain directions. West African goddesses, though more common now than they were in the early days of the movement, are still far down the list after Greek, Mesopotamian, Hindu, Egyptian, Celtic, Buddhist, Norwegian, Hawaiian, and Native American goddesses. The probability is that this lapse is due to the fact that the predominantly white population of the feminist spirituality movement is afraid of offending African-American women. Indeed, there are a lot more African-American women around to offend than there are Tibetans, Japanese, ancient Sumerians, medieval Celts, or even Native Americans.

The fate of Jewish religious elements in feminist spirituality lends credence to this theory. In early issues of *Womanspirit*, Jewish women sometimes contributed feminist versions of Jewish myth and ritual, and meditations on the Shekhinah, which they reinterpreted to be "the female half of the deity." But when non-Jewish women tried to use Jewish religious elements in a positive way (or rejected Judaism with the same breath they used to dispose of Christianity), their Jewish sisters called them on the carpet for their misinterpretations and distortions.[45] Jewish feminists continue to use Jewish symbols, even while in their capacity as members of the feminist spirituality movement, but Jewish symbols have not earned the seal of approval for inclusion in feminist spirituality liturgies. When there is a possibility of alienating a living, breathing, Jewish feminist who is there in the same room by invoking Lilith or the Shekhinah, it seems the better part of wisdom to call on Sarasvati or Cerridwen. The same is also true of Christian religious elements, though there seems to be less desire on the part of spiritual feminists to include them in the first place. Rather than risk offending the Christian—or anti-Christian—sensibilities of participants (and even those not present), feminist spirituality typically dispenses with Christianity altogether.

If all this politeness begins to feel too constraining, there is always another option: imaginative invention. Morgan Grey and Julia Penelope have done just that in *Found Goddesses,* a collection of brand-new goddesses tailor-made for the needs of the current day. Their first and most famous new goddess was Asphalta, the parking goddess. As they reasoned, "Why, after all, would Artemis or Demeter wander so far from their ancient spheres of influence to materialize parking spaces?" Grey and Penelope describe Asphalta as follows:

> Asphalta, goddess of all roads, streets, and highways, and guardian of those who travel on them, is best known for Her miraculous powers of finding parking places. The formal Parking Place Invocation to Asphalta, chanted by Her devotees around the world, and never known to fail when sincerely uttered, even in impossible-to-park-in cities like New York and Montreal, is:
>
> > Hail, Asphalta, full of grace:
> > Help me find a parking place.
>
> This invocation should be intoned at least two blocks before you want to park, although it has been known to work on very short notice. . . . Asphalta is one of the most widely-worshipped of all modern Found Goddesses. Her major temples are located wherever road construction is underway, and are attended by Her High Priestesses, who usually wear jeans or overalls, boots, hardhats, and colorful scarves or handkerchiefs about their necks or heads, as well as vestments of Her sacred color, day-glo orange.[46]

The pantheon of *Found Goddesses* obviously started in fun, but its authors note that invoking these goddesses has also worked, bringing them parking spaces and money when these are needed. This is perhaps truly the oldest religious tradition: taking old things and making them unrecognizable, because they are so new. It is here where feminist spirituality has shown its true brilliance: wherever spiritual feminists have gone for inspiration, when they have brought it back home, religion has become something new in their hands. This imaginative and often contradictory mixture of religious elements is being molded into a spirituality for those women who are willing to enter the fray and see what it can do for them.

· 5 ·

Encountering the Sacred

Feminist spirituality is a religion of doing more than believing. What spiritual feminists have created for themselves upon the skeleton of the alternative religious tradition, fleshed out with materials selected from a global storehouse of religious and cultural artifacts, is a religion focused on ritual practice. There is much discussion of goddess and who she is, and efforts to understand the relationship between the goddess, women, nature, and human history. But this discussion is the backdrop against which feminist spirituality takes place. Center stage is occupied by women petitioning Pele, welcoming the summer solstice, and ritually marking menopause.

Over the course of an interview, spiritual feminists were often reluctant to engage in any analytic precision when discussing the nature of the divine. But they became animated and specific when relating their ritual practices and the feelings and dispositions these practices engender in them. What they do and how they feel doing it is what feminist spirituality is for them; how they interpret and describe these experiences may be important, but is distinctly secondary.

That practice should dominate faith in feminist spirituality is no doubt related in part to the great diversity of "faiths" present in the movement. Belief is not likely to be central in a religion where there is little agreement on that in which one is to believe. Conceptions of the goddess are so varied and personal that they provide insubstantial common ground for spiritual feminists. If spiritual feminists are to come together to form covens or groups, or to exhibit sufficient unity of purpose to form a socially recognizable movement, there must exist a stronger glue than thealogical doctrine. This glue is ritual.

The ritual practices of feminist spirituality are tools for many things: worship, supplication, celebration, personal transformation, ecstatic experience, and management of both psychic and material reality. Most obviously they are a vehicle through which women make contact with the sacred. Not all such contact occurs through ritual; some experiences of communion with the sacred are spontaneous. For example, Hallie Austen Iglehart describes a "spontaneous enlightenment experience" that occurred as she was sitting in an ordinary restaurant on a day like any other. As she narrates it: "My mind is almost completely silent, and when I do hear it, it is like a far-away voice trying to get my attention. I feel total love and acceptance for all I see, yet I can still discriminate between suffering and nonsuffering." Though this experience felt sudden and unbidden to Iglehart, it came only after eleven years of spiritual work including Hindu visualization, chanting, and breathing; Zen meditation; karate; Jungian inner guide meditation; bodywork; Malaysian Senoi dreamwork; and consultations with psychic teachers. Following her "spontaneous" experience in the restaurant, Iglehart learns "to stimulate mini-versions of my 'Good Earth Experience' with certain music, light, circumstances."[1] Iglehart's response to her experience in the restaurant epitomizes the central goal of spiritual feminist ritual: to feel contact with the sacred, and to be able to produce that contact at will; to not only glory in the sacred when it comes knocking at one's door uninvited and unexpected, but to enter into the realm of the goddess whenever one feels the need to visit there.

If laying down pathways to the sacred is ritual's first raison d'être, its most important subsidiary interests are social. Ritual is the primary way in which spiritual feminists help each other to find a meaningful place in the world, to experiment with new and different social values, and to build a sense of community among themselves. Catherine Sharp defines ritual as "remembrance," saying that ritual's purpose is "to remember who you are and what you're doing and where you are in relationship to the universe." Spiritual feminists also use ritual as a method of expanding habitual patterns of thinking, of widening our options as a culture beyond those they deem no longer satisfactory (if indeed they ever were). These women argue that language and abstract concepts can only go so far in inculcating new values or even imagining them, and that if new values—particularly those pertaining to women—are to become truly viable, they must be introduced into deeper levels of the pscyhe via ritual. As Gloria Feman Orenstein remarks: "Ritual permits us to live a new myth, to experience its cosmogony, its symbols, its traditions, its modes of expression. As we enter the world of the ritual, we begin to 'embody' these new knowledges and new feelings."[2]

Ritual can be, and often is, performed alone. But even women who work alone generally do so in such a way that they are symbolically joined to others who perform the same rituals or celebrate the same holidays. Spiritual feminist handbooks frequently reassure the solitary practitioner that she is never truly alone in her practice, that "uncounted thousands of other women" are working with her.[3] Spiritual feminists' first choice, however, is most often to perform ritual with other women, when this can be arranged, and this type of ritual is the communal soul of the feminist spirituality movement. It is through collective ritual that spiritual feminists intensify their bonds to one another, that they transform themselves from a collection of individuals to an organic spiritual group.

Occasions for Collective Ritual

Group rituals are of two basic types: those that honor particular events in and aspects of women's lives, and those that correlate with lunar or solar cycles or other holidays. The specific events spiritual feminists most often choose to focus on in ritual are precisely those they feel are demeaned by mainstream society: events relating to the female body and the female life cycle. In *The Holy Book of Women's Mysteries*, Zsuzsanna Budapest offers a series of rituals to mark bodily events in a woman's life, including puberty, menopause, conception, motherhood, abortion, miscarriage, gynecological surgery, middle age ("queening"), and cronehood.[4] This list is fairly comprehensive; most spiritual feminists put the largest emphasis on menstruation, particularly its beginning in puberty (menarche) and its end in middle age (menopause).

Menstruation is described as an opportunity for women to connect to nature, and particularly the moon; to recognize their own divine life-giving powers; to exercise psychic powers that are supposedly heightened during or before menstruation; and to experience death and rebirth on a monthly basis. Spiritual feminists extol menstruation in words like these: "Our bodies wax and wane with the moon monthly, continually through the phases of our lives. We contain the ability to conceive, carry, and give birth to life. We are divine!" Menstrual blood is described as "liquid flesh" as "the primal matrix which becomes babies, and becomes milk," and women herald themselves as having the ability to "bleed without dying," to participate in "woman's transformation mysteries," and to incorporate the power of the heavenly bodies into their own bodies. Many commentators suggest that the relationship between the phases of the moon and the phases of the menstrual cycle is more than accidental: they say that women who are regularly exposed to moonlight ovulate at the full moon and menstruate at the new moon. Some spiritual feminists endeavor, insofar as it is in their power, to shift their menstrual cycles to match the cycles of the moon.

For spiritual feminists, it is almost as though the "problem that has no name" to which Betty Friedan alluded in *The Feminine Mystique* is actually the problem of menstruation ignored and debased. The neglect of the rhythms and power of the menstrual cycle are, according to Monica Sjöö and Barbara Mor, "a major cause of mental illness, and a major barrier against self-realization." Demetra George cautions that if "we do not heed our inner Lilith need to retreat during our bleeding time, and instead force ourselves to externalize and continue meeting the expectations of others, Lilith protests as the raging bitch."[5]

Remedying the situation begins with menarche. Several women have published blueprints for or accounts of menarche rituals, and advocated their use as a way of encouraging pubsecent girls to regard their bodies and their new bodily functions in a positive light. Susana Valadez suggests the purpose of such a ritual in the words she recommends to mothers whose daughters are approaching puberty:

> Mothers may explain to their daughters that when the womb sheds its lining for the first time, the young girl will undergo a complete transformation. Like the butterfly that emerges from the cocoon in beauty and flight, so is she who bleeds and blooms now a caretaker of the magical and transformative blood of life, and her womb a fertile seed chamber. She is a guardian of Mother Nature, and her uterus a chalice carrying the life force that women have embodied through the ages.[6]

For adult women, menstruation is honored through the moon lodge. Borrowing from the Native American menstrual hut (and from similar practices in other cultures), spiritual feminists are championing the withdrawal of menstruating women from day-to-day society and their gathering together in a site where they can commune with one another and with the sacred powers to which they are presumably close when they are menstruating. The vision of what a moon lodge could or should be is spun out in numerous tales. In *Daughters of Copper Woman*, Anne Cameron records this description of a Native American menstrual hut given by "Granny," a woman of the native tribes of Vancouver Island:

> Every month, when the moon time came for you, you'd go to the waitin' house and have a four day holiday, or a party. Most of the women had their moon time at about the same time of the month, and you'd sit on a special moss paddin' and give the blood of your body back to the Earth Mother, and you'd play games, and talk, and

if you were havin' cramps there was a special tea you would drink
and they'd go away, and the other sisters would rub your back.[7]

Brooke Medicine Eagle is the woman most instrumental in turning
spiritual feminist attention to the sanctification of menstruation
through the moon lodge. She modifies the moon lodge concept to
allow for the necessity of holding down regular jobs, keeping up with
other activities, and taking care of families that might be unable to
cope with a woman's absence for several days or a week out of every
month. Instead of spending twenty-four hours a day of every day of
menstruation in a specially designed moon lodge, she encourages
women to set aside an extra bedroom or garage space in someone's
home as a moon lodge and to try to spend at least the evening of the
first day of menstruation there, if not the whole night. The ideal she
recommends is to "spend your moontime . . . out on the earth. . . .
to find moss, or find something soft, and simply sit yourself down so
that your blood, the creative life-possibility that that blood means is
gifted back into the earth to cycle around again." Pragmatically, she
suggests an alternative: that women use a menstrual sponge to collect
their flow, and then squeeze the sponge out onto the earth to accom-
plish the same ritual act of giving their blood back to the earth.[8]

Some life cycle events that spiritual feminists mark through ritual
are events specific to their own lives. They may be going through a
difficult time with a sick child or a dying parent, with a boring job or
a hostile landlord. Or they may wish to rejoice in a new home, a job
transfer, or a reunion with old friends. Ongoing ritual groups will
sometimes take turns being the focus of particular rituals, or ad hoc
groups will be formed for a special ritual. One woman interviewed
gathered her closest friends for a ritual when she began therapy to
deal with the father/daughter incest she was subjected to as a young
girl. The ritual was designed to increase her feelings of safety and to
support her decision to overcome the lasting psychological effects of
the sexual abuse.[9]

Rituals for life cycle and personal events may be occasions for ritual
by themselves, or they may be practiced within a ritual calendar of
lunar and/or solar cycles. For example, a new moon ritual may double
as a menstruation ritual, or a spring equinox ritual may honor new
mothers. Solar or lunar events may also be sufficient cause for ritual by
themselves. Life cycle events and nature's cycles are linked in spiritual
feminist thinking. Some spiritual feminists argue that all ritual, whatever its cosmic referent, is ultimately derivative from menstruation:
that women's cycles are the model on which ritual is built. For example,
Elinor Gadon writes that "the word ritual comes from *rtü*, Sanskrit for

menses. . . . The earliest rituals were connected to the women's monthly bleeding." Because of the similarity between menstrual and lunar cycles, some feminist spirituality groups choose to meet on or around the new moons and full moons each month for rituals that are sometimes called "esbats." Brooke Medicine Eagle describes new moon rituals as quiet affairs, concentrating on silent meditation and dreaming, and full moon rituals as very energetic, filled with dancing, shouting, drumming, and the welcoming of new faces. Some feminist witches interpret lunar rituals as particularly well suited for female-only groups and for building up a rapport within a small group. In *The Spiral Dance*, Starhawk defines lunar rituals as belonging to the goddess and solar rituals as belonging to the god. Between this tradition and ties to menstruation, lunar cycles are commonly thought of as "feminine."[10]

Ironically, however, for all the "femaleness" attributed to the waxing and waning moon, spiritual feminist groups are more likely to meet on the solstices, equinoxes, and the four cross-quarter days that fall between them—collectively known as "the sabbats."* This is the solar cycle spiritual feminists adopted from neopaganism. Many neopagans understand this "wheel of the year" as a replaying of mythological events: The goddess gives birth to her son, the horned god, at the winter solstice; he grows and eventually becomes her lover in May; he flourishes through the summer and then gradually weakens with the harvesting of crops until he expires at Halloween; the goddess mourns, but the god is reborn again as her son at the next winter solstice. Mainstream neopagans use this myth to conceptualize the solar cycle as a gradual rising up and falling away of male power or the male principle. Spiritual feminists generally reject this interpretation. They speak instead of "the earth's rhythms," of "the Earth as she moves back and forth between the polarities of inward and outward activity," bringing the focus back to the ostensibly female earth and away from any male dynamic.

Cycles of lightness and darkness are often treated as metaphors to indicate the type of activity appropriate for the various seaonal rituals. For example, at the autumnal equinox, spiritual feminists may speak of going in for the winter, of gestating projects, while at the vernal equinox they may talk of rebirth and renewed energy. The most important of the sabbats is generally agreed to be Halloween (often called

---

*The sabbats go by a variety of names, but these are the most common: winter solstice or Yule (December 20–23), Candlemas (February 2), vernal equinox (March 20–23), Beltane (May 1), summer solstice (June 20–23), Lammas (August 1), autumnal equinox (September 20–23), and Hallowmas or Samhain (October 31).

Hallowmas or Samhain), which is referred to as the witches' New Year's Eve. Spiritual feminists—along with mainstream neopagans—say that this is the night when the veil between the worlds (our world and that of the spirits, or the world of the living and that of the dead) is thinnest and psychic and ritual work is likely to be most effective. Most spiritual feminists are happy to hold their rituals some time in the vicinity of these solar events, at a time convenient to all those attending. But a few insist on the power of the exact astrological moment and hold their rituals at four o'clock in the morning when necessary.[11]

A full ritual calendar, both lunar and solar, would include a total of at least thirty-two holidays (which might begin to explain the spiritual feminist preference for solar holidays over lunar holidays; it is easier to schedule eight rituals than twenty-four). But the sabbats and esbats are not the sum total of the spiritual feminist ritual calendar. Marah, a peddler of incense, oils, potions, and a correspondence course in witchcraft, publishes an almanac eight times a year listing the major and minor neopagan holidays that spiritual feminists might choose to celebrate. In the almanac covering May 1 to June 21, she lists twenty-one holidays—some ancient, some from other cultures, and some American favorites like Mother's Day and Memorial Day. Zsuzsanna Budapest's *The Grandmother of Time* is another encyclopedia of potential spiritual feminist holidays. The thirty-one days of March, for example, hold nineteen holidays.[12] Clearly, not all holidays are celebrated by spiritual feminists, or even meant to be. The intention rather is to make every day a special and unique opportunity to commune with the sacred, and to illustrate the plethora of ritual possibilities our ancestors and neighbors have bequeathed to us. The occasions for ritual are almost limitless, waiting only for the inspiration of spiritual feminists to bring them to life.

Characteristics of Collective Ritual

The design of spiritual feminist ritual is a participatory creative exercise. Variety and inventiveness in ritual are encouraged in all the major texts of the feminist spirituality movement.[13] Women take this advice to heart, and compose their rituals from written sources, techniques they have seen successfully used by others, and their own inspirations. Marguerite Keane leads rituals for all the major sabbats, rituals she assembles from her research in Greek, Roman, and Celtic mythology, her training in Hindu and Buddhist meditation, and an appreciation for Episcopalian liturgy. She builds ceremonies that aspire to a pacing and majesty more reminiscent of a church service than an encounter group. Barbara Otto, on the other hand, creates rituals that are lighthearted in mood, "more like pep rallies, not that kind of ritual where you have to wear long white gowns and do an ode to the north and an ode to the east. . . . I try to be very funky and very silly and very nonthreatening and accessible."[14]

Rituals may be large and open to the public or tiny and restricted to a few friends; they may be indoors or out; carefully orchestrated or spur-of-the-moment. Almost all rituals are led by one or more individuals, though occasionally a group that has been meeting for some time will develop a ritual form that is easily repeated and requires no preparation or official leadership. However, it is an axiom of spiritual feminist religious organization that all women are leaders, each a priestess in her own right.[15] This attitude toward leadership is held in place by a strong distrust of religious authority figures. Having struggled to free themselves from traditional religions and from personal relationships in which men were granted automatic authority over them, spiritual feminists are suspicious of anyone telling them what to do. Women, they believe, must no longer be victimized by authoritative individuals, female or male: each woman should come into her own power. Starhawk in particular has been adamant on this point. In *Dreaming the Dark*, she argues:

> A spiritual organization with a hierarchical structure can convey only the consciousness of estrangement, regardless of what teachings or deep inspirations are at its root. The structure itself reinforces the idea that some people are inherently more worthy than others. It doesn't matter what guru we follow. The fact that we are following anyone else will prevent us from coming to know the spirit, the power, within.[16]

There are pressures that complicate feminist spirituality's ambition to live out the "all are leaders, none are led" ethos. Many spiritual feminists honestly have no interest in leading groups. It is not that they are reticent or intimidated by stronger women; they just don't want to put in the effort, and they are grateful when other women come prepared to lead.[17] On the other hand, some spiritual feminists want very much to lead. They feel they have the knack for it, they certainly have the interest, and they sometimes find themselves frustrated trying to pretend that they are not leading the group when they are, or watching as the group drifts along aimlessly when they know that it is in their power to lead.[18] Groups in which no one is willing to lead tend to disintegrate into apathy and directionlessness.

Many small groups balance the need for leadership with their commitment to a strict equality among their members by rotating leadership. Leaders may change from meeting to meeting, or from year to year; they may work in pairs or trios or alone. Leaders are usually responsible for planning rituals and activities and for bringing in any necessary materials, but from there it becomes a more or less open forum.[19] There are a few women who, as exceptions to the rule, are proud to claim a special role for themselves as leaders. Marguerite Keane says: "I have responsibility as the spiritual leader for the content, although I may solicit other people's input. Because that is my responsibility, because I know what I'm doing. I have the feel for it. To have the right tone, and say the right things." Zsuzsanna Budapest is another exception to the rule. She says, "My ministry is my gift and my divine act; it is where I am Goddess." In her ritual calendar, *The Grandmother of Time*, she includes this entry: "Also on this day, January 30, Zsuzsanna Emese Budapest, founder of the Women's Spirituality Movement in the United States, was born in Hungary." But this sort of self-promotion is not the norm, and even women such as Keane and Budapest who make strong claims to leadership are diligent about soliciting others' participation and restraining their own authority.[20]

The attempt to imbue all women with leadership capacities adds greatly to the movement's appeal to its participants. Women who might be restricted to teaching religious school or occasionally reading a portion of scripture during services in a traditional religious organization, are set free in feminist spirituality to write their own liturgies, compose their own goddess music, decorate altars, and sculpt sacred objects. Rarely the passive recipients of ritual, spiritual feminists are often its architects. This flood of creative activity is in itself a gift to spiritual feminists, giving them a sense of their many talents. As Ann Forfreedom explains, "I learned [through feminist witchcraft] to do things I had always thought were impossible for me: to compose Witchcraft chants and songs, to create Goddess-oriented prayers and feminist poems, and to perceive the artist in me."[21] Carol Schulman feels this openness to individual creativity is a major benefit of feminist spirituality:

> So much of the way that we live, especially in a big city like New York, is that we sort of have the best of everything here, so you stop trying to make your own art. And you lose a lot that way. So in my little group, or when I plan a ritual for friends, it's like an art form. You really come up with some beautiful stuff sometimes. And it's very satisfying to do art that has a purpose. I mean, the reason that I stopped drawing was that I wasn't good enough to be an artist. It was almost make-work to take out the sketch pad and sketch so that I would stay in practice. But now if I'm drawing something that's like

an image that I want to meditate on, it's meaningful. It's much more satisfying.[22]

As a result of this loving attention, spiritual feminist rituals are frequently islands of beauty and magic in a sea of ordinary time.

The mood of spiritual feminist rituals depends largely on the attitude of leaders and the women present, but rituals are often very playful. Even rituals that take a serious tone can become occasions for shrieking and howling, for hugging trees and pounding walls, for dancing uncontrollably and embracing total strangers. In the late 1970s, Jeannie Garawitz participated in a couple of ritual groups, and attributes her continued attendance to this: "It was really a chance to play. I always felt like a little kid when I went to these things because there were so many opportunities to play. We'd dance and crawl and roll around on the floor. It was really fun."[23] Particularly at longer feminist spirituality retreats, a summer camp atmosphere prevails: activities include arts and crafts, campfires, shared meals, swimming at the lake, and so on.

Rituals are also a feast for the senses. Not only are the relatively chaste senses of vision and hearing engaged in spiritual feminist ritual, but also the so-called proximity senses of touch, taste, and smell.[24] Incense, herbs, and scented candles are burned; chalices filled with wine or juice are savored and passed from woman to woman; ritual circles are in almost constant physical contact, holding hands or putting their arms around each other's shoulders or waists. Proximity senses are emphasized even further when, as often happens during rituals, participants close their eyes and purposely shut out the predominant visual sense so that they may more richly appreciate other sensations. Ritual nudity, or going "skyclad," is de rigeur in some neopagan circles; it is not so in feminist spirituality, but neither is it unusual. Complete nudity is rare, but often there will be a few women who take off their shirts or shoes. Partial or complete nudity is sometimes advocated as a way of appreciating and acknowledging female physicality, and it lends another degree of intimacy and relaxation of inhibition to spiritual feminist rituals.[25]

Elements of Collective Ritual

Because rituals are almost always the creations of the women who lead and participate in them, each is unique. Even rituals that are designed and led by a single person may change from one enactment to the next, owing to the improvisations of different participants. However, certain patterns do emerge. Once one has attended a few feminist spirituality rituals, one gains a feel for the structure and pacing of ritual acts and can anticipate some of what will follow. The outline of a feminist spirituality ritual can be summarized like this: First the ritual space is prepared. Altars are constructed or decorated, ritual tools and "power objects" are brought into the space, the leader may give a brief description of what is to follow and allow time for women to introduce themselves to one another. The ritual itself begins by "casting a circle," creating sacred space and time. Often women are "purified" or "cleansed" as they enter the circle, which is then formally cast by "calling in the directions." At each of the four major compass points, individual women or the circle as a whole will invite the goddesses or powers appropriate to that direction to come into the circle and be a part of the ritual. This action closes the circle, after which the ritual work proper begins. This may include chanting, dancing, meditation, trance, blessings, brief sermons or recounting of important myths, healing, group discussion, role plays—whatever the group or its leaders feel is appropriate to the occasion. The centerpiece of ritual (and the fall-back option when there is nothing special planned in advance) is "raising power" or creating a "cone of power." Usually via a combination of chanting, dancing, or drumming, the group becomes increasingly loud and ecstatic until at some point the energy or power generated is "sent" to a specific purpose. The energy is then "grounded," the group relaxes, and the ritual is completed by "closing the circle": saying farewell to the goddesses or powers of each direction, and often reciting a final benediction. Rituals are usually followed by casual conversation and sharing of food and drink, and a milling about the ritual site as the participants retrieve their ritual tools and any discarded clothing, and work together to restore the space to its original appearance.[26]

Preparing for Ritual
With this broad-brush map in hand, each of these ritual elements can be examined in greater detail. A ritual begins with the space in which it is held. This space is almost always a matter of convenience: someone's living room in an area where the neighbors are unlikely to complain at the sound of peculiar yelps and shouts; a park or national forest where a group can find a modicum of outdoor privacy; a camp or retreat center where a feminist spirituality event is being held. Groups meet in offices, garages, shops, barns, and gardens. Small groups that meet regularly almost always meet in one another's homes; larger groups and organized spiritual feminist events often find lecture halls, schoolrooms, or camps for their rituals. Some women feel that ritual must occur outside, where communion with nature is enhanced,

and will go to some lengths to find places where they can worship on the earth and under the open sky. Most compromise and make do with whatever semiprivate space they can find. In her book *Grandmother of Time*, Zsuzsanna Budapest bemoans the lack of specialized ritual space, saying she has been praying "that a wealthy woman or man would step forward and donate a mountaintop or just a lovely piece of land to us, a place where the goddess could be worshipped by women from all over the world." Starhawk makes a similar complaint in *Truth or Dare:* "Our rituals take place in a field or on the beach, in public halls or our living rooms. Rarely do we have the luxury of celebrating ritual in a space designed for our forms."[27] And yet there is a certain romance to creating sacred space out of ordinary space, to taking a place that has no apparent reason to be suffused with divine power and making it into a temporary funnel for the sacred.

Preparation for ritual, however casual and offhand it may appear, is an essential component in the creation of sacred space. Even the simplest of rituals will be adorned with a candle, a stick of incense, a crown of ribbons; something to evoke a space and time set apart from the ordinary. More often, there is a surfeit and more of flowers, fruits, and ritual objects. Some objects are brought to rituals because they are already felt to carry something of the sacred in them; others are brought so that they might be infused with the sacred and be carried home as reminders. Even in large rituals, where the leader or leaders have decorated an altar in advance of the participants' arrival, everyone present is generally invited to add something of their own to the altar.[28]

Once the space has been prepared and the ritual is about to begin, the leader will usually offer a preview of what is to come. One pronouncement is ubiquitous at workshops, and is offered within the first few sentences of official speech: "This is a safe space for women." This is elaborated to mean that women should feel free to interrupt with questions, to register complaints if they have them, to refuse to do or say anything that makes them uncomfortable, and to ask the group to limit itself to activities in which they can participate: if, for example, one woman cannot stand, then the entire group will sit. Where the women present are unfamiliar with each other, the leader may ask each woman in turn to introduce herself and say something about why she is attending, what she hopes to get out of the ritual, and what special concerns she might have. In groups where the women present have worked together before, the introductions are left out, but there is still an opportunity for each woman to speak in turn and say how she is feeling and what has been happening in her life since the group's last formal gathering. This preparatory sounding out of all the participants is included in even quite large rituals, though at some point introductions are either limited to saying one's name or are left out altogether.

Casting the Circle

If women have been introducing themselves, they are probably already seated in a circle, but this is not the same as *the circle,* which requires a ritual invocation and a definite demarcation from nonritual time and space. (Circles are themselves sometimes celebrated by spiritual feminists as uniquely female forms; for example, Diane Mariechild describes the ritual circle as "symbol of the uterus, the creative force.") The circle is usually "entered" before it is formally "cast," and then only after each woman has undergone a ritual purification. Diane Stein recommends the following methods: "sprinkling with salt water, stroking each other's auras with a large feather or stalk of wheat, or with a burning incense stick or smoking cedar branch, or with a live flower." Another method is to inscribe a pentagram in the air in front of each woman as she enters. Ann Forfreedom (and others) also recommend that each woman should say aloud that she enters the circle "in perfect love and perfect trust."[29]

Once all the participants have entered the circle, the circle is cast by invoking the four cardinal directions. This portion of the liturgy is pervasive in spiritual feminist rituals whether they are drawing on neopagan, Native American, or voodoo sources. Generally all participants turn toward each direction in turn with their arms upraised, while one woman (or a different woman for each direction) recites an invocation. When the last direction has been called in, the circle is pronounced closed, and all present have entered sacred time and space. Diane Stein and other feminist witches refer to this state as being "between the worlds," and indeed this is the feeling that the circle casting promotes. It is as though for that period of ritual time—which is timeless—the rest of the world sleeps, and it is in this one unassuming place alone that there is any action taking place. To preserve this sense of sacred time and space, once the circle has been cast, women do not leave it until it is formally closed at the end of the ritual. This prohibition is taken with different levels of seriousness in different circles. In some very informal or large settings, women will drift in and out without any notice being taken. In other circles, if a woman must leave the circle for some reason, she will symbolically trace a doorway in the air in front of her, and step through it. When she returns, she traces another doorway, steps in, and closes it behind her.[30]

There are many published versions of the invocations, and some groups will read from these, using the same invocations each time they meet. Others will extemporize, or write poems of their own with which to call in the directions. The cardinal directions have a lengthy set of correspondences in spiritual feminist lore, being assigned an element, a group of goddesses, and a realm of human characteristics and areas of human endeavor over which to rule. These are the correspondences that are most frequently included in the invocations, but other correspondences are plentiful, including animals, signs of the zodiac, chakras, colors, crystals and gemstones, seasons of the year, times of the day, geometric symbols, phases of life, geological phenomena, and so on.[31] The correspondences provide excellent raw material for poetry and prayer. To give an idea of the variety present in spiritual feminist liturgy, here is a complete circle of invocations, each one drawn from a different source:

East
Hail, Guardians of the Watchtowers of the East,
Powers of Air!
We invoke you and call you,
Golden Eagle of the Dawn,
Star-seeker,
Whirlwind,
Rising Sun,
Come!
By the air that is Her breath,
Send forth your light,
Be here now![32]

South
blue flame
and the five pointed star
blue flaming star
blue pulsing door of the sun
tower of fire the south
raise the wand alloyed
of metal heat
raise the sparkling wand
electric as the shocks
that raise a mind
raise the cone of will
lioness
bright orange and gold
burning summer of the veld
candle flame
lightning rod
desert whirling wind

volcano flow and hearthside
combustion molten stars
the noonday glare
of solstice singing cells
hail goddess lady ishtar
star of tower south[33]

West
Great liquid Mother
whose reflection dances
each evening with the light
                  of the Great Goddess.
Come to us—
Come dance with your children
                  tonight—
Bless us with your presence.[34]

North
Hail to thee, corner of all powers! Great Demeter, Persephone, Kore,
Ceres! Earth Mothers and Fates! Great sea of glass! Guard our circle
and bear witness as we perform our rite according to your heritage.[35]

Raising Energy
When the directions have been invoked, and the circle thus cast, ritual
work begins. It is in this portion of spiritual feminist ritual that there
is the greatest amount of variation. From here until the closing of the
circle, the ritual may resemble anything from an encounter group to a
one-act play, or all manner of things in between. The "cone of power"
is the simplest and most common ritual practice, and in many ways the
template from which other alternatives are drawn. Even when other
elements are added to the main body of the ritual, they frequently
mimic the gradual building and sudden releasing of energy found in
the cone of power.

The cone of power is usually built by chanting and singing, and
sometimes dancing and drumming as well. The circle will stand or
walk while holding hands, with eyes closed. A chant or song will
begin, and then gradually increase in volume and tempo. If women
are dancing, they will often dance faster; if they are drumming, they
will drum faster. As the chanting reaches a dramatic pitch, the participants will raise their hands until, at a signal from the leader or by
common consensus, they will fling their arms wide, and "send the
power" to its appointed goal. The goal is announced or discussed in
advance, and women are instructed to visualize this goal while chanting or dancing, and to see this goal being attained as the cone of power
is "sent." Sometimes the energy raised is sent to political goals, such

as ending sexism or child abuse; sometimes it is sent to personal goals, such as healing for an absent member. It is most often directed either toward the healing of the earth (from wounds inflicted on it by human—typically male—mismanagement) or to the personal healing of the women present.[36]

The chants used to raise power are musically very simple: a few words on a few notes, readily learned by newcomers and open to virtually endless repetition as needed. Some favorites have these lyrics:

> She changes everything she touches, and everything she touches changes

> We are the flow, we are the web, we are the weavers, we are the web

> Isis, Astarte, Diana, Hecate, Demeter, Kali, Inanna

> The earth is our mother, we must take care of her, hey yanna, ho yanna, hey yan yan[37]

Drumming is increasingly used by spiritual feminists as an accompaniment or substitute for chanting. Retreats often include workshops on drumming, and many women have become proficient at African, Middle Eastern, or Native American forms of drumming. Many others happily bang out simple rhythms on whatever is at hand—including cookie tins and pots and pans—when the ritual fever is upon them.[38]

Dance is much lauded by spiritual feminists as an important part of ritual. In rituals I have seen, most invitations to free-form dance result in a performance by a few of the most uninhibited and/or well-trained among the participants, while the remainder sway or walk a bit before either stopping or gradually making their way to a wall against which they can lean. Nevertheless, the emphasis on movement appears to be important to spiritual feminists, ecstatic performer and wall-leaner alike. Dance is described as a way of linking mind and body and opening up to new ways of experiencing one's body and its relationship to everything ordinarily defined as not-my-body. Ayla Heartsong, a ritual dance leader, gives this answer to the question "Why a dance?": "Dance is a form of altered consciousness. Dancing helps the body 'tune in' to the rhythm, helping to shut off the 'brain.' . . . Dancing has been used thru all time as a way to connect our material, physical existence with the more immaterial, psychic energies of our universe. Dancing can be a vehicle to feelings of joy, ecstasy, and realizing that your energies *are* united with all energies in the cosmos."[39]

However far spiritual feminists have proceeded with the raising of power, from a fairly restrained humming and shuffling to a wildly abandoned leaping and spinning with a chorus of animal noises, once the energy has reached a peak and been thrown out to the skies, women will immediately drop to the ground, sometimes kneeling and placing their palms on the ground, sometimes lying prostrate. This is called "grounding," and as Starhawk describes it, it is a way of "giving [the power raised in ritual] back to the earth, letting it flow down through our bodies, and releasing it." The amount of time spent grounding the energy is usually proportional to the amount of time spent raising it. If a circle has chanted for four or five minutes before sending out a cone of power, ten or twenty seconds of palms placed on the floor suffices. But when ritual has run long or been ecstatic, it takes more time to come down from the ritual high. After one particularly elaborate ritual I attended where fifty women chanted, drummed, danced, keened, and wailed for upwards of an hour, the entire group streamed outdoors and fell down on the grass, lying prone for ten or twenty minutes. Some women got up when it began to rain, but many could not be moved even by this, and lay on the grass still longer.[40]

Closing the Circle
The circle is closed by return visits to each of the four cardinal directions, and a ritual thanking and releasing of the spirits and powers associated with these directions. These blessings are usually shorter than the invocations used to open the circle. Sometimes they are dispensed with entirely, and the closing is summed up in a single benediction. Many groups recite, either singly or in unison, a "traditional" witchcraft benediction that has been expanded and popularized by Starhawk:

> By the earth that is Her body,
> And by the air that is Her breath,
> And by the fire of Her bright spirit,
> And by the living waters of Her womb,
> The circle is open, but unbroken,
> May the peace of the Goddess go in your heart,
> Merry meet and merry part, and merry meet again.[41]

Even after the energy is grounded and the circle closed, women do not rush off to their next engagement or hurry home for their favorite television show. The lingering fragrance of the divine is savored in an element of ritual sometimes formalized as "cakes and wine." Meals ranging from a few peanuts and some juice to groaning boards of fruits, breads, cheeses, wines, salads, and even casseroles are served up and consumed by the ritual group. Zsuzsanna Budapest has recommended that this ritual meal begin with each woman feeding another her first bite of food and her first sip of water, saying, "May you never hunger! May you never thirst!"[42] Some groups follow this practice; others simply dig in with an appetite whetted by their taxing excursion into the divine. As they eat and relax, women talk to one another about the ritual, but also about their jobs, lovers, homes, vacations, and families. As the hour grows later, and the energy generated in the ritual dissipates, the participants pack up their ritual tools, dismantle the altar, and set about the often long and arduous post-ritual task of scraping candle wax off the floor and exchanging information on the best methods of extracting paraffin from carpets and clothing.

Talking Circles and Guided Meditations

Rituals are customized to suit the occasion for which they are performed. The altar may be decorated with wildflowers or evergreen boughs; the invocations may refer to the waxing of the moon or to the growing shortness of the days; energy raised may be sent to any number of goals. Rituals are further customized by the inclusion of additional elements. The most popular of these are talking circles and guided meditations. The "talking circle" or "women's council" is a virtual duplicate of the process used in the consciousness-raising groups of the late 1960s and early 1970s. Women speak in turn, uninterrupted, usually about personal matters: how they are feeling, where they have been on their spiritual journey, what their current worries and concerns are. To clarify who is commanding the group's attention at any particular moment, the speaker will often hold an object in her hands—a feather, a stone, a rattle—and as long as she holds it, she is the only one who can speak. When she has finished, she will pass the object to the next woman, or return it to the center where whoever wishes to speak next can retrieve it. This process is not unique to feminist spirituality and is much in vogue throughout the emergent religious tradition as well as in many therapeutic settings. Indeed, a therapeutic flavor pervades these councils, and women talk of surprisingly private subjects, often crying in despair or shouting in anger as they do so.

The specific revelations of women's councils are deemed confidential, but I will relate one story, told to me by Sara Copeland, of her own experience in such a circle. Sara was part of an all-night solstice ritual in which the women's council continued until dawn. She was very nervous going into the ritual, because she had experienced a serious clinical depression several years prior to this during which she could neither eat nor sleep regularly, and spent most of her time trying to swallow enough food to stay alive. Having finally established normal eating and sleeping patterns, she was reluctant to disturb them with an all-night ritual. And yet she decided to participate. As she tells it:

> When the rattle went around the first time, I was about halfway around the circle, and it was pretty late into the night. I had planned a couple things that I might do, but when the rattle came around to me, I was so full of all these fears . . . oh, and then we were supposed to sing everything. And I have no voice, I can't carry a tune. I have this really weak little voice. So when the rattle came around, I just kind of sang all my fears in this shaky little voice. And then I was silent, and [the leader] said, she sang to me, "What do you want? What can we do?" And I asked for the whole group to give me a big hug, which everyone did. And people were just beaming at me, and they sang me this nice song. It was really just a very powerful, moving experience.[43]

Often this component of ritual, in which individuals speak in turn, is transmuted into a form that is less talk therapy and more ritual action. Women may take turns lighting candles and invoking blessings or burning scraps of paper on which they have written words describing the unhappinesses in their lives. But whether a woman relates her most painful experiences to a silent group or leaps over a steaming caldron and makes a wish to cries of "Blessed be!" the basic impact is the same: ritual is personalized. Every participant is given the opportunity to inject something of herself and her concerns into the ritual, and to see these met with the support and encouragement of the group.

Group meditation during ritual is almost always meditation on specific images rather than a generalized effort to enter a meditative frame of mind. It is usually guided by one woman (or by a prerecorded voice on a cassette tape) who leads participants through a set of images or on a fantasy journey. Some guided meditations are routine and are used as a regular part of ritual, but most are more detailed, plot-driven, and subject to personal interpretations. After being gradually led to relax, women are taken through dramatic landscapes: along a windswept beach, to a tiny cabin far back in the woods, through a labyrinth of caves, to a mountaintop on another planet. They meet spirit guides, power animals, fairies, and goddesses, and receive the wisdom these spiritual beings have to impart. They build castles, plow fields, lead pilgrimages through strange lands. They discover jewel-encrusted boxes or earthenware jars and open them to find an object or message intended especially for them. This meditation by Hallie Iglehart Austen is typical of the genre:

Close your eyes, and imagine that you go to your favorite Goddess site or natural setting. Allow yourself to rest there for a while, letting yourself relax into the spirit of the place. Suddenly the Goddess, as you know her, appears. What does she look like? How is she dressed? What does she have to say to you? Ask her what she would like you to do in the world to help make her presence better known . . . Request a gift from her to help you fulfill her wish. When you are ready, thank her for all she has given you, and say goodbye. Slowly bring yourself back to your everyday reality, carrying with you the presence of the Goddess.[44]

In the context of ritual, such a meditation is usually followed by a discussion of what participants saw or experienced during the meditation. What did the various goddesses or spirit guides look like? What did they advise? What gifts did they bestow on the seekers? Sometimes the guided meditation will segue into an arts and crafts session as participants draw or paint their impressions of the experience.

In some of these rituals, there is nothing one can easily point to and say: "Here is the feminist element." But most spiritual feminist rituals do pay some attention to the female, and given the notable absence or subservience of female images in traditional religions, this may be considered in itself to be feminist. Several women told me about participating in "womb meditations" where they were directed to imagine themselves becoming very small and swimming up their own vaginas to explore their uteruses, fallopian tubes, and ovaries. Sara Copeland remembers this meditation as a very emotional experience for her: "I think . . . there was this sense of those places being colonized already by culture in a way that had made me feel like it wasn't mine, and so reclaiming was very powerful." Menstruation rituals also carry an obvious emphasis on the female. One such ritual, designed by Diane Mariechild, involves participants lighting red and white candles to signify strength ("I bleed and am not wounded") and pure spirit ("I am virgin, one-in-myself"). This is followed by the passing of a dish of menstrual blood, into which women may dip their fingers and make a mark on their foreheads, saying, "This is the blood of my body, the blood of renewal, the blood of life." A length of red yarn is then used to weave the circle of women together, to represent their blood ties to one another. At the end of the ritual, each woman is given a piece of the yarn to tie around her wrist and take home as a reminder of this symbol of women's power. A ritual Carol Christ describes in *Laughter of Aphrodite* is also aimed at the celebration of femaleness. In this ritual, each woman in turn is ensconced among the roots of a large tree, where she curls up in a fetal position and is encouraged to feel herself being nurtured in the womb of the earth. When she is ready, the other women help her to be "born," shouting, "It's a girl! It's a girl! Oh good, it's another girl!"[45]

Some rituals are more aggressively feminist, demanding an end to the second-class status of women and choosing specific abuses as appropriate targets for participants' rage. Zsuzsanna Budapest has designated Hallowmas for this righteously angry work, and others have followed in her footsteps. The ritual Budapest recommends for Hallowmas uses a pomegranate to symbolize rapists. The names of rapists known to the women present are read aloud, and then the high priestess "thrusts her knife into the fruit so that it drips like blood." The pomegranate is passed from one knife to another around the circle, to the sound of women cursing the men who have hurt them. Jeannie Garawitz remembers a three-hour-long feminist ritual she participated in at the Michigan Womyn's Music Festival. While a circle of women drummed and clapped, one woman at a time jumped into the middle of the circle and chanted a story of something abusive that had happened to her: her brother had raped her, a policeman had molested her. As she finished her story, she would rip off her clothes and all the other women would cheer for her. Rosemary Sackner remembers the high point of one feminist ritual being when the assembled women painted themselves with lipstick, "reclaiming these oppressive, very sexualized feminine things and making them into war paint."[46]

· 6 ·

Magic and Other Spiritual Practices

Collective ritual is the socially dominant form of spiritual feminist expression, but it is by no means where spiritual feminist activity ends. Group ritual gives women ample opportunity to introduce their own needs and concerns, to share their experiences, and to take over certain leadership functions. Other spiritual feminist activities continue this emphasis on the self, if anything in a more pronounced way. The various religious practices of feminist spirituality—whether solitary or in communion with others—all point toward an effort to develop and refine the self, to identify who one is and how one can grow in positive directions. In modern parlance, this concern with the self would be called a manifestation of the therapeutic ethos, and indeed many spiritual feminists draw a straight line between their spirituality and therapy. (Some, in fact, are professional therapists who use spiritual feminist techniques with their clients.[1]) Many, if not most spiritual feminist practices are aimed at buttressing a fragile, incomplete, or unsatisfactory sense of self, or at unraveling an old identity deeply scarred by experiences of abuse and constructing a new, less assailable one in its place.

In the present climate, to say that something is part of a "therapeutic" culture is to denigrate it, to paint it in the bland colors of self-indulgence and superficiality. But the effort to discover an authentic self, to strip away layers of alienation and culturally imposed identity and find a soul in clear, unimpeded communion with the sacred is consonant with spiritual quests throughout the ages. Spiritual feminists, no less than medieval mystics, are searching in the ways made available to them through their culture to separate themselves from everything in their hearts and minds that puts them at odds with the divine plan (and therefore with their own best interests), and to find a true harmony between themselves and the universe. How they describe their present anguish, to what they attribute it, and what corrective measures they envision taking for themselves all serve to locate them within the particular framework of late twentieth-century feminism and the emergent religious tradition; for the way out of their anguish is mapped over the terrain of New Age and occult practices of divination, healing, magic, meditation, and solitary ritual, appropriately modified to suit feminist insights.

Spiritual Feminist Practices

Solitary Ritual
Solitary ritual gives women a home-based practice to complement their group's rituals, or more often, a substitute for the lack of a ritual group with which to practice. The most common solitary ritual described in the pages of spiritual feminist handbooks is the "self-blessing ritual," and its purpose is self-affirmation, the "celebration and reinforcement of the Divine within you."[2] An early version of the self-blessing ritual by Zsuzsanna Budapest appears to be the model upon which other versions are based. Budapest's ritual begins with preparation of the altar, which is covered with a white cloth and topped with two white candles anointed with oil and a chalice filled half with wine and half with water. Salt is sprinkled on the floor, the woman stands naked and barefoot upon it, and lights the candles, saying, "Blessed be thou, creature of fire." She lights incense, and then proceeds according to these instructions:

> Dip your two forefingers into the chalice; touch your forehead, say: "Bless me Mother, for I am thy child." Dip your fingers again and touch your eyes, saying: "Bless my eyes to see your ways." Dip again and touch your nose, saying: "Bless my nose to smell your essence." Dip and touch mouth, saying: "Bless my mouth to speak of you." Dip and touch breasts, saying: "Bless my breasts, formed in strength and beauty." Dip and touch genitals, saying: "Bless my genitals that create life as you have brought forth the universe." Finally, dip and touch feet, saying: "Bless my feet that I may walk on your path."[3]

The self-blessing ritual is especially designed to focus on the female body, and to give women a love of and an appreciation for their own bodies, however they may be formed. As Luisah Teish explains: "This exercise is important because women have been taught to be supercritical of their bodies. If you are alienated from your body, this will help you to overcome that alienation. If you already like your body, you'll feel even better."[4]

Other solitary rituals are similarly directed at sanctifying the self and embodying the goddess. In *The P.M.S. Conspiracy*, Felicity Artemis Flowers offers a ritual to be used when menstruating. In one part of the ritual, she recommends lighting a red candle and saying:

> Blessed am I by the blood of my womb.
> Sacred Ambrosia of Immortality
> Blessed be my cyclic transformation of Self.[5]

Flowers suggests that this menstrual ritual be done before a mirror, "seeing your divinity." Diane Stein's self-blessing ritual, Zsuzsanna Budapest's "self-realization ritual," and Hallie Iglehart Austen's meditations are also performed before a mirror. Austen offers this advice in *The Heart of the Goddess*, a picture book of goddess images: "I encourage you to take the pose of a Goddess in order to find out more about her and the qualities she conveys. . . . Try moving as she might move, speaking what she might say. This posture might be as simple as the hand gesture of Diana of Ephesus or as complex as the pose of Vajravarahi. Let yourself become her, and let her become you. . . . seeing yourself in the pose of the Goddess usually adds a new dimension to your awareness of your body's potential."[6]

That solitary ritual can in fact be a powerful means of self-transformation is clearly seen in the life of Diane Turcott. After sixteen years of prostitution, when Diane finally developed the will and resources to break free from this life and create a new one for herself, she moved out to the country in upstate New York. As she tells it: "I went off into the woods and metaphorically took my head off and shook everything out and laid it on the floor here and said to the trees and the butterflies and the woods, 'I think I was taught a lot of crazy stuff in my life; what should I put back in my head?' And they said very emphatically, 'Nothing.'" Diane then began to develop her own rituals to encourage her in her process of self-transformation. She would drive off to the mountains on the weekends, and there she found a quiet place by a stream. She lay down in the stream with the water pouring toward her head and prayed to the water to "wash away from me all old outdated belief systems and attitudes." She found a mountain topped by a large meadow with a rock in the center, and in an effort to work through her feelings of guilt, she "crawled naked up the side of the mountain, over rocks and stones and lizards and things." At the top, she climbed onto the rock and spoke aloud, "I call the four directions to witness what I am saying, I ask the wind that blows across this mountaintop to blow through me and take out the cobwebs in the places of pain, blow through me, mother wind, and blow me free."[7] Like the self-imposed trials of Christian and Muslim ascetics, Diane's rituals gave her the strength to see herself in a new light: as the child of the goddess, deserving of respect and all the blessings the world has to bestow.

Altar Building

Altars are constructed as part of group rituals, but they are also constructed by individual women for use in their own homes. Every woman interviewed said she had an altar in her home, and sometimes another at work. In fact, several women said they had altars in every room of their home.[8] What women choose to put on their altars is largely a matter of personal taste. Some guidelines are offered in spiritual feminist literature: Reba Rose, for example, says that a symbol of each of the four elements should be included on an altar, as does Luisah Teish. Zsuzsanna Budapest specifies which objects to use as symbols of the elements, as do Diane Mariechild and Shuli Goodman in their "Keepers of the Flame" workshop. Some women take these instructions to heart, but go on from there to add objects that they find particularly meaningful or that correspond to a goal they are seeking in their spiritual work.[9] Others—probably the majority—ignore these standard setups altogether, and go with whatever attracts them.

Different women are attracted to different things, but altar-making is an identifiable art form whose creativity occurs within certain parameters. There are no required elements, but most altars include candles and images of the goddess (figurines, drawings, or symbolic representations such as flowers, shells, or photographs), along with natural objects like crystals, shells, stones, and feathers. Beyond this, a variety of objects of special significance to the individual may be included: poems, pictures, postcards, tarot cards, ritual tools (wands, swords, knives, cords, drums, rattles, caldrons), gifts from family and friends, and so on. Special altars may be set up for special events. For example, when Carol Schulman was pregnant, she designed her altar to focus on childbirth, and included various symbols and objects to indicate fertility and health.[10]

That altars are subject to individual inspiration is crucial to their function. They represent to women who they uniquely are, and how they fit into the world. As Luisah Teish explains: "An altar is a perfect opportunity to express the Goddess within. Your altar is your personal signature. Here's a place where you need not be scared you're gonna do it wrong. An altar can be made of anything that appeals to you." Altars are vehicles for self-expression, but more than this, they are frequently a medium of self-representation. The altar is the self, symbolized and idealized, and set in right relationship to the world. Many women are very literal about placing their identities on their altars, resorting to mirrors or photographs of themselves, often along with photographs of people close to them or objects that belong to these others. Altars frequently change as their creators feel themselves to change, or as they seek change in different directions. As Karen Whiting notes: "When something no longer holds a sense of living symbol or living presence to me, then I take it off."[11]

Meditation and Dreamwork

Many women also practice meditation on a regular basis, and many more have practiced it at some time in the past. Some have learned Buddhist or Hindu forms of meditation and rely on these; others use forms they have found in spiritual feminist literature. Marguerite Keane, whose meditation practice is derived from Buddhist sources, describes meditation as a way of opening to the divine within herself, to the goddess, and to the bodhisattvas of Buddhism. Sara Copeland has experimented with different forms of meditation, but is currently practicing transcendental meditation (TM). She understands this meditation as a way to "have direct knowledge and direct experience and being able to get centered and get in touch with a core, a core that I also feel is very much larger than myself."[12]

Dreams are also believed to be a potent source of information, and to provide an opportunity for growth. Through dreamwork, women are invited to direct their dreams in such a way that they are able to confront problems or antagonistic persons in their sleep and emerge victorious, giving them the confidence to do the same in waking life. Spiritual feminists interested in Jungian thought advocate taking sequences from dreams and then continuing them in conscious imagination, or taking dream images and investigating their various mythological associations. Diane Stein recommends that women hold a crystal as they sleep in order to have dreams that are symbolic and/ or precognitive and to better remember them. In *Womanspirit*, Hallie Austen Iglehart writes that the same goals are achieved by making a dream pillow and stuffing it with mugwort and psyllium seeds.[13]

Some spiritual feminists insist that the deepest form of meditation is that which makes ordinary work a spiritual exercise. This consecration of work is perhaps best summed up by Luisah Teish in a discussion of dishwashing. Teish says that "washing your dishes can turn into an exquisite ritual" with the proper music, and a sink of dishwater "to which has been added an ounce of river water, an ounce of ocean water, an ounce of rain water, and some lemon oil." She concludes: "Woman's work has been degraded and it never should have been. It's what preserves life. When you start to make your everyday work a ritual, you become re-empowered as queen of the manor."[14]

Healing
In spiritual feminist thought, it is a given that all women need healing: if not from specific illnesses or infirmities, then from the pains suffered as a result of growing up female in a patriarchal world. Spiritual feminists aspire to healing themselves and their sisters through a variety of less than medically and psychotherapeutically orthodox techniques, including homeopathy, chakra balancing, massage, Bach flower remedies, acupressure, and so on. Healing, physical as well as spiritual, has long been linked to religion, particularly in the emergent religious tradition in the United States.[15] In the present day, spiritual feminist healing is almost identical to healing as it is found in the New Age movement. Not only are specific practices duplicated in both movements, but the overall philosophy of holism and of emphasizing positive well-being rather than amelioration of symptoms of disease is also found among both spiritual feminists and New Agers. Disease is widely regarded as the result of individual choice: people subconsciously choose illness to draw attention to problem areas of their lives and provide themselves with an opportunity for insight and change. Through printed charts and word-of-mouth folklore, spiritual feminists can diagnose the true origin of their particular symptoms: headaches may indicate "feelings of inadequacy" or "pressure to conform or be perfect"; ulcers are a result of fear; arthritis strikes those who have "difficulty releasing/expressing anger."[16] Spiritual feminist healing eventually parts ways with New Age healing in its increased emphasis on women as the possessors of natural healing knowledge and in the level of attention it gives to uniquely female bodily functions.

The most popular form of healing in feminist spirituality has to do with chakras, a way of understanding the human body and spirit derived from Hindu sources (though spiritual feminists claim that the chakras are more universal than this, having developed as well in Tibetan and Native American cultures). The chakras are seven "energy centers" corresponding to various locations in the human body, and corresponding also to particular colors, emotions, activities, and types of disease or health. Chakras are "cleansed," "balanced," or "opened" through use of meditative techniques, massage, chanting, and placement of crystals on the body. If, for example, a woman is suffering from kidney disorders, she would concentrate on her second chakra, located in the abdomen, and would visualize the color orange, which is associated with this chakra. She might also wear orange clothes, eat orange foods, and burn orange candles to send the appropriate healing energy to her kidneys.[17] Another popular form of healing is that which falls under the broad heading of "bodywork," and includes therapeutic touch, Rolfing, reflexology, shiatsu, polarity massage, and acupressure. Internal counterparts to these external forms of healing are such things as homeopathy, herbal healing, and a virtually limitless set of diets designed to enhance health, control moods, symbolize a reverence for nature, and "change the cellular structure." When healing involves more than one party, as in the laying on of hands, one is usually designated as healer and the other as client, but even where there is transfer of money, spiritual feminists are quick to insist that the healer is not "doing" the healing. Rather, she is channeling universal energy (goddess or earth energy) and allowing the person healed to take that energy if she so chooses.[18]

Some women become interested in feminist spirituality through its emphasis on healing, particularly women who have faced serious illness.[19] More often, however, healing is valued in a broader, more spiritual sense. "Healing" finally becomes a metaphor for any form of self-transformation, whether physical, emotional, or mental: it is the name given to the overall effort to gain self-knowledge and marshal personal power. It is here that the justification of healing practices takes on a distinctively feminist tone. As Chellis Glendinning writes in "The Healing Powers of Women":

> For women to heal ourselves is a political act. To reclaim ourselves as whole and strong beings is to say "No" to the patriarchal view of women as weak and "misbegotten." To call upon the natural healing ways is to say "No" to the patriarchal obsession with controlling, directing, and enacting "cure." To heal ourselves is a reclamation of the power we all have as living beings to live in harmony with the life energy and to fulfill our potentials as creatures among many on this planet.[20]

Some spiritual feminists argue that women are natural healers who, before their historical oppression at the hands of men, were able to control menstruation, abort fetuses, and shrink tumors in a nonintrusive, low-technology manner (principally with herbs). There are a number of attempts underway to rediscover this knowledge, and particularly to apply it to women's reproductive cycles. For example, in a workshop titled "Releasing Spirit Life Within the Womb," Deborah Maia teaches women how to effect a miscarriage through herbs and rituals, thereby circumventing the need to undergo clinical abortion in the event of unwanted pregnancy.[21] Whatever the form of healing advocated or the technique used, spiritual feminist healing is devoted to reinstating women as the architects of their own bodily experiences, extending their opportunities for self-transformation, and understanding the organic integration of the individual's mind and body as a microcosm of a harmonious universe.

Divination
Another area of extensive overlap between the feminist spirituality and New Age movements is that of divination. Most of the occult techniques used in New Age circles to gain insight into the self and to assist in life choices have their counterparts in the feminist spirituality movement, sometimes modified for feminist use and sometimes practiced as is. The most popular form of spiritual feminist divination is tarot card reading, but there is also extensive use of astrology, the *I Ching*, runes, aura reading, past life regressions, automatic writing, pendulums, Ouija boards, numerology, dowsing, and scrying (seeking visual images from crystal balls, bowls of water, mirrors, the flames of a fire, or the moon). Individual women have their especial favorites, but generally speaking, any available divination technique is adopted enthusiastically by the feminist spirituality movement. Women who identify themselves as Anglo-Saxon witches turn to the Chinese *I Ching* for advice; authors who are devoted to auras and the tarot will let their readers know the astrological positioning of heavenly bodies at the time of their writing.[22] More than once in the course of interviews, women wanted to know my astrological birth sign before scheduling a favorable date for an interview or agreeing to sign a consent form.

As the feminist spirituality movement has grown and flourished, specifically feminist or female versions of many divination techniques have been released and gratefully received by women who find standard occult sources incompatible with their feminist worldview. This is especially true of the Tarot, the *I Ching*, and astrology. Spiritual feminists have also set about designing runes and feminist means for their interpretation, and have occasionally created new systems of divination (such as Erica Langley and Shirley Schnirel's Goddess Channeling Cards, a deck of twenty images of goddesses from thirteen different cultures).[23]

The justification for "feminizing" divinatory techniques goes beyond the simple observation that existing forms of divination are often full of references to things with which spiritual feminists have a difficult time identifying: male rulers, male gods, war, the conquest of nature, hierarchical class relations, and so on. It is also argued that the most popular divinatory techniques were created in prepatriarchal times, and that within them lies the wisdom of goddess-worshiping cultures. Zsuzsanna Budapest traces the runic alphabet to "the time of the matriarchies"; Jade suggests that the *I Ching* was an oral tradition of matriarchal, goddess-worshiping cultures that was "masculinized" when it was written down in the third millenium B.C.E. Though the earliest known tarot deck in Europe dates from 1390 C.E., spiritual feminists believe that it too is far older. Diane Stein suggests that it "may have come from the goddess religion in Africa or Egypt," though she also discusses possible links with China, India, and the Hebrew Kabbalah.[24] The most popular theory of the tarot's origins comes from Zsuzsanna Budapest, who says she heard this story from her mother:

> Mother said [the tarot] was originally designed about 2,300 years ago, when Alexander the "Great" burned down the matriarchal libraries. Scrolls of knowledge and ancient wisdom perished in the flames, especially at the largest library, in Alexandria. The existing scientists, partially matriarchal and partially (new) patriarchal, gathered at a conference to resurrect the living knowledge still in their heads. Being from different parts of the world, they had a language problem, so they devised the Tarot deck to communicate with each other through symbols they had all agreed upon. Thus, the human condition was reduced into twenty-one forces [the major arcana], and later enlarged to seventy-eight pictures.[25]

The challenge is for spiritual feminists to locate and free up the goddess genius that lies sleeping within the tarot, astrology, the *I Ching*, and the runic alphabet, and this is the task spiritual feminists have taken on in creating new and modified means of divination.

Most spiritual feminists stress that divination is not principally a matter of disembodied spirits or goddesses telling the querent what will happen in the future. The knowledge that spiritual feminists access through divination is often held to be internal knowledge, the province of a "higher" or spiritual self. Processes that appear random—the order of cards in a tarot deck, the selection of a particular rune stone from a bag, the results of a coin toss—are actually controlled by the seeker's inner guide (or occasionally by external helpers). For example, in giving instructions as to how to use their Goddess Channeling Cards, Erica Langley and Shirley Schnirel write: "Shuffle the cards and spread them out face down. . . . Choose a card intuitively . . . knowing that your highest inner self will lead you to draw the Goddess card that will assist you in what you are working on at this moment."[26] Women interviewed spoke about divination in much this way: they did not seem to feel that they were requesting information from powerful outsiders, but rather felt that they were consulting the wisest and best part of themselves.[27]

Art, Music, and Theater
Feminist spirituality is a religion profoundly oriented toward both representation and performance, and the arts flourish within its embrace.

Artists in the movement supplement their income by selling visual representations of the goddess: pictures for calendars and appointment books, prints, small statuary, pendants, and rings. Some artists have undertaken more ambitious projects to envision the sacred world of feminist spirituality. Rowena Pattee has made a series of "shamanic robes" under the instruction of spirits who tell her how to design and construct the robes and even what to eat while she is making them. She believes these robes will have a function in the future: they will be used for rituals at "sacred centers" and will participate in a plan "for the regeneration of humanity." Spiritual feminist art has also entered the world of architecture with the design of goddess temples. Mimi Lobell, an architect at Pratt Institute, and her student Christine Biaggi have built a prototype for one such temple: from the exterior, it is an irregular mound, but from the interior, it is hollowed out in the shape of a woman. The entrance, located where the woman's vagina would be, is painted red.[28]

There are as many musicians as artists in the movement, and they have a wide and expanding market for their compositions. Individuals purchase spiritual feminist music for their own consumption, and also use this recorded music in rituals or as background music for massage. Kay Turner, a professional flutist, has developed a musical scale and form she calls "the Sapphic mode" which, she says, is more natural to women and women's bodily experiences than traditional Western musical scales. Lisa Thiel, composer and performer of feminist spirituality songs (such as "I Am the Goddess," "Moon Mother," and "Rainbow Woman"), receives these songs as direct transmissions from the spiritual world. And, as with visual art, in addition to the efforts of professionals, every woman in the movement is encouraged to develop her own simple chants or drum rhythms. There has even been some effort to organize female-only choruses to perform goddess-related music.[29]

Where ritual and performance art intersect, there is another area of spiritual feminist expression: ritual theater. At times spiritual feminist theater is scarcely different from the spiritual feminist workshop: the "audience" is drawn in, and they dance, chant, and paint their bodies along with the "actresses." At the other end of the spectrum are theater pieces in more traditional dramatic form that address spiritual feminist topics. For example, a two-woman organization called WomanShine Theatre performs a play titled "Women of the Gateway" that tells the story of two women who meet "in a 9th century village of women healers and artists" and find each other again and become lovers in a subsequent lifetime in the twentieth century. Other performance pieces fall somewhere in the middle: they involve the audience, but never pretend to be spontaneous ritual. Several of these pieces are explicitly feminist, such as those created by Mary Beth Edelson in the late 1970s: "Your 5,000 Years Are Up" (referring to the patriarchy) and "Memorials to the 9,000,000 Women Burned as Witches in the Christian Era." The latter, performed on Halloween night in New York, consisted of a long litany of names of women who were executed as witches in the middle ages, and eventually led to a procession through Soho of people chanting, "The Goddess is here; the Goddess is us." A more recent performance piece occurred in 1989 in Cambridge, Massachusetts, where a group called "Witches' Return" put the "Patriarchy on Trial." Larger-than-life puppets were constructed to represent specific patriarchs: priests, pornographers, rapists, serial killers, and academics, among others. Each puppet was put on trial individually, and eloquent and poetic statements were read detailing their crimes. A triumverate of judges (one of whom was Mary Daly) ruled in the case, sentencing the patriarchs to death, with assistance from the hundreds of women in the audience who obligingly booed and hissed at appropriate intervals.[30]

Pilgrimages to Sacred Sites

In recent years, the feminist spirituality movement has increasingly drawn attention to sacred centers, places where divine power (of the goddess or the earth) is found in concentrated form. Indeed, throughout the New Age movement there seems to be a trend toward identifying certain spots on the earth's surface as conduits for the divine. Martin Gray, an archaeologist and environmentalist, has conceptualized this theory as "planetary acupuncture." He argues that there are particular geographical sites around the globe that are "power points" that human beings can stimulate through their presence and loving meditation to help heal the earth's body. Spiritual feminists are receptive to such theories, and are also busily creating their own. They are likely to envision the entire natural world as a shrine, but there are always some places that seem more sacred and powerful than others. For spiritual feminists, these places are frequently sites of ancient goddess worship that retain, for the modern believer, some flavor of a culture they believe was devoted to living in harmony with nature and celebrating female power. Carol Christ and Christine Downing have written of their spiritual experiences and the rituals they have performed at ancient Greek temples such as those at Delphi and Eleusis.[31] The desire to visit these sacred sites becomes for many women a pilgrimage, a holy quest to bring their relationship to the goddess and to themselves as women alive. Patricia Reis was a graduate student in fine arts when she conceived the idea of embarking on a spiritual pilgrimage:

One day in the UCLA library, I came upon pictures of the Venus of Willendorf and other female figurines from the Paleolithic era. My body became electrified. I began to realize that this was the beginning of an answer. These objects held a haunting mystery filled with sacredness. They were saying something about a time when those three aspects, art making, femaleness, and the sacred, which felt so sundered in me, were once unified. . . . Slowly, my profound lack of female groundedness was made clear. . . . I spent the rest of the summer devouring books and decided to take a leave of absence from school and go to Europe on a quest for the Great Goddess.[32]

The results of such a pilgrimage can be dramatic. Miriam Sidell says of her journey to Avebury in England: "It caused a kind of inner explosion in me. I felt it gave me imagery and permission to see the divine within myself as a woman."[33]

Spiritual feminist pilgrimage has today become something of a business enterprise. As Gloria Orenstein notes in *The Reflowering of the Goddess*, one can now "buy packaged tours to the Goddess sites, and, equipped with majors and minors in women's studies, one can arrive at Delphi or Eleusis in a tourist bus." An advertisement for one such prepackaged pilgrimage, this one to England, reads: "I felt the sacred stones of the Goddess at Avebury and Stanton Drew. I drank in her sacred waters at Chalice Well and Bath. England allows me to see, and truly know, there was a time when the feminine was honored and respected. I'll be returning in May . . . join me!" Those who wish to make the pilgrimage on their own now have a resource to help them on their way: a long, thin handbook titled *Goddess Sites: Europe* that as efficiently as any Baedeker's or Fodor's highlights how to get there and what to see.[34]

Magic

The most controversial of spiritual feminists practices is magic, and it occupies a special place in the movement. For many spiritual feminists, ritual is magic and magic is ritual: the two are virtually synonymous. Any effort to come into contact with the sacred, to infuse ordinary time and space or ordinary consciousness with the scent of the divine is seen as a magical act of transformation. Others are less comfortable with this equation of ritual and magic. They are squeamish about the use of the term "magic," but comfortable with the term "ritual." The source of this disjunction is most probably a result of customary understandings of these two terms. "Ritual" implies a formal set of actions, which in religious settings are geared toward participation in the sacred. "Magic" involves a formal set of actions as well, but it implies a desire not only to participate in the sacred, but to harness its power for specific—and often nefarious—purposes. Those women who claim magic as a spiritual feminist art are diligent in stripping the term of its foul connotations, but not of its powerful ones: magic is conceived of as divine power accessed and directed by the will and the actions of its practitioners. There is an ambivalence about such power and its appropriate uses in the feminist spirituality movement, an ambivalence that sometimes erupts into real conflict. Still, magic occupies an honored place. Some women choose not to practice it, but almost all spiritual feminists acknowledge the existence of magic and respect its power.

The Mechanics of Magic

If spiritual feminists agree that magic works, what they do not agree on is what causes it to work, what the processes are that link the invocation of magical power with its intended result.

Magic is regarded by spiritual feminists to be a form of technology, and the analogy certainly fits. Technology relies on harnessing the forces of nature. When one takes a sledgehammer and pounds in a railroad spike, the railroad tie is successfully fastened to the ground in part through the force of gravity. In the same way, magic is believed to work through the existence of natural (occasionally supernatural) forces, proved over time to be efficient in translating certain actions into predictable results. The overall spectrum of possible magical mechanisms ranges from a power-of-positive-thinking approach at one end to the manipulation of unseen forces and/or personages at the other.*

At the end of the spectrum that is least at odds with commonly accepted scientific understandings of the universe is the belief that magic works by changing the practitioner's thoughts and feelings. As a result of these internal changes, she behaves in new ways. Her new behavior elicits a new response from the world around her, and between the two, magic has happened. For example, if I make a charm to protect myself from muggers and hang it around my neck, I may feel less vulnerable. As a result, I walk with greater confidence and less fear, and may therefore look like an unattractive target to the mugger in search of a victim. The magic has worked: I did something to protect myself from muggers and I have not since been mugged. But the only direct effect of the magic has been on my internal state.

---

*The various forces that spiritual feminists propose to explain magic are not mutually contradictory; a single woman can, and many women do, hold that many forces are operative to ensure the success of magical means. But most women will alight on a theory or two and leave the others behind.

From that point on, ordinary mechanisms of behavior and response have taken over. The reason spiritual feminists believe a charm may help to protect me when the simple determination to walk with confidence may not is that they believe symbolic means speak more directly to the subconscious mind than does everyday language.[35]

However, it is difficult to convince the subconscious mind that one is being protected from muggers by a charm when one's conscious mind rejects the possibility that a charm alone could have any such impact. One is unlikely to have an adequate faith in something that one believes to work through faith alone. (Even Christian healers, so determined to say that faith alone is required for healing, believe that when healing occurs, it does so because the believer's faith is rewarded by God.) So most spiritual feminists move on from the theory that magic involves a simple change in consciousness to speak of additional ways in which magical acts change reality.[36] The most popular way of conceptualizing this "something more" is to speak of the power an individual's mental state has not only to change her own behavior but to change the world. With the phrase "thoughts are things" as their watchword, these spiritual feminists argue that since there is no hard and firm boundary between the material and the spiritual, spiritual change can effect material change directly without ever proceeding through the halfway house of the individual's changed behavior. In this theory, it is specifically thoughts that are capable of affecting the universe: it is not the ritual action itself that creates change, but the thoughts that are elicited by it. Lady Miw elaborates:

> Thoughts are things, and thoughts manifest. A thought is a real, tangible thing you can hold in your hand—that real. You get a little picture in your mind, a little film, seeing things as you want them to go, then you raise your energy with this little film, and when you send that energy back up into the universe, where there's all that loose energy where it can connect, then that little film can make manifest on this plane of reality.[37]

All of this is premised on a cosmology in which everything is deeply interconnected, and finally reducible to one primary "stuff" that is capable of taking on different forms. Like the nineteenth-century mesmerists who believed all life is permeated by a "magnetic fluid" that can be manipulated by those who are aware of it, twentieth-century spiritual feminists believe the entire universe is composed of "energy" and those who are sensitive to this can engage in acts that will produce apparently unrelated—though in reality profoundly related—results.[38] As Diane Mariechild explains:

The universe is composed of whirling energy vibrating at different frequencies. The patterns and forms vary: some are matter and some vibrations. But it is all energy and can be neither created nor destroyed, only transformed. . . . Human beings are also energy forms, and as such emit waves of energy which respond to and interact with countless other waves of energy. The energy in your body and the energy in the universe are the same.[39]

And as Starhawk concludes: "When our own energy is concentrated and channeled, it can move the broader energy currents."[40]

The question then becomes one of appropriate technology, one of successfully accessing this energy and manipulating it to produce the desired results. For this, spiritual feminists rely on a system of correspondences and affinities similar to that used in the ritual calling in of directions. For example, to attract love, I might choose a red candle; to attract money, I might choose a green candle. Similar correspondences exist for everything else a practitioner might use in her magical work: herbs, oils, objects, chants, days of the week, phases of the moon, and so forth.

Spiritual feminists differ on why these correspondences are efficacious in making magic. Some say that it is because our minds are filled with a catalog of images that are associated with one another in various ways. If I live in the United States, money is green, both in actuality and in the popular imagination. So if I wish to direct my subconscious mind to form thoughts that can move out into the energy of the universe and bring money back to me, I burn green candles or wrap an herbal charm in green cloth. This theory assumes that the images used in magic are effective because they focus the mind of the practitioner, whoever she may be and however her mind may operate.[41] If she thinks of money as purple and love as black, she should use those correspondences rather than the traditional ones to make successful magic.

But most theories of magic root a system of correspondences considerably deeper in the human mind. If not laid down in our chromosomes, such symbolic correspondences are at least woven into the collective unconscious, honed for thousands upon thousands of years of human civilization. They may not be truly universal, but for all practical purposes they are. Luisah Teish explains: "Symbols work because they evoke responses that lie deep in the human psyche. . . . Therefore it is essential to respect all symbols. If you have the *akuba*, the west African fertility doll, lying around, it will evoke the desire to reproduce no matter what your ancestral culture is."[42]

Other theories of magic say that symbols are truly universal, and this because correspondences and affinities exist not only within the human mind, but in the external world as well. Red and love are importantly connected, not just because we perceive them to be, but because the universe and the energy or deities within it are designed such that they actually are. Magical expertise consists in knowing how to manipulate these connections accurately.[43] As Rosemary Sackner explains:

> It's definitely not just a process of suggestion. In other words, if I call someone up and say, "I put a curse on you," and then he gets sick, it's not just [a process of suggestion]. Because I feel like I could put a curse on someone . . . and not tell him, and he would get sick if that's what I was trying to get to happen. I think what I would say is that you ally yourself with certain powerful forces, and those forces make a house call on that person. You affect some plane that can really fuck with people.[44]

For some who rely on "unseen forces," the mechanisms of magic are lawlike. As Zsuzsanna Budapest advises: "Your spell will work fine even if you don't believe in it. Witchcraft is not a matter of faith, it is a matter of observation. We work with natural laws. You can think the sun won't rise or the moon won't shine, but they still do whatever they're supposed to do in the universe, regardless of what you believe."[45] For Budapest, if the practitioner moves the right levers, the universe will respond, even if in her mind she is thinking that she is foolishly wasting her time.

This last conception of magic is not held in wide repute in the world of feminist spirituality. Most spiritual feminists are in agreement that magic ultimately—and usually sooner rather than later—points back to the practitioner and her ability to focus her mental powers. Luisah Teish writes that in practicing candle magic "your sincerity and intention are 89.98 percent of the drawing power of the candle work." This leaves an undefined 10.02 percent effect, something that cannot be reduced to the practitioner's thoughts. Presumably this 10.02 percent means that magic will not work unless you move the right levers. Still, moving the levers will not do the trick without firm faith and concentrated mental power, and this is the true engine that drives spiritual feminist magic.[46]

These are the theories of magic, and every spiritual feminist has one or more of these that she can draw on to explain and legitimate her magical practice (or occasionally, her lack of one). And yet the theories are only the shadow of the practice itself. Many women who are enthusiastic practitioners resist pinning magic down to any explanation of how it works; to do so seems to them to rob it of its mystery, of that which makes it "magical." As Starhawk says of magic, "We can swim, but not measure, its depths."[47] Indeed, most women approach magic with a desire to learn the backstroke but no desire to learn the mechanics of how force and fluid dynamics propel a backstroking body through the water. And so spiritual feminists generally disclaim any certain knowledge of how magic works, preferring instead to give illustrations of how it has worked for them. Through magic, Suzanne Courveline has brought a long-lost cat home, Sharon Logan has prevented (at least temporarily) automotive breakdown, Del McIntyre has protected her home from damage when a tornado passed over wreaking havoc in her neighborhood. One standard pagan warning regarding magic is to "be careful what you ask for, you may get it." Carol Schulman remembers a time when out of gratitude to a dear friend, she prayed that she should be able to do something for him someday. Within twenty-four hours, he was on the phone telling her he was sick and needed her help.[48]

But magic does not *always* work, and spiritual feminists are aware of this fact. Just as Christians must explain how you can pray to God to bring you a baby sister for Christmas and find a puppy under the Christmas tree instead, spiritual feminists must give some account of why magic sometimes fails. Christians typically resort to the will-of-God argument to explain unanswered prayer: you can ask God to bring you a baby sister, but God knows what is best for you, and maybe what is best for you is a puppy. Spiritual feminists sometimes use exactly the same argument: the goddess is wiser than we; if we seek something we shouldn't have, she will keep it from us in spite of our magical efforts. As Esther Hoffman says, "I do rituals . . . for things I want. If I don't get them, then I figure the Goddess doesn't need me to have them right now." Luisah Teish asserts that "Magic does not 'fail'; it tests our faith, causes us to clarify our desires, and directs our attention to other avenues." Starhawk explains failure by cautioning her readers not to overestimate the power of magic: "It does not work simply, or effortlessly; it does not confer omnipotence."[49]

Some spiritual feminists, however, claim that magic fails because it is ineptly practiced. Ideally, the perfectly trained, spiritually powerful, and sensitive practitioner could achieve anything through magic, but in reality, we are all far clumsier than this. Failure is an opportunity to learn what one has done wrong in order to make failure less likely in the future. Jade counsels: "If the results [of magical practice] are not what was intended, the process is repeated and refined until one is able to consistently send out a certain type of energy and receive a specific result." Suzanne Courveline also blames the failure of magic on unskillful practice, but she sees it not as the result of the practitioner's inexact manipulation of the universe's energy, but as a problem of addressing the wrong deities. It is a problem easily solved: "If you go to the elder gods, and they don't come through for you, you just don't sacrifice to them anymore. They're out the door."[50]

Practicing Magic

When spiritual feminists choose to use magic, they must make two fundamental decisions: how to use it and what to use it for. Fortunately, they are alone in neither of these decisions: there are resources within feminist spirituality to assist even the most confused and indecisive woman in finding her way through the world of magic. There is a wide range of things that women might want magical help in getting, but human needs are not so different that these cannot be reduced to a relatively short list. In her writings, Zsuzsanna Budapest includes magical spells for (among other things) health, love, money, finding a home, getting a job, studying productively, improving relationships with lovers, stopping harassment, and also for psychic purposes such as astral travel, seeing fairies, summoning the departed, and so on. Women interested in making magic can consult these recipes, and also ones found in other spiritual feminist handbooks.[51]

Magical recipes are sometimes simple and open-ended; at other times, extremely precise and detailed. In general, the more firmly a book is within the world of feminist spirituality (rather than mainstream paganism or the New Age movement), the more likely it is to give only general guidelines and leave much room for imagination and improvisation. Angela Price finds much of the fun in magic to consist in comparing various magical recipes and designing her own variants to suit her specific task. She explains: "Basically when I do spells, I do herbal spells. And the thing that I really love is going through all the literature and sitting with the plants and figuring out what plant energies are appropriate to what it is that I'm working on." Suzanne Courveline also finds a creative outlet in developing magical spells, though her usual process is to imagine what might work first, and then check this against written sources. Suzanne relies heavily on her intuition: "You just sort of sit, and you open yourself up, and you let things come to you. And you write them down. . . . The really nice thing about it is that later on you get synchronicities with things that are very ancient, and you'll find that it came to you when you didn't know about it at the time. And that's nice, because it sort of validates what you do."[52]

Magic is available for many purposes, but probably the most popular spells are protection spells. Women magically protect themselves, their friends and loved ones, their homes, their places of work, even their

cars. In *Mother Wit*, Diane Mariechild testifies to the effectiveness protection spells can have:

> One afternoon before leaving my apartment I circled it [to protect
> it] as usual. Later that night I returned to find a water pipe had
> broken and the hallway was filled with water. It had not yet begun
> to go under my front door. When I checked the basement, water had
> leaked on things people stored there but my things were unharmed.
> Another time while on vacation in the Canadian provinces I circled
> my car. When we returned I forgot to use the daily circle. That same
> day the line to the gas pedal broke. Fortunately I was close to home.
> While those instances may seem like coincidences at first, each new
> "coincidence" is harder to label this way.[53]

In other protection spells the object is more narrowly defined in regard
to specific threats to the practitioner. For example, Starhawk describes
an herbal charm that can be used "to win in court": "Use a square of
blue cloth, filled with bay laurel, High Joan the Conqueress Root, St.
Joan's Wort, and vervain. If you are being persecuted by an enemy,
add a pine nut or part of a cone, some tobacco, and some mustard
seed. Put in a small picture of an open eye, so that justice will look
favorably on you. Tie with purple thread." Luisah Teish offers a different spell, this one designed to protect one from gossip. To carry out
this spell, one buys a cheap beef tongue, and splits it from the base to
near the tip; then writes the name of the gossiper on "virgin parch-
ment" saying, "May the wagging tongue of (name) burn till bitter turns
to sweet." The paper is placed in the tongue, which is covered with
black pepper, folded over, and fastened shut with nine steel pins. The
tongue is wrapped in a black cord, set on a black cloth, and placed in
a closet or under a piece of furniture. Then the practitioner is to "rise
every morning at 6 A.M. and whip the tongue with [a] leather strap.
Think of the disharmony caused by the gossip as you beat the tongue.
Do this every day until the tongue begins to decay." The spell is completed by covering the tongue with salt, wrapping it in the black cloth,
and tossing it into a large body of water. Teish advises: "Return home
by a different route. Wash your hands with salt and water, rinse your
mouth with salt water, and eat a piece of something sweet."[54]

Another popular type of magical work is the wish-fulfillment spell.
Whether to find love or money, a home or a job, these spells are designed to make the practitioners wishes come true. Diane Stein suggests that women make a "wishing box" a permanent part of their altar.
Taking a small lidded box, the practitioner writes down her wishes on
slips of paper, wraps a bay leaf up in each wish, and places it in the
box. She then visualizes the wishes, seeing them first as pieces of

paper, then as thought concepts, and finally as the wishes themselves fulfilled. She states these fulfillments aloud, saying, for example, "I have the perfect apartment," "I am a healer," or "I own the finest guitar." When these visualizations have borne fruit, the fulfilled wishes are removed from the box and new ones added. Love magic also falls under the category of wish-fulfillment spells. Jeannie Garawitz claims to have met her husband as a result of her magical acts. She was searching for a soul mate, using the image of a red thread tying her heart to a spiral to which was attached another red thread that led to her soul mate's heart. Her future husband, it turns out, was also visualizing spirals, searching for love. Just before they met, he had spent several days meditating by the ocean, and was planning to stay even longer, but he got a "message" that his soul mate was calling for him, so he came back to the city and attended a party where he met Jeannie.[55]

The use of magic can be understood to be implicitly feminist. Part of what it means to be female, spiritual feminists believe, is to be vulnerable, to be targeted for abuse. To take advantage of magical power to protect oneself is to claim one's right to be safe, to have one's personal dignity respected, and is therefore a feminist act. Occasionally, magic is explicitly feminist as well. In her article "Contemporary Feminist Rituals," Kay Turner relates this story from Margi Gumpert, a witch who makes magic in public bathrooms:

> I often notice that the mirror reflects an image which makes me question myself, feel critical or dissatisfied with my appearance. I don't ignore it as trivial, because I recognize that the mirror is infested with a very common political poison, virus hollywoodius or televisioniensis, subtle pressure to measure up to a pattern designed to enslave. Just to free myself of that pressure isn't a magical operation. But hundreds of other women will use that mirror. So after I have cleared my own image of that false cloud, I usually perform some sort of magical activity to neutralize the poison. I pour suggestive energy into the mirror, encouraging anyone who might look in it to see herself in her true beauty. I reinforce the suggestion with all the power of my will and call on the Goddess of Beauty Herself, blessed Aphrodite, to banish that which would deny Her, as She exists in all of us.[56]

The Hexing Controversy

Spiritual feminists practice magic so that they may be at the helm of their own lives rather than haplessly towed along by outside forces. This is a motivation with which many people can identify. The conviction that people can be in charge of their own lives is so deeply ingrained in the American psyche that one need not go so far as the feminist spirituality movement to find people who champion it. Yet many people would hesitate to call their attempts to control their lives and environment "magic." A large part of the divergence of attitudes toward magic is a semantic one: it is not a question of who practices magic, but of who uses the word "magic" to describe her practices. This divergence is very similar to that found between women who call themselves witches and those who don't. Like "witch," the term "magic" signifies strength and competence, it tastes of power as it trips across the tongue. Moreover, in its common usage, the power of magic is naked, unbridled power: it is the capability to kill or to heal, to curse or to bless. Magic is morally neutral, a simple cause-and-effect process that knowledgeable practitioners can tap for their own ends. The ability to use magic is not then equivalent to the ability to use it wisely; in the wrong hands, magic could be like a thermonuclear device in the trunk of a terrorist's car.

Some spiritual feminists, aware of the threat that such unmonitored power could pose—especially to their own credibility as spiritual persons—do what they can to demystify both the term and the practice. They deny that what they call "magic" is anything like its traditional definition. They explain the relationship between a magical act (such as making a charm for material abundance) and a magical result (such as receiving an unexpected check in the mail) in ways that make magic seem as mundane as brushing one's teeth to prevent tooth decay. They may even describe it as a lower form of spirituality, as nothing but juvenile card tricks when compared to the quest to develop the goddess within.[57] They may dispense with it altogether.

If these women seek to defang magic, there are other women who are eager to restore its tooth and claw and the fear these inspire. To practice magic and to call it by its name is to claim a power that women, as a dispossessed minority, desperately need to enhance their effectiveness in the world. If outsiders are frightened by spiritual feminists' claim that they are practitioners of magic, so much the better. Magic is a means of arrogating the energy of the universe to one's cause (a cause that is assumed to be righteous), and those determined to stand against that cause need to take notice that unorthodox weapons will be disturbing their peace. This attitude toward magic is not always so confrontational, but it does insist that magic involves substantial power, power intended for the chosen few who penetrate its secrets, and that it is this alone that recommends it for spiritual feminist use.

This variation forms a controversy in the feminist spirituality movement, as participants struggle to determine the proper uses of magic. According to Jade, a principal actor in the female-only Re-formed Congregation of the Goddess, divisiveness between "Aradians" and "Positive Practitioners" may "cause the first major thealogical split among women of spirit." In her terminology, Aradians are those women who believe that magic may be used to manipulate, curse, or hex individuals or social systems that oppress women, while Positive Practitioners "believe that there is *never any* reason for negative manipulative magic." The heart of their disagreement is this: "The Positive Practitioners believe that the Aradians . . . have adopted the tools of the enemy, while the Aradians feel that the Positive Practitioners are not willing to stand up for the rights of women."[58]

The hexing/positive magic controversy is the result of an unresolved tension in feminist spirituality's worldview. On the one hand, spiritual feminists are enthusiastic about the possibility of manipulating the world through magic and gaining a degree of power women have not yet known. On the other hand, a world in which people can cause each other grievous harm through unseen forces is a scary place to be. For many spiritual feminists, the world is scary enough as is: why add the threat of psychic violence to the threat of physical violence they feel walking past a rowdy bar or a porno theater? The challenge for spiritual feminists is to find a way that they can control reality through magic and yet be protected from others' efforts to control them. The desire to control reality demands a strong theory of magic; the desire to be safe and protected wants a weak theory of magic. The trick for feminist spirituality is to find a logic by which both are possible simultaneously, to somehow ensure that magic cannot hurt women but can definitely help them.

Spiritual feminists offer two theories that limit magic's power to do evil, while leaving it free to do good. The first theory is that the universe has a preference for the good, and will reward magical attempts to enhance life and frustrate magical attempts to harm it. Diane Mariechild explains: "The amount of energy available to you is in direct proportion to the universality of your motives. Each time you come from a space of fear, anger, greed or envy, you limit the flow of energy. Each time you are motivated by love and work towards the higher good, the energy available to you increases." Quite simply, good magic works, and evil magic either fails, or works poorly. Some spiritual feminists suggest that the mental and spiritual power it takes to work magic is only attained by means of a process that also creates good, humanistic motives in the practitioner. People who use magic for bad ends do so clumsily and ineffectively, and are therefore not to be feared. Mariechild takes this one step further to say that whatever negativity is transmitted from one person to another is only transmitted with the deep psychic permission of both parties. So not only is one protected from evil magic because evil magic is weak, but if one has no desire to be affected by it at all, one will not be affected. In her words, "You cannot receive anything you don't agree to. No one can do anything to you without your permission." To those who do not recall granting any such permission, Mariechild says, "Often the permission is given at a deep unconscious level so that it may feel that you are getting something you didn't ask for."[59]

This theory offers maximal protection, but at the expense of robbing magic of its sharp savor of power and danger. A second, more popular theory of magic that retains greater power while still restricting magic's ability to do evil is karma. The term is borrowed from Hinduism, though the concept, according to mainstream neopagans, is found in their tradition at least as far back as medieval witchcraft. It is embodied in this "traditional" witchcraft saying that spiritual feminists have adopted, sometimes called the Three-Fold Law: "What you send, returns three times over" (in some versions, ten times). In other words, if you send out negativity through your magic, that negativity will come back to you, whether directly or indirectly, and you in turn will be harmed. The universe is so constructed that evil is returned for evil, and good for good—sometimes in very complex, difficult-to-trace ways, but reliably. The doctrine of karma offers a measure of protection against the potential abusive power of magic, since those who seek to harm spiritual feminists magically will find their evil intentions cast back on themselves. They will suffer, and, one can hope, will learn not to use magic for malicious purposes. Of course, unscrupulous magicians are still able to inflict suffering on others, even though they themselves will suffer as a result, and this is why karma provides only a measure of protection from magical harm rather than an inviolable suit of armor.[60] But karma is still attractive to spiritual feminists because it purchases a more potent form of magic at the price of sacrificing a degree of safety. Magic is not maximally safe, but greater control is delivered into the hands of the practitioner, who can now choose whether to use magic for good or ill rather than leaving that choice to a universe that has ordained that only positive magic will work.

This makes magic a greater arena of personal autonomy and a greater threat to those who would meddle in spiritual feminists' lives. But it also returns the burden of ethical decision-making to practitioners of magic. Having negotiated a balance between feeling safe and feeling powerful, spiritual feminists must move on to the question of how power can be used appropriately. Karma serves a function here as well. It gives the practitioner an excellent reason to refrain from harming others. Rosemary Sackner, for example, has been tempted to hex others with her magic, but has always refrained from fear that she would suffer negative consequences as a result. As she says: "The thing that stopped me from doing spells is not because I thought they wouldn't work. . . . Because a lot of times I've wanted to put a curse on someone or something like that, but I don't do it, because I feel like it's not good karma, and I do believe it's gonna come back on me, rather than that I think it wouldn't work."[61]

Another "traditional" witchcraft saying spiritual feminists use is "Harm none, and do as thou wilt."[62] Though virtually all spiritual feminists subscribe to this aphorism, they differ greatly on what qualifies as "harm." Some spiritual feminists have so refined their moral sensibilities through attention to possible karmic effects that the magic they can morally justify is very limited indeed. Even certain kinds of positive magic are deemed inappropriate because they violate another's free will. For example, it is wrong to do a love spell to make a specific person fall in love with you, because they must be allowed to fall in love with you or not at their own choice. By this theory of magic, it is even inappropriate to attempt to heal another person of illness without their consent. Carrie Washington tells of an unfortunate experience she had with a coven that tried to heal one member's father of cancer. The father died in spite of the healing ritual, and many coven members became disillusioned with the practice of magic. But as Carrie tells it, the fault was with the coven: it was they who had the temerity to try to heal a man who was probably deciding of his own free will that he needed to die. As Diane Stein remarks succinctly, "Everyone has the choice of their illness, and for whatever reason has the right to refuse [healing]."[63]

If love and healing spells are hedged about with restrictions for most spiritual feminists, negative magic is out of the question. Diane Mariechild addresses the morality of negative magic in this hypothetical example: "You have been raped. Should you send negative energy to the rapist, hoping that he will break his leg, or worse? No, to do that would only perpetuate violence as well as bind you to him because of the intense emotion. If you use mental violence against someone, you are leaving yourself open to being the recipient of someone else's mental violence." She suggests that the rape victim instead surround herself in white light and use affirmations to achieve a positive state of mind.[64] For these theoreticians of magic, however justified one's anger, doing magical harm is never permitted, for both moral reasons (it "perpetuates violence") and for self-interested ones (it "binds you to him" and creates negative karma).

Others have a very different definition of what "harm" consists of in the phrase "Harm none, and do as thou wilt," and very different ideas about when and how magic may be morally justified. To these spiritual feminists, if it were not so pathetic, other women's reluctance to hex a rapist would be almost comical. This is what magic is for, they say: to administer justice when ordinary systems of justice fail. If a rapist is on the loose, there is no better use of magic than to curse him so that he can be tracked down and convicted. In *Jambalaya*, Luisah Teish recalls an incident in which she and some other women were discussing a serial rapist, and one of the other women said, "Well, my way of dealing with it has been to surround him in white light." This enraged Teish, who offers this hex addressed to the goddess in place of the other woman's "white light":

> I want this man to *stop raping women*, immediately, if not sooner. I pray that the next time he crawls through a window to strip some woman of her dignity, his foot slips. I beg You, break his leg! Let the woman he intended to harm pour hot grits down his back, and shove him through a window pane. May there be three angry policewomen standing near the rosebush where he falls. Let him confess in the tears of fear and guilt. May he be confronted by those he has harmed. Let them call him foul names and spit in his eyes. Let him fall on his knees and beg forgiveness. May he be tried by a jury of thirteen rape survivors in the court of a virgin fundamentalist Christian elder-mother. May he be sentenced to twenty-one years of hard labor. May he have time to review his hideous crime. Let the Sirens of night invade his dreams, may he toss and turn and find no rest for 365 nights for every woman he has damaged. May the men in prison threaten him, intimidate him, and cause shame to possess him. May he run to the showers to scrub himself clean as those women did when he abused them.
>
> Then let him surround *himself* in white light. Let him swear at the foot of the Goddess of Change to never abuse another woman. Let him utter a sacred oath to Obatala [a Yoruban deity] in an attempt to compensate for his wrongdoing. Let him share his experience, serve as a counselor to other men who are possessed by the demon misogyny. May he preach on the street corners in the rain, testifying to the beauty and power of all womanhood. May he be reformed. May he become a good person! This is justice. *So mote it be.* [65]

Teish obviously wishes some harm to this rapist. But, she argues, this is morally justified. This is her rule of thumb: "Hexing is appropriate when you seek to stop an abusive action for which you would be willing to receive the same punishment if you committed the same crime. Be clear about that!" Zsuzsanna Budapest, who also approves of hexing in certain circumstances, explains: "If you attack the innocent, it returns tenfold. This is the Law. If you don't attack the innocent, if somebody actually harms you, you can return that harm." She is particularly intransigent in the case of rape, as is Teish, and she reassures her readers: "Know that rape is the foundation of patriarchy, and to attack the rapist is not black magic, because you are not attacking the innocent."[66] But Budapest qualifies this in important ways: one of the reasons it is legitimate to hex criminals is that the magical practitioner is acting in the criminals' best interests, even if the criminals do not understand this. She explains: "Killers exist only on the physical plane and their souls are saddened by the evil they are doing. We can call on their very own souls to stop the evil, and their own souls will make them make 'fatal' mistakes so they can be apprehended and taken out of circulation." In this understanding, hexing is just an unusually strong form of moral persuasion. Without conversation or even face-to-face interaction, the magical practitioner convinces the criminal that crime is not a good idea.[67]

The majority of spiritual feminists limit themselves to positive magic or do not practice magic at all. In the hexing controversy, the Positive Practitioners are winning. There is an unshakable minority committed to using magic to harm those who harm women, but most spiritual feminists find that intentionally doing psychic harm to others is a little too strong for their blood. Most spiritual feminists prefer to give up a little magical power in exchange for a sense of security: they think that toying with magic, particularly negative magic, is playing with fire, and they fear getting burned. Those who do practice negative magic are, it seems, women who have been victims of a sufficient amount of abuse in their lives that safety does not exist for them in being magically harmless and believing that others are or will be harmless too. Abuse is the reality, and this being the case, safety comes only in self-defense, in being prepared to retaliate against those who would do them harm.

·7·

Not Just God in a Skirt

Up until the time some enlightened college professor or Eastern guru tells you otherwise, chances are you have been made to understand that you can't have religion without gods, and that you can't have a really good religion unless you have only one god: one very big, very powerful, universal (and probably male) god. Those who make their living trying to understand religion have shied away from defining religion solely in terms of supernatural beings or forces, for it is possible to have something that looks very much like what we call religion without belief in any gods at all. Having made this proviso though, people who study religions spend much of their time trying to outline what religionists believe about the realm of the sacred: whether they have a deity or deities (or what they have in their place) and how these divine beings interact with human beings. If what is unique about religion is its concern with the sacred, how better to understand a religion than by examining what its faithful perceive as sacred? This quest to understand the divine has long been the centerpiece of the study of religions. It is the so-called queen of the sciences: theology.

Spiritual feminists are involved in the thealogical task of defining the divine as well. But spiritual feminists are iconoclasts: they love to flout the rules of the theological discipline, to challenge the categories usually used to think about the sacred. They don't think most of these categories apply to what they experience anyway. Or rather, they think all of them apply indiscriminately, even those categories that were originally set up to be mutually exclusive. Do spiritual feminists believe in one goddess or in many goddesses? Both, they answer, both at the same time. Is their goddess within them, a part of them, or is she completely outside of them, looking in? Both, they answer, both at the same time. Does this goddess exist independently of human beings or did spiritual feminists invent her? Both, they answer, both at the same time.

On the face of it, talking thealogy with spiritual feminists sounds unrewarding, kind of like trying to play Monopoly with someone who doesn't see why she can't put a hotel up on Boardwalk just because Park Place is mortgaged to the bank. But spiritual feminists are actually very competent players of the theological game. They are surely not the first to suggest that deities are so far beyond the constraints of human intellect that it is an insult to them to pretend that they must adhere to human rules, even to human rules specifically developed to apply to divinity. This is a common refrain in theological debate. For every theologian who develops a formulation for god, there is another—or even the same one—to say that this formulation is partial and inadequate, and is doomed to be so because it is only a human invention. Spiritual feminists are sensitive to the limitations language imposes, and seek to escape them to some degree by thwarting all attempts to pin the goddess down with theological labels. As Shoshana Hathaway writes in a letter to the spiritual feminist quarterly *Sage-Woman:* "To 'write the truth of the Goddess' seems impossible to me, since Her truth encompasses *all* truth. We can touch and present a piece of it, but it is a truth from our perspective only."[1]

Keeping the goddess free from definitional capture is part of what keeps her divine. In Western religious traditions, much of what we experience as numinous is so because it is not simply explained or directly analogous to other types of human experience. The sacred has the flavor of mystery; it is not completely subject to the canons of rational thought. Because the experience of the sacred is a powerful one—and frequently one believed to have important implications for how life should be lived—the compulsion to share it with others is nearly irresistible. But this most often necessitates putting it into words, and while words communicate, they also constrain. All of theology takes place between the twin impulses of explaining divinity in words and setting divinity free from human language altogether. This makes theology a tricky enterprise. Words are used to point to things that words cannot say. It is no wonder then that theological rhetoric is so often characterized by paradox, and that words like "ineffable" and "inexpressible" are so frequently heard. If spiritual feminists seem a bit confused about just who their goddess is, it is well to remember that traditional religions are similarly "confused." Spiritual feminist assertions that goddess is both one and many, both personal and impersonal, both dependent on human belief and radically independent of it serve to move her existence to a deeper level than that which human beings ordinarily occupy. They make her truly goddess.

However, part of feminist spirituality's resistance to applying specific theological labels to the goddess is due more simply to the fact that systematizing goddess thealogy is not a priority for spiritual feminists right now. Feminist spirituality is a young religion and a loosely organized one, interested in remaining open to different women's experiences of goddess. Because it emphasizes the experiential over the thealogical, feminist spirituality can afford to remain flexible about its precise beliefs. Carol Christ, whose academic preparation in theology taught her to ask and answer such questions as "whether Goddess is one or many, personal or impersonal, whether she is nature or more than nature," has found that these questions are not truly relevant to her experiences in feminist spirituality.[2]

Although systematic thealogians and dogmaticians are not much in evidence in the feminist spirituality movement, there is much discussion of goddess (along with goddesses, gods, and other divine players), and certain trends emerge: she is in nature, she affirms life and sexuality, she is in each woman. There is still much variation within this picture, but certain positions have attained currency while others are gradually receding from view. Together these form a composite picture of who the goddess is (and who she is not), how she interacts with human beings, and over what sort of cosmos she presides.

Who Is the Goddess?

Monotheism and Polytheism
One very real difficulty in writing about feminist spirituality is deciding whether to use the singular or the plural in referring to the divine. Most spiritual feminists use both, depending on the context. Among the more common responses to the interview question "Do you believe in a goddess?" was the reply "*A* goddess? I believe in *many* goddesses." But in subsequent discussion, the phrase "the goddess" would continue to come up with regularity. Clearly, both "the goddess" and "many goddesses" are realities for most spiritual feminists. And the domain of the divine expands even farther than this. Marguerite Keane explains:

> I don't make those kind of distinctions that you hear about, they don't make any sense to me. You can say it's the Great Goddess, and that's the one Goddess, but she's also all of the many goddesses, and that's true. And she's everywhere. She's immanent in everything, in the sparkle of the sun on the sea, and even in an animistic concept. I think certain objects can embody that force and power. So I worship the Great Goddess, and I'm polytheistic and pantheistic and mono-

theistic too. And I also have a feeling for nature spirits and what we call the realm of fairy, which can be misconstrued as being cute, but I feel it. And the earth elementals, and the guardian spirits of the home . . . I feel all of those, and I feel in contact with all of those different realms.[3]

This generous mixture of theisms is widespread among spiritual feminists. The most convinced polytheists believe there are discrete goddesses that occupy different spheres of the spiritual world, and who are no more related to one another than are various human beings.[4] In feminist spirituality, this type of polytheism is very unusual. Almost all spiritual feminists believe that the relationship between various deities is closer and more significant than this. Many more spiritual feminists collect at the opposite end of the spectrum, where the goddess is worshiped in many aspects and invoked by many names, but in the front of the practitioner's consciousness is the conviction that the goddess is truly one. As Karen Whiting says, "My personal experience and belief is that there's one Goddess who manifests in different forms."[5] A quick review of the titles of thirty-two books on female deities indicates the prevalence of some type of modified monotheism in feminist spirituality: twenty-five titles refer to goddess in the singular ("the goddess," "our mother," "the great goddess") while only seven are explicitly plural ("goddesses"). This is particularly telling in that even books that contain hard-hitting critiques of monotheism refer to a singular goddess in their titles, and several of those that refer to plural goddesses in their titles quickly note that the plurality is only apparent, the many goddesses being but names or aspects for the one goddess.[6]

Yet if the idea of a single great goddess has lasting appeal for spiritual feminists, the concept of many goddesses proves nearly as irresistible. In its most restrained form, goddess polytheism emerges in the image of the "triple goddess" who has aspects corresponding to various phases of a woman's life and likened also to the phases of the moon: maiden, mother, and crone (waxing, full, and waning). Borrowing from the Greek pantheon, these aspects are sometimes given the names of Persephone, Demeter, and Hecate, and there are stories told and rituals concocted around the interaction of these three deities.[7] But goddess polytheism usually takes much more flamboyant forms, and spiritual feminists exult in stringing the goddess's many names together into litanies that seem to have no end. It is a polytheism whose spiritual juice is the celebration of divine femaleness. Goddess names are female names, and they are names of power. Their existence is in itself an epiphany: nothing more is required. Charlene Spretnak gives a striking example of this love of the goddess's names in her article "The Politics of Women's Spirituality." Between a paragraph on feminist spirituality's sacred history and one on patriarchal myths lies a paragraph neither introduced nor explained, composed entirely of goddess names and set in italics:

> *Anat, Aphrodite, Artemis, Asherah, Astarte, Athena, Attor, Au Set, Blodeu-wedd, Britannia, Britomaris, Changing Woman, Demeter, Dictynna, Gaia, Hathor, Hecate, Hera, Ananna, Ishtar, Isis, Ix Chel, Kali, Kuan Yin, Magna Mater, Nut, Pandora, Persephone, Rhea, Rhiannon, Saraswati, Selene, Tara, Themis, White Goddess.*[8]

Alongside and intertwined with a polytheism that thrives on the simple plenitude of goddess names is another polytheism that is greedy for details: who is each goddess? where does she come from? what are the myths people tell about her? what does she look like? what symbols are associated with her? what can she do for those who worship her? The knowledge spiritual feminists have of their many goddesses is often surprisingly encyclopedic. In workshops on goddess lore, it is not only the leaders and coordinators who are able to identify a particular goddess's image, the mythology surrounding her, and elements of her worship. Many women present, women who have other occupations in life besides the cross-cultural study of female deities, will deliver long discourses on any number of goddess figures. This is not knowledge that is lightly acquired through participation in spiritual feminist activities: it is knowledge that requires study and research, and an impressive amount of memorization. For women who make this sort of effort, the many goddesses are more than a proclamation of the one goddess's grandeur; they are individual deities, goddesses useful to the believer in specific ways having to do with their unique qualities.

Individual women often choose specific goddesses to interact with, goddesses whom they feel particularly akin to or who personify forces that they wish to embody in themselves. For example, Angela Price has long felt close to Demeter, but has done most of her spiritual work with Hecate; Isis Mendel more or less restricts herself to invoking Kwan Yin; Luisah Teish, who worships many gods and goddesses, considers herself the daughter and priestess of Oshun.[9] But again, this is not an inveterate polytheism, for virtually every spiritual feminist is quick to note that all goddesses (and sometimes gods as well) are part of a larger, overarching divinity, a goddess/god/cosmic force that is one. This pattern of an ultimate monism coupled with an intermediate or functional polytheism is a pattern found in several world religions (among them Hinduism and Buddhism), and according to Robert Ell-wood, it is also typical of the alternative religious tradition in America.[10]

Gender and the Goddess

That the goddess is female is clear enough; what should also be clear by now is that there are male deities wafting in and out of the picture. Not all spiritual feminists worship male deities or even acknowledge their existence. But many spiritual feminists say gods exist, though they choose not to deal with them; some will worship or invoke gods when they are doing rituals with men; a few even worship gods on their own.[11] That spiritual feminists refer to male deities at all is worth noting, but perhaps more interesting is to explore the position these male deities occupy in the overall thealogical scheme of feminist spirituality. Where does gender come into the god(dess)head? There is no consensus among spiritual feminists on this question. For some women, it is anathema to even consider the possibility that maleness could be polluting the divine; it is bad enough that men exist on the earth plane. Others see male deities operating on an intermediate level, but believe they are secondary or subservient to the goddess, who is the ultimate divine force in the universe. Still others believe that the ultimate is without gender, but that gender either comes in at the intermediate polytheistic level or can be arbitrarily assigned to suit the needs of the practitioner or society as a whole. In any case, whether for reasons of ontology or choice, the goddess is always the central figure in feminist spirituality's thealogy.

Part of the reason spiritual feminists keep coming back to female imagery (apart from its obvious feminist appeal) is that the goddess is representative of many qualities that have long been regarded as "feminine," not only by spiritual feminists or their comrades in the alternative religious tradition, but by Western society in general. The nexus of values gathered under the goddess's skirts include the sanctity of nature, the earth and the moon, the life of the body, and sexuality. The goddess is a deity who is close to hearth and home, who cycles with the seasons, whose presence is tangible in things that traditional religions have considered profane. She is a deity who bestows respect and admiration upon the spheres women have traditionally occupied. She is an invitation to human women to proudly claim a special female identification with nature and the body, with sexuality and childbirth, and to see this as a source of women's strength rather than their weakness. Her femaleness is not solely a matter of biological sex (or some spiritual counterpart), but is an identification with things denigrated as feminine and an opposition to ideals uplifted as manly.

Elizabeth Dodson Gray writes of patriarchal religion: "The goal of this old 'sacred game' is to get away from the ordinary, the natural, the 'unsacred'—away from women, fleshly bodies, decaying nature, away from all that is rooted in mortality and dying. 'Up, up and away' is the cry of this religious consciousness as it seeks to ascend to the elevated realm of pure spirit and utter transcendence where nothing gets soiled, or rots, or dies."[12] In contrast, what gets soiled, rots, and dies (and is also born anew), what is female and fleshly, is precisely what is most valued in feminist spirituality. The "sacred game" for feminist spirituality is immersion in the natural world rather than escape from it.

Pantheism, Nature, and the Earth
The goddess is the movement's most powerful symbol for nature. For many women, in fact, the goddess is not a symbol for nature, but *is* nature. As divergent as women's understandings of the goddess are, few would disagree with the portrayal found in Doreen Valiente's "Charge of the Goddess" (as adapted by Starhawk):

> I who am the beauty of the green earth and the white moon among the stars and the mysteries of the waters, I call upon your soul to arise and come unto Me. For I am the soul of nature that gives life to the universe. From Me all things proceed and unto Me they must return. Let My worship be in the heart that rejoices, for behold—all acts of love and pleasure are My rituals. Let there be beauty and strength, power and compassion, honor and humility, mirth and reverence within you. And you who seek to know Me, know that your seeking and yearning will avail you not, unless you know the Mystery: for if that which you seek, you find not within yourself, you will never find it without. For behold, I have been with you from the beginning, and I am that which is attained at the end of desire.[13]

Several themes overlap in this invocation: nature worship (with particular attention to the earth and moon); affirmation of earthly life; cycles of birth and rebirth as a divine process; respect for beauty, love, and sexuality; elevation of the individual spiritual seeker; and denial of external spiritual authority.

Perhaps the best broad categories under which these themes can be subsumed are pantheism and immanence, and it is here that spiritual feminist thealogies often begin. Starhawk makes immanence the core of her thealogy, defining it as "the awareness of the world and everything in it as alive, dynamic, interdependent, interacting, and infused with moving energies: a living being, a weaving dance." She suggests that this is the wisdom of tribal cultures around the world, "that the sacred is found here, where we are, immanent in the world."[14] As the earth, the cosmos, and everything in it, the goddess is also present in human beings (at least in women; men's status is less sure). Esther Hoffman describes her own sense of goddess as being "one big breathing human mass, or world mass, not even just human—animals, trees, forests . . . we're all gods and goddesses, the words are interchangeable."[15] Such a view, that the divine is in everything, is usually termed pantheism, and spiritual feminists are happy to claim the term.

Many spiritual feminists want to say that the goddess is specially embodied in the moon and the sun. The moon is seen to be particularly linked to goddess, because the moon has often been called female in mythology.[16] Yet some spiritual feminists are not content with the moon, but want the sun too; though the sun has often been male in mythology, spiritual feminists such as Hallie Iglehart Austen asert that "in most primal cultures the sun is female."[17]

It is the earth, however, that is the centerpiece of feminist spirituality's nature worship. Both nature and the goddess are usually understood to be greater than the earth on which we stand, but it is to the earth that spiritual feminists most commonly return in enunciating their thealogy. The view that the earth is a living being is extremely common among spiritual feminists, along with the view that this being is somehow female. Some women are reluctant to attach a gender to the earth in the same way that they are hesitant to call ultimate divinity female. They prevaricate, saying, "It's much more complex than that," "It's not gender specific," "The earth is more primeval than that," or "I don't know that it necessarily has a gender." Yet gender does come creeping back in. As Angela Price says, "I would not want to name [the earth] as only female . . . but I would want to say that her name is probably female." Nancy Robison concludes, "I think we have a need to grasp something. . . . And I have chosen to view that as a her."[18] Others are more certain that calling the earth "she" is something more than individual preference or arbitrary choice. The earth is feminine, they argue, because it shares characteristics in common with women: qualities of nurturing, creating, sustaining, giving birth. As Jeannie Garawitz says, "Women give birth in their wombs and the earth births trees, mountains, nature." Helen Littlefield remarks: "I'm trapped in the metaphor of my physical body. . . . from [the earth] springs food . . . she is what carries me, she is what I walk upon. . . . I think our experience of these things is at a very cellular level . . . we all spring from the mother."[19] Many spiritual feminists subscribe to the Gaia theory, proposed by British atmospheric chemist James Lovelock, who argues that the earth has a personality and a consciousness along with a body. He calls this being Gaia, after the Greek earth goddess of the same name.[20] Spiritual feminists use the goddess title more literally than Lovelock does: for them the earth is the living body of the goddess. This is graphically illustrated in a drawing by M. Lynn Schiavi titled "Only Goddess Can Make A Tree." The drawing shows a pair of breast-shaped hills, one of which is topped with a nipple, the other with a nipple from which grows a tree.[21]

Because the goddess is portrayed as an immanent deity, one who is in nature and inseparable from it, it is not transparently clear how she could have created it. And indeed, creation stories play a less important role in feminist spirituality than they do in many other religions.[22] On the rare occasions when a creation story is told, it is a story of birth. Birdwoman offers this version of the creation of the world in the pages of *SageWoman:*

> Once upon a time, this space between the stars was pregnant. Full, heavy, ripe with atoms, energies, and light. SHE convulsed, and birthed out the matter of planets.
> Shrouded in their embryonic veils, new bodies found their places. Resting together were Earth and her sister Moon. . . .
> Gaia breathed and sang, "I AM!"
> Then, as children come from mothers, came we all: the winged, the four-legged, those that swim and creep. Even the two-leggeds. . . .[23]

Emily Erwin Culpepper calls this "a cosmogony of parthenogenesis."[24]

Built in here at the ground level is a respect for sexuality that permeates the feminist spirituality movement. There are some spiritual feminists who are dubious about *hetero*sexuality; but I have never encountered any antisex sentiment in the feminist spirituality movement, and paeans to the glory of sex and the miracle of childbirth are ubiquitous. Sexuality can be abused—usually by men—but in itself it is not only acceptable, but sacred. Goddesses such as Aphrodite, Artemis, and Oshun are used as representations of a positive, untamed female sexuality. Spiritual feminists have reinterpreted "virginity" (such as that attributed to Artemis) in what they call "a pagan sense," according to which virginity is not sexual innocence, but sexual self-possession: virgin goddesses are those who are free to relate sexually to whomever they choose.[25]

The Goddess and the Unification of Oppositions

For spiritual feminists, the goddess serves to unify all manner of what we ordinarily think of as opposites, and not just the obvious opposition between monotheism and polytheism. A basic feminist critique of patriarchal culture has been that it continually carves human experience into dualisms. Spiritual feminists join in this critique, and bring the goddess in to bridge the gap. Gloria Orenstein, author of *The Reflowering of the Goddess*, sees this as goddess spirituality's primary virtue, that it does not separate "heaven and earth, spirit and matter, human and animal." Monica Sjöö and Barbara Mor attribute this ability to the goddess's triple aspects (maiden, mother, and crone), and suggest that she is also able to bring together the transcendent and the immanent. Perhaps the most important synthesizing task the goddess performs is that between what we ordinarily think of as good and bad. The goddess is often described as "positive and negative," "creative and destructive," "light and dark." It is typically through analogy to nature that this good-and-bad dyad is portrayed, and the terms used to describe it are not so morally charged: the goddess is not "good and evil" but "birth and death (and rebirth)." The goddess is negative in the way that winter is negative, or storms or earthquakes are negative, or death is negative. Yes, people suffer and die, and their suffering and death are not something for which the goddess apologizes. But these events are all part of a process that includes spring, new life, regeneration—and often, reincarnation. Nothing is lost in the goddess. What appears evil is incorporated into an organic cycle that is ultimately good and positive. Death does not overwhelm the goodness of life. It cannot even be said to be truly evil, for it is life's other side, that aspect of life which serves to give it greater meaning.[26] Karen Whiting gives an example:

> When the goddess Demeter makes the land barren and threatens to starve out the human race, it's for the purpose of getting her daughter back from the underworld, and rescuing her both from patriarchy and a certain vision of death. If you were the human beings starving, you wouldn't necessarily find that palatable or acceptable, but . . . it seems to me that what we call evil, in the realm of the Goddess, is often in the service of the good.[27]

The Goddess and the Women Who Relate to Her

Belief in the Goddess

In seeking to understand the relationship of spiritual feminists to their goddess, the orthodox Judeo-Christian model of human relationship to God is of little help. Jews, and even more so Christians, tend to speak of God wanting humans to believe in him and express that belief in worship and praise. A key virtue for many Jews and Christians is the ability to believe in God without any proof of his existence and in spite of experiences that might lead to a contrary opinion. Spiritual feminists, on the other hand, often claim that "belief" is an irrelevant category when speaking of the goddess. If the most common answer to the interview question "Do you believe in a goddess?" was "*A* goddess? I believe in *many* goddesses," the second most common answer was "*Believe* in her? No. I *experience* her." Starhawk makes the paradigmatic statement of this position in *The Spiral Dance*, and many spiritual feminists cite her answer:

> People often ask me if I *believe* in the Goddess. I reply, "Do you believe in rocks?" It is extremely difficult for most Westerners to grasp the concept of a manifest deity. The phrase "believe *in*" itself implies that we cannot *know* the Goddess, that She is somehow intangible, incomprehensible. But we do not *believe* in rocks—we may see them, touch them, dig them out of our gardens, or stop small children from throwing them at each other. We know them; we connect with them. In the Craft, we do not *believe* in the Goddess—we connect with Her; through the moon, the stars, the ocean, the earth, through trees, animals, through other human beings, through ourselves. She is here. She is within us all.[28]

This seems to be true to the experience of many spiritual feminists, who say that their belief or lack of belief in the goddess is a question that is comfortably, even purposely, shelved. As Catherine Sharp says: "I don't agree with the word belief. I would just say I relate to archetypal forces which might be called goddesses. . . . I don't believe in it. It's something I do." Similarly, Sara Copeland reports that though she enjoys invoking goddesses, she doesn't "necessarily like to go around with beliefs," and doesn't "feel the necessity to really grapple with what my beliefs are and how I feel the universe works."[29]

The fact that many spiritual feminists do not find it necessary to believe in the goddess does not mean that she is considered to be only a figment of the feminist imagination, a convenient construct of the mind. As Starhawk suggests, the reason one does not have to "believe" in the goddess is that she can be experienced directly. But not everyone does experience the goddess. Most spiritual feminists explain this by saying it is only a question of semantics: everyone experiences goddess, but not everyone chooses to call her that. Evelyn Hart, for example, implies that we all experience the goddess, because we experience nature, and they are—if not identical—at least profoundly related.[30] "Believing" in goddess is more a matter of adopting a new term for an old experience to call attention to its sacredness and its femininity.

This is the closest thing one gets to a consensus thealogy in feminist spirituality, but it does not truly do justice to the thealogies that grow up all around it. All apologetics aside, some women believe in the goddess (or in many goddesses) not because she is a dynamic concept, but because she talks to them and grants them favors, knows their troubles and comforts them. Other women cringe a little when saying they "believe" in the goddess because it is their conviction that feminists have invented her: she is nothing more than a useful fiction. Thealogies cover the entire spectrum, but it seems that most spiritual feminists grant the goddess a much more substantial existence than one of concept, symbol, or linguistic device. For most of the women interviewed, the goddess was divine presence: she existed before they were born, before they became aware of her existence, and will continue to exist whether they or anyone else notices her or not. As Karen Whiting remarks, "Divinity is big! . . . No divinity is limited to being perceived!"[31] Even those who are insistent that goddess is purely an invention of the human mind are still disinclined to say she was invented in 1971 for feminist reasons. For these women the goddess is so deeply embedded in the collective unconscious of humanity and is so ancient in provenance, that whatever her origin in human thought, by now she takes up real cultural space and can influence both thought and action.[32]

Even those women who are consciously aware of having invented the goddess to suit their spiritual needs are frequently surprised at how well she fills them. Eleanor Haney describes the transformation she experienced as she traveled the road from Christian feminism to feminist spirituality: "As I moved more and more into feminism and then into participation in feminist spiritual community, my language shifted to goddess imagery and names and feminine pronouns. At first, that use seemed artificial and trivial, which, of course, was to be expected. But gradually, trivialness and pretense gave way to power and at the same time to new directions for questioning and understanding."[33] Whatever problems feminist spirituality may have, clearly a lack of a robust experience of the divine is not among them.

Goddess and the Self

One of the reasons the goddess is so readily experienced by spiritual feminists is that she is taken to exist within each individual woman. Litanies of goddess names are intended not only as a means of glorying in the goddess's multiplicity, but as a way of showing each woman her participation in the divine, her goddess nature. As Zsuzsanna Budapest explains: "The Goddess has 10,000 names, shared by women around the world. . . . Her name is every woman's name—Carly, Doris, Lily, Catherine, Sharon, Susan. All of the personal names of women derive from Goddess names, as all women without exception are the expressions of the Mother—Goddess-on-Earth-Manifest."[34] Many spiritual feminists change their names or adopt second names for use in spiritual settings to emphasize their identification as goddesses. Amongst the Janets and Jennifers of feminist spirituality, one finds Artemis Bonadea, Lunaea Weatherstone, Joyful Moon, Airstream Night Womoon, Blackberry, Terra Mountain Star, Shanti, Singing Blue Dolphin, Eclipse, Carol SheBear, Willow Femmechild, Lizard, Brigit Firebringer—a veritable dictionary of female self-definition.[35]

For some spiritual feminists, identification with the goddess is paramount. As Lynn Andrews says, "I'm always amazed when people come to me and talk about the Goddess as if I'm not one! Who do they think the Goddess is? She's you! She's me!" These women emphasize the divinity of human women, and they worry that attention to some external or greater-than-human goddess will diffuse that emphasis. Sonia Johnson, eager to avoid what she sees as the pitfalls of patriarchal religions, is particularly diligent in keeping the focus on human women. She explains: "Goddess worship is not really worshipping the goddess, it is really worshipping women and ourselves, and saying we're peers, we are what creates everything, we are the creator and the created." Hallie Austen Iglehart is somewhat more tolerant of an externalized goddess, but only as a transitional stage in the progress toward a more perfect deification of human selves: "Ultimately . . . to be truly whole, we must recognize that there is no goddess beyond ourselves in the rest of creation. We are part of that great natural whole. It may be helpful in our movement to wholeness to refer to a female divine force, but only if we remember that it is a step in our process of reclaiming our own divinity as part of the vastness of the natural world."[36]

The notion of self-as-goddess is further strengthened by widespread spiritual feminist belief in reincarnation. Because spiritual feminists are continually reincarnating, they are not narrow beings confined to the limits of a particular life, but at least semidivine, if not fully divine beings. It is not at all unusual to hear spiritual feminists (or for that matter, anyone in the general population, one-quarter of whom believe in reincarnation[37]) make reference to their past lives or those of others. A veteran of many lives on earth, Diane Turcott has long found herself responding to information gained in other incarnations, particularly information about witchcraft: "I have been a witch in many lives. I know that from flashbacks from previous lives, and psychics have been telling me that for over twenty-five years. I've been burned at the stake, probably more than once, I've been stoned to death, I've been drowned, I've been left out in the desert to die. But I just keep doing it. It goes back for many, many lifetimes." Belief in reincarnation serves to expand the significance of the self almost infinitely. Although occasionally a woman will report a rather dull and pedestrian past life, far more often one hears—as in the case of Petey Stevens—of lifetimes as a citizen of Atlantis, a Montauk Indian, and an Egyptian Winged Pharoah.[38]

The Mother Goddess

Spiritual feminists are adamant that the goddess not be restricted to any one single image, and she is worshiped in an enormous variety of aspects. But if one image predominates amidst the manifold incarnations of the goddess, it is that of mother. When the goddess is referred to in the singular, she is often "the great goddess," but nearly as often she is "mother goddess." Her role as mother is crucial to her identity. It is her ability to give birth and to nurture that justifies the attribution of feminine gender to the earth and to the divine for many spiritual feminists. Parent imagery for god—though it is almost exclusively male—is pervasive in Western religious thought. So it is not surprising to find that the goddess is worshiped as a mother, and that practitioners define themselves as her daughters.[39]

Some spiritual feminists say that having a divine mother is a way of compensating for the frailties of human mothers, giving women a more perfect mother, one who will never separate from them or prove herself inadequate to her daughters' needs. Just as Freud has suggested that human beings create god to project the child's view of the father onto the universe, some spiritual feminists claim that the goddess is the child's image of the mother projected outward. The goddess may exist prior to this projection, or she may not—depending on who you ask—but the projection is an expression of the human need for divine mothering. Spiritual feminists hope that this great mother goddess will have a transformative effect upon the social valuation of motherhood, and will ease strains in actual mother/daughter relationships.[40] Sharon Logan, for example, notes that "Adrienne Rich or Gloria Steinem, somebody very well known, said there isn't a mother alive that could mother me in the way that I need or want to be mothered. And I think that's true for most women. . . . So the idea of being able to call on or have a deity that can embody these qualities that we need in our lives, that are missing in our lives, is extremely valuable." Lunaea Weatherstone, publisher of the spiritual feminist journal *SageWoman*, has written a fairy tale to express this relationship to a mother goddess. The central character is a young princess who loses her mother, the queen, when she is only four years old. She grieves unceasingly until she is nine years old. Finally, with the kingdom at war, her father, the king, sends her to live in a tower overlooking the sea where she will be safe. The princess lives there for years in a kind of dream state, pining for her mother, forgotten by her father. When she is seventeen, she awakens from this dream, leaves the tower, and wanders on the beach. As she lies on a sand dune, thinking of her long lost mother, the princess hears a voice that says to her, "I am Mother Dea, Mother Goddess . . . I am the singing sea, the dancing stars . . . I look down on you when you look at the Moon . . . I hold you in my arms when you lie on the warm sand . . . My sweet daughter, I am your mother, and I am always with you." The princess's mother goddess gives her a new name, and tells the princess she can see her whenever she likes, for her home is everywhere. At the end of the tale, the princess "took a deep breath, spun around one more time, and began to walk. It didn't matter which way she went. Her Mother was with her."[41]

One of the most popular goddess myths in feminist spirituality is that of Demeter and Persephone, and in feminist retellings, its focus on motherhood is intensified and the male players drop out entirely. For example, in Diane Stein's version of this myth, Demeter creates the world, and then, "lonely for female companionship," gives birth to Persephone parthenogenetically. They live in great happiness together until one day Persephone wanders into the underworld (rather than being abducted and raped by Hades) where she meets Hecate. This wise old goddess tells Persephone that she can learn from her, but cannot stay long, for Demeter misses her terribly. So Persephone returns to Demeter, who in Persephone's absence has turned the world into a cold, infertile place. When they are reunited, spring comes once again.[42] Some spiritual feminists find in Demeter a model for their own mothering, but more often, whatever their age or maternal status, they find in Persephone a chance to experience daughterhood in an ideal way, to be adequately mothered.[43]

Merging with the Goddess
Whether mother or not, spiritual feminists often express a heartfelt desire to merge with the goddess, to be absorbed into her. Chants to the goddess express these longings: "I am she, she is me"; "We all come from the Goddess, and to her we shall return, like a drop of rain flowing to the ocean."[44] In a fragment of her poem, "Hymn to Kali," Jennifer Paine Welwood writes:

> Come swallow me like night, you ageless mother,
> Come drown me in the blanket of your tide;
> Dissolve me in your blackness, then uncover
> What lingers on when all the rest has died.[45]

For all their talk of the goddess within and of being able to experience her directly without needing to believe in her, it is clear that the experience of many spiritual feminists continues to be one of alienation and separation from the goddess, of hungering for an embrace that is more often wish than reality. In thealogical terms, spiritual feminists are inseparable from the goddess, and yet in experiential terms they know the anguish of being parted from her. The spiritual feminist ideal is the sort of frictionless communion described by Susan Griffin in her article "This Earth is My Sister": "My body reaches out to [the earth]. They speak effortlessly, and I learn at no instant does she fail me in her presence." But Griffin also speaks of an awareness of "all that has come between us, of the noise between us, the blindness, of something sleeping between us."[46] The religious yearning to see these obstacles between the human and the divine dissolve is hauntingly expressed in this poem by Janet R. Price, "Liturgy Circa 1976":

> Look, Goddess,
> can I call You God for short,
> or is that too butch for You?
>
> I don't know what to call You
> let alone how to serve You—
> I've lost touch with the ritual.
>
> Goddess, Mother, Mistress of the world,
> my faith is strong
> but my theology is floundering.
>
> I want to love you perfectly.
> I want to wear my hair for You
> like a Nazarene.
>
> But I don't know how to dress or walk
> or where to put my hands
> or who to give my body to.
>
> Should I love a woman?
> Could I come close to You
> by coming close to someone close to You?
>
> Or should I love a man
> to flatter You by imitation
> of Your boundless Motherhood?
>
> Or should I be chaste for You,
> lest I throw myself at idols
> because they make me come?

I mention this last
just to show the lengths I'd go
if I knew what lengths to go

to get to You.[47]

Other Characters in the Divine Play

Spiritual feminists include a number of spiritual beings in their pantheon who are not quite equivalent to the goddess, and are not referred
to by her names. Among these one finds disembodied spirits (some
of whom act as spirit guides), ancestors, power animals, and the occasional evil spirit or deity. Marion Weinstein describes this wealth of
spirits "in the Invisible" as including "loved ones we knew in this life
. . . ancestors in linear time, people we knew in other incarnations
who are not in Form during this lifetime, spokespeople from other
cultures, animals, and even—yes, sorry to say—troublemakers." Jade
includes "discarnate individuals, psychic energy, spirits, elementals,
auras, plant divas, and many more such energies" in what she terms
"the less-commonly-perceived realm."[48]

Out of this crowded spiritual population, those whom spiritual feminists most commonly choose to interact with are those they call "spirit
guides." Spirit guides are encountered through meditation, visualization, or auditory hallucination. Some women believe they are con-
tacting their own subconscious wisdom in a personalized spirit form
when they commune with spirit guides; others believe, as Jade puts it,
"spirit guides are actually separate, non-form entities who have taken
an interest in an individual woman or who have agreed to assist her
with her sojourn on the Earth plane." Hallie Austen Iglehart takes the
first option, saying that a spirit guide—or in her terminology, an "inner
guide"—is "the 'imaginary' personification of the wisest, most centered part of ourselves." More commonly, however, spiritual feminists
interact with spirit guides who are other than and outside themselves.
Working within a theory of reincarnation, spiritual feminists assume
that spirit guides have at various times been incarnated as human
beings on earth, but that while they are between incarnations, they
may act as guides to those who are presently inhabiting human bodies.
These spirit guides may not have bodies, but they do have personalities, along with other characteristics we usually attribute to those with
bodies: gender, ethnicity, and even physical appearance. In her psychic
manuals, Diane Mariechild says she receives information through two
spirit guides: "an Egyptian woman and an Asian man." Petey Stevens
recalls her first contact with one of her spirit guides: "One day while

I was reading my *I Ching*, a large Chinese spirit voice boomed in my head, 'Can I be direct with you?' Not knowing what else to say, I said 'Yes' so he explained himself to me. It seemed that I had inherited a group of spirit guides back in the 1960s along with the *I Ching* book. Although I was unaware of their presence, the guides were at work with my best interests in mind."[49]

Some disembodied spirits take a particular interest in an individual woman because she is their blood descendant. Luisah Teish, for example, receives rituals and spells from her ancestors (to whom she in turn offers ritual reverence). More often though, spiritual feminist reference to "ancestors" is more generic than this, including all spirits who have come before oneself. Melanie Engler is in more or less constant conversation with spirits who are now disembodied, not only during her self-induced trances, but in everyday life. Sometimes she goes to the "land of the dead and land of the spirits" to commune with them, and she refers to them as "people on the other side." She attributes their interest in her to her willingness to listen, but says that the spirits have an interest in and an effect on everyone, regardless of whether or not they acknowledge or are aware of this influence. Some women also report being in contact with disembodied spirits who are requesting access to their wombs to incarnate again as their children. Judyth Reichenberg-Ullman, who has experienced two miscarriages, recalls that during her pregnancies she "was surprised at how easy it was to communicate with the being inside of me. Through asking her such questions as why she had come to us, how had we known each other in previous lifetimes, what was her purpose this incarnation, and what could we do to facilitate her entry, we came to know her quite intimately."[50]

Other connections in the spiritual realm are not to anything human at all, whether embodied or disembodied. Drawing alternately on Native American traditions and on the demonology of medieval witchcraft, spiritual feminists have developed an interest in "power animals" or "animal familiars," animals to whom seekers have a spiritual relationship. Spiritual feminist workshops advertise the ability to connect women with their power animals, and spiritual feminists themselves are notorious pet enthusiasts (especially where cats are concerned). Marion Weinstein describes animal familiars like this: "These may be cats, dogs, rabbits, mice, toads, rats or any animal which *volunteers* for the work. A familiar is not a pet; it is an equal from the animal realm, and it is a co-worker for the witch. . . . A psychic link exists between the witch and the animal, which is apparent to both and transcends speech—such as appearing frequently in each other's dreams and thoughts, and acting with total understanding of each other's needs."[51]

Feminist spirituality generally has little use for demons or devils or Satan. It is particularly concerned to draw its boundaries such that Satanism falls well outside (particularly in a climate where Satanic ritual abuse of children is garnering increasing feminist and media attention), so it is only very rarely that some notion of supernatural or spiritual evil comes into play.[52] Luisah Teish, Marion Weinstein, and Zsuzsanna Budapest are exceptions; they all recognize the existence of malicious spirits. Teish calls these "hants," and provides an emergency ritual for dispelling them; Weinstein names the phenomenon "psychic attack," and gives instructions for repelling it; Budapest says that goddess religion has no demons or devils, but that Christianity does, and because people can be possessed by Christian devils, she offers exorcism as a remedy.[53] In all these cases, however, the hants, demons, devils, or perpetrators of psychic attack are less powerful than the goddess, and are even encompassed by her, in the same way that a bothersome human being is included within the realm of the goddess. Evil spirits may be more powerful than the particular individual they torment, but only temporarily. Teish notes that hants "tend to choose the vulnerable, unprotected, sick, and depressed person as their host"; Budapest attributes demon possession to "the sad madness that comes from an overdose of Christianity." With a bit of effort, evil spirits can be driven away or transformed, and they prove to be no real threat to the universality of the goddess. As Weinstein explains:

> We believe . . . that each one of us is a perfect manifestation of The Goddess and The God. That our own Power is equal to the Power of whoever might have sent the attack, and that since a misuse of this Power could have caused the attack, a rightful use of this Power can end the attack. The Universal Power is basically neutral; the way in which it is used is what makes it seem to be good or evil.[54]

Suzanne Courveline provides an unusual dissenting voice to the spiritual feminist consensus about the absence or ultimate harmlessness of evil spirits. She is convinced that Jehovah exists and that he wishes her—and indeed the entire world—no good. She describes him as "a manifestation of the hatred and fear and killing wish of the patriarchal principle," and says, "I think that he has been thought about and invoked so often that he's completely insane, and I think he's out to destroy everything." She has experienced his intervention in her own life, saying that when she has exercised her natural psychic powers most freely, "it's like patriarchal god wakes up and thinks he has to kill me." Morgan Grey and Julia Penelope also have a single hostile god among their pantheon of "found goddesses." His name is

Quietus and he is "the demon of male-identification, and his symbol is the forked tongue of doublespeak. . . . He is often found skulking around the celebrations and revelations of Lesbian gatherings. He feeds voraciously on vibrant gynergy and has shown himself adept at hitching rides on in-spiration."[55] Though the portrait is made in jest, it does seem to point to an evil that is not easily eradicated, one that is not embraced by the goddess or her devoted women.

In fact, Quietus is a stand-in for the enormous inertial power of the patriarchy, and the relationship between the goddess and the patriarchy remains a problematic one. Spiritual feminists tend to envision a universe in which there are no accidents, nothing that does not occur in conjunction with some larger plan. As Zsuzsanna Budapest writes: "Nothing escapes the ordered, complicated, sensitive, and effective chain of events—the Wheel of Changes. . . . All is subject to the Law of the Way."[56] Although the goddess as portrayed by spiritual feminists is able to incorporate much of what we regard as evil in her divine unity, it is not at all clear that the patriarchy itself—for most spiritual feminists, the very definition of evil—is part of her ultimately beneficent being. There is some explicit discussion of this dilemma in feminist spirituality, and it creates an even greater wealth of subterranean tension. It is this tension more than anything else that feeds interest in feminist spirituality's central story: the myth of the fallen matriarchies.

· 8 ·

The Rise and Fall
of Women's Power

I n every corner of the feminist spirituality movement, a story
is being told. It is "our" story. Listen:

In the olden times, the Goddess had many groves and wimmin
served her freely and in dignity. The Goddess' presence was everywhere, and her wimmin knew her as the eternal sister. The patriarchal powers burned down her sacred groves, raped and killed her
priestesses, and enslaved wimmin. Her name was stricken from history books, and great darkness of ignorance descended upon womankind.[1]

It is now commonly known that there was [sic] at least 30,000
years, pre 15th Century, B.C.E. of matristic civilization worldwide,
before the onslaught of the patriarchal revolution. . . . In Indo-
Europe, over roughly a period of 2000 years, between 4500 and 2500
B.C.E., hordes of rebellious sons came in waves to propagate their
values of power-over women and the life force through conquering
the matristic tribes. The takeover was accomplished through acts of
terrorism: murdering/enslaving the men of those cultures, raping/
marrying the women and co-opting the psyches of the future generations of those tribes by teaching the children a new religious mythology, which totally eradicated the notion of female divinity. . . . We
are the children of those lost matristic tribes, violently invaded, co-
opted and enculturated.[2]

The rhythm of this story is unmistakable, moving in a great wave
pattern across human history. Respect for the female surges, then ebbs;
perhaps it will surge again. This rhythm is the heartbeat of the feminist
spirituality movement. It pulses out into the greater culture where it

gradually leaches into the popular mentality as something between folk wisdom and historical fact. I have overheard conversations in trains and restaurants of the "Did you know?" variety: "Did you know that everyone used to worship goddesses?" "Did you know that women used to run society?" I have listened to professors in fields from English to economics comparing notes on how to introduce students to the revelation that male social power is a recent innovation in the history of human civilization. These conversations take place outside feminist spirituality circles: inside, this is a story ceaselessly told, a favorite yarn worn smooth and sweet around the edges with its multiple recountings.

With apologies to Mircea Eliade, I call this story the movement's "sacred history." In *The Myth of the Eternal Return,* Eliade describes how the concept of time functions in different societies and how this is encoded in religious belief and practice. Speaking of "archaic" societies, Eliade writes: "[The] 'history' of the Cosmos and of human society is a 'sacred history,' preserved and transmitted through myths. More than that, it is a 'history' that can be repeated indefinitely, in the sense that the myths serve as models for ceremonies that periodically reactualize the tremendous events that occurred at the beginning of time."[3] Spiritual feminists are little interested in the creation of the cosmos, but tales of early human societies function in feminist spirituality in a way similar to creation stories: These early societies were the domain of the goddess. Under her devoted beneficence, the human race had its true beginnings. Spiritual feminists return to these times in art and imagination, seeking inspiration and sustenance, learning the taste and feel of being human on earth when civilization and nature were in synergy, not competition. The story of how this Shangri-la was wrenched apart at the seams is feminist spirituality's "myth of origins" for the patriarchy, an understanding and a critique of male-dominated society in a single package. The entire cycle, from bliss to destruction to rejuvenated hope, is a narrative that functions religiously: a sacred history. It explains who we are, how we came to be, where we are going, and how to get there. In a few simple lines, one finds a thealogy, a values system, and a political agenda all interleaved.

Feminist spirituality's sacred history is a new story on a preexisting model. The idea of matriarchy has long been a part of Western consciousness. In a society with strongly differentiated sex roles, there is a natural urge to imagine what society would look like if the roles were reversed, and to develop legends and fairy tales to explore this premise. This exercise in imagination was taken one step further by nineteenth-century cultural historians such as Frederich Engels, J. J. Bachofen, Sir E. B. Tylor, and Lewis Henry Morgan who developed a theoretical case for the existence of ancient matriarchies. These "armchair anthropologists" argued that early societies, who had no sure means of determining paternity, were of necessity matrilineal, determining a child's kinship through the mother's line. The primal social unit was a mother and her children. Since economic and social power usually pass through kinship lines, these thinkers reasoned, in a matrilineal society all power would be channeled through women. Women may not have retained all power and authority in such societies, they said, but they would have been in a position to control and dispense power. And so in the eyes of these nineteenth-century cultural historians, prehistoric societies could properly be called matriarchal, meaning that the final social authority belonged to mothers, or more generally, to women. Matriarchy came to an end (and patriarchy was born), they suggested, when men took control of reproduction by enforcing monogamous marriage. As Engels writes in *The Origin of the Family, Private Property, and the State:* "The first class opposition that appears in history coincides with the development of the antagonism between man and woman in monogamous marriage, and the first class oppression coincides with that of the female sex by the male."[4]

According to this early theory of matriarchy, the dominance of women in society had its reflection in myth and religion, where female deities or a monotheistic goddess reigned supreme. Assuming the primacy of maternity, and combining this with a near-universal human tendency toward ancestor worship, the ultimate mythical ancestor would quite naturally be a mother goddess. Anthropologists and folklorists of the twentieth century, such as Sir James Frazer, Robert Briffault, Robert Graves, Margaret Murray, and Erich Neumann, fleshed out this theoretical matriarchal religion by examining mythological images of women and goddesses. Working on the assumption that "primitive" cultures are living remnants of human prehistory, these thinkers looked at myths from living cultures, and also the tattered remains of ancient mythologies, and concluded that goddesses were indeed preeminent in prehistoric societies. Their theories were further buttressed by a spate of archaeological findings, conducted mainly in the post-World War II years, that indicated widespread goddess worship in the ancient Near East.[5]

With such rich soil to till, spiritual feminists have not tarried in bringing together these diverse sources to germinate a myth that is both historically plausible and religiously useful. With growing feminist interest in a theory of ancient matriarchies, more and more women have educated themselves in the niceties of archaeological research and have begun to interpret—and even to find—their own evidence. Others, equipped only with their imagination and desire, have filled in details where those were lacking and created a sacred history filled with poetry, grace, and numinous delight.

Feminist spirituality's sacred history is not a matter of doctrine or scripture; it is a living story remade in every telling, by every teller. It is a story frequently written down. There are entire books devoted to reconstructing just one phase of this sacred history: for example, the worldwide existence of ancient matriarchies or the persecution of women as witches in Europe in the sixteenth and seventeenth centuries. Other books treat the entire sweep of feminist spirituality's sacred history and assess its significance for society today. But even books that focus on other topics, say magic or ritual, will include a couple of paragraphs summing up the movement's sacred history. This sacred history is seldom merely referred to: it is told, and told again, as though each reader were hearing it for the first time. Sometimes it is told in poetic form, as in this excerpt from "Non sumus qualis erasmus" by P. M. Pederson:

> We are not now as once we used to be,
> Anna, Athana, Anantis, Urana,
> For we are slaves, whom once you knew as free,
> Nina, Innina, Nanna Innana . . .
> Blind fathers of blind sons, they cannot see,
> Dictinna, Diti, Hera, Diana,
> Whilst we are slaves, they never can be free,
> Nina, Innina, Nanna Innana.[6]

Feminist spirituality's sacred history is not only or even primarily a literary story: it is an oral one. There are two major study curriculums, *Cakes for the Queen of Heaven* and *The Partnership Way*, whose main task is to teach this sacred history. Reporting on alumnae of the former curriculum, journalist Christina Robb says the legacy of their study is this insight: "Before the religions of Judaism and Christianity and before the God-heavy pantheons of ancient Greece and Rome, paleolithic and neolithic people all over the world worshiped a goddess in three persons—maiden, mother and crone." A number of women have developed slide shows filled with goddess images from cultures the world over, and use these in public lectures to track the progress of goddess worship from its earliest relics up until its demise at the hands of the patriarchs.[7] Feminist spirituality's sacred history has even made its way onto the airwaves: A four-part radio series titled "The Return of the Goddess," authored by Merlin Stone and broadcast in Canada, begins with this "once upon a time" story spoken by a deep male voice:

A long, long time ago, in the very beginnings of human life in Europe, Asia, and Africa, people revered the mother of all life. Just as they'd been born from their own mothers, they envisioned a mother who had given birth to the cosmos and the very first people in the world. The Creator was the first Mother. Goddess worship, so widespread in ancient periods, was gradually suppressed and obliterated by later religions that worshipped male deities. This period of patriarchy began about 5,000 years ago. As male gods took precedence over the ancient goddess and her female clergy, men assumed the right to make all the major decisions, because the male god had given them that right. What was left of the powerful images of the female god was diffused in the beliefs of classical Greece and Rome, where the goddess was fractured into many parts, each subservient to the male god Zeus, the father that replaced the mother as the ultimate deity.[8]

Priestesses and other ritual leaders are also oral transmitters of sacred history, making it clear that this is something more than an alternative theory of Western history: it is a model from which women may order their lives. In *Laughter of Aphrodite*, Carol Christ describes a "womanhood" ritual that she and a friend designed for her friend's twelve-year-old daughter. The ritual was held in an ancient Greek temple, but its preamble occurred during the taxi ride to the temple. Says Christ:

I tell [the daughter] about the Paleolithic Goddesses with huge breasts and bellies, the givers of life. I speak of the time when women invented agriculture, and weaving, and pottery, all great mysteries, and of how the Goddess came to symbolize the creative power women knew, of how there was a time when we were not afraid but walked upright, confident in our powers. Briefly I speak of how and why this power was lost, of how religion became the domain of fathers and sons. . . . We tell [her] how lucky she is to be becoming woman now when women are beginning to understand again that our bleeding is not curse but mystery, sacred gift.[9]

The key elements of sacred history are included here: ancient goddess worship, a patriarchal revolution, and the incipient return to female-centeredness. In this economical, mythic way, thealogical teachings are also transmitted: women are creative and powerful, and endowed with special bodily gifts (menstruation, childbirth, lactation) that are properly valued in a goddess-worshiping religion.

Feminist spirituality's sacred history is a synecdoche of the entire movement. If one were given a catalog of the many tellings of this story, one could do a creditable job of reconstructing the religion. And, befitting its brilliant encapsulation of sometimes subtle religious "truths," it is this story that is the central vehicle of feminist spirituality's evangelism to the cultural mainstream. The story of ancient matriarchies and their destruction by men, while not created sui generis by spiritual feminists, is the hallmark of the movement. In it, the key concerns of feminist spirituality are carried like so much ideological freight to the outside world.

And apparently, the trains are arriving on schedule. Women and men who have never heard of croning rituals are familiar with the concept that matriarchies predated patriarchies and that goddesses were worshiped before gods. This change in public consciousness is due in large part to the publication of Riane Eisler's *The Chalice and the Blade*. Heralded by critics as "the most significant work published in our lifetimes" and "as important, perhaps more important, than the unearthing of Troy or the deciphering of cuneiform," it is said by some to be "perhaps a key to our survival," something that "might make the future possible." In roughly five years of publication, *The Chalice and the Blade* sold 181,000 copies in softcover and 24,800 in hardcover.[10] *The Chalice and the Blade*, like a number of other works, combines archaeological evidence with anthropological speculation and culture criticism to devise a lengthy telling of feminist spirituality's sacred history. Where Eisler's work differs from these others is that she has made several key concessions to the cultural mainstream that other authors have been unwilling to make. The first of these is that she has substituted other terms for the highly charged "matriarchy" and "patriarchy," terms that are not unavoidably connected to gender. In place of "matriarchy," Eisler uses either "partnership" or "gylany" (a word she has coined from Greek roots: *gy* for women, *an* for men, and an *l* to link the two). Where others speak of "patriarchy," Eisler refers to either "dominator" societies or "androcracy" (the rule of men).* In both cases, there is a strategic (if partial) distancing of these two types of social structures from actual men and women. Presumably you could have a "dominator" society where women dominated; hence, this appears to be less of an assault on men than reference to "the patriarchy." And "partnership" societies make it transparently clear that Eisler is not advocating the rule of women.

This goes far toward making feminist spirituality's sacred history more palatable to men, and to women who fancy themselves less "radi-

---

*Other writers have also sought substitutes for "matriarchy" and "patriarchy" for some of the same reasons, but have not moved so far as Eisler. Virtually everyone else has retained the term "patriarchy," and only softened the term "matriarchy" (with substitutes like "matristic," "gynocratic," and "gynocentric") without removing its decisively female connotations.

cal" than the average spiritual feminist. In addition, Eisler has devoted the better part of a chapter to recreating Jesus as a feminist hero, a "gylanic" man bringing a message to "dominator" society. In Eisler's hands, this becomes Jesus' primary mission, a mission that failed only because his successors were unwilling to see or act upon the true implications of his teachings. Eisler thereby invites Christians into the spiritual feminist fold, including a substantial group of people who would otherwise be alienated by feminist spirituality's frequent claim that Christianity is a misogynistic religion. Finally, Eisler, unlike some more radical spiritual feminists, is not antitechnological. She does not romanticize close-to-the-land tribal society as the ideal to which we should all return. Instead, she says that the basis of all the technological advances we have enjoyed was laid in prepatriarchal societies, and so concludes that advanced technology cannot possibly be in conflict with a return to "feminine" values. In this way, all those people who were hoping to keep their microwaves and VCRs can rest assured that adopting feminist spirituality's sacred history will not condemn them to pounding out the day's grain between two heavy stones.

But perhaps most significant of all, Eisler—along with several other thinkers—has detached feminist spirituality's sacred history from its original roots. She has made it possible for people to celebrate a "partnership" past and condemn a "dominator" present without feeling any compulsion to worship a goddess, practice magic, or meditate on menstrual fluid. Through their companion study guide *The Partnership Way*, Eisler and her partner, David Loye, provide curriculum materials that they recommend for use in high school and college classes and addiction and recovery groups (such as 12-step programs), as well as religious or spiritual groups.[11] Eisler has allowed feminist spirituality's sacred history to be marketed to whole new constituencies that might not have been receptive to feminist spirituality itself. She has, in turn, had an impact back in the direction from whence she came: feminist spirituality. More "moderate" spiritual feminists are now in the habit of talking about "gylany" and "the Chalice," "dominator" societies and "living in partnership."[12]

If Eisler is one of the movement's most captivating storytellers (especially to those outside the movement), she is only one. Every woman interviewed was willing to speculate about the details of feminist spirituality's sacred history, to say how *she* would tell the story (even in cases where she discounted her own authority). With some exceptions, spiritual feminists regard their sacred history as history, pure and simple. They offer evidence that they deem to be archaeologically and historically sound, and believe that any reasonable person will accept this evidence as proof that the basic outlines of their story are verifiable.

However, all of the evidence spiritual feminists offer in support of their sacred history is open to differing interpretations. Some of these interpretations do not uphold the thesis that ancient societies were either matriarchal or goddess-worshiping, that a patriarchal revolution ever took place, or that the persecution of witches in the Middle Ages was motivated by the desire to suppress either women or alternative goddess-worshiping religions. Some spiritual feminists, sensitive to the inconclusive nature of most of the evidence for their sacred history, are content to view the story as a religiously and politically useful myth. I will here be treating this story as a myth, not questioning the questionable evidence spiritual feminists tender in its support,[13] but simply presenting it. For whatever the status of the historical evidence, this story of matriarchy and patriarchy is the central myth of the new religion that is feminist spirituality.

Ancient Matriarchies

The story of feminist spirituality's sacred history begins in ancient times, times too ancient to be recorded in written language. Most spiritual feminists assume that goddess worship began with the first human societies, of which we have no records whatsoever. But since they cannot begin to prove anything about the religious or social practices of cultures that have left nothing but bones, spiritual feminists usually date ancient matriarchies back to the first archaeological evidence they can find for goddess worship. Merlin Stone, author of *When God Was a Woman*, initially dated goddess worship from the beginning of the Neolithic period, approximately 7000 B.C.E. Based on her continuing research, she pushes the date back farther and farther. In her Summer 9990* (1990) newsletter, *A Letter from Merlin*, she reports on goddess figurines dating from the Upper Paleolithic period in Russia, "from as long ago as 30,000 B.C.E." More enthusiastic spiritual feminists hearken back to even earlier times. Morgan McFarland, for example, claims that "the oldest known site of Goddess worship is on the banks of the Desna River in Russia," that it is "constructed of mammoth skulls and tusks," and "dates back to 70,000 B.C.E."[14]

Spiritual feminists assert that ancient goddess worship was universal. As Elizabeth Gould Davis writes: "In *all* myth throughout the world, from the sun's rising beyond the farthest shores of Asia to its

---

*Stone uses a dating system that counts 8000 B.C.E.—when women presumably invented agriculture—as the year zero. Others in the feminist spirituality movement have adopted her dating convention as a more "feminized" way of reckoning history than the standard one that counts from the advent of Jesus.

setting west of the farthest islands of the vast Pacific, the first creator of all is a goddess." In spite of this purported universality, spiritual feminist literature has been concentrated almost solely on Europe and the ancient Near East. However, there is a growing effort among spiritual feminists to defend the proposition that all ancient cultures worldwide were goddess-worshiping and/or matriarchal. As Hallie Iglehart Austen assures her readers: "All of us, no matter what our racial or spiritual heritage . . . have spiritual and blood ancestors who revered the Goddess. She is an important part of the heritage of every person on the planet."[15]

Spiritual feminists find several types of evidence for ancient goddess worship and/or the social power of women in ancient societies. Often the basis of their matriarchal theories is conceptual, as was that of nineteenth-century cultural historians. Women's ability to bear children, spiritual feminists say, gave natural cause for ancient peoples to image their creator deities in the form of a woman. As Rosita Veracruz reasons: "When our ancestors came out of caves, what did they think? Of course, woman gives birth. Whatever gave birth to us is a woman." Superadded to this is women's menstruation, their "ability to bleed rhythmically with the moon's phases," which spiritual feminists believe gave our ancestors "evidence of [women's] intimate relationship with the mysteries of the universe." In an article titled "She Who Bleeds, Yet Does Not Die," Rosemary J. Dudley suggests that menstruation led to the primacy of women because ancient peoples noted that "a wounded person, suffering loss of blood, inevitably weakened or died." Because women could bleed without dying, their blood—and presumably themselves along with it—was regarded as sacred and powerful.[16]

The theory that matriarchy should follow from women's ability to bear children is further strengthened by the frequent spiritual feminist contention that ancient peoples were ignorant of the connection between sexual intercourse and pregnancy. Because of this, it appeared that women "brought forth life alone and unaided." Many spiritual feminists assume that ancient peoples did not understand the mechanics of conception as we do because some preliterate cultures in the modern world also understand them differently, believing, for instance, that men may assist pregnancy by "opening" the woman's womb, but that the fetuses that eventually grow there are the result of actions by either the woman herself, "returning spirits of dead kin," or "the future child's spirit." Some spiritual feminists reject or modify this theory that prehistoric peoples saw no connection between sexual intercourse and pregnancy. They say that ancient *men* were ignorant of their role in reproduction, but ancient *women* were not; or that the facts of reproduction were shared knowledge, but that paternity was still uncertain because women had multiple sexual partners. On the fringe of spiritual feminist thinking are those who say that ancient societies did not recognize men's role in reproduction because men had none: reproduction was by parthenogenesis. Some women even suggest that there were no men at all in prehistoric societies, that men only entered the human race much later as the result of genetic mutations, hormonal imbalances in pregnant women, or incursions from other planets.[17]

Spiritual feminists also theorize that ancient societies were matriarchal because they relied on hunting and gathering and, later, agriculture for subsistence. It has been shown in modern hunting and gathering societies that the largest and most dependable portion of the tribe's diet comes from women's gathering work, not from men's hunting work. So, suggest spiritual feminists, those responsible for the gathering in ancient societies—women, they assume—had greater social power than those who were not so key to the tribe's survival. In agricultural times, they say, if anything this divergence was exaggerated. They suggest that women were the logical inventors of agriculture, having discovered the principles of plant reproduction in the course of their work as gatherers. Having invented agriculture, "women came to control the new food supply and the wealth it generated," and consolidated for themselves both economic and social power.[18]

These theories are all conceptual, based on extrapolation from what we know of our own society and those for which we have historical or anthropological information. They do much to make the idea of ancient matriarchies plausible to spiritual feminists (and others). However, the real excitement for spiritual feminists comes from archaeological evidence for ancient goddess worship and women's social power. The leading light of spiritual feminists' reconstruction of ancient societies as goddess-worshiping or matriarchal is Marija Gimbutas, an archaeologist and folklorist who calls her work "archeo-mythology." Gimbutas was the first archaeologist to suggest that artifacts from post-World War II excavations in Europe and the Near East supported the conclusion of widespread ancient goddess worship in this area of the world.[19]

Archaeologists have long theorized that the multitude of female figurines they have uncovered in Paleolithic and Neolithic sites have religious significance. However, they have (possibly as a result of their sexism) assumed female figurines were fetishes used in "primitive fertility cults." Spiritual feminists reject this theory and propose one of their own. These figurines are representatives of the goddess in her many forms, they say. Properly understood, they reveal "that the female deity in the Near and Middle East was revered as Goddess—much as people today think of God." Through the work of Gimbutas and others, a putative iconography of the ancient goddess religion has been composed such that not only are female forms representations of the goddess, but so are wavy lines, chevrons, triangles, snakes, butterflies, birds, fish, spiders, eggs, and even—amazingly—phalluses.[20] So defined, ancient Europe and the ancient Near East are awash with goddess imagery.

Spiritual feminists typically assume that evidence of ancient goddess worship also indicates that ancient societies were matriarchal, "woman-centered," or "equalitarian." The same one-to-one correspondence spiritual feminists see between male gods and male social power in the modern world leads them to believe that in the ancient world goddess worship equates to female social power. Elizabeth Gould Davis finds this truth recorded "in all myth" where "the goddess is synonymous with gynocracy: where the goddess reigned, woman ruled." Some spiritual feminists even suggest a cause-and-effect direction for this correlation: they say that goddess worship evolved directly out of women's social power in ancient societies. An early theorist of ancient matriarchies, Sophie Drinker, expresses this point of view in her 1948 article on women's goddess worship: "The women of the ancient world of seven and eight thousand years ago—in China, India, and on the Mediterranean shores—were themselves the prototypes of the deities. The hierarchy of divine and semidivine spirits represented the institutionalized role of women in that type of society."[21]

The only archaeological evidence spiritual feminists advance regarding women's social status in ancient societies (apart from that which they infer from ancient goddess worship) is from two southern European sites and one—Çatal Hüyük—located in present-day Turkey. Gimbutas describes the southern European evidence: "In the 53-grave cemetery of Vinca, hardly any difference in wealth of equipment was discernible betwen male and female graves. . . . In respect to the role of women in the society, the Vinca evidence suggests an equalitarian and clearly non-patriarchal society. The same can be adduced of the Varna society: I can see there no ranking along a patriarchal masculine-feminine scale."[22] The evidence from Çatal Hüyük is also based on burial patterns, but is somewhat different. Çatal Hüyük was a Neolithic "city" that flourished in the seventh millenium B.C.E. with an estimated population of between 3,000 and 10,000 people. It enjoyed 800 years of continuous settlement, and archaeologists have excavated "twelve successive layers, the remains of twelve different cities, one built on top of the other." Women in Çatal Hüyük were buried with "mirrors, jewelry, and bone and stone tools"; men were buried with "their weapons, rings, beads, and tools." What is more significant for spiritual feminists than grave goods (which do not, after all, seem to suggest greater social power for women or even an atypical division of labor) is the location of the graves. Women (and sometimes children together with them) were buried under large sleeping platforms located in a uniform place in each room; men and children (not together) were buried under smaller sleeping platforms located in varying places in each room. Elinor Gadon interprets this to mean that the people of Çatal Hüyük reckoned descent through the mother (since children were sometimes buried with women, but never with men); Gerda Lerner interprets it to mean that the people of Çatal Hüyük were matrilocal (husbands settled with their wives' families).[23] Again, most spiritual feminists translate matriliny and matrilocality into female social power; those most reluctant to make a direct translation suggest that if it cannot be shown that women were powerful, respected, or venerated in the ancient world, neither can it be shown that women were subordinated. If ancient matriarchies are not a certainty, at least they are a possibility, and this is enough to go on.[24]

Whatever the evidence for it, this is the content of feminist spirituality's myth of matriarchy: there was no war,[25] people lived in harmony with nature, women and men lived in harmony with one another, children were loved and nurtured, there was food and shelter for all, and everyone was playful, spontaneous, creative, and sexually free under the loving gaze of the goddess. People were in touch with their bodies and the seasons, there were no rich and no poor, homosexuality (particularly lesbianism) was as valid or more so than heterosexuality, and as Heide Göttner-Abendroth says, "the ability to bear children was just as sacred as intellectual creativity" and "a love affair was as much a performance of matriarchal spirituality as was a temple service."[26] Numerous cultural innovations were introduced during this time, ones that continue to be valued to the present day, including agriculture, writing, spirituality, law, animal husbandry, metallurgy, government, medicine, architecture, textiles, ceramics, wheeled vehicles, chemistry, astronomy, and mathematics.[27]

Spiritual feminists are nearly unanimous in saying that matriarchy, if it can be called that, is not the reverse of patriarchy. As Gloria Feman Orenstein argues: "Contrary to the ways in which patriarchal religions disempower women, the Goddess tradition does not exclude men. The Goddess religion does not turn patriarchal religion on its flip side and offer a matriarchal hierarchical system." Matriarchy is typically reconstructed as a society that includes men, that in fact gives them a more secure (if less exalted) place than that they hold in patriarchal society. But men did have to forego the power of fatherhood for the delights of sonship. According to Heide Göttner-Abendroth, in ancient matriarchies "men are well accepted and integrated as sons, brothers and uncles, but they have no importance as husbands or fathers." This is perceived by spiritual feminists to be no sacrifice at all, because men share with women the best status of all: being children of the goddess. Felicity Artemis Flowers explains: "Males were considered children of the Goddess and were woman-identified; the mother, who bore him and birthed him into this world was his frame of reference for existence. He was a Sacred Son of the Goddess and part of Her. She gave him a door into this Life, and he lived in respect and reverence for Her as the source of his being. Woman, the Sacred Female, was worshipped by the culture as the Mother of All Life." For spiritual feminists, this primacy of motherhood does not necessarily imply that women dominated society. Riane Eisler grants that "this certainly gave women a great deal of power," but says that "it seems to have been a power that was more equated with responsibility and love than with oppression, privilege, and fear."[28] Whatever spiritual feminists speculate about how ancient matriarchies treated men, these societies were not destined to last. Men were soon to seize the upper hand. How they did so—and most perplexing of all, why—is the second installment in the story of feminist spirituality's sacred history.

The Patriarchal Revolution

In dating the patriarchal revolution, spiritual feminists encounter a dilemma: On the one hand, they must date it early, before historical records that might complicate or discredit their picture of a worldwide goddess-worshiping matriarchy. On the other hand, they must date it late, to make the patriarchy appear even more short-lived in the long course of human civilization. Some spiritual feminists also have a stake in redeeming early Christianity and/or medieval witchcraft as the products of egalitarian or matriarchal cultures, and so they set the date even later. Dates for the patriarchal revolution range from 8000 B.C.E. at one extreme to 1600 C.E. at the other, with the majority of spiritual feminists citing 3000–2000 B.C.E. as the crucial turning point between matriarchy and patriarchy. Most say that the process was not instantaneous, that patriarchy caught on only gradually in the ancient world. Some say it did not fully consolidate its power until the modern era, but most believe that it was solidly in place by the classical era.[29]

Like the ancient matriarchies, the patriarchal revolution is believed to have been a global phenomenon. Obviously, if all societies were matriarchal, they all had to make the transition to patriarchy at some point if the world is indeed as universally patriarchal today as spiritual feminists claim. But again, when spiritual feminists tell the story of the patriarchal revolution, the emphasis is almost entirely on Europe and the Near East, particularly the Mediterranean cultures, the so-called cradle of (Western) civilization. It is for this region that spiritual feminists offer a well-developed theory of when the revolution happened, how, and—to some extent—why.[30] The most difficult of these questions to answer is why the patriarchal revolution took place, given that the ancient matriarchies were utopian or nearly so, and both women and men were happy within them. Many spiritual feminists express frank puzzlement over how such an event could come to pass. When asked in interviews where the patriarchy came from, spiritual feminists often responded with laughter, or with remarks like "I really don't know," "Good question!" or "Oh dear, I don't know how to answer that."[31] But most spiritual feminists find the question irresistible, and wonder aloud over various possibilities.

Some spiritual feminists say that the patriarchy developed as the result of increased population density and economic scarcity. They suggest that there was a period of drought, earthquakes, volcanic eruptions, and tidal waves, catastrophes that affected the food supply. Men's hunting skills became more important, and so their stock in society rose accordingly. Also, scarcity produced intertribal conflict, and men's role as warriors came to the fore.[32] A few spiritual feminists place the patriarchal revolution earlier, and attribute it to the agricultural revolution. They say that once people learned to take dominion over the land and its productive capabilities, men saw that they could take dominion over women and their reproductive capabilities. More commonly, spiritual feminists trace the patriarchal revolution to the practice of animal husbandry. This theory, put forward in an early work by Elizabeth Fisher, *Women's Creation*, says that men learned the facts of reproduction by breeding animals, and once they realized that as males they had a role in reproduction, they forcibly reduced women to the status of incubators for their sperm.[33]

One surprisingly popular theory of the origin of the patriarchal revolution—given that most spiritual feminists believe that men were treated well in matriarchal societies—is that men within the matriarchal cultures rebelled against their second-class status and violently seized power over their former rulers. The key proponent of this theory is Elizabeth Gould Davis, who in *The First Sex* says over and over again that men fomented a revolution in revenge for the neglect and ill treatment they received as the underclass of the matriarchies. Davis writes that under "feminine supremacy," men were forced "to wear false breasts and female attire" whenever they were given positions of minimal authority, and had over the ages been driven to sacrifice "mountains of foreskins, penises, and testicles" to the goddess. Davis believes the seeds of the revolution were sown when groups of dissatisfied men began to leave the matriarchies and form their own nomadic, barbaric, "marauding bands of adult males" that were "womanless except through seizure and rape." Women foolishly collaborated in their own downfall, according to Davis, by choosing these "phallic wild men" over "the more civilized men of their own pacific and gentle world" because the "wild men" had grown larger penises as a consequence of their carnivorous diet. Once these tribes had grown to sufficient size and power, they initiated a violent overthrow of the matriarchal societies.[34]

Zsuzsanna Budapest also supports this theory as at least one reason the patriarchal revolution took place. However, she suggests that the "hordes of males reacting violently to their position vis-à-vis matriarchal cities and matrilinear families" were not the well-endowed specimens Davis envisions, but rather men expressly rejected as inferior sexual partners by the matriarchal women. Other spiritual feminists wonder if perhaps mythological reports of early male sacrifice are accurate, and if men might not have been revolting against their victimization. Some fear that women's importance, never intended to take anything away from men, nevertheless left men feeling ignored and excluded. As Sara Copeland muses: "I wonder if maybe some group of guys was like feeling left out. They can't give birth like women, and what use are they really? And so, you know, they decided to make themselves kind of self-important."[35]

A tiny minority of spiritual feminists believe that the patriarchal revolution resulted from planetary influences, as the earth moved from the lunar, feminine age of Taurus, to the solar, masculine age of Aries. An even smaller group of spiritual feminists believe that the patriarchal revolution was initiated by extraterrestrials. Some believe these beings from other planets came as missionaries who sowed discord among the men of the matriarchal societies and incited them to rebellion; some believe that these beings from other planets were what were to become human men, heretofore unknown on planet earth, which was then populated exclusively by females. In this theory, men's hostility to nature and the earth is attributed to the fact that they come from outer space and continue to get their "energy" from outer space, while women, the original inhabitants of the earth, get their "energy" from the ground up.[36]

All these theories are present in spiritual feminist discussion of sacred history, but none is the authorized version most often promoted by women in the movement. The authorized version—and the one most easily defensible in terms of archaeological and mythological evidence—is that patriarchy was brought to the matriarchal societies by means of invasion. Tribes that were already patriarchal conquered the lands where women and men lived in harmony with the goddess, and they imposed a new and destructive social order on these formerly happy peoples. This story is virtually always told in reference to what happened in Europe and the Near East (occasionally India as well, and less often Africa, the Americas, and the Far East). In its standard tellings, the invaders came from the north, speaking an Indo-European language that has since become the basis for human languages from Europe to the Middle East to Russia and India. They were warlike and nomadic; they were cattle-herders rather than farmers. When they began to covet the fertile lands to the south, they drove in on their chariots and took them by force. These people, alternatively called Indo-Europeans, Kurgans, or Aryans, were "tall, big-boned, and light-skinned." They "swept down in huge hordes from the regions of the Russian steppes and the Kazakh" and "looted, killed, and enslaved the smaller, darker, agricultural Goddess-peoples, who were trying to live in their bloody pathway." According to Marija Gimbutas and Riane Eisler, who both draw on radiocarbon-dated archaeological evidence, the Indo-European incursion came in waves, occurring in roughly 4400–4300 B.C.E., 3400–3200 B.C.E., and 3000–2900 B.C.E. (Gimbutas's figures). The Indo-Europeans moved quickly to establish their dominance, and it was only on a few island communities such as Crete, Thera (Santorini), and Malta that the earlier matriarchies survived awhile longer. As Riane Eisler says poetically, "Like fingerprints in the archeological record, we see evidence of wave after wave of barbarian invaders from the barren fringes of the globe. It is they who bring with them their angry gods of thunder and war, and who everywhere leave destruction and devastation in their wake."[37]

The invasion from the north is the leading explanation of the patriarchal revolution, with the directions appropriately adjusted for other parts of the world (for example, the patriarchal revolution in the Far East is said to have come from the west). But in the pivotal case of Europe and the ancient Near East, there is a second invasion, this one from the south. In theories sometimes flagrant in their anti-Semitism, spiritual feminists say the Hebrew tribes came into the ancient Near East from the south bringing their patriarchal ideology with them. The goddess-worshiping cultures were caught in a vise grip between the Indo-Europeans and the Hebrews, and could find no escape. Elizabeth Gould Davis describes the Jewish contribution to the patriarchal revolution:

> The Semites never achieved a civilization of their own. . . . The Hebrews imbibed a modicum of culture from their long sojourn in civilized Egypt; and they were later shrewd enough to adopt the

civilization of Canaan, but to this already established culture they contributed nothing. . . . Yet it was these people, cultureless and semi-civilized, who first upset civilization in the ancient East by over-throwing the city states and later by dethroning the ancient goddess and enthroning male strife in the form of Yahweh.[38]

This theory is predictably annoying to Jewish feminists and to the many spiritual feminists who sympathize with them. Fortunately for sisterly cooperation, most spiritual feminists concentrate on the Indo-Europeans as the primary patriarchal invaders.[39]

The first steps in the patriarchal revolution, according to most spiritual feminists, were those characteristic of any violent conquest or uprising. People were murdered or forced into slavery; lands were taken; libraries of "matriarchal knowledge and wisdom" were burned down; women were raped and forced into oppressive marriages.[40] But however effective force and infiltration were in the short run, in the long run the patriarchy could only work its evil will by changing the way the goddess-worshiping peoples thought. Only in this way would the ancient matriarchies forget their happy past and consent to their oppression.

Patriarchal indoctrination in the early days of the revolution took the same form that spiritual feminists believe it still takes to this day: religion. Spiritual feminists emphasize again and again that the religion of the goddess did not simply lose out to its competitor from the north: rather, it was persecuted out of existence.[41] Spiritual feminists track the advances of the patriarchy through changes in mythology. They consistently detect (or construct) a protomythology in all recorded myths and separate this "original myth" from its "patriarchal overlay." The changes between early and late mythologies provide evidence to spiritual feminists about how the patriarchal revolution took place and indeed, that the patriarchal revolution happened at all. As Monica Sjöö and Barbara Mor put it: "Myth records the real history of the ancient preliterate world."[42] The patriarchs accomplished their aim of destroying the goddess by rewriting the myths to make the goddess gradually less powerful and finally subservient, and by installing male deities in her place. Among the patriarchal tactics spiritual feminists cite are the forcible marriage of the goddesses to powerful gods; the transformation of beneficent goddesses into minor, "petulant," or evil goddesses; the transfer of goddesses' powers to their male consorts; and the insistence that the goddesses are the daughters of father gods, born of them in miraculous ways. Some attacks on the goddess resulted in her death, as new male gods slayed the older goddesses to take their power.[43]

The upshot of these mythological changes is that via a corrupted, dual-gendered paganism, the way is paved for the monotheistic, exclusively male god that finally takes over and rules the West in Judaism and Christianity. This male monotheism is "the most radically patriarchal position possible," and its triumph is recorded for posterity, say spiritual feminists, in the Bible: particularly the Hebrew Bible or Christian Old Testament. The Bible is, they say, perhaps the best documentation we have of the religious conflict that ensued when patriarchal and matriarchal cultures clashed: it is a book written as a political tract aimed at destroying the last remaining underpinnings of matriarchal culture. Spiritual feminists pay special attention to the myth of Adam and Eve. Eve's sin is the desire for knowledge and power, the knowledge and power spiritual feminists say she had by birthright up until the time the ancient matriarchies were invaded by patriarchs from the north. She is tempted by a serpent: an ancient symbol of the goddess, according to spiritual feminists. And the punishment she receives for her sin is, in a phrase, "patriarchal marriage": childbirth is no longer a woman's goddesslike creative miracle, but her cruel destiny of suffering and pain; her husband is no longer her delight freely chosen, but her master appointed over her. Even more telling, say spiritual feminists, Adam is not born of Eve, in the way that all men are born of women; rather, Eve is born of Adam, in a way the world has never seen before or since. Human reproduction, central to the goddess's former power, is now made a male prerogative. With this manual of patriarchy in hand, the Christian church carried patriarchy north to western Europe, to cultures as yet untouched by the Indo-Europeans (who apparently missed a few places on their rampage southward).[44]

The patriarchal revolution instituted a new world order. And if the ancient matriarchies were characterized by harmony, the patriarchy, from its inception to the present day, is characterized by discord. The first discord—the foundation of all the others—is that which was instituted between the sexes. Under patriarchy, say spiritual feminists, women became men's chattel. Gerda Lerner describes the characteristics of the patriarchal family in ancient Mesopotamia:

> The father has the power of life and death over his children. He had the power to commit infanticide by exposure or abandonment. He could give his daughters in marriage in exchange for receiving a bride price even during their childhood, or he could consecrate them to a life of virginity in the temple service. . . . A man could pledge his wife, his concubines and their children as pawns for his debt; if he failed to pay back the debt, these pledges would be turned into debt slaves.[45]

Contemporary America has seen a few changes from this picture, but spiritual feminists say these are largely superficial; the specifics have changed, but the underlying ethos remains the same. Lady Miw describes the modern patriarchal family like this: "A woman's place is in the home, a woman's place is in the kitchen. Make my food, put my dinner on the table, I'm the breadwinner, I get laid when I want to get laid. You know the old story. . . . This is how far it's come in two thousand years. . . . There are some cultures where a vagina is sewn up, and cut open when he wants to get laid." The relationship between men and women in the patriarchy is described by some spiritual feminists as that of "vampire" to "energy source." Women are "batteries," and men "come and plug in and get a little energy out of you." Audre Lorde describes women's status in the patriarchy as the holders of emotional, nonrational, erotic power and says, "Women are maintained at a distant/inferior position to be psychically milked, much the same way ants maintain colonies of aphids to provide a life-giving substance for their masters."[46]

Another feature of the patriarchy is its continuing effort to discredit menstruation (which in the ancient matriarchies was a revelation of female creativity and power). The old menstrual hut where women could gather to relax and commune with one another and offer their menstrual blood to the goddess became under patriarchy "a declared *punishment,* a banishment for 'uncleanness.'" But this patriarchal denigration of menstruation is only where the trouble began. Women were forcibly alienated from their bodies' mysterious powers, but men, out of their boundless envy of women, created a male menstrual ritual that now threatens the survival of the planet: namely, war. Many spiritual feminists find the genesis of war in men's desire to mimic women's natural bloodshed. Sal Frankel says that when men started taking over the religion of the goddess, "they didn't have blood to give freely, so they sacrificed other people's blood, and they sacrificed animals, and they sacrificed women, and sacrificed other people." Diane Stein calls war "patriarchy's parody of women's monthly bloodshed,"and as Charlene Spretnak explains, "The bloody red badge of courage that warriors wear signifies man's only honorable access to flowing blood."[47] Whether war stems from men's inability to menstruate or other sources, spiritual feminists are nearly unanimous in the belief that warfare is a patriarchal invention. As Riane Eisler says, "Societies orienting primarily to the dominator model are characterized by the force-backed domination of one half of humanity by the other . . . and a high degree of institutionalized social violence, ranging all the way from child and wife beating to warfare."[48]

But the new world order that is patriarchy is more than the subjugation of women and the invention of warfare. Spiritual feminists give very broad diagnoses of what is wrong with the patriarchy. Women interviewed offered these summations of the principal characteristics of the patriarchy: "domination, hierarchy, the trying to manipulate and control things, beings"; "excessive desire to be first, excessive competition, which results in oppression, hurting others to your own betterment, control over everything that's external: control over the environment, the earth, control over other countries, other peoples, control over women, control over animals"; "aggression, inability to listen . . . total obsession with power and power hierarchy . . . abusive, insecure, emotionally inept, and trying to cover up for that through violence and through abuse of women." Patriarchy is obviously horrible for women, but spiritual feminsits say it is not beneficial for men either. Men were happy in the ancient matriarchies; they were loved and cared for, they were free and spontaneous. Under patriarchy, according to Barbara Walker, man "inadvertently produces many frustrations for himself, in addition to a world where love seems to have little or no practical value; a world where the generally desirable rewards are gained by cruelty or, at best, callousness. As a social system, patriarchy hurts men too."[49]

The story looks extremely gloomy at this stage. Women have lost their cultural battle for respect for all people and harmony with nature; men have seized abusive power, which they wield to everyone's detriment; the goddess and her religion are dead. Or are they? From here on, feminist spirituality's sacred history keeps its narrative percolating on seemingly equal proportions of hope and desperation. The desperation growing out of the patriarchal revolution is evident; what is not as evident, but also present, are the seeds of hope the story carries. For it turns out that the goddess was not so easy to kill. It took the patriarchs centuries to make real headway against the goddess, and even when they triumphed, they could not eradicate her entirely. She continued to feed an underground river of rebellion. Some spiritual feminists locate persistent reminders of the religion of the goddess within Christianity, which soon became the predominant religion of the West; all spiritual feminists locate at least a few surviving ideals of this religion outside Christianity.

Within Christianity, many spiritual feminists are especially eager to except Jesus from any criticisms they make of what they feel to be an otherwise overwhelmingly patriarchal religion.[50] Jesus is a hero; the church (sometimes personified in the figure of Saint Paul) is the villain. Rosita Veracruz suggests that "Jesus was crucified because of his feminist leanings"; Renee Landau believes that Jesus "was basically macrobiotic, believe it or not"; Lady Miw says that "Christ really loved women and the Goddess" and goes on to relate theories she has heard that "Jesus himself was a pagan, and a Kabbalist, and studied eighteen years in Tibet and Nepal, and was a fine magician."[51] Further hope within Christianity is found in the figure of the Virgin Mary. To many spiritual feminists, she is the direct descendant of the powerful mother goddesses that once ruled the ancient world.[52] Mary has, of course, been the victim of patriarchal dimunition, but to spiritual feminists, her survival attests to the enduring power of the divine female in the human psyche. A few spiritual feminists have redeemed Mary just as they have Jesus (though she is less in need of redemption among spiritual feminists, since she is female) by suggesting that her mission was a feminist one. I have heard several women propose that the Virgin Mary was a witch, "a keeper of the women's mysteries." She saw that women's situation was deteriorating and realized that over the next couple of millennia only a man's voice could be heard, so Mary trained her son Jesus to spread the message of women's power and harmony with nature.[53]

Outside Christianity, the religion of the goddess retained its hold over "the country people," even after the patriarchal revolution. These people were "the faithful who practiced their rituals in small bands and preserved their knowledge of nature's teachings." Some spiritual feminists believe these goddess-worshipers were intentionally preserving matriarchal culture in the hope that it could one day be revived when the patriarchy weakened. Others believe they were just following the old ways, seeing no reason to switch to the new.[54] The patriarchal revolution, as all-encompassing as it was, did not consign the religion of the goddess to oblivion. One could hope for its rebirth, the destruction of the patriarchal powers, and a return to the bliss of the ancient matriarchies. But alas, things were to get worse before they got better.

Medieval Witchcraft

The next chapter of feminist spirituality's sacred history serves to illustrate just how unrelentingly hostile the patriarchy is toward women and goddess worship. The persecution of witches in late medieval and early modern Europe is for spiritual feminists the second grand assault of the patriarchal revolution. It is an attack on what remained of the religion of the goddess and the social status of women after the first invading patriarchs rested from their dirty business.

The historical documentation for the European witch burnings is far more extensive than that for ancient matriarchies or the patriarchal revolution, but still requires spiritual feminist interpretation. As Marion Weinstein notes, the only historical evidence of the witch burnings available is that left by the persecutors. She reasons, "A responsible occult historian would no more accept an Inquisitor's history of witchcraft than a modern religious historian would accept a Nazi's history of Judaism."[55] Indeed, the accounts of witchcraft given by the persecutors and recorded in the confessions of the persecuted are not ones spiritual feminists could possibly savor as representations of the noble history of women and the religion of the goddess. In his essay "The European Witch-Craze of the Sixteenth and Seventeenth Centuries," historian H. R. Trevor-Roper summarizes the purported activities of European witches according to the inquisitors:

> Every night these ill-advised ladies were anointing themselves with "devil's grease," made out of the fat of murdered infants, and, thus lubricated, were slipping through cracks and keyholes and up chimneys, mounting on broomsticks or spindles or airborne goats, and flying off on a long and inexpressibly wearisome aerial journey to a diabolical rendezvous, the witches' sabbat. . . . Sabbats were found to take place on Monday, Wednesday, Friday and Sunday, and soon Tuesday was found to be booked as a by-day. . . .
>
> And what happened when the witch had reached the sabbat? . . . First, she was surprised to observe nearly all her friends and neighbours, whom she had not previously suspected to be witches. With them there were scores of demons, their paramours, to whom they had bound themselves by the infernal pact; and above all, dominating them all, was the imperious master of ceremonies, the god of their worship, the Devil himself, who appeared sometimes as a big, black bearded man, more often as a stinking goat, occasionally as a great toad. . . . They kissed him in homage, under the tail if he were a goat, on the lips if he were a toad. After which, at the word of command from him, they threw themselves into promiscuous sexual orgies or settled down to a feast of such viands as tempted their national imagination. In Germany these were sliced turnips, parodies of the Host; in Savoy, roast or boiled children; in Spain, exhumed corpses, preferably of kinsfolk; in Alsace, fricassées of bats; in England, more sensibly, roast beef and beer. . . .
>
> In the intervals between these acts of public devotion, the old ladies had, of course, good works to do in the home. They occupied themselves by suckling familiar spirits in the form of weasels, moles, bats, toads or other convenient creatures; by compassing the deaths of their neighbours or their neighbours' pigs; by raising tempests, causing blights or procuring impotence in bridegrooms; and as a pledge of their servitude they were constantly having sexual intercourse with the Devil. . . . [56]

The witch persecutions in Europe got underway in the early 1400s and received church sanction in December 1484, when Pope Innocent

VIII issued the papal bull "Summis Desiderantes Affectibus" authorizing the inquisitors to stamp out witchcraft. He apparently did so at the behest of Heinrich Institor (Krämer) and Jakob Sprenger, two Dominican inquisitors. These two published the infamous handbook of witchcraft, the *Malleus Maleficarum*, or *Hammer of the Witches*. The *Malleus* was released in 1486 and became the authoritative work used by the witch hunters to identify, extract confession from, and punish their prey. Prior to this papal ruling, the official position of the church was that witchcraft did not exist, and that it was a heresy to believe in its possibility. (In fact, in the eighth century, Charlemagne ordered the death penalty for anyone who "burnt supposed witches.") With the position of the church reversed in the late 1400s and the energies of the inquisitors running high, the witch persecutions began in earnest in the early 1500s. The Protestant Reformers picked up the practice when Catholic witch persecution waned and took it to even higher proportions. The peak of the witch persecutions came in 1630, after which the practice dwindled until the 1680s, when it was all but abandoned.[57]

As early as 1835, Jacob Grimm, a scholar of the European witch burnings, suggested that medieval witchcraft was actually the remnants of an ancient Teutonic religion. In two early twentieth-century works, Margaret Murray, a British folklorist, developed the theory that what the church persecuted was a thriving underground religion, and proceeded to detail what the religion involved by extrapolating from confessions of accused witches. Her critics have called her theory "vapid balderdash," and say that any similarity found in the confessions of accused witches "can be explained by a combination of identical questions and intolerable pain." They assert that medieval witchcraft was nothing more than the fantasy of the inquisitors. Some scholars seek a middle ground, saying that there were survivals of pre-Christian paganism practiced in medieval Europe, and that these were in part what the inquisitors sought out and punished, but that many witchcraft practices existed only in the churches' imagination.[58]

In the main, spiritual feminists take this last position. They believe that medieval witchcraft (insofar as it existed) was the underground survival of the religion of the goddess that flourished in the ancient matriarchies.[59] But suckling familiars, murdering babies, and eating corpses are rejected out of hand as politically motivated inventions on the part of the persecutors, as is worship of the devil, and most spiritual feminists believe that the great majority of women killed as witches were not practitioners of any religion other than Christianity. These women were, they say, only the tragic victims of the church's misogyny. Spiritual feminists argue that the church was reacting to a rise in women's status in the Middle Ages, to the continuing existence of pockets of matriarchal culture in the countryside, and to the rise of Mariolatry (the worship of the Virgin Mary in preference to devotion to Jesus or the heavenly Father).[60] The ultimate referent in all these situations was women; the solution the church saw, according to spiritual feminists, was to eliminate some of these women and terrify the rest into subservience.

Starhawk portrays the victims of the witch burnings as "the elderly, the senile, the mentally ill, women whose looks weren't pleasing or who suffered from some handicap, village beauties who bruised the wrong egos by rejecting advances, or who had roused lust in a celibate priest or married man." Some spiritual feminists claim that what the patriarchs were attempting to rid society of was a particular type of woman: one who was not thoroughly controlled by a man. Thus widows and the never-married were at special risk, say spiritual feminists, as were women who rebelled against the strictures of the feminine role. But many spiritual feminists emphasize the complete arbitrariness of witch accusations. They conclude that the only crime committed by accused witches was that of being a woman in a patriarchal society. As Anne Carson writes, "Even the most cursory glance at the historical evidence makes it plain that a great many women lost their lives at the hands of the male authorities of Church and State simply because of their sex." Mary Daly quotes early feminist Matilda Joslyn Gage as recommending that the significance of the European witch burnings can best be grasped by substituting the word "women" for the word "witches."[61]

The church's special motivation in their persecutions of witchcraft, say spiritual feminists, was to regain male control of reproduction and women's sexuality. The *Malleus Maleficarum* is filled with descriptions of the bizarre sexual practices of witches, and says in one passage frequently quoted by spiritual feminists, "All witchcraft stems from carnal lust, which is in women insatiable." Vicki Noble, Zsuzsanna Budapest, and Mary Daly all say that the portrayal of women's sexuality prominent in the witch trials is the product of "the perfervid imaginations of the celibate Catholic priests," or of "the demented, sadistic fantasy life of the male collective consciousness in the repressed sexuality of two Jesuit priests." Many spiritual feminists see a connection between the female-dominated profession of midwifery in medieval Europe and the frequent charge that witches killed babies or aborted fetuses. They conclude that women were being persecuted for their ability to control reproduction. Other spiritual feminists say the witch persecutions were part of a more general effort on the part of the patriarchs to exploit and control nature and the lower class of society in the interests of "professionalization and a new kind of economics of land ownership and production." Women, historically believed to be closer to nature (and believed by most spiritual feminists to be in fact closer to nature), were especially vulnerable in this patriarchal crusade.[62]

Spiritual feminists report that a huge number of women were killed as witches during the European witch craze. The standard figure in spiritual feminist literature is nine million.[63] The first reference to this figure appears in Matilda Joslyn Gage's 1893 book *Woman, Church and State*. This number is not supported elsewhere, and is never to my knowledge found outside spiritual feminist literature. Scholars of the European witch burnings place the numbers far lower, the lowest estimate being thirty thousand and the highest "several million," though all agree that firmer numbers cannot be determined.[64] There is more agreement between spiritual feminists and other scholars as to the predominantly female composition of those murdered as witches. Spiritual feminists almost always say eighty or eighty-five percent female; Elizabeth Gould Davis says the proportion of women to men who were burned as witches is "as much as ten thousand to one." Jean Bodin, himself a witch hunter, gave a ratio of fifty women to every man accused of witchcraft in 1580; other of Bodin's contemporaries estimate the ratio from a low of twenty to one, to a high of one hundred to one. Scholars tend not to quantify, though Richard Kieckhefer, author of *European Witch Trials*, estimates that two-thirds of the accused were women. But even those scholars who refuse to speculate on the proportion of women to men consistently use female-gendered language to refer to witches (as does the *Malleus Maleficarum*). Since this is a clear departure from the usual convention of using male-gendered language when gender is uncertain, it seems obvious that those persecuted as witches are assumed by everyone to be predominantly female.[65]

The European witch burnings work both as a persecution history for women and as a symbol of the resilience of women and their goddess-loving religion. As a persecution history, the witch burnings intensify spiritual feminists' sense that they are anathema to the patriarchal powers; it bolsters their conviction that feminism is a question of life and death, of the very survival of women. Several spiritual feminists have told me that they remember former lives as persecuted witches, and that this feeds their commitment to feminism and to feminist spirituality. Kathryn Theatana includes this excerpt from her journal in an article titled "The Priestesses of Hecate": "We know each other's faces from past times of horror—when we lost each other to the flames, to the rack, to the sword, to the sea. The sorrow from those times has lived on within us . . . has affected our every motion in this life. We have lived in constant fear of separation." Women who remember no such past incarnations as witches still feel the weight of this persecution history pressing close to their lives. Barbara Walker remembers happening upon a book about the witch persecutions in her college library and becoming physically sick as she read of these horrors. It was a feminist awakening for her: "I thought the unspeakable martyrdom of 9 million women ought to have been remembered more clearly than that of one man [Jesus], who may or may not have existed. . . . I thought the woman hatred that fueled these real martyrdoms ought to be comprehended and dealt with, instead of being buried out of sight." Esther Hoffman notes that the history of the witch burnings is not a distant history, but a near one: "It was only ten or eight generations ago. . . . My great-great-great-grandmother might have lived in that time. My grandmother's mother, or her mother." She feels that women today may not consciously fear the stake, but that it continues to have an impact on their subconscious and fosters "that whole philosophy of women being silent and not being heard and not being at the forefront and being second-in-command . . . the silence." In *Gyn/Ecology*, Mary Daly describes the treatment of young girls during the witch persecutions. When they were not killed outright as genetic carriers of witchcraft, they were flogged in front of the fire in which their mother was burning. As Daly concludes, "The horrors branded upon their memories must have carried over for many generations."[66]

But if the European witch burnings are a history of persecution, they are also a testimony to the strength and survival of women. One spiritual feminist song, "Allu Mari Mi Portate," pays homage to women in the Middle Ages who committed suicide en masse rather than risk being tortured and accusing friends and relatives of witchcraft. The chorus of the song is in Italian, and is taken from a nineteenth-century work. It is purportedly the hymn these women sang as they rushed into the sea together to drown themselves, proclaiming their love for the goddess. The English verses, authored by Catherine Madsen, are as follows:

> To the sea, to the sea let me follow
> to save me from burning and heal my sorrow.
> Taking the way of sand and water,
> the tide way, the last way to love my Mother.
>
> Down the dunes with sister and stranger
> the wicked women who dance in their danger
> craving the blessing altogether
> of grass and seaweed, shell and feather.

So in love does my lady enjoy me
that death by drowning cannot destroy me.
Life on the tide will run before me,
the long wave, the grey wave, will cry my story.[67]

Lady Miw also sounds a note of bitter triumph and heraism (the spiritual feminist version of "heroism"). She recites the terrors of the witch burnings: "When they buried the Goddess, between the twelfth and I guess fifteenth centuries, it took about three hundred years to wipe out nine million European women, and a lot of books went with it, and all our mysteries went with it, and all the churches were built on top of Diana's altars, on top of Diana's temples." In spite of all this, Lady Miw has hope, for she concludes: "They buried [the goddess], and buried her so deep that they swore up and down she'd never be found again. But they didn't bury her deep enough. They didn't bury her deep enough."[68]

The First Wave of Feminism

Most spiritual feminists do not linger long on anything in between the final (apparent) triumph of the patriarchy in early modern Europe and the present day, but some take a quick side trip to claim early feminists as a part of their history, as the foremothers who blazed a trail for the spiritual feminists who came after them. Spiritual feminists see in these women the faint dawning light that they hope will soon break into the day of a new era for women and for the goddess.

Elizabeth Gould Davis, in *The First Sex*, gives the most extensive coverage of this phase of feminist spirituality's sacred history, beginning with Mary Wollstonecraft and the publication of her book *A Vindication of the Rights of Women* in 1791. Others date the first wave of feminism—as many contemporary feminists do—to the 1848 Women's Rights Convention held in Seneca Falls, New York. However, they, unlike nonspiritual feminists, say the convention was divinely assisted by the goddess and that it was especially significant as an early insight into the bankruptcy of patriarchal religion. Zsuzsanna Budapest includes the dates of the convention, July 19–20, in her book of holidays: "On this day the most important love-gift to both sexes was conceived—equality. The Goddess moved our sisters Susan B. Anthony and Elizabeth Cady Stanton to begin the liberation of women then at Seneca Falls. . . . There is no doubt in my mind that with all that politicking, they instinctively called on the higher powers." Diane Stein writes: "The first wave of feminism, whose beginning is marked by the 1848 women's rights convention at Seneca Falls, New York addressed the issues of women's rights, of patriarchy and religion. With an awakening in women of who they are and always have been in society, a re-cognition of what had gone wrong and why, came the forerunner of the re-emergence of the goddess." Also mentioned as founders of this protofeminist spirituality are Matilda Joslyn Gage, Virginia Woolf, and Theosophists Madame Blavatsky and Annie Besant.[69]

The Present Moment and the Future to Come

Spiritual feminists are of two minds about the nature of the present— patriarchal—moment. Some are certain that there could be no point lower in the course of Western history than the one in which we are living. The patriarchy, they say, is now more entrenched, better defended, and more everlastingly violent and hateful toward women than at any other moment the world has seen to date. Others believe that the low point of Western history came with the European witch burnings, and that once women recovered from the shock imposed by these persecutions—no mean feat; many women have not yet recovered, spiritual feminists believe—they began to rebel against the patriarchal powers. Others feel it is futile to compare one era of patriarchy to another. The present moment is bad, the time of the Seneca Falls Women's Rights Convention was bad, the witch burnings were bad, and the patriarchal revolution was certainly no picnic. It is wise, these spiritual feminists counsel, not to be distracted by any fluctuations in women's freedom and power: as long as the patriarchy rules, any freedom and power women have is only contingently permitted to them and can be snatched away at a moment's notice.

The real significance of the present moment, however, is what it bodes for the future. And what it bodes for the future turns out to have little to do with how the present moment is conceptualized. Whatever spiritual feminists say about the present moment, there is one position on the future that dominates in feminist spirituality, and it is this: We are at a crossroads as a planet. Destruction or salvation are equally likely outcomes, and the die will soon be irretrievably cast. Things are growing worse, the times are increasingly perilous. But there are grounds for hope, and these grounds are female. The serious, united effort of women to transform planetary culture can win the day (perhaps with the assistance of the goddess) and usher in a new age of peace and prosperity.

Only a few spiritual feminists are willing to go on record as saying that a new age is definitely coming, that the patriarchy will soon be history. Of those who do, most say this is so because the planets and stars have decreed it. Marion Weinstein has argued that as we leave the Piscean Age and move into the Aquarian Age, we can expect the patriarchy to give way. Says Weinstein, "We can afford to be optimistic about Aquarius! It has long been heralded in occult lore as a Golden Age for the planet." A different astrological theory says that the patriarchy will fall and the feminine rise—indeed that it is already happening—because human beings journeyed to the moon recently and "excited that [female] energy." (As Angela Price says in an aside, "God help us if we ever land on Mars.")[70]

Other dissenters from the spiritual feminist norm are those who think the patriarchy can be defeated only gradually, and that it may take a very long time to complete the process. Marguerite Keane's prediction is that it will take fifteen hundred years to "emerge from patriarchy"; Nancy Robison says the patriarchy might end "a few thousand years from now"; Esther Hoffman says, "I don't think it will happen in my lifetime; it's gonna take a few generations." For some, this is not as depressing as it sounds, because they believe that change is already taking place and will continue to take place until the patriarchy is eventually dismantled. Suzanne Courveline predicts that "we'll chip away here, and change a phrase there, reeducate, make new stories, begin to say no, begin to reclaim, begin to reclaim our history." Others are more fatalistic, believing that nothing they say or do can exert any real pressure against the patriarchy. These women tend to be resigned to working for a possibly futile cause, consoling themselves with the thought that they are making their lives and those of other women more tolerable in an intolerable situation.[71]

The majority of spiritual feminists share this pessimism, but they mix it with an even more profound optimism than that of those who favor gradualism. For them, it is clear that we are living in a time when a momentous choice must be made: either we will leave control to the patriarchs and kiss the human species and Mother Earth good-bye as we all perish in a nuclear holocaust, or we will demand a change just in time to save ourselves and the planet from certain death. As Vicki Noble poses the dilemma: "Will we go ahead into nuclear suicide, or will we change our direction and learn to follow the advice of our spiritual guides?" The outcome is usually believed to be uncertain. Again, Noble says, "We may become extinct . . . [we] may or may not survive this crisis." Some spiritual feminists offer time lines for the peril we are facing, saying that we have only a few years in which to dramatically alter our course before the consequences become catastrophic. In 1989, Starhawk wrote: "The health of the earth has declined alarmingly over the last ten years, and the next decade may see us take an irrevocable turn, either toward destruction or toward regeneration." Lady Miw gives us nine years; Barbara Otto says we have ten years, noting that "every scientist I've read lately says that's about the deadline." All these estimates put the point of no return within a year of the new millennium. Spiritual feminists, like many other alternative religionists, sometimes argue explicitly that the year 2000 is the pivot around which history will turn, for good or ill.[72]

If triumph over the patriarchy is not inevitable in most spiritual feminists' thinking, deterioration of the patriarchy is. Things are getting worse, and they will continue to get worse before they get better—if they get better. In one spiritual feminist's words, the patriarchy is "at the end of its rope." Unfortunately, it has no intention of letting go: the patriarchy is bent on clutching the world in its death grasp. As Monica Sjöö and Barbara Mor write: "We have only to look around us, to see [the patriarch's] vision for us: Robots. Computer hearts. Satellite missiles. Ground zero. Cruising nuclear penises targeting cities in barbed-wire bondage. . . . He has so abstracted himself from the female imagination and the cosmic-material 'fetters' of Mother Nature that he is just about to blast himself entirely *out of the picture.* And everything with him." Spiritual feminists predict innumerable nightmares to befall us as the patriarchy flails about in its death throes: the polar ice caps will melt; innocent animals will die; there will be "massive deaths" among humans; nuclear waste will befoul the planet; poverty and starvation will rise; AIDS will infect more people; the bubonic plague and leprosy will return; the stock market will fluctuate wildly; tornadoes and earthquakes will strike with greater frequency; violence against women will continue to increase. Elizabeth Gould Davis sums up and draws the natural conclusion from this state of affairs: "The ages of masculism are now drawing to a close. Their dying days are lit up by a final flare of universal violence and despair such as the world has seldom before seen. . . . Any and all social reforms superimposed upon our sick civilization can be no more effective than a bandage on a gaping and putrefying wound."[73]

Metaphors of disease and healing are frequently applied to this rising misery that is the consequence of patriarchal values being taken to their logical extreme. Dhyani Ywahoo explains that the current situation is "like the crisis of malaria fever, the time when all the sickness comes to the surface."[74] Some feel the disease is so serious that the living earth and humans as cells in her being are having "a collective near-death experience." Old and new philosophies and religions are cropping up everywhere and people are seizing them in desperation. Melanie Engler explains:

> They've done studies that when people . . . sort of died, but they
> lived, they went through this whole past life thing. Are you familiar

with the thing where the whole life goes before their face? Well one of the theories on why that happens is that the brain or the mind is looking for a way to deal with the situation. . . . I feel that as a species and a planet . . . that the Earth is rapidly doing the same thing . . . this rapid searching through to find the tools and elements that will create that balance to bring us back.[75]

The situation is dire and growing worse. Yet spiritual feminists are not feeling hopeless and fatalistic. Spiritual feminists predict terrible years ahead, catastrophically terrible, but they believe that the potential for revolutionary change is proportionately high. As Riane Eisler writes: "What may lie ahead is the final bloodbath of this dying system's violent efforts to maintain its hold. But the death throes of androcracy could also be the birth pangs of gylany and the opening of a door into a new future." Spiritual feminists are living in the time of the "paradigm shift," and in ways, they are loving it. As Sonia Johnson exults, "How lucky we are to be alive now in history's most fecund hour. . . . Learning moment by moment to be free in our minds and hearts, we make freedom possible for everyone the world over." Sally Gearhart also feels the thrill of living in dangerous times: "Every now and again I get overwhelmed by the significance of the times I am living in. I have been waiting, it seems, all my life, all my lives, for the movement that is now happening among women, for the birth of the womanpower that is presently on the rise."[76]

If anything can save the planet at this late stage, according to spiritual feminists, it is women. As Sally Gearhart goes on to say: "I believe that [womanpower] is on the rise *now* because the human species and its planet home are at a critical point in their interrelationship; history needs now the different energy that only conscious women can bring to it." Almost all spiritual feminists agree that women are uniquely suited to the task of transforming culture and averting disaster. Lady Miw feels that "it is up to we women now, to pull together and save what's left." Charlene Spretnak concludes her massive anthology, *The Politics of Women's Spirituality*, with these dramatic words: "The authentic female mind is our salvation." Whether women are able to save the world or not has partially to do with whether they willingly and in sufficient numbers take on that responsibility. But a far larger factor in the failure or success of this transformation is whether men take a breather from their wanton violence and destruction and give women a chance to steer the ship of culture. In the thinking of many spiritual feminists, men do not need to do anything more than this; indeed, are incapable of doing anything more than this. Others feel that men can be made to understand that the patriarchy must be eradicated for the good of everyone, including themselves. Such men, spiritual feminists hope, can at least be a booster squad for those women working for change. Perhaps they can even be fellow workers in the revolution.[77]

There is a notable absence in most spiritual feminists' program for the defeat of the patriarchy: the goddess. In many religions that predict an imminent apocalypse, the hope for salvation lies not in human beings, female or otherwise, but in divine intervention. In feminist spirituality, this is rarely the case. The goddess may be a resource, but change must be initiated and effected by human beings. The goddess is simply not interested in mandating a paradise, if indeed she is capable of doing so at all. But some spiritual feminists believe that she is sorely grieved by what the patriarchy has done, and the catastrophes that now befall us and those that spiritual feminists anticipate as part of our worsening lot over the next ten years are the goddess's doing. She is angry, and she is lashing out. Lady Miw marvels at this patriarchal insolence toward Mother Nature: "How can you be against and beat up your own mother? How can you sodomize your own mother? So now either she's gonna die, or like a wounded animal, she's gonna get up and say, 'Oh yeah? Have some lava!' . . . You can only push your mom so far before she's gonna pick up a rolling pin." Angela Price remembers someone saying of the goddess, "One of these days, she's just gonna shake the fleas off her back."[78] Spiritual feminists who attribute a degree of benevolence to the goddess say that she is not just punishing us, she is trying to be heard, trying to bring the human species back to its senses. Merlin Stone hears the goddess saying, "Open your eyes. Look at what you're doing, before it's too late." Kim Chernin asks: "Is it possible then? The female God is coming back to the world. . . . Unearthing herself from the female psyche? Making a claim to us? Taking us by the hair? Calling out when we try to ignore her? Bringing us to our knees?"[79]

The bottom line is that the goddess has no responsibility toward human beings, but human beings have a responsibility toward her. The goddess may help or inspire human beings in their efforts to save her, but she does not take responsibility for the outcome. Throughout the feminist spirituality movement one is presented with images of the goddess awakening. For thousands of years she slept; now she is awakening. The untutored might wonder how she managed to sleep through the patriarchal revolution, only to awaken now. But the goddess is not this sort of deity. She did not decide to take a five-thousand-year catnap, say spiritual feminists, so much as we decided to ignore her (or were forced to forget her in order to survive in the patriarchy). It was human beings, says Starhawk, who "turned away from the Goddess" during the patriarchal revolution, who saw her "fettered, beaten, raped, tortured, burned, poisoned, and dismembered." Her "awakening" now is really we waking up to her, ending "the dark night of Her exile under patriarchal domination."[80]

What would the world look like, according to spiritual feminists, if the human race managed to avoid patriarchal nuclear holocaust and strike out boldly in a new direction? Tellingly, spiritual feminists spend remarkably little time discussing the final chapter of their sacred history. Their story is not a murder mystery, finishing with all the loose ends securely knotted up. Rather it is a story whose final chapter has not yet been written. Spiritual feminist visions of the future are shrouded in a dreamlike haze, kept purposely fuzzy so that women may unite together to fight the patriarchy without bickering over the precise nature of a future that may, in truth, never arrive.* When spiritual feminists do venture descriptions of the future, they are wishful fantasies meant more to inspire than to blueprint. Riane Eisler's description of what will happen when we "resume our interrupted cultural evolution" is a liberal feminist utopia. It is the remedy to all the ills that beset us. By changing our underlying ethos, we can expect "a decrease in the seemingly endless array of day-to-day problems that now plague us, ranging from mental illness, suicide, and divorce to wife and child battering, vandalism, murder, and international terrorism." Starhawk's vision of the future is more lyrical, and lifts up themes of racial and religious pluralism, decentralized government, small-scale cooperative farming and child rearing, a predominantly trade economy, and a creative combination of the low-tech and the high-tech: skateboards and bicycles on the one hand, computers and precision tools on the other.[81]

Spiritual feminists permit themselves few of these trips to dreamland. The focus is continually brought back to the present moment, fraught with possibility and danger. Starhawk ends one of her tellings of feminist spirituality's sacred history by refusing to go beyond the recent rebirth of goddess religion, saying that the end of the story is beyond our knowing. She closes on this somber, challenging note: "Has the Goddess reawakened only to preside over the destruction of the earth? Or will our awakening come in time? For unlike other deities, the Goddess does not come to save us. It is up to us to save her— if we so choose. If we so will."[82]

---

*It is likely that spiritual feminists would not agree on just what sort of society they would like to see replacing the patriarchy if it were a frequent topic of conversation. Zsuzsanna Budapest has advocated "a socialist matriarchy"; others have insisted that once women lead society away from patriarchy, social power will be distributed without attention to sex.

Two things spiritual feminists will say about the future they dream of: it will not be patriarchal, and it will not be any simple return to the culture of the ancient matriarchies. Reconstructions of the ancient matriarchies are crucial for giving spiritual feminists hope, showing them that human beings have lived in successful nonpatriarchal societies in the past, and for giving them models of what those societies might look like. But much has changed since the time of the ancient matriarchies, and few spiritual feminists want to go back. Some do. They can imagine nothing preferable to living in small tribal communities, working with other women to gather the day's food and raise the children, presiding over seasonal rites in the tribe's ritual center. Most spiritual feminists, however, may enjoy living off the land for the duration of a spiritual feminist weekend retreat, but they have no intention of living their entire lives this way. Oceana Woods stresses the importance of the ancient matriarchies for providing inspiration, but indicates that what she wishes for is something radically new, something more compatible with today's technological sophistication and expanded population:

> [The existence of ancient matriarchies] gives me the hope that we don't always have to live the way we live now, in a male-dominated—not even male-dominated, the fact that someone dominates, that there are so many people oppressed, that there is a hierarchy of personhood. It gives me hope that we can get out of this. That we've had it another way. And we can create it. We don't have to go back to the way it was. I mean, that's not going to be appropriate. We have mass quantities of people now, the population is totally different, the world is different. We have advanced so much in terms of industry and electronics and mass communication, international communication; it's very different now. But we need some other models; this model doesn't work. And not only that, we don't have to buy the argument "Well, it's always been this way."[83]

This is, in capsule, the function of feminist spirituality's sacred history. No longer is the patriarchy the only system the planet has ever known. Not only that, the patriarchy is reduced by means of feminist spirituality's sacred history to a brief aberration in human civilization, an accident that was preceded by untold millennia of female power and peaceful harmony with nature, and an accident that will—with luck and effort—be corrected in the coming years (possibly in as little as ten years).

Apart from a tiny coterie of radical lesbian separatists seriously committed to eliminating men from the planet, spiritual feminists are certain that the future they work toward will have a place for men, a place in which they can be happy and productive, if not necessarily powerful and in control. Most spiritual feminists would not even withhold social power from men, once men could be trusted not to reinstate the patriarchy. The dream of a matriarchal revolution, if it can be called that, is not a revenge fantasy. As Charlene Spretnak reassures her male readers: "Fortunately for the patriarchs, the female mind uses power in more positive life-affirming ways than the patriarchal 'an eye for an eye, a tooth for a tooth.' In short, justice and cultural sanity interest us, not vengeful degradation and reverse oppression."[84]

What will come in the future, if spiritual feminists are allowed the opportunity to apply the values of the ancient matriarchies to contemporary society is yet to be seen. This is an experiment, spiritual feminists say, and the results are unpredictable. But we can know that they will be preferable to anything we have endured over the last five thousand years. Given how bad things are now and have historically been, stepping off the edge into something new—however ill-defined it may be—is not much of a risk.

·9·

Feminist Politics and Feminist Spirituality

A lawyer sits alone late at night in her firm's law library, searching for information she needs to argue an upcoming case in court. Tomorrow she must try to convince a jury that her client, who lost her job as a waitress at a four-star restaurant when the management decided to switch to an all-male wait staff, was the victim of sex discrimination.

A nurse, having finished a short shift at the city hospital, takes the bus to a local shelter for battered women. The facility's live-in administrator takes her from room to room, where she meets with women and children and attends to their simpler medical needs. She shows one woman how to clean and bandage her child's burned hand, and checks another woman's recently broken arm to make sure it is healing correctly.

A college student sits eating dinner in the cafeteria with a group from the women's center. Together they plan an abortion rights rally to be held on campus next month. They discuss possible publicity ploys, trying to decide if it is wise to hand out flyers after a local lecture by a right-to-life activist. They finally agree to send a small delegation who will rely on their best judgment of the situation at the time.

A high school softball coach calls a friend on the phone to work out the details of the ritual they are planning as part of a feminist educators' conference. Since there have been sexual harassment scandals at both their schools this year, they want to make this the theme. One suggests that they hang "one of those old lechers" in effigy, but they decide instead to ask all the women present to be silent and listen for the pain of young girls victimized by their male teachers. They plan to follow up the ritual with a discussion of how to be sensitive to the signs of possible harassment.

A child care worker arrives home late, as usual. There are always parents who seem too busy to pick up their own children from the center, and so she stays and tries to comfort them while they wait. Tired from her long day at work, she draws a bath, adding rose petals and sandalwood oil. She lights two white candles and standing naked before her bedroom mirror, she says to her reflection: "You are goddess."

All these women consider themselves feminists. But they do not always consider each other feminists. As it happens, those women who steer clear of anything that looks too spiritual are on firmer feminist ground in most people's minds. Women whose feminism consists of designing equinox rituals are not viewed in the same light as those whose feminism consists of raising a campaign fund for a pro-choice political candidate. One has impeccable feminist credentials; the other has some explaining to do.

From the time feminist spirituality first emerged on the American cultural scene, it has been charged with abandoning a feminist social conscience in favor of a mindless feel-good spirituality. It has, say its critics, sliced off its political roots and ascended into the airy heavens where oppression is meaningless and women never have to run for president. Many religions, both traditional and alternative, would take such a charge in stride. "Why care about politics?" they might say. "We are interested in people's souls, in the nature and destiny of the universe. Why divert ourselves from such weighty topics with the frivolity of politics?" Feminist spirituality has never had recourse to this easy answer. The movement wants to continue to lay claim to the term feminist.* To do so successfully, it has to hash out the meaning of this term with those who are more typically seen as its true holders: the feminist movement proper. Wherever spirituality may fit into the feminist movement, it does not hold the unquestioned prominence accorded to politics. The burden of proof is on spiritual feminists to demonstrate that their religion is neither hostile to nor indifferent toward politics. It is a burden most spiritual feminists take on happily.

Criticism of feminist spirituality as insufficiently political has come in several guises. Probably the most common critique is that spirituality is overly personal and can therefore never address the concerns of women as a class. Feminist spirituality is at best a waste of time and at worst a serious distraction from more important political pursuits;

---

*This is true of the movement as I have defined it. However, there are women who are nominally a part of the movement who prefer to speak of "women's spirituality" and who object to being called feminist. They may have no special interest in how women are treated in society, and want only to talk about "the feminine" and how this is expressed in their own lives.

it may help individual women, but it does not have the power to change the status of all women. Another critique is that feminist spirituality is "a cultural luxury of mostly white middle-class women," that interest in spirituality only emerges for women when their basic survival needs have been met. Such critics find it unconscionable that women fortunate enough to be comfortably situated should turn to the idle pursuits of spirituality when other women are still struggling to attain a minimal level of economic and physical security. The strongest criticism of feminist spirituality comes from those who argue that alternative religions are always the ally of the ruling classes. Whatever they may preach, what alternative religions actually do is to contain dissent, to reroute it to places in the social body where it is robbed of its ability to stand as a real challenge to the status quo. Alternative religions are not clumsily or ineffectively political, as the movement's more tepid critics charge; they are politically regressive. In a biting critique of the very basis of feminist spirituality, anthropologist Sally R. Binford asserts: "The function of myth is the same in all societies: to rationalize the *status quo*. . . . The powerless dream of and long for a mythic past and waste precious time attempting to document its reality. The bottom line of power and authority has to do with who owns and allocates goods and services, not with the gender of the deities we choose to worship."[1]

Those who take this position liken feminist spirituality to the Ghost Dance movement that sprang up among the Oglala Sioux and other Plains Indians in the 1890s when their culture was in imminent peril of being destroyed at the hands of the American government. Ghost Dancers "thought that ecstatic ritual and magical 'ghost shirts' would make them invulnerable to soldiers' bullets." They soon learned differently at the battle of Wounded Knee. Critics of feminist spirituality fear that this new religion for women is falling into the same trap, inventing a mythic power that is belied by women's actual social status. Because they falsely believe themselves to have magical and spiritual powers, say critics, spiritual feminists do not seek the real social power with which they might better the position of women, and so women's actual status remains the same or deteriorates.[2] Such feminist critics imagine the patriarchs laughing up their sleeves at the sight of women dancing and chanting under the moon, calling for the patriarchy's downfall. They are right where the enemies of feminism want them to be, venting their rage to the empty skies: utterly harmless and more than a little silly.

Critics of the feminist spirituality movement tend to picture it as a regressive element that emerged out of and then separated from a politically progressive feminism. In their eyes, political feminism came first, and then, sadly, gave birth to this spiritual aberration. The feminist movement was making rapid gains, they argue, until it fell victim to an internal split between spiritual and political feminists.* As a result of this political/spiritual split, "political" feminism—the true feminism—saw its ranks diminished and its message chilled. This story is an almost exact parallel to that often told about the youth movements of the 1960s. First came the highly political civil rights and anti–Vietnam War movements. But just when it seemed that real power could be marshaled against the establishment, large portions of the youth movement splintered off to follow Hindu gurus, drop acid, stare at lava lamps, and make daisy chains. The failure of the political movements to attain their full promise is blamed in this story on the emergence of an escapist counterculture.

The story has its political uses, but it does not seem to be an accurate portrayal of how the feminist spirituality movement came to be. Feminist spirituality did not gain its own identity until the early 1970s, and so seems to be a latecomer to the feminist scene and not the heir apparent to the early women's liberation movement. But spiritual feminism grew up alongside political feminism, and the tensions that later caused them to split were present in the feminist movement from the start. For example, the consciousness-raising movement, even in its heyday, was controversial for feminists. Some feminists described CR meetings as "hen parties," and insisted that they were "trivial" and "non-political."[3] It is these same charges, of course, that were later applied to feminist spirituality. Women who wanted only to face off against mainstream society and demand change were from the beginning at odds with women who wanted to explore their life experiences and develop their personalities in more powerful ways.

The debate between spiritual and political feminists began in the early 1970s and peaked in the late 1970s and early 1980s, though it continues to this day. Women who became involved in feminist spirituality during this time found, often to their surprise, that their new interests were not always greeted with delight and reciprocal interest by their feminist sisters, but with anger and outright hostility. As Zsuzsanna Budapest recalls: "Feminism, which you would think to be a natural ally of the women's [spiritual] traditions, resisted for many

---

*The terms "political feminism" and "spiritual feminism" juxtaposed to one another seem to imply that feminist spirituality is not political, an implication that spiritual feminists resist. I continue to use these terms, in spite of their inadequacies, because they were the terms used in the early debate between these types of feminists. Readers may wish to think instead of "political feminism" as "politics-alone feminism" or "anti-spiritual feminism," and of "spiritual feminism" as "spiritual-and-political feminism" or "politics-through-spirituality feminism."

years with all of its political might. We were called 'bliss bunnies,' nonpolitical, examining our navels. . . ." Jeannie Garawitz remembers that in the late 1970s conflict between spiritual and political feminists shook up the women's community in the city where she lived. She reports: "There were some women that were very, very, very political, who were like 'This is bullshit! we need a Take Back the Night march, we need legislation, we need more police protection, and you guys are sitting there going "om, om, om, om." ' "[4]

Part of the reason for the early conflict between political and spiritual feminism was that these two worlds occupied the same social space. When the feminist spirituality movement first developed, it tried its best to infuse the feminist movement with its new insights. Women began to meet in spirituality groups and to convene spirituality conferences, but they also tried to hold rituals and workshops at feminist conferences and to incorporate ritual elements into feminist political actions. The Bloodroot Collective, a feminist bookstore and vegetarian restaurant formed in 1977, is a good example of this merging of political and spiritual visions. As partisans of the feminist movement, the members were eager to start a feminist business, to be role models of female economic independence, to give women a place to meet and organize, and to spread the message of feminism through their bookstore. But as budding spiritual feminists, they felt the Collective's project came about for more than these clear, pragmatic reasons. There was "something in the air"; it "came out of a dream." Early business decisions were informed by tarot card readings and the *I Ching*.[5] In the same way, when the Susan B. Anthony Coven No. 1 was formed in Southern California in 1971, this obvious expression of spiritual interest was well salted with political intent. Zsuzsanna Budapest remembers the first coven ritual in this way:

> We sang regular women's liberation songs, because there were no goddess chants then as there are today. . . . Katlyn worried that when this idea caught on, women would just want to use it as an excuse to have a great party. To make sure we would never forget how politics and religion are used together, she named the newly formed coven Susan B. Anthony Coven Number 1. . . . Since we were steeped in public service, most of our spells concerned political freedoms for all oppressed people: free Chile, grant women control over their bodies.[6]

Spiritual feminists in these early days worked hard to keep a political vision alive partly out of consideration for their sisters in the feminist movement. Women who had discovered feminism together and who hoped to forge into the future together were loath to be torn apart.

There was a visible strain developing between political and spiritual feminists, but because there was a desire on all sides to overcome their differences, there was an open forum of debate on the topic of spirituality. Those convinced that spirituality was leading feminism into a dead end did not hesitate to tell spiritual feminists that; spiritual feminists, for their part, offered defenses for spirituality and championed its political relevance. This debate is no longer so lively. Spiritual feminists believe this is so because political feminists conceded victory to them. They say that the priestesses are now being called home to minister to their political sisters, that at long last their feminist legitimacy is not in question. Zsuzsanna Budapest exults: "No longer are Goddess worshipers mocked as silly in the Feminist Movement; no longer are we seen as threatening clouds on the political horizon, but as the very essence of Women's Politics." As is clear now, says Budapest, "we [spiritual feminists] were the new wave of feminism. . . . In fact, it is the only kind of feminism going on twenty years later that permeates the entire women's culture. . . . The old politicos who swore that we were distractions and not serious feminists have long since stopped working, burned out, dropped out of the history-making stream, and blended into the fabric of the mainstream." Jade closes her discussion of the political/spiritual split on the same note of triumphalism: "Today women's spirituality is seeing a tremendous rise in interest, while the traditional women's movement, which disavowed the concept of women's spirituality, seems to have almost burned itself out."[7]

The debate between political and spiritual feminists has cooled, but not, I believe, for the reason spiritual feminists claim. The tension between the two is simmering gently rather than boiling over, not because one walked away with the victor's spoils, but because the two camps have worked out a mutually satisfactory separation agreement. Spiritual and political feminists no longer need to argue with one another because they are no longer best friends.* Most political feminists do not meet spiritual feminists as they go about their political business. They are not watching women they believe to be sisters in the revolution suddenly adopting strange religious beliefs and practices. This is not because the feminist spirituality movement has not grown as they feared it would, because it has. But when the National Organization for Women holds its annual conference, it does not include a special

---

*An important exception to this is found in the lesbian community, where women opposed to spirituality work side by side with women who practice it. Spirituality is more accepted by "political" feminists in the lesbian community than it was in the 1970s, but the debate also remains much more heated there than in the feminist movement generally.

session on introducing goddess worship in the elementary schools or an opening ritual in which participants are smudged with cedar and sage. And when the Re-formed Covenant of the Goddess holds its annual conference, it does not include a keynote speech on recent Supreme Court challenges to *Roe* v. *Wade* or a workshop on strategies for ensuring that Title IX legislation is respected in the local schools. The two worlds have grown apart.

Individual women continue to live in both worlds. There are certainly spiritual feminists who are professional activists and who are strongly identified with feminist politics. But chances are that though they may discuss their spirituality with their political peers, it is mainly something that they save for themselves and the members of their coven, if they belong to one. As with many religions, feminist spirituality has become for some of its practitioners one in a series of identities that do not compete, and may even feed one another in private ways, but that do not interact in the public world for all to see. That political feminists can tolerate sister activists who burn incense to Hecate does not mean that they share their conviction that such actions have any meaning. If a consensus has been reached between political and spiritual feminists, it is not that spirituality is political, but that it is not a clear and present danger to the feminist cause. It may or may not help, but it probably does not hurt either.

This superficial reconciliation of political and spiritual feminists disguises a wealth of continuing disagreement. In spite of the many individual women who function as both, there is a deep divide in feminist thought between the mind-set that might be called "political" and that termed "spiritual." And yet there are broad commonalities as well, areas of agreement not always obvious to those more conscious of their differences. Both spiritual and political feminists are intent on creating a feminist revolution, and even their political agendas are not so far apart. Where they truly come to an impasse is over their differing methods for bringing this agenda to fruition.

Feminist Spirituality's Political Agenda

The key points of feminist spirituality's political agenda are environmentalism, feminism, nonviolence, and community. Feminist spirituality's political agenda is most strongly distinguished from that of political feminists by its attention to ecology, and via this, to the oppression of women. When spiritual feminists were asked if they felt there was a political agenda associated with the movement, the answer was almost always yes. When asked about specifics, the first answer was most often one of these: "environmentalism," "animal rights," "green politics," "ecology."[8] One might anticipate that the first response would be something having to do with the treatment of women in society, given that this is the *feminist* spirituality movement. But for spiritual feminists, the fate of the earth and the fate of women are intimately bound up with one another. To be working for the environment is ipso facto to be working for the cause of women. Both women and nature have been oppressed and exploited by men, spiritual feminists argue, and this joint oppression has not been accidental. Women and nature have a special relationship, according to spiritual feminists, and the oppression of one quickly becomes the oppression of the other.

Feminist spirituality's position on the related oppression of women and nature has had a strong boost over the last decade from the growing ecofeminist movement. The term *ecofeminisme* was coined in 1974 by Françoise d'Eaubonne, a French writer, and quickly adopted in the United States. Ecofeminists trace the beginning of their movement to a conference in Berkeley in 1974 titled "Women and the Environment," and believe it burst into flower in 1980 with a conference in Amherst, Massachusetts, titled "Women and Life on Earth: Ecofeminism in the 1980s."[9] Ecofeminism shares feminist spirituality's basic premise that the oppression of women and the abuse of the environment are mutually reinforcing phenomena. As Arisika Razak writes in her article "Toward a Womanist Analysis of Birth":

> The physical rape of women by men in this culture is easily paralleled by our rapacious attitudes toward the Earth itself. She, too, is female. With no sense of consequence and scant knowledge of harmony, we gluttonously consume and misdirect scarce planetary resources. With unholy glee we enter "virgin" territory. Nature is *naturally* threatening—she must be conquered, reduced, put in her place. She can be improved on. The Earth must be entered, emptied, changed. She can be made to "yield up her secrets." We *will* have from her what it is that we need.[10]

The same relationship is detailed by Monica Sjöö and Barbara Mor, who write: "What can be done, under patriarchy, to one female body can be done, under world patriarchy, to the entire body of the earth. The pornographic images of women trussed up in chains and barbed wire, of female flesh bruised and bloodied and beaten raw, are really our species' maps of the mutilated earth, who for four thousand years has been tortured for power and profit."[11]

Most spiritual feminists would willingly identify themselves as ecofeminists. As Oceana Woods notes, "The ecofeminist stuff I read sounds so much like the women's spirituality stuff that I read, it's almost like I'm reading the same thing." The reverse is not true. Ecofeminists do not all consider themselves to be spiritual feminists, and some even criticize the movement. Where ecofeminism and feminist spirituality separate is that the latter is more forthrightly religious. This gives spiritual feminists even more reason to uphold ecology as the first point on their political agenda, for it is not only a cultural, or even a biological link that joins women and nature, but a religious one. The earth is the body of the goddess, so in Merlin Stone's words, "One of the most pressing political issues that those who revere the goddess are taking on today is the threat to the goddess herself."[12]

In the context of feminist spirituality's worldview, putting ecology on the political program quickly translates into putting feminism on the program along with it. However, it is significant that spiritual feminists mention ecology first—and not feminism—when they outline their political agenda. An obvious conclusion is that spiritual feminists value the environment more than they value women. For some spiritual feminists, this is probably true: just as many Jews or Christians would argue that God is more important than humankind, so some spiritual feminists believe that it is the earth, the goddess, that goes on and on while we only walk for a time on her surface; therefore her preservation is vital, while ours is only of contingent importance. But there are other reasons why it is ecology that receives top billing among spiritual feminists. One reason is that some spiritual feminists regard the relationship of humans to nature as the model for the relationship of men to women. If one is to truly pull sexism up at the roots, it is the relationship of humans to nature that must be addressed, for the relationship of men to women is just another of many repetitions of this first, fundamental theme. It is only sensible then to make ecology the top priority and let feminist political gains follow naturally from this.

But some spiritual feminists take the view that the more fundamental violation is the violation of women, that the male/female relationship is the model on which all social ills—racism, heterosexism, imperialism, capitalism, and the exploitation of nature—are based. And yet these women often persist in addressing ecology first, and feminism only secondarily. The impetus to do so, I believe, is not that environmentalism is a more basic issue, but that it is a more "user-friendly" one. Women whose ultimate goal is ending sexism concentrate on environmentalism as a way of reaching people who might be resistant to more direct feminist appeals. As Oceana Woods explains: "Maybe dealing with the environment and how we're destroying the earth is maybe the first step to changing all the [patriarchal] institutions and looking at our whole values system. That's a safer place to start, for many." Environmental politics is, specifically, a way of reaching men: the theory being that they will find it easier to identify with and care about the suffering of the earth than that of human women. Sal Frankel voices the hope that becoming involved with the ecology movement will bring men to understand something "that's more female in context," and will teach them to behave in more nurturing ways, thereby lessening their inclination to "fuck up women."[13] Environmentalism can bring together what feminism, unfortunately, pulls apart, and so it is simple political strategy for spiritual feminists to form a partnership with the ecology movement.

Some spiritual feminists do begin their political program with feminism, and all get there eventually. The issues they choose are those they share with the broader feminist movement: abortion, child abuse, the sexual objectification of women. Of these, the one spiritual feminists mention most frequently is abortion. "Pro-choice" falls right after ecology in spiritual feminists' descriptions of their political agenda. Abortion rights has been a tremendous rallying point for feminists over the past twenty years, but spiritual feminists feel a particular need to emphasize abortion rights, given that their thealogy and sacred history are heavily dependent on the glories of childbirth. Spiritual feminists are eager to ensure that women's ability to reproduce does not necessitate their actually doing so, and certainly not when they have not chosen this. In *The Grandmother of Time*, Zsuzsanna Budapest gives a religious argument in favor of abortion rights: "Where does it say that every little soul that manages to land a fertilized egg is entitled to occupancy? Abortion is the prerogative of the Dark Mother; she aborts us monthly; it is called menses. The shadow of motherhood is abortion, which is also our responsibility, making the choice of life and death as much a part of the Goddess as her life-giving good nature." Some spiritual feminists use the issue of abortion to make a more general feminist point: that women should have choice in all areas of their lives, not only in their reproductive capacity.[14]

Feminist spirituality has traditionally focused on rape as an important political issue; it is rapists either individually or as a class (perhaps composed of all patriarchal males) that focus spiritual feminists' anger. Rape is still used by spiritual feminists as a metaphorical stand-in for all maltreatment of women and the earth: it is the calling card of the patriarchy, they say. Spiritual feminist literature frequently mentions rape and its effects on individual women and on women as a class, and awareness of the issue is high within the movement. For example, a store in Seattle that sells spiritual feminist goods hands out bookmarks that have the 1968 WITCH manifesto (see chapter 2) printed on one side, and on the opposite side, this message:

> Almost any woman walking toward almost any man on almost any sidewalk: She automatically evaluates whether he looks dangerous; what shoes she has on; whether there are other people around, and of what sex; what time of day it is; what neighborhood it is; whether there are blind doorways in the buildings alongside; and more. He automatically knows she is fearfully evaluating him. He automatically feels the power difference, just as she does. (If he is walking behind her, then triple all the above feelings.) She's more likely to find and stick with a "safe man" because she knows there are rapists.[15]

Recently this focus on rape has been expanded to include child abuse and especially child sexual abuse. The Women's Spirituality Forum has made "ending the cycle of child abuse" its political commitment for the 1990s. This involves "raising consciousness about this issue and healing the spiritual hurts of the many who are affected." It also involves raising money for child abuse prevention agencies.[16] Certainly incest and child abuse survivors form a real presence at feminist spirituality conferences and workshops, and work to bring attention to the problem.

Probably the greatest statement of feminist spirituality's feminism is its use and interpretation of the word "witch." Certainly many women (and men) call themselves witches with no more feminist intent than they might have in calling themselves Presbyterians or Scientologists. But for spiritual feminists, being a witch, saying one is a witch, is most often a feminist statement, the symbolic encapsulation of a feminist political program. The witch is the powerful outsider, the despised and excluded person that is threatening to the established order. All women are witches, according to some spiritual feminists, whether they want to be or not, because they possess natural (female) powers linked to childbirth and their intimate communion with nature, and they are therefore compelled to be outsiders to male-dominant society. To choose witch status is, for spiritual feminists, to recognize that true inclusion is not possible for women in society as it is, that women are outsiders not by accident or happenstance, but by the nature of the game. By proudly acknowledging their exclusion, spiritual feminists demand their inclusion. For the outsider's power is threatening only to a narrow, oppressive oligarchy of men; it is evil only in the eyes of those who relegate it to the margins of society. In itself, it is good power, the best power: it is woman's power. For this reason, many spiritual feminists speak of "reclaiming" the word "witch." To do so is to stand in solidarity with the class of women across the span of history, calling attention to women's historic exclusion and persecution and proclaiming it illegitimate. As Angela Price says, "I think of myself as a witch because I claim that name for all the women who were killed." Or in Starhawk's words: "To be a Witch is to identify with 9 million victims of bigotry and hatred and to take responsibility for shaping a world in which prejudice claims no more victims."[17]

The remaining points on the spiritual feminist political agenda, non-violence and community, derive from this basic stance. If women are not to be shoved out of the human community, the community needs to expand. And in order to ensure that the human community never forces anyone else outside on the basis of their race, gender, religion, and so on, there need to be general prohibitions against the use of violence. Spiritual feminists often put world peace high on their political wish list, and talk specifically of the need for nuclear disarmament and a new defense strategy. This is tied to feminist spirituality's thealogy: As Starhawk explains, "If we are all interconnected parts of the body of the Goddess, then pain in any part, no matter how small or how far away, is in some measure felt by all."[18]

Building up the human community is the ultimate goal of feminist spirituality; the proximate one is the creation of a women's community where women can lend one another courage and support as they work to transform society. Feminist spirituality aspires to give women a place where they can come to know and use their special powers, and to provide a model for how human community can function.[19]

None of these spiritual feminist goals are antithetical to what political feminists seek. Political feminists may not call themselves witches, but they say that women are cut off from important roles in society—however much they may want to pretend otherwise—and that if they are to win inclusion, it will be because they work in solidarity with one another to demand it. Ecology and nonviolence are not always priorities for political feminists, but neither are they outside the feminist purview. As Barbara Otto sums up the political agenda of feminist spirituality: "Obviously choice, obviously antiwar and weapons corporations, obviously ecologically concerned, obviously people concerned . . . everything that's been cut out of the budget [during the Reagan/Bush years] is what I believe in."[20] Most feminists, spiritual, political, or otherwise, could subscribe to this.

The Political Methods of Feminist Spirituality

The greatest differences between spiritual and political feminists surface over the question of what political methods they deem useful. It would seem that spiritual feminists are working with a more expansive definition of politics than that in common feminist usage, since they count spirituality as political. This is the sticking point for political feminists. Spiritual feminists may have political motivations and an excellent political agenda, say political feminists, but they do not have a useful method. All the candle wax in the world cannot convince men that there is something wrong with rape, or the government that there is something right about economic parity between the sexes. Political feminists do not fault spiritual feminists for bad intentions, but for ineffective methods.

Spiritual feminists defend their methods from this charge in two basic ways: they argue that there are either indirect links between spirituality and politics or direct ones; for most spiritual feminists, there are both. When the links are indirect, politics is defined as advocacy, protest, holding or seeking public office, and the like, and spirituality is seen to support this by giving women additional motivation and energy to engage in these activities. This is a fairly noncontroversial position. With the exception of a few intransigent critics, most political feminists would not view spirituality and politics as a strictly either/or opposition. After all, one woman can both worship the goddess and lobby Congress. And if one woman chooses to boost her self-confidence by taking a shamanic journey to discover her power animal while another does the same by spending five mornings a week in a psychoanalyst's office, why should one be more "feminist" than another? If one woman spends her weekends refinishing her furniture while another spends them sewing herbal charms, why say one is feminist and the other not? As long as both are spending some portion of their time furthering the feminist cause and neither are proving an embarrassment to it, what they do in their free time is not at issue. Though political feminists might not themselves choose spirituality to heighten their political strength and motivation, if it works for other women, they feel no need to criticize.

However, direct links between spirituality and politics is the more favored option for spiritual feminists. Religion for most spiritual feminists is no hobby; it is not a purely self-indulgent avocation to be partitioned off from their "real" political work. Spiritual feminists say that their religion itself is political. Worshiping the goddess, reconstructing Western history, and creating feminist ritual are all political acts with political consequences. This position is not so easily digested by political feminists.

Indirect Links: Traditional Politics
Spiritual feminists who argue that their spirituality enhances their traditional political activity say that at the simplest level, feminist spirituality can be seen as a rest-and-recreation break from feminist politics

that is "energizing, restorative, regenerative" to those who participate in it. According to these women, spirituality is a necessary part of a full feminist program that must treat its activists as whole persons who are occasionally in need of nurture and support. Many spiritual feminists credit their spirituality for their continued political activism. Rosita Veracruz, who has "fought tooth and nail to make sure that our uterus wasn't claimed by the state," says: "What informs my strength in doing that is my spirituality, my understanding that I am every bit as much an individual on this planet as anybody else, any male."[21]

Spiritual feminists also claim that spirituality suggests the pathways down which politics should travel. For example, Corinne Foster says she has become more aware of the environmental impact of her actions since becoming involved with feminist spirituality. She reports that before she realized that there "is energy and vibration in everything," she was "disrespectful" of the land, throwing trash out of her car windows and so on. Now, she says, she could never do this, "because it would be like hitting a person." Barbara Otto suggests that once "you can feel yourself as being an interrelated part of this whole fabric of the universe . . . then it certainly makes the idea of war unthinkable, certainly makes the idea that farmers here burn wheat and people somewhere else in the world are starving—all this stuff becomes just incomprehensible."[22]

Many spiritual feminists are in fact involved in traditional political pursuits.* They go on pro-choice marches, they write letters to their representatives in Congress about animal rights, they put together newsletters for lesbian rights or against sexual harassment. Some women have combined their spirituality and politics in creative ways. They participate in traditional political actions, but spice them up with ritual elements acquired from feminist spirituality. Corinne Foster remembers one such combination ritual/political demonstration she participated in that was held in Connecticut. A group of women chained themselves together, and on their chains they wrote inscriptions such as Toxic Waste, Oppression, and Racism: "all the things that the hierarchy and the patriarchy represented to us." After a march through a local park, they arrived at an outdoor stage, gathered together in a circle, and to heartfelt shouts of "No!" they broke their chains. Barbara Otto continues this tradition to the present day with her plans for an Arbor Day celebration in which she hopes to plant an apple tree in

---

*And, it should be stressed, many nonspiritual feminists are not. Many women who consider themselves political feminists are not particularly activist, or were in the past, but are not now. Yet this kind of inactivity does not seem to be as threatening to political feminists as the inactivity of spiritual feminists, whom they believe to have been bought away from the political struggle by the promise of narrowly personal rewards.

soil brought from all neighborhoods in all five boroughs of metropolitan New York and use this not only as a statement "about the earth and taking care of the environment and nature and loving trees and all that, but also [to] have it symbolize our community and our interdependence."[23]

The general assumption of spiritual feminists is that political activism follows spirituality naturally and inevitably. But some women feel that the links between spirituality and politics are sufficiently indirect that they are not automatic, and so spiritual feminists must make the extra effort to stay involved in politics and to keep important political battles alive. Starhawk has been the most prominent spokesperson in the feminist spirituality movement for keeping the bonds between spirituality and politics strong. She believes that feminist spirituality can neglect politics while pursuing spirituality, and she warns: "It is not enough to confront our self-haters, to change our inner psychic structures, to spin new myths and new stories. As long as we feel powerless in the political and social arenas, we cannot be free." Starhawk has written extensively of her own political involvements, particularly in the antinuclear movement, and has served as a model for many spiritual feminists of how to merge spirituality and politics. She has also served as an indication to some spiritual feminists that there is no certain connection between spirituality and traditional politics, if only because they know so many women who do not follow Starhawk's example.[24]

Direct Links: Mechanisms of Social Change in Feminist Spirituality
Some spiritual feminists find in spirituality just the strength they need to stay in the political game. But for many others, the links between spirituality and traditional political action break down. They may feel guilty about being apolitical, and voice the hope that in the future they will be more political. But most spiritual feminists, pressed to defend their lack of traditional political activism, wish to say that they are feminists not because of what their spirituality inspires them to do in the political arena, but because of what their spirituality does of its own accord when set loose in the world.

Traditional political activism itself is critiqued by some spiritual feminists. It is not neglect or laziness that keeps them out of the political arena, but a belief that traditional politics cannot get society where they want it to go. For these spiritual feminists, traditional politics is a seductive mine field: it appears to be a good way to win feminist victories, but it contains hidden dangers that can blow the women's movement apart. Women may become unwitting token patriarchs, they may "feed the machinery by resisting it," they may lose their feminist ideals as they take on nonfeminist methods for social change. Politics, say these spiritual feminists, is a patriarchal enterprise. It is well suited to battling over distribution of the pennies in the zero-sum game of patriarchy, but it can never implant a new social system that will benefit all. As Sonia Johnson notes: "The planet will be a little radioactive ember blowing about in the void eons before we can begin to make the necessary transformations using the old anachronistic and corrupt tools. . . . The problems caused by patriarchy cannot be solved through the patriarchal system with the tools that system hands us. The blood dripping from them will corrupt everything they touch."[25] As an alternative, spiritual feminists offer spirituality.

The basis of spiritual feminists' conviction that spirituality has a role in promoting social change is the belief that spirituality and politics are truly two sides of the same coin, and that the split between them is a false and patriarchal one. To heal this split, to bring spirituality and politics together, say spiritual feminists, is to cause the exponential growth of personal and social power.[26] Spiritual feminist discourse is peppered with redefinitions of power: women seek "power-from-within," "power-with," "power of presence"—not the patriarchal power of coercion and dominance (which spiritual feminists often associate with politics as it is practiced in America), but a power that does not derive from anyone else's lack of power.[27] Power thus marshaled has political results, but it is first a spiritual power.

There are a number of models that spiritual feminists propose for understanding the direct links between spiritual power and political results. These include: divine intervention, magic, changing consciousness, cultural feminism, and alternative cultures. Divine intervention is the least favored of these mechanisms for social change among spiritual feminists. The goddess is not, in most spiritual feminists' perceptions, an intervening deity. But some spiritual feminists do believe that goddesses will help to create social change if women will only ask them to do so. For example, in *The Holy Book of Women's Mysteries*, Zsuzsanna Budapest offers this invocation asking for divine help in achieving political ends:

> Great Rhea, Mother of all living, turn the wheel of fortune to the betterment of women and their liberation. You alone have power over patriarchy in this time of oppression. I invoke You and call upon You, o mighty Mother of us all, bringer of justice, fruitfulness! I invoke You by the vestal fires in our cauldron, by the passion in our hearts, by the intense flames of the pyres that burned Your witches not long ago. Descend upon our enemies in Your fury. Avenge the wrongs, halt the rapes, illuminate the minds of our leaders and judges with your eternal fire. So mote it be![28]

One lesbian separatist spiritual feminist also suggests that divine intervention can further the feminist cause (as she interprets it). She recommends this as a technique for ending the heteropatriarchy: "Asking our amazon ancestors and amazon spirits, with full respect and seriousness, that earth be a female-only planet and earth males become extinct as soon as possible and that we all be safe, prosperous and happy in the transition and after."[29]

A more commonly cited, and related, spiritual feminist mechanism for social change is magic. The only real difference between this and divine intervention is that the powerful forces one calls on to produce social change are not personified, and sometimes not even externalized. They are the forces of one's own mind, one's own female energy projected out onto the world, and possibly multiplied by the forces of the universe that one can successfully channel. The universe is not necessarily sympathetic to women's causes—as it is in the divine intervention model—but neither is it unsympathetic, and the technicians of magic can manipulate the universe's energy to move in the directions they choose. Spiritual feminists do use magic to work toward political ends: they attempt to heal the earth, create global peace, protect animals from abuse, free political prisoners, and end the oppression of women through magical means.[30] Lady Miw and her coven are actively involved in cleaning up toxic waste through their visualizations. She explains:

> I pictured [toxic waste] as this sludge, this slippery slime that's just coating the ground. And I could see it and feel it burning her, like itching: "Get it off me, all this toxic waste and ooze and stuff that you guys created, this chemical mishmush. I don't even know what it is, you don't even know what it is." . . . What came to me is: dry it up. So I used the male energy of the sun to bake down hard, that sunlight, onto the female earth, and bake it, this oozy stuff, to where it would crust and crumble. And I just pictured it as scabs, just falling off of her, like dried out, harmless scabs, where it had no more radiation, no effect, but just kind of scabbed off. And we've been working that way a lot.[31]

One of Zsuzsanna Budapest's strategies for reaching feminist political goals is to use women's magical abilities to prevent the conception of boys. As she explains: "I'm advising people and telling my witches to aim for lowering the birthrate of males. The female principle can do that. The collective unconscious can do miracles. Even if we had a ten-year gap in bearing male children, we could start over again and take it from the beginning and train them differently." This particular program has not yet been successful, but many spiritual feminists claim success for their efforts at magical social change. Melanie Engler, who participated in an all-night ceremonial dance "to end the chain of violence against women and children" (for which everyone prepared by fasting for the three days prior to the dance), notes that "we began to see a lot of things change after that"—for example, abuse of women and children received increasing media attention.[32]

A number of prominent spiritual feminists describe magic as the effect of concentrated thought, of "changed consciousness." Starhawk, who has popularized Dion Fortune's definition of magic, "the art of changing consciousness at will," likens magic to politics, saying, "I also think that's a very good definition of political change—changing consciousness on a mass scale in this country."[33] This is one of the more common mechanisms spiritual feminists propose for social change. To change themselves (through spiritual knowledge and practices) changes the world. Development of the self is therefore a political act. Its translation to the political realm is automatic. Sonia Johnson explains: "We need to concentrate now upon learning about ourselves and the powers of our spirits. We need to concentrate upon changing our internal reality, knowing that as the foundations of oppression inside us crumble, external patriarchal reality must give way." This is a lesson Hallie Iglehart Austen learned the first time she did a meditation on her inner guide. During her meditation, she met "a young androgynous figure" who took her to see the High Priestess: "She wants me to realize that whatever I do as a strong woman contributes to feminism, even if I can't directly see the connection. Even if I spend a lot of my time meditating and just living a normal life, I will be filling that part of the world with new ways for women to be." Simply living as a changed individual has an inexorable impact on the world, pushing it in the direction feminists desire. It is a matter of—to borrow a Christian metaphor used by Austen—"letting our light shine," revealing "the brilliance of our inner light . . . so that we may each recognize our own radiance, come out of our caves and shine our light onto the world."[34]

Spiritual feminists expect changed consciousness to change the world because the world is ripe for change and women ripe for changing it. The old dry husk of patriarchal convention need only be shaken off for the fresh young seeds of feminist spirituality to sprout and take root. Even those who give a more grave estimate of the accumulated strength of the patriarchy believe that feminist spirituality is so superior in innate power (via its alignment with the earth, "womanpower," universal truth, or the goddess) that it can triumph with only a tiny number of individuals committed to its practice. As Barbara Starrett writes in "The Metaphors of Power," "We are far more powerful than we know, so powerful that only a minority of us, if we know what we are doing, could stop the death machine." Or as Mary Daly explains: "Since we have been conditioned to think quantitatively, feminists often begin the Journey with the misconception that we require large numbers in order to have a realistic hope of victory. This mistake is rooted in a serious underestimation of the force/fire of female bonding." Brooke Medicine Eagle even sets a number to this. In a vision, she saw "hoops of eight," and realized that an eight turned on its side is an infinity sign. She encourages women to meet in groups of eight because "when eight of us get together, when eight of us put our intention together, then it's infinite, it's literally that infinity sign of infinite power. We have the ability to do everything we need and want."[35]

Spiritual feminists also work institutionally for social change, though not in the institutions that political feminists recognize as those most relevant to the feminist cause. If political feminists have found government, economics, and law to be the proper foci of efforts at feminist social change, spiritual feminists have found their focus in "culture": in art, music, literature, language, mythology, folklore, and most importantly, of course, religion. Believing as they do that it is patriarchal religion that makes it possible for the patriarchy to exist, it is only ىensible for them to feel that a nonpatriarchal society cannot come into existence without a nonpatriarchal religion to support it. Feminist spirituality *is* this nonpatriarchal religion, in its adherents' eyes. It is the religion Sal Frankel is searching for when she remarks that "we're safer in a religion that says no, you can't oppress women. And that's like a real bold-print, first-page document. Ten commandments: one, you cannot oppress women; two, you cannot rape women; three, you cannot treat women as property. . . ." As Zsuzsanna Budapest says, religion is "the supreme politics," and "culture-makers are the soldiers of history, more effective than guns and bombers."[36]

Both of feminist spirituality's major models for the relationship of spirituality and politics—changing consciousness and cultural feminism—leave women who are searching for immediate feminist change hungry for something more. If these methods are sure, they are sometimes slow, and so spiritual feminists are still vulnerable to the charge that they are having no political impact. Spiritual feminists take refuge from these charges by saying that they are creating alternative cultures. What creating alternative cultures typically entails is withdrawal from patriarchal society. Joan Maddox sees this as the only realistic course, to "refuse support": "Not folding socks, not typing letters, not fucking them, not doing any of it." Sally Gearhart also counsels withdrawal, saying: "Who is the enemy? There may be no 'enemy' except a system.

How do we deal with 'the enemy'? As seldom as possible. . . ." Ruth-Inge Heinze, a spiritual feminist who grew up in Germany when Hitler was coming to power, comments: "Living under a dictatorial government one has to learn to cope. One learns how to defend life, and everything that is precious. One can commit suicide, or die in the process of speaking out, or learn how to raise an invisible shield."[37] The latter is the choice that some spiritual feminists have made. In their eyes, the patriarchy they live in is no less ruinous to them than was Nazi Germany to its victims. Not wanting to commit suicide, exhausted from speaking out and frightened by it as well, they take up feminist spirituality as their invisible shield, and crouch behind it to look out at the world. Here they devote themselves to healing their wounds and those of others and to staying out of the way of future danger.

If all of this sounds less than political, it is important to remember what spiritual feminists are doing behind their invisible shield, for they believe that the "negative" act of withdrawal is more than counter-balanced by the positive act of building an alternative culture, readying it for the day when the world may be receptive to it. In the meantime, they are offering a safe haven for women who have been deeply wounded by the patriarchy, and a place where other women can come to gather strength. Anne Kent Rush hopes that "women's spiritual groups can become birth centers for social change." Heide Göttner-Abendroth is part of an effort to create such a birth center, a separatist commune where women "work autonomously on nonpatriarchal models" and begin to live out their "concrete matriarchal utopia."[38] The insights of alternative cultures may never be incorporated into mainstream social institutions, but if—when, for many spiritual feminists—these institutions collapse, viable alternatives will already be in place, other models for living. Though these spiritual feminists step farthest from what are usually regarded as the centers of political power, their feeling is that they are still very much political; and given the state of the world, they believe they stand a better-than-even chance of being politically effective.

Utopian Politics

One reason political and spiritual feminists find themselves talking past each other when the goals they seek lie in the same direction is that their political analyses are set on different time scales. Feminist spirituality's is a religious time scale. It is not primarily interested in political successes that must be secured this year to the next. It is more interested in a vision that—once realized—will end forever the need for incremental political successes. By adopting this long-range focus, feminist spirituality frequently sacrifices an absorbing interest in day-to-day politics, just as its critics charge. But it does not thereby lose its political passion. Many spiritual feminists voice the conviction that they are in politics for the long haul. This implies several things, all of which are supported by feminist religious constructs. First, apparent defeats are not final defeats, and a backlash against feminism does not signal its end. With this wisdom in hand—a divine wisdom derived from the cyclicality of the goddess and nature, who move endlessly through days and seasons—one can be patient. Second, not only *can* one be patient, but one *should* be patient, because short-term gains are meaningless if they slow the process of long-term victory. Lady Miw cautions: "We have to remember to enlighten and educate, especially in politics, because we can get branded and ripped down real quick. We have to do this very slowly and very carefully. . . . We can't be the spouting politicians, with ferocity. We have to be gentle, firm, clear, and intelligent." This carefulness, this determination not to rush things, is assisted by attention to a sacred realm that provides perspective on the sometimes fleeting political issues of the day. As Starhawk explains: "Political awareness can become a tyranny of its own, not least because it locks us into the issues and perspectives of a particular time. But when we are looking at questions of the sacred, we move beyond time. To create the changes in consciousness needed to transform society at a deep level, we need insights broader than those the issues of the moment can provide."[39] Third, if one is to stay in politics for an indefinitely long time, one needs resources to replenish one's energies and motivation. In her article "Daughters of the Theris," Sandy Boucher writes that she sees feminist spirituality functioning in this way:

> The messianic enthusiasm and belief of the latest wave of feminism have now banked down into a lower, steadier flame. Many women committed to politics have come within the last few years to the realization of a need in themselves for something deeply sustaining and nourishing with which to enlarge their lives and support their commitment. The struggle for equality is long and can often be dis-heartening. To sustain it some women need to reach a place in themselves that can only be called "spiritual."[40]

Religion, spirituality, myth: these are ways in which people express and remember long-term truths. Feminist spirituality is committed to feminist politics, so committed in fact, that it has sought out the appropriate languages and religious practices to elevate feminist politics to a cosmic significance.

It is a very sober religion that says that individual women must work for a future they will never see and live out their lives in a world that conspires to demean them. Feminist spirituality is not this sober. Its final stroke of religious genius—one with many precedents in the history of religions—is to translate defeat into victory by saying that total revolution will be preceded by total collapse. Each and every political defeat can then be seen as a sign that the tables will soon be turned, that we are nearing the time of the paradigm shift. The next-to-last installment in feminist spirituality's sacred history is global crisis, but this crisis does not necessarily portend final destruction, but rather final redemption. Cosmic events do not happen overnight; it takes years of hard work and sacrifice to ensure progress. And yet when change finally comes, when the old order can no longer tolerate the strains imposed on it by the new, the birth of a new world does take place overnight, in an instant. Fortunately for those asked to tolerate apparent political defeats, spiritual feminists say this time is at hand.[41]

This apocalyptic vision is not one that is shared by most political feminists. Ironically, it is spiritual feminists—not political feminists— who have set their sights higher. In political feminists' eyes, the situation for women and society is grave, but not *that* bad; enormous changes are required, but not quantum leaps. For political feminists, a feminist future is a vastly improved version of the present; for spiritual feminists, the present they live in and the future they desire are as night and day.

Feminist spirituality practices a utopian politics. It is "the system"— the patriarchal system—that is the target of feminist spirituality's political program; and just as "the system" is a totalistic conception of a corrupt world, feminist spirituality's alternative is a totalistic conception of an ideal world. This devotion to the ideal leads to a parallel devaluing of the not-so-ideal: that which may be an improvement over the status quo but could not be described as paradise. One ritual I attended invited women to envision a feminist future by calling out their completions of this sentence: "I see a world where . . ." Responses included: "there is no codependence," "women are respected," "the earth is protected," "there is caffeine-free chocolate," and "no one is hungry." To test the political waters, I said: "I see a world where they pass the ERA." Immediately after, one woman said, "I see a world where we don't even need an ERA," and another quickly interjected, "I see a world where we are far beyond the ERA."[42] The order of the day is visionary; intermediate goals are perceived almost as irritants, distractions from more far-reaching social change.

Lest this be perceived as a tyranny of the dreamable over the achievable, it is worth considering that a reverse tyranny may obtain in political feminism: that of the achievable over the dreamable. Political feminists tend to regard discussions of what utopia would look like as a good way of setting themselves up for disappointment. For them, it is most important to keep their eye on the hurdle immediately in front of them: get abortion rights signed into law, for example, or even more narrowly, see to it that women desiring abortions are conducted safely past demonstrators. Spiritual feminists, on the other hand, think that such tasks are of limited value if they are not part of a larger plan to create a society in which abortion rights are granted to women as a matter of course. Political feminism sometimes looks to them like digging the same ditch every day and waiting for the partriarchy to fill it back up overnight. To break out of that cycle requires a distancing from immediate goals and an asking of long-range questions.

It is this distancing that worries political feminists, and it worries many spiritual feminists too, who are eager to strive for some type of balance between envisioning the future and negotiating compromises in the present. Sally Gearhart, who advocates separatist communes as a means of building a feminist utopia, still cautions:

> If we get too far into this attitude [that we can only worry about our own change, and let other women change themselves], we will not be political at all but only "groovy," "far-out" women, each doing her own thing and assuring each other every now and again that by living our mellowed-out lives we are thus doing our bit, creating the atmosphere, *tra-la!*, in which Toots and Amy and the governor's wife and the woman hanging out diapers in Middle America are all someday going to blossom into feminists—re-sourcement feminists, at that.[43]

Spiritual feminists are sensitive to this danger, and they work to avoid it. Direct political action is part of their strategy for social change, whether it is they themselves who are engaged in the action or not. All they ask is that other feminists accept that working to change consciousness and build alternative cultural forms is feminist work too, that it is the necessary groundwork for a coherent, sustainable feminism.[44]

Why Feminist Spirituality?

Women continue to discover the feminist spirituality movement every day, and to find things there that keep them coming back for more. Feminist spirituality does not hold on to every woman that samples its wares, but new women are constantly being introduced to their goddess selves, to the ritual raising of energy, to the icons of ancient matriarchies. Women committed to feminism find a spiritual context for their feminist convictions; women who have never thought of themselves as feminists find a religion that speaks to them anyway, and which may gradually nurture their unarticulated feminist sensibilities. Feminist spirituality's unique contribution to individual women is empowerment, and empowerment in a particular form: empowerment as a woman. Other spiritual movements are eager to give their adherents a sense of personal power, and may even offer that power in gendered terms, but none is as strong as feminist spirituality in providing a sense of identity, mission, and meaning that is indissolubly linked to femaleness.

The Experience of Empowerment

Power Deprivation
Sociologists of religion have long speculated on why some people are drawn to alternative religions while others are not. Theories have run the gamut from defective individual theory (that alternative religions are the final resting place for society's oddballs) to social disorganization theory (that alternative religions crop up and attract members when mainstream society is found wanting) to deprivation theory (people deprived of money, social standing, physical health, or feelings of self-worth are the population from which alternative religions are formed).[1] These theories are not mutually contradictory; probably all

contribute to the creation and growth of emergent religion. Feminist spirituality can be seen to conform to all these theories: Women are, as a class if not always as individuals, deprived of money, social standing, and self-worth; it is even possible to argue that they are deprived of physical health insofar as being female in a sexist culture militates against their having positive body images. The feminist spirituality movement came into being during a time of considerable social unrest, particularly around appropriate gender roles, and continues to attract interest in proportion to society's still heated and unresolved "battle of the sexes." And though most women in the feminist spirituality movement are highly functional by anyone's standards, there are also some very peculiar women inhabiting the spiritual feminist subculture.

If all these theories of alternative religions are at least remotely applicable to feminist spirituality, they are not equally explanatory. Defective individual theory is a stretch as an adequate account of feminist spirituality's appeal. It is true that I have met some strange women at feminist spirituality events, but I can remember finding an eccentric or two or three at every church or synagogue I have ever attended (not to mention those that have surfaced in classes, at workplaces, and so on). Feminist spirituality certainly has no corner on the misfit market. Social disorganization theory seems more promising as an explanation of the social forces behind feminist spirituality. At the least, social disorganization may be an important precondition for the movement's emergence. If mainstream society and mainstream religions were operating smoothly, fulfilling everyone's needs for bread and meaning, alternative religions would likely not develop. If gender roles were so clearly defined and thoroughly justified as to be beyond question, feminist spirituality would likely be stillborn. But social disorganization theory still does not explain why some women have adopted feminist spirituality as their religion and others have not. I believe that deprivation theory can.

To make the case that spiritual feminists are suffering from some type of social deprivation that makes them susceptible to feminist spirituality's appeal requires a more nuanced version of deprivation theory. The largely white, middle-class population from which feminist spirituality draws its adherents may, statistically speaking, be deprived of money, status, self-worth, and so on when compared to men of the same race and class, but compared to society as a whole, these women are doing well for themselves. Women who would on all counts seem much more deprived are resistant to the appeal not only of feminist spirituality, but of other alternative religions as well. It would seem that deprivation theory needs to be qualified to account for this.

In a 1972 article, David Aberle refines deprivation theory, calling it "relative deprivation" and defining it like this: "Relative deprivation is . . . a negative discrepancy between legitimate expectation and actuality."[2] Spiritual feminists are near-ideal candidates for relative deprivation according to this definition: nurtured on the women's movement of the early 1970s, these women came to expect a great deal that society has not given them. Reality seems a far cry from the perfect equality and perfect freedom that the women's movement demanded and believed was right around the corner in its early days. The discrepancy must loom particularly large in the eyes of white middle-class women who were inclined to believe that the American dream their brothers had apparently been living would soon be theirs. These are women with seemingly realistic dreams that are somehow just out of their grasp. Women from races and classes whose men were nearly as deprived as themselves were probably more circumpsect in their dreaming, never developing the very high expectations against which reality appeared so lacking.

Further refinement of the concept of deprivation can elicit a stronger explanation of why feminist spirituality attracts those it does. In his article "The Role of Deprivation in the Origin and Evolution of Religious Groups," Charles Y. Glock suggests that the effort to overcome social deprivation can be either religious or secular. He reveals a strong bias toward secular solutions to social problems, saying that those who work through religion are perceiving the nature of their oppression inaccurately and dooming themselves to failure. They may compensate for their feelings of deprivation, but they will never eliminate the sources of these feelings. But Glock also notes that people favoring religious solutions are "those experiencing the deprivation [who] are not in a position to work directly at eliminating the causes" while those who favor secular solutions "have the power, or feel they have the power, to deal with it directly."[3] That spiritual feminists are not working directly at eliminating the causes of their social deprivation is contrary to their own self-understanding. But it does seem true that spiritual feminists are women who have felt stymied in their more direct political attempts to work their will on American society, and that they have felt correspondingly disempowered. I believe that feminist spirituality is, to a great extent, a response to this feeling of disempowerment and an effort to redress it.

Thomas Robbins, in "The Monstrous Regiment of Women," suggests that disillusionment with political feminism lies at the heart of feminist spirituality's appeal. He notes that feminist spirituality grew in popularity after the "defeat of political feminism" he sees symbolized in the failure of the Equal Rights Amendment to pass Congress. Many spiritual feminists have, in fact, spent years as political activists, and typically they feel that they have nothing to show for those years, no tangible advances in the causes they have championed. They have been caught up at times in the fever of imminent political victory or disaster, and have lived as though the future of the world depended on their success. In spite of all their devotion and effort, the feared disasters have happened: bills improving women's lot have not passed Congress, women's wages have not been equalized with men's, rape and other forms of sexual violence continue unabatedly. These women were supposed to go on living as though the world had not ended; even more, they were supposed to pick up the pieces and wage yet another— probably equally doomed—political battle for feminism. It is a prescription for political burnout, and this is what many women suffered. They did not burn out from losing sleep over xeroxing flyers and attending Take Back the Night marches; they burned out from losing sleep to no apparent end and from the feelings of frustration and futility those experiences engendered.[4] Women who did not themselves have this experience often witnessed it, and they have suffered disillusionment by proxy.

In feminist spirituality, this thwarted political desire is plowed under to fertilize a different kind of feminism: one that uses religious vehicles to carry its dreams of social power. Thus it is a particular type of deprivation that gives rise to feminist spirituality: power deprivation. It is not money or physical health that is absent; even social status is available to most spiritual feminists if they are willing to take status where society offers it to women. What is lacking is the conviction that their thoughts and actions can make a difference, that when they speak, people listen; that when they articulate a legitimate grievance, society apologizes and makes recompense. R. Laurence Moore suggests that it is exactly this sort of power deprivation that motivated nineteenth-century middle-class, European-American women to become involved in religion. In *Religious Outsiders and the Making of Americans* he writes:

> As pampered creatures whose virtues were tenderly praised, but whose actual power was limited to certain realms within the household, many women were surely unhappy. Even though they had middle-class husbands who provided them with economic comfort and social status, they felt useless and expendable. . . . Although barred from running the churches because of their sex, they constituted most of the membership of both large and small denominations. They taught the church schools, organized the social life of the church community, and overwhelmingly, with their children, filled the pews on Sunday morning. Religion offered not only an

outlet for unfulfilled emotion, it was also one of the few nondomestic spheres of activity open to women where they could imagine they were doing something useful and creative. Religious life became one of the ways in which women searched for power or learned to do without it.[5]

Women are no longer as bound to hearth and home—and church—as they were in the nineteenth-century middle class, but much of this analysis still applies. White middle-class women have more avenues of power open to them than they did a century ago, but they still have not achieved parity with men, and for many the discrepancy has become intolerable. Immersing themselves in a religion where women are primary, where women's equality is a forgone conclusion and women's superiority a real possibility, spiritual feminists find a realm where they can exercise power, feel powerful, and compensate for the lack of power they experience in their daily lives.[6]

The feminist spirituality movement is filled with claims of power, allusions to power, pleas for power. Rituals, songs, poems, literature, even academic analyses of feminist spirituality speak with one voice on the desirability—and usually the reality, albeit neglected—of women's power. An invocation by Katherine LeMaster reads in part:

> Omnipotent, Omniscient, Omnipresent
> Infinite and Eternal are We.[7]

A favorite spiritual feminist song has these lyrics:

> Woman am I, spirit am I,
> I am the infinite within my soul [or "self"].
> I can find no beginning, I can find no end,
> All this I am.[8]

Women in feminist spirituality have truly become goddesses, with all the power and invulnerability that this term usually implies. As one spiritual feminist writes in a lesbian separatist publication: "I believe with all I know and all I feel that wimmin have a power among us that far surpasses any power against us. . . . Power is after all, the issue . . ."[9]

Empowerment as a Woman

The use of gender in spiritual feminist references to power is not accidental. For spiritual feminists, it is not enough for a woman to think of herself as a strong and powerful person who happens to be female; she needs to think of herself as a powerful woman. It is as women that spiritual feminists feel they have been scorned and oppressed; it is as women that they must be liberated. If it is women's bodies that have been the basis of a cultural mythos that denies women power, then women's bodies must be seen as the very source of true power. If women's sexuality has been regarded as dangerous, then women's sexuality must be regarded as the essence of life. If emotional qualities of empathy and nurturance are seen to make women poorly suited for public life, then empathy and nurturance must become the foundation of a radically restructured society.[10] Feminist spirituality is a religion for women who view accepting a traditional (inferior) feminine identity and seeking a traditional (superior) masculine identity as mutually unacceptable options. Feminist spirituality gives them the means by which to make the traditional feminine superior, and the traditional masculine feminine (where masculine traits are desirable). It does this most strikingly through its image of divine femaleness, the goddess, and what she symbolizes to the women who have found her.

The primary symbolic function the goddess has for spiritual feminists is as female self-image. The goddess, the many goddesses, are external projections of a new, desirable internal conception of self. They are figures that reflect back to women what they already—if imperfectly—are: powerful women. The goddess is, in Elinor Gadon's words, "first and foremost a model of empowered selfhood," or as Carol Christ sums up, "The legitimacy and beneficence of female power" is "the simplest meaning of the Goddess symbol." What the goddess does for women is to give them power in their femaleness, not apart from it, to make womanhood itself a powerful quantity. It is a divine redemption of femaleness. One woman, speaking of her initial encounter with the goddess, reports: "I could actually feel my last prejudices against my own female mind and body falling away." Sal Frankel explains the impact of the goddess on her life, how she has come through the goddess to feel that power can belong to her as a woman: "There is something that develops in you, where you are echoing [the goddesses] more completely; the more you visualize them, the more you experience them, the more you can feel a sense of how to act like them in your own life."[11]

Another of the goddess's symbolic functions, according to those who have a spiritual relationship to her, is that she broadens the scope of activities and personality traits that can be understood to be feminine, the appropriate province of women. Not only does she join femaleness and power, she joins femaleness to other qualities formerly categorized as male. The feminist spirituality movement uses the figure of the goddess to push the definition of "feminine" beyond culturally stereotyped "femininity": weakness, coyness, prettiness, deference. The goddess is not often portrayed with pink bows in her hair and modestly downcast eyes. Instead, she is strong, principled, aggressive. Rosemary Sackner explains her attraction to feminist spirituality's goddess images: "I need to have these strong images of women in nonstereotyped ways. I need to know that the deity of wisdom is a woman. And the deity of death is a woman. . . . I really want to see goddesses that can do everything. . . . these images of strong women in different areas, some of which are traditional for women, some of which aren't."[12] Jean Shinoda Bolen, a Jungian therapist, criticizes Jungian psychology for inaccurately compartmentalizing the feminine and offers a spiritual feminist reframing of his theory:

> Jung's psychology of women was essentially kinder than Freud's, but it was sexist. It assumed that if a woman thought clearly or thought well, had spiritual aspirations or considerations, was assertive or competitive, that it wasn't her that was doing whatever it was in this area, but it was her animus, her male component that was doing it for her. He felt that all women were by nature nurturing, people-oriented, receptive, and passive, and that any of these other characteristics that had to do with thinking or assertiveness in the will was done by her animus. . . . So it meant that if a woman was naturally a thinking-type woman, she would end up (if she knew this theory) feeling that it was being masculine to do this. And to find that rather than it being masculine, it's not only an innate part of her, but that innate part of her in thinking clearly resembles the pattern of Athena, the goddess of wisdom, who was strong and beautiful and thought well and was feminine, rather than it being some masculine part of her, makes a great deal of difference.[13]

In *The Goddess*, Christine Downing offers a similar perspective on the goddess Athena and her ability to "feminize" women's sense of their own power. She explains: "Athene is not just a goddess who takes on the role of being man's anima—she serves also, I am coming to recognize, as an anima image for women, and thus as a goddess who provides us women with a singularly confirming understanding of our own creative powers as feminine powers."[14] Through the example of the goddess's broadening of femininity and her linking of femaleness and power, spiritual feminists learn that all their characteristics, appropriately incorporated into their identities, are feminine characteristics.

Attaining this "true womanhood," this complete femininity, is crucial for many spiritual feminists, and at first glance it seems odd that it should be so. Why should women who denounce society's construction of womanhood and the limits it imposes be so intent on clinging to femaleness, in whatever transformed fashion? Ironically, I believe, it is because femininity has caused them such pain. Feminist spirituality is the attempt to transform handicaps into blessings, to take negative identities that have been imposed on one and convert them into positive identities that have been freely chosen. It is the path taken by those who believe, for whatever reason, that their gender either cannot or should not be transcended.

Spiritual feminists are surely right in thinking that cultural femaleness is difficult if not impossible to transcend. Gender is highly determinative of individuals' identities, so much so that there are simply no models available for how one experiences life as a woman or man whose sexual differences are not interpreted as the stamp of social inferiority or superiority. It goes without saying that there are no models for living as a gender-neutral person. Experimentation in going beyond gender is just that: experimentation, imagination. The virtue of feminist spirituality is that it gives women something far more tangible with which to work. It is a religion that responds to women's desire to be respected as the women they are, as the women they have been born and raised to be. At the same time, it works to free women from the tightest strictures of cultural femininity without branding them as unfeminine or unwomanly.

This is a real fear for many spiritual feminists, being taken to be or actually being, in Kim Chernin's coinage, "pseudomen."[15] For femaleness, even in feminist spirituality's very permissive construction, is not the effortless property of all women. If nothing else, the patriarchy has intervened, and made it difficult for women to express their natural femininity, their womanhood. The experience of Claire Jones, described by her in the spiritual feminist journal *SageWoman*, illustrates just how high and how numerous can be the barricades between spiritual feminists and the powerful womanhood they seek for themselves. Walking on the beach, Jones hears a voice—possibly that of the goddess—speaking to her. The voice tells her: "You are not a man. Enlighten yourself with Women's Ways. Embolden yourself with Women's Ways. Learn the ways of the flesh." Jones describes her reaction: "What does this mean? I wondered from my man-programmed, overbound mind. What does this mean??"[16]

Many spiritual feminists seem to have this experience, this longing for a femaleness that eludes them. As Lynn Andrews says of herself: "Towards the end of my twenties, I couldn't define myself as a woman at all. . . . When I met [my Native American mentor] I saw something in her that I knew I needed to be a total woman."[17] Though biologically female, though raised as a woman in her culture, Andrews feels that authentic womanhood has somehow escaped her and that she cannot be complete without discovering it and including it in her self. Others seem to share Andrews's experience and to be motivated toward feminist spirituality for this reason. They do not like the model of femaleness that their culture has handed them. By mainstream measures of femininity, they feel that they fall dismally short: they are not cute and flirtatious; discussions of recipes and hairstyles leave them cold; they may enjoy traditionally male pursuits or feel more comfortable with men. It is this feeling of being at odds with culturally defined femininity that has often led them to be feminists in the first place, since they feel the female role model is too narrow for them. And yet even after rebelling against society's vision of what women are good for, there remains a sore spot in their lives, a sense of self that remains unassimilated to notions of gender, that leaves them uncomfortably in the no-man's (or woman's)-land between masculinity and femininity.

Feminist spirituality provides a means by which these women can reconcile themselves to being female. Femaleness is given a positive and powerful meaning in feminist spirituality. These women can at last feel themselves to be "feminine" without consigning themselves to what has been for them the hell of cultural femininity. In a world where gender is a crucial determinant of social identity, feminist spirituality spares its adherents the pain and anomie of falling into the interstices of gender definition. It gives them a femaleness that they can relate comfortably to their own lives. Carol Schulman is a spiritual feminist who fits this pattern. She describes herself as someone who always identified more closely with her father than her mother, who followed out traditionally male academic pursuits, and who "lived in her mind" rather than her body. Many of her friends were male, and "femininity" seemed foreign to her. But by becoming involved with feminist spirituality, Carol made a conscious decision to "get in touch" with her "womanly nature," to learn more about her "feminine aspects." Esther Hoffman also says that feminist spirituality has given her "a peace and serenity, and a sense of power in being a woman." She recalls: "I grew up hating being a girl. I was a tomboy. I liked to climb in trees, I liked to ride bikes and play baseball, and the guys got to do all this stuff, you know? . . . It was like the guys got everything, just because they were guys. . . . So I think I really hated being a woman, and I couldn't see the sense of it. Here I was married, I had kids, and I was really not [happy] being a woman." Now feminist spirituality has given Esther the context in which she can "want to be a woman, for a change." Jeannie Garawitz remembers her entrée into feminist spirituality being accompanied with a soaring self-esteem as she left the strictures of "femininity" behind: "Here we are strong, got our muscles, we don't have to wear high heels or makeup. I used to pluck my eyebrows when I was eighteen, nineteen; I'd pluck them and cry. You know, I don't have to do that anymore! I mean, it was just a total, like hallelujah, I can just let go of all that. And I always felt so fat, and then it was OK to be fat; in fact there were a lot of women who thought fat was great. So that was so empowering because I had such big food issues all my life."[18] Sara Copeland also felt frustrated and ill at ease with mainstream notions of femininity. She remembers her childhood like this:

> Up until I was about ten years old, I was this extremely outgoing and self-confident child, completely unselfconscious, really out there. . . . But I skipped fifth grade, and that was right around the time of puberty. It was really prepuberty for me, I was still very much a child, very much a tomboy, and the girls in my new grade were already wearing makeup and talking about boys and their periods, and it was like . . . it really changed my personality entirely. I became extremely withdrawn, and in a way that's when the depression began, and I've sort of been struggling all these years to recapture the self that I was as a child.[19]

A good friend of Sara's told her that when they first met in college, she thought that Sara "was the most male-identified woman" she had ever met. Sara agrees that she was, saying, "I was struggling about my own identity and the ways in which I was so hard on myself in terms of how feminine I was . . . feeling like I ought to be [more feminine] but knowing there's no way. And feeling awful about that." In feminist spirituality, Sara says that she is "learning a way to be a powerful woman."[20] She, along with the other spiritual feminists she works with, is creating a new kind of womanhood, one that is not oppressive to her and does not require that she be disempowered. Her unique gifts as a person are socially validated through feminist spirituality, validated not simply as her quirky traits or even as admirable human powers, but as an expression of her divine femaleness. In the embrace of feminist spirituality, she and many others like her find a way to be "authentically female" and feminist at the same time.*

Spiritual Feminist Identity

Religious Outsiderness

The theory of power deprivation and the desire for a powerful sense of one's femaleness are clearly crucial factors in explaining why feminist

---

*Many spiritual feminists, like those cited here, seem to experience this need because they have felt very ambivalent about being women prior to any involvement with the movement. They do not want to feel like freakish imitation women; short of expensive

spirituality attracts the women it does. But some disillusioned and frustrated feminists, even those who yearn for a sense of specifically female power, never find their way into feminist spirituality. I think there can be no completely satisfactory answer to the question of why they do not, except to say that religious resolutions of psychosocial dilemmas do not seem to be for everyone. For reasons that defy easy explanation, some people seem to be more religiously inclined than others: religious rituals that leave others indifferent will move them profoundly; questions about the meaning of reality that strike others as idle entertainments will eat away at them unmercifully. In explaining feminist spirituality's appeal, there does seem to be some room for, if not a defective individual theory, then at least a special individual one.

Robert Ellwood describes the experience of those in alternative religions like this: "They experience a subjective turbulence and acute self-consciousness which seems to make them more complex than others. To put it another way, they have not only a social identity like everyone else, but also a dissonant non-social identity in some way not placed by the ordinary structures of society, which needs to be reified."[21] Spiritual feminists frequently experience this alienation, this out-siderness in regard to their spiritual selves. Any preexisting alienation is aggravated by the conditions of being female in a male-dominated society (and even further aggravated by being lesbian in a heterosexist society). Where at least some men who are spiritually gifted find a socially sanctioned role for themselves as wise and holy men, most women so inclined are viewed as peculiar and slightly pathetic, and lesbians so inclined are completely beyond the pale. Luisah Teish comments of her early life: "I wanted to be an asset to my community, to contemplate the meaning of existence and produce beauty. But literally everything in the society told me I was a useless nigger wench. I was someone who was best forgotten and destined to be destroyed. I was caught between my soul's desire and society's dictates."[22] Being a spiritual feminist is for women like Teish a way to bring the outside inside, to take their "dissonant non-social identity" and make it not a source of shame and derision, but of distinction, of chosenness.

Some indication of how deep this sense of differentness goes for

surgical interventions, they cannot be men. But neither do they want to be the type of women of whom society approves. Other spiritual feminists seem to arrive at their desire for female validation from the opposite psychological extreme. They feel very comfortable with femaleness as society describes it. They were not tomboys as children, but easily feminine little girls. Their only complaint is that they should be made to feel lesser than men for what are, in their eyes, equally if not more attractive traits. A feminism that emphasizes a complete abdication from cultural femininity is asking them to give up something they hold dear. Feminist spirituality, because it does not request this sacrifice, is especially appealing to them.

spiritual feminists can be seen in the fact that once they find a religious community where they are with others like themselves, they still do not shed their sense of differentness. Participation in feminist spirituality does not erase feelings of specialness and separateness; it confirms and strengthens them. The spiritual feminist is no longer alone in her experience of moving between an ordinary social identity and a dissonant nonsocial identity, but she is still special: her sisters in feminist spirituality tell her that her hunches have been true, that she is privy to authentic and cosmically significant religious experiences to which most people remain impervious. Her outsider identity remains, though interpreted and experienced in a more affirming way.

Much as they romanticize it, spiritual feminists tend to be very ambivalent about their marginal social status. It is the mark that both distinguishes them and separates them from normative society. They have the unique pleasure of viewing and participating in an intricate and beautiful alternative reality of goddesses, spirits, and an enchanted nature, but this pleasure is inseparable from the pain of being different, of sensing an impenetrable wall between their own experience and that of the average individual. This ambivalence is key to understanding spiritual feminists' attitudes toward evangelism, for most spiritual feminists are not enthusiastic about preaching the good news of the goddess. They may plaster their cars with bumper stickers reading In Goddess We Trust and My Other Car is a Broom, but they are not likely to post themselves outside the A&P clutching a sweaty handful of flyers encouraging people to worship the goddess before it is too late. This does not stem from any deficit of true belief; many spiritual feminists believe that it is only their ideas—if not in the specific form of feminist spirituality, then in a similar one—that stand between the human race and its destruction. But spiritual feminists' long history of feeling like outsiders makes them cautious of being laughed at or betrayed by the insincere. Before laying their precious gift upon the table, they want to have some reassurance that those they are speaking with are kindred spirits, or at least open-minded and tolerant.[23]

Although spiritual feminists fear and avoid persecution, they also thrive on it, or at least on the threat of it. Persecution, after all, means that people take them seriously; it means that their set-apartness has been recognized; it confirms them in their sense that they are indeed powerful people who pose a threat to established social conventions. Feminist spirituality is not a movement rife with martyrs, but there is clearly a magnetic attraction for spiritual feminists to the feeling that they are women under seige. Zsuzsanna Budapest has gotten much mileage out of her arrest by the Los Angeles police in 1975 for fortune-telling. It is a story she loves to tell, one she clearly feels authenticates her calling as a wiccan priestess. As she herself notes in one such retelling: "There was a silver lining to this crisis, however; women's religion was suddenly seen as politically threatening to the patriarchy."[24]

This does not mean that it is pleasant for spiritual feminists to contemplate being badgered or bullied or even burned at the stake, but it is better than being ignored; it is better than being written off as a harmless nutcase. In "Womanpower: Energy Re-sourcement," Sally Gearhart responds to her own worries that her spirituality is socially irrelevant with this comforting thought: "When I lapse into thinking how easy and mellow it is to be in the re-sourcement mode, I remind myself that when the backlash comes it will be weirdo women who will be chased down first, arrested, and separated from each other. That thought sobers me and keeps me from getting lazy."[25] It is a sign of Gearhart's power and importance that the game she plays is a dangerous one. Though the danger is not in itself desirable, the power and importance are. And in the patriarchal society in which spiritual feminists believe themselves to be living, women's power and the danger of patriarchal reprisals are inextricably bound together.

A popular song by Chris Carol, "The Witches' Warning," captures this mood of power, danger, and persecution that suffuses the more intensive forms of feminist spirituality:

> They're gonna come, they're gonna come;
> They'll come for us in the morning.
> They're gonna come, but we'll be gone;
> We've heard the witches' warning! [CHORUS]

> They snatched away our children dear
> They took away abortion;
> They wiped the wildflower from the field
> And covered us with poison.

> Now childcare costs our weekly wage
> We're prisoners in our homes;
> The welfare barely feeds the flesh
> And starves our woman's soul.

> They cast our Goddess from the earth
> Subdued with rape and burning;
> But every spring the new corn sprouts
> The old ways we're learning.

The night watch now, the daylight soon
The struggle brings the glory;
The lives we lead, the songs we sing
Will be our woman's story.

The sooner fight, the sooner win;
Why wait a moment longer?
Our deadliest weapon is our hope
And we are getting stronger.[26]

I think it is fair to say that spiritual feminists are far less persecuted than they imagine themselves to be, but they come by their subjective experience of persecution honestly. Research by R. Laurence Moore and by Luther Gerlach and Virginia Hine indicates that alternative religious movements "often perceive more opposition to their cause than seems to exist objectively."[27] The evidence for feminist spirituality supports this claim. When asked how the people around them respond to their feminist religion, women were practically uniform in saying that others were benignly tolerant of their beliefs and practices. They said that people sometimes found them a little strange, or thought their activities were a little silly, but that for the most part, they didn't have much to say about them one way or the other. Unlike the case with some other alternative religions, I have never heard of anyone trying to "deprogram" a convert to feminist spirituality; rarely have I even heard of a parent, spouse, or friend being deeply upset by a woman's practice. In fact, several women mentioned that family, friends, and co-workers who know of their religion are at first amused, but later, when they feel a need for a spell or a charm or a ritual, they know whom to call.[28]

This kind of reaction is in stark contrast to the embattled self-perception many spiritual feminists have. It bears more resemblance to the spiritual feminist's hidden fear—that she is irrelevant or ignored—than to the more commonly voiced fear that she may be denied jobs, arrested, or tortured for her religious identity. Angela Price reconciles this public disinterest with her sense that her spirituality is dangerous to the patriarchy (and to her as its sworn enemy) in saying, "I think we have to be very careful not to have them take us seriously. . . . It's good they should not take us seriously. It's good that they should think we're silly. It really is. Because the minute they take us seriously there will be really, really bad trouble." She returned to this theme more than once during her interview, and cautioned me to be careful not to make feminist witches sound too powerful, for fear that it could lead to persecutions and prevent feminist witches from carrying out their important spiritual work against the patriarchy.[29]

The reality is undoubtedly somewhere between the visions of all-out slaughter that some women see hovering in the not-too-distant future and society's apparent disinterest in spiritual feminists and their strange religious practices. Persecution is not entirely unknown. Suzanne Courveline's story of attempted exorcism and book burning is the only such story I have heard, but other women have spoken of being avoided or socially ostracized. And as Sharon Logan points out, saying one is a witch or a priestess in metropolitan New York is one thing, while saying it in rural Florida, where she grew up, is quite another. She notes that fundamentalist radio stations there regularly announce that people who meditate are organizing to kill fundamentalist Christians, that the harmonic convergence is the work of the devil, and so on.[30] And though hundreds of years have passed since the last of the witch persecutions, it is a fact that vast numbers of women have been murdered by the church and state on the presumption of witchcraft.

Further contributing to the spiritual feminist sense of persecution is the reality that women are not very safe in American society, that they are subject to harassment, rape, and domestic violence at alarming rates. The solution society typically recommends for avoiding such abuse is "being a good girl": that is, staying off the streets at night, wearing one's skirt long enough, being demure and self-effacing, and so on. These are behaviors that spiritual feminists are giving up, in spirit if not in letter, in the very act of becoming spiritual feminists. They are declaring themselves to be powerful women, women who do not intend to follow society's rules. Though there may be no immediate connection between their choice to be spiritual feminists and any painful consequences, the feeling is that violations of the rules will eventually and inevitably be punished.

Apart from any actual persecution or immediate threat of it, it is important to understand that it is nevertheless the perception of spiritual feminists that they are courting danger. The perception may not have a strong basis in "fact," but it does have a strong basis in experience. Remember that spiritual feminists are women who have not felt at home in the world, who have long believed that they are misunderstood, who have had a sense of themselves that the world around them has not shared. This is a frightening position to be in, whatever the source of the feeling. When one's own internal perceptions of self and society are continually at odds with what society is mirroring back and what it claims for itself, self-images swing from genius to fool and back again at alarming rates. This in itself is a form of persecution (though it is not clear who is guilty of doing the persecuting).

The anxiety spiritual feminists feel around this unstable self-definition is apparent in Jade's discussion of what she calls "the witchie-in-the-night syndrome." In instructing an audience of novice spiritual feminists in how they should go about finding other women with whom to practice, she explains that one needs to be on the lookout for women who are not reputable witches, but "witchies-in-the-night." She details how these pseudowitches behave, how they look, what they talk about. For example, she says that while it is accepted in the neopagan community for witches to wear robes or flashy clothing or even to go naked in ritual, some women take this too far, and wear extremely peculiar clothing all the time. These are women who are not to be trusted. Jade offers many pointers of this type, all of which are intended to draw a line between those whom society regards as deviant—but who are really prophets and seers and wise women—and those who really are deviant, who are beyond the margins of feminist spirituality's marginality.[31] By locating women who have tripped beyond the outer limits, Jade is able to offer reassurance to those who remain within that they, like she, can rest secure in a spiritual specialness that will not be confused with insanity.

Relationship to Judaism and Christianity

The effects of spiritual feminists' feelings of marginality are perhaps most acutely present in relationship to traditional religions, where spiritual feminists exhibit a striking ambivalence. This ambivalence was in full flower at one workshop I attended on feminist witchcraft. Discussion during the workshop had been full of casual slurs on Christianity: how wonderful Europe had been before it was Christianized; how the church denied and punished women's sexuality; how the crucifix was a perfect illustration of how men fetishize pain. Finally, one woman began to speak with great agitation about how difficult it was for her when other women criticized Christianity. She said that though she recognized the church had some serious problems where women were concerned, she thought it unfair for spiritual feminists to characterize the church as the unrelieved enemy of women, and she said she found it personally hurtful when women around her called the pope "an asshole."

Almost all the women present immediately retracted earlier statements, apologized for having upset her, and said that they had no intention to speak ill of her religion, which was in fact a beautiful religion. Some expressed regret for having felt driven to leave Christianity themselves; some said that while it was not for them, they did not want to dictate anyone else's choices; others praised her for sticking it out in the church and standing up for women in an arena where women's voices were so desperately needed. But at last, two women intruded on the apologetics to say that though they were sorry it hurt her, they had to stand firm: the church hurt women, historically and currently, and women needed to have that shown to them. Though they tried to be delicate in their phrasing, they intimated very strongly that women who remained within Christianity were collaborating in their own oppression and that of other women.[32]

The majority of spiritual feminists seek out a precarious balance between slamming traditional religions at every opportunity and allowing that traditional religions have redeeming characteristics and every right to exist and propagate themselves. Christianity, in particular, is the object of truly virulent rhetoric: it is "a curse," it is "sado-sexual" (with praying on bent knee likened to fellatio); it is "necrophilic," "fascistic," "nihilistic," and of course, misogynistic. Zsuzsanna Budapest describes Christianity like this: "It is an incestuous male homosexual concept that excludes the Mother, the female principle of the universe, and the creator. And of course the entire semen theology of the Pope, barring ordination of women, is completely supporting this."[33] And yet spiritual feminists are constantly proferring their respect to Christian feminists, to women working inside the church for change, and they frequently qualify their attacks on Christianity by talking about its "good side": its pagan elements, its fine art and music, the "feminism" of Jesus, and the cosmic truth of his teachings.* The

---

*Judaism, in contrast, is something of a special case: even women who are extremely harsh toward Christianity and other patriarchal religions sometimes—though not always—make an exception for Judaism. It is especially interesting to note that both Jewish and Christian women make this exception. Incorporation of Jewish elements into feminist spirituality is more widely practiced and tolerated than any parallel incorporation of Christian elements (see, for example, Zsuzsanna Budapest's *The Grandmother of Time*, which includes virtually all of the Jewish holidays, while mentioning only a very few Christian holidays). Some women argue that this differential exists because Judaism is a richer source for women's spirituality, because it already includes rituals around menstruation and the moon, is less hostile toward women's sexuality, and prescribes specific spiritual duties for women. Though Judaism undeniably provides useful material for feminist spirituality, I suspect that the reason it is more widely tolerated than Christianity in spiritual feminist circles has more to do with the position it occupies in American society. However patriarchal Judaism may or may not be, it is not the dominant religion in the United States, and so it escapes some of the taint of being allied with the patriarchal establishment in a way Christianity cannot. For Christian women, Judaism is not "their" religion, and so they are less personally injured by it and more circumspect in criticizing it. And because Christianity is the mainstream religion in the United States, ironically, it is easier to reject it. Just as white women are in a better position to ignore race than are black women, so Christian women are in a better position to ignore religion of origin than are Jewish women. For most Jewish women, Judaism is not an identity that can be easily cast aside. As Tzivia writes in the pages of *Womanspirit*: "Christian women I know are able to leave behind their family's traditional rituals and call themselves ex-Catholics or ex-Protestants. I know that I can never call myself an ex-Jew because I am a Jew and the world allows me no choice" (Tzivia, *Womanspirit* 37 [1982]).

attack on Christianity is the natural extension of what was a real impetus for the birth of feminist spirituality in the first place: an analysis of traditional religions that argues that they are the central cultural legitimators of the oppression of women. In light of this, what is curious is not that spiritual feminists should despise traditional religions (as some do), but that they should be so relatively tolerant of them (as most are).

This mixed reaction to Christianity stems, I believe, from the same ambivalence about religious marginality that informs spiritual feminist attitudes toward secrecy, persecution, and martyrdom. Because spiritual feminists are proud of their outsider status, they rail against Christianity as an abomination, a perversion of all that is good and true, a reversal of everything cherished by goddess-loving peoples. But because spiritual feminists are pained by their outsider status, they are at some level envious of the solidity and simplicity of ordinary society. Out of these feelings of pain and alienation come a grudging respect for Christianity or parts of it, and a tolerance—even admiration—of those women who can feel at home in the mainstream. Behind all the rhetoric of critique and censure spiritual feminists mount against Christianity is a poignant plea to be left alone, to be left free to pursue alternative spiritual truths without the weight of the mainstream constantly pressing down with its exclusive claims to cosmic truth. Spiritual feminists try to establish room to move within a dominantly Christian culture by unilaterally granting a certain amount of religious space to Christianity. The most common strategy spiritual feminists take is to say that Christianity is not bad at its roots, that its truths are indeed universal, sometimes even identical to feminist spirituality's own. The problems with Christianity are then problems of superstructure, not foundation, and so the quarrel between feminist spirituality and Christianity becomes a resolvable one.[34]

Of course, making space for Christianity and other traditional religions is also motivated by a desire not to further fragment the ranks of feminism by writing off women in traditional religions as reactionaries.[35] In *Laughter of Aphrodite*, Carol Christ paints the choice between traditional religions and feminist spirituality as one "based on complex questions of judgment" having to do with where women find spiritual sustenance, where they can have the greatest impact, and whether traditional religions are reformable. Critical judgment undoubtedly plays a role, but as Mary Jo Weaver suggests in her article "Who Is the Goddess and Where Does She Get Us?" religious autobiography probably plays a bigger one. Spiritual feminists do make considered decisions to leave traditional religions, and to stand in positions of opposition to them. But they also feel driven to leave them, or feel that they have never belonged and never will. Esther Hoffman speaks with some regret about abandoning Catholicism: "I was so down that I had to grab so hard onto [feminist spirituality], and I went so deeply that I couldn't possibly do both [Catholicism and feminist spirituality]. . . . I had trouble for a long time . . . even just stepping into a church, a patriarchal space, because it's so inundated with memories of what the church meant." Karen Whiting has fond memories of being involved in liberal Christian churches, their youth groups and choirs and political activism. But she concludes, "I liked it a lot, but that's when I realized that I was truly a heretic. I mean, from the church's perspective, there was no way that I was ever going to be a Christian in a church sense. My experiences were simply outside of what was being taught." In a similar vein, Susan Ackley muses, "Since the day when I was overwhelmed by the concept of the Goddess, and all my earlier religious instincts suddenly made sense, I have carried out my religious 'work' quite outside the Christian belief in which I was raised."[36]

The Gift of Feminist Spirituality

As full of ambivalence as spiritual feminists sometimes are about their identity as religious outsiders, the rewards of spiritual feminist practice have, they say, been tremendous. When asked if feminist spirituality helped them to reach personal goals, women's responses were immediate, enthusiastic, and overwhelmingly positive. Where their pasts have been seriously traumatic, spiritual feminists say that their spirituality has given them a base from which to construct a new sense of self. Where their past experiences have not been seriously traumatic, spiritual feminists say that their spirituality has given them new strength in setting their priorities, approaching life with greater confidence, and integrating their fragmented identities. Marilyn Gordon says that feminist spirituality makes her feel "valuable and legitimate," where before she felt "somewhat peripheral." Carol Schulman reports that "having spiritual practices has made me feel happier and more confident and more powerful. . . . I still get upset over things, bad things still happen, but I seem to be able eventually to reach some kind of philosophical adjustment to things." Corinne Foster says that "[Feminist spirituality] gave me the courage to continue to live the way I wanted to live. It made sense of what I was doing earlier in my life, my struggles to be myself. . . . And it gave me more direction and more focus, and a lot of support. . . . It really stopped the conflict within myself."[37]

The movement as a whole works to strengthen women's identities and to give them confidence in themselves. Virtually every handbook on feminist spirituality advises women to heed their "inner voice," to know that their intuition is trustworthy. Many times recipes for rituals or spells are followed by the advice to ignore instructions if you, the practitioner, feel that other techniques will be more effective. For example, in her manual on the *Motherpeace* tarot, Vicki Noble writes: "Your intuition is more critical to reading the Tarot than all the books available on the subject, including this one." Or as Ann Forfreedom explains in a discussion of "Major Wiccan Tools": "Underlying the uses of all these different tools is a fundamental tool, without which most of these tools are valueless. That fundamental tool is *you*—your beliefs, your self-confidence, your knowledge of yourself and the universe."[38]

Much of the actual religious practice of feminist spirituality is devoted to understanding and expressing the self's uniqueness. In spiritual feminist handbooks, women are encouraged to regard their tarot deck, pendulum, or crystals as being intimately connected to their essence, as "filled with their energy." They are instructed to treat their divinatory tools with special care, wrapping their pendulum in a special cloth or making a special box or pouch for their tarot cards, and are further instructed never to let anyone else use their tools and to periodically "clean" them of other people's vibrations. In addition to her personal energy field, each woman has her own aura, her own astrological chart, her special "significator" card in the tarot deck; she may have her own "power animal" or a particular goddess who is in effect her patron saint; she has an unending array of past lives in which her unique essence has interacted with the world in an infinite variety of ways.[39] This is a self not limited by time, death, ethnicity, vocation, or particular relationships, and yet it is not without content. It is a self that has a power and a presence, some indefinable core that marks an individual as truly herself, whatever contingent factors of identity may intervene.

Externally, individuals are supported by a community of other seekers that echo their singularity back to them, while still holding them safely within a net of relationships. Several feminist spirituality songs and chants consist of many short verses, each sung to an individual woman. The group sings a woman's name to her, perhaps her mother's name as well: "Susan is beautiful, Susan is strong"; "The goddess's name is Karen, her mother's name is Charlotte." In a write-up of a women's solstice summer camp, Georgette Psaris and Marlena Lyons stress this individual-in-solidarity aspect of feminist spirituality:

> Once you have entered the circle and stood beside and across from yourself, you have crossed a threshold where you experience, perhaps for the first time in your life, enough. You become a part of a large mirror into which you pour yourself and see yourself reflected

back in all your facets. . . . You are finally merged with a hoop of women that is a sisterhood that we all dream about and never allow ourselves to experience and to join. You have to take the action to say you want to be a part of the hoop. It is not a secret society that quietly chooses the best, brightest, and most beautiful. It is there for each of us. You only have to choose to take your place in the circle.[40]

The individual's place is already waiting; all she need do is fill it. Many spiritual feminists say they have found just this type of sisterhood in the movement, and see it as one of the greatest rewards of their participation. Rosita Veracruz reflects: "I am really happy that I have been exposed to all the wonderful wisdom that I've gained from other women, through their writings, through their friendship, through their love. It has touched everything in my life. Every major aspect of growth has been because I've been able to connect spiritually with women and with my own inner self."[41]

If some forms of empowerment in the feminist spirituality movement seem a little exotic—gender validation or sisterhoods of revolution—the bottom line for spiritual feminists is oftentimes much more familiar. Like all religions, feminist spirituality's principal legacy to its adherents is a sense of mission and meaning. It is here that the benefits of feminist spirituality are brought vibrantly to life. When asked how their involvement in feminist spirituality had changed or influenced their life and why their identification as spiritual feminists was important to them, women often became surprisingly eloquent. Those who had had little to say would become expansive; those who had been prolix would offer pithy summations. Even women who were more subdued in their answers conveyed a strong sense of having undergone (or expecting to undergo) personal transformation as the result of their spiritual feminist practice. A couple of women spoke of the comfort afforded them by faith in the goddess, their sense that they are cared for and protected by divine powers. Others said they find in their religion a relationship to themselves and a home within the divine. Many women said that what they get from feminist spirituality is the belief that their lives are meaningful and that the universe is operating in an orderly fashion. As Angela Price says, "It is *incredibly* important to me to have things make sense sometimes. I really need that."[42]

Spiritual feminists are women for whom a sense of personal destiny is crucial. They are loath to feel that they are simply bumbling through life, another face in the crowd, all their choices accidental ones. And so they devote themselves to solving the puzzle of what their life's purpose might be. Some less meaning-hungry individuals may respond to the question "Why am I here?" with the answer "Who knows? I am, so I may as well enjoy it." But spiritual feminists feel compelled to give a substantive answer to that question, and to keep on asking and answering it whenever they are threatened with feelings of meaninglessness. Many take it as an article of faith that their life (and the lives of others) have a purpose, that all they need to do is discover it. Some talk of having "chosen" their life or their life circumstances from some other spiritual realm for specific reasons they must now remember. Again, Angela Price says: "There was a reason I said I would be in a body this time here, and do this stuff. And it had to do with my learning, it had to do with what it is I said I would learn here. . . . I mean, there were things that I said I'd learn. I rarely know what they are. Sometimes I have a sense of what they are . . . so I'm very concerned with doing my job." Many spiritual feminists are very specific about what their mission in life is: they are here to restore consciousness of our links with the natural world and to return humanity to an appreciation of the feminine principle. Renee Landau describes herself as part of a critical shift from yang to yin, from masculine to feminine, that is currently taking place on a planetary level. Helen Littlefield says: "I've had lovely pictures of the largest, most inclusive feminine that I can think of, for a very long time. I sensed that it was my task to unfold, with the feminine, with the goddess as a witness." Whatever the specifics, feminist spirituality is permeated by talk of "what I have to do," "my purpose," "my work," "what my life is about," "the gift I can offer the world." Barbara Otto describes her choice to remain in New York and try to infuse the city with spiritual and ecological awareness as a mission. She pokes fun at herself, saying, "I know that that sounds like I'm a total case: 'This is my *mission*. I am on a holy mission from Spider Woman.' But I believe that, I really believe that this is what I'm supposed to be doing."[43]

In feminist spirituality, these women have found a place where they receive at least partial answers to the questions that torment them and always a respect for their ongoing search. Oceana Woods credits feminist spirituality for taking her from being an eighteen-year-old single mother living on welfare to having "an abundance in my life . . . a totally different view on myself, and many possibilities open to me." Marguerite Keane says: "I can't imagine my life without [feminist spirituality]. . . . It seems to embody the best part of me." For some, feminist spirituality has been and continues to be a matter of survival. Diane Turcott credits witchcraft with saving her life. Lady Miw exclaims, "I don't know how I ever lived without it . . . if they ever wanted to take the mother away from me, I would rather die. If they ever tried to take the green away, the animals away, or told me I couldn't worship a female mother goddess, then I would not want to live." Luisah Teish describes the transition she has experienced: "What [spirituality] has done for me—it's taken me from being someone who found my life tolerable at best, to somebody who can say, 'Even when I'm broke, even when I'm sick, even when the people I care about most are mistreating me or misunderstanding me, when the political situation is crummy, and there's steam coming out of my nose, no matter what's going on—I may bitch and complain and fight, but there's still a place I can say, "I *love* my life." ' "[44]

It is not always pleasant, spiritual feminists stress: their spiritual quests involve frustrations and challenges and constant tests as often as they involve hope and reassurance. But the end result is growth and added strength to enrich their own lives and impact the lives of others and the world. As Oceana Woods remarks: "Just like anyone else, I get depressed, and I sometimes have doubts. But inside me it's a system of beliefs that works. And I've seen it work. I've seen myself transformed through my own spiritual empowerment as a woman. . . . And I've seen it work for other women too."[45] If the central goal of feminist spirituality is the empowerment of women as women, for those who call themselves spiritual feminists the religion seems to be fulfilling its promise.

Interview Sample[1]

Pseudonym	Year of Birth	Place of Birth	Religion of Origin[2]	Education[3]	Occupation[4]	Sexual Orientation[5]	Marital Status	Children[6]
Grete Bjorkman	1943	Sweden	Lutheran	M.A.	Librarian	H	M	N
Sara Copeland	1963	N.Y.	Protestant	B.A.	Research assistant	H	S	N
Suzanne Courveline	1948	D.C.	Methodist	Some college	Artist	H	S	Y
Melanie Engler	1949	Hawaii	Baptist	M.A.	Administrator	H	S	N
Debra Fleming	1950	Ga.	Episcopal	B.A.	Restaurant owner	L	S	N
Corinne Foster	1944	Conn.	Catholic	M.A.	Therapist	L	S	N
Sal Frankel	1956	Conn.	Catholic	Some college	Artist	L	S	N
Jeannie Garawitz	1958	Wis.	Jewish	M.A.	Dance therapist	B	M	N
Marilyn Gordon	1944	R.I.	Unitarian	Some grad.	Artist/Writer	H	M	Y
Sally Hargreaves	1951	Mass.	Episcopal	B.A.	Restaurant owner	L	S	N
Evelyn Hart	1943	Hawaii	Congregational	B.A.	Nonprofit administrator	L	S	N
Esther Hoffman	1944	Conn.	Catholic	M.F.A.	Artist	H	M	Y
Marguerite Keane	1949	Singapore	Anglican	J.D.	Lawyer	H	M	N
Renee Landau	1948	Calif.	Catholic	M.A.	Carpenter	L	S	N
Rachel Laura	1935	N.Y.	Jewish	B.A.	Restaurant owner	L	D	Y
Helen Littlefield	1949	Conn.	Congregational	—	House cleaner	H	D	N
Sharon Logan	1952	Fla.	Episcopal	B.A.	Musician	H	D	N
Joan Maddox	1944	Conn.	Catholic	Some college	Restaurant owner	L	D	Y
Del McIntyre	1955	Md.	Catholic	M.Div.	Bookstore clerk	L	S	N
Isis Mendel	1963?	N.Y.	Jewish	—	Signer for deaf	L	S	N
Lady Miw	1951	N.Y.	Catholic	Some college	Store owner	L	S	N
Barbara Otto	1945	Ohio	Jewish	M.A.	Artist	L	S	N
Angela Price	1944	N.Y.	Catholic	M.A.	Teacher/Writer	L	D	Y
Nancy Robison	1950	Mich.	Catholic	Ph.D.	Academic administrator	H	S	N

Name	Year[3]	State[1]	Religion[2]	Education[3]	Occupation[4]	[5]	[4]	Children[6]
Rosemary Sackner	1963	Va.	Episcopal	M.A.	Teacher/Student	H	S	N
Carol Schulman	1949	N.Y.	Jewish	M.A.	Teacher	H	M	Y
Catherine Sharp	1946	Tex.	Methodist	B.A.	Dancer	H	S	N
Diane Turcott	1937	Miss.	—	—	Massage therapist	L	D	Y
Rosita Veracruz	1949	Cuba	Catholic	Some grad.	Educator/therapist	H	S	N
Carrie Washington	1966	Calif.	Episcopalian	—	Student	B	S	N
Karen Whiting	1944	Wis.	UCC	M.A.	Therapist	H	D	Y
Oceana Woods	1965	Conn.	Catholic	Some college	Student	H	S	Y

---

[1]Formal interviews were conducted between June 1989 and April 1991 in the following states: Maine, Massachusetts, Connecticut, New Jersey, New York, and Washington. All interviewees were Caucasian except Washington, who is African-American, and Veracruz, who is Hispanic-American. All interviews were conducted by the author, except for Frankel, Gordon, Landau, Mendel, Price, Veracruz, and Washington, who were interviewed by Faulkner Fox, and Fleming, Hargreaves, Laura, Maddox, and McIntyre, interviewed by the author and Faulkner Fox together.

[2]Response to the question "Did your family have a religious affiliation when you were growing up?" A dash indicates no response.

[3]Highest educational level achieved. A dash indicates no response.

[4]Current and/or past occupation, as reported by interviewee. Some interviewees requested greater anonymity, so some of the listed occupations are purposely vague.

[5]H = heterosexual; L = lesbian; B = bisexual. All interviewees made comments about their sexual orientation in the course of interviews, but they were not directly asked to give their sexual preference. These classifications are based on their comments.

[6]Where Y = yes; N = none. One interviewee had three children; the others with children had either one or two.

· APPENDIX B ·

Interview Guide

BACKGROUND
Birthdate?
Birthplace?
Education?
Profession?
Religious background?
How did you become involved in feminist spirituality?
    (books / journals / newsletters
    groups / covens / classes / workshops
    friends / mentors)
To what extent are each of the above important to your current practices?
Have you had other religious affiliations?
Do you have any other current religious affiliations?
    (and/or spiritual, personal growth, etc. affiliations)
Are you currently in a feminist spirituality group?
    How long has this group been together?

BELIEFS
Do you believe in a goddess?
    If so, what is she like? (pantheism, monotheism, polytheism, animism, triple
        goddess?)
    Does the goddess have male aspects? Do you worship a god?
    Why is it significant that the goddess is female?
    Is the goddess capable of controlling historical events? Does she?
    Does the goddess exist even for those who don't believe in or recognize her?
Do you see the Earth as living? as female? Why?
    How does this connect to belief (or lack thereof) in goddess?
Do you believe there was ancient goddess worship?
    What were goddess-worshiping societies like? for women? for men?
    Why is their existence significant for you?

Where does the patriarchy come from?
> How long has it been around?
> Why did it arise?
> What are its principal characteristics?
> When will it end? How will it end? What will replace it?

Are women more spiritual than men? In what way? Why?

Is there a connection between women's spirituality and sexuality? What is it?

Do you see feminist spirituality as being incompatible with Judaism and/or
> Christianity?
> Eastern religions?
> If so, how? If not, why not?

PRACTICES
(for those practicing in groups):
> How often do you meet?
> Where do you meet?
> What do you do when you get together?
> Are there any leaders?
> What kind of authority do leaders have?
> Are there any men involved?

Do you have an altar?

What is on your altar?

Do you do any rituals? any kind of prayer / meditation?

How do you decide what to incorporate in your practice?
> Do you think it's problematic to borrow from other cultures or religions?

How do you feel about secrecy and evangelism in regards to your spirituality?
> How does your family feel about your involvement in feminist spirituality?

Do you practice magic?
> How do you define it?
> How do you practice it?
> How does it work?
> Can it be abused?

Do you believe what you believe because it works, or because it's true?

IDENTITY AND THE MOVEMENT
Do you call yourself a witch? Why or why not?

Are you separatist in your practice? Why or why not?

What is women's spirituality? witchcraft? feminist spirituality?
> Who is included? Who is excluded?
> How old is the movement?
> Where does it come from (geographically / culturally)?
> Is it connected to the New Age movement? If so, how?
> Why is it happening now?

In what sense is it feminist and how important is that?

What kind of politics does it support, if any?
    Does it set particular political agendas?
    Does it help you/us reach political goals? directly? indirectly?
    Does it help you reach personal goals?
How has feminist spirituality changed or influenced your life?
Why is your identification/practice important to you?

Notes

Detailed information on the women interviewed for this study can be found in appendix A. In the notes, interviews are cited by the last name of the pseudonym assigned to the interviewee. When several women interviewed share the sentiment of the source quoted in the text, I have included their names in the notes after the word "also." The reader will not be able to consult these interviews, but I have cited their names so as to build a fuller picture of each individual interviewee in places where extensive quoting was not practical.

Several spiritual feminist publications are intended to circulate only among women and/or lesbians. When citing well-known figures in the feminist spirituality movement who have written for these publications, I have cited author and title and left the publication anonymous; when citing women whose writings I have not encountered outside of these publications, I have made both the author and the publication anonymous, and referred only to the title of the piece.

Chapter 1: Feminists on Spiritual Quest

1. This ritual was held at the Feminist Spiritual Community's Tenth Anniversary Celebration, Camp Mataponi, Naples, Maine, June 9, 1990 (hereinafter referred to as "FSC Retreat, June 1990"). The Feminist Spiritual Community meets weekly in Portland, Maine.

2. Passing reference to controversies involving feminist spirituality's construction of gender and its theory of ancient matriarchies is made in these pages; a more extensive treatment can be found in my forthcoming book, *Gender Politics and Feminist Religion.*

3. See, for example, Russell Chandler, *Understanding the New Age* (Dallas: Word Publications, 1988), 121–23.

4. In classifying feminist spirituality in this manner, I am indebted to Jonathan Z. Smith's discussion of taxonomies in *Imagining Religion: From Babylon to Jonestown* (Chicago: University of Chicago Press, 1982), 2–4.

5. The empowerment of women and the movement's version of Western history are characteristics more unique to feminist spirituality than the others, and for this reason I would weight them more heavily in making decisions about how to classify individuals in borderline cases.

6. Because of the extensive overlap between feminist spirituality and other alternative religions, there are times and places where men and women meet as mixed groups and operate with a more or less equal distribution of authority. However, I would argue that

at these times, what they are doing is defined as something other than or additional to feminist spirituality (such as goddess worship, paganism, etc.). When it is the nature and future of feminist spirituality that is at stake, women's voices are the only ones that count.

7. Ursula King, *Women and Spirituality: Voices of Protest and Promise* (New York: New Amsterdam, 1989), 118–119. For an assessment of the geographic scope of the feminist spirituality movement and an account of the development of the neologism *thealogy,* see Emily Erwin Culpepper, "Contemporary Goddess Thealogy: A Sympathetic Critique," in *Shaping New Vision: Gender and Values in American Culture,* ed. Clarissa W. Atkinson, Constance H. Buchanan, and Margaret R. Miles, Harvard Women's Studies in Religion Series, no. 5 (Ann Arbor: UMI Research Press, 1987), 51.

8. Spiritual feminist literature occasionally reports plans for women's spiritual communities and solicits contributions. For example, *Of a Like Mind,* a newsletter published by the Re-formed Congregation of the Goddess, has published articles on "Waxing Moon Healing Village," to be located in British Columbia, and "The Grove," to be located in Wisconsin (*Of a Like Mind* 6/1 [Summer 9989 (1989): 4–5]. One spiritual feminist, Cedar Spring, is publishing her own newsletter and raising funds to fulfill her dream of creating a spiritual monastery including a "women's village" that she intends to call Delphos Wilderness Sanctuary (Cedar Spring, newsletters and flyers on Delphos Wilderness Sanctuary, Minneapolis). One commune that has apparently left the drawing board is Hagia, an "academy" founded by Dr. Heide Göttner-Abendroth, located on a farm in the Bavarian Forest two hours east of Munich (Heide Göttner-Abendroth, "Hagia: Academy and Coven," anonymous spiritual feminist publication). Dates such as "9989" are part of a revised dating system used by some spiritual feminists in which counting begins in 8000 B.C.E., when agriculture was invented, presumably by women. These dates are sometimes followed by the designation A.D.A., meaning "After the Development of Agriculture."

9. Frankel; Hart; Washington; Schulman; Boehnert; Copeland; Woods; Turcott; Engler; Courveline; Veracruz; Foster; Otto; Keane; Whiting.

10. The RCG is modeled on the Covenant of the Goddess, an organization headquartered in Berkeley that provides the same services for the broader neopagan community. The RCG caters specifically to the women's community, and is located in Madison, Wis. Women in Constant Creative Action was inactive as of 1989. Two more successful operations of this type are sponsored by the Unitarian Universalist Association and the Center for Partnership Studies in Pacific Grove, Calif. Both provide curriculum materials for study groups of limited duration (Shirley Ranck, *Cakes for the Queen of Heaven* [Boston: Unitarian Universalist Association, 1986]; Riane Eisler and David Loye, *The Partnership Way: New Tools for Living and Learning, Healing Our Families, Our Communities, and Our World* [San Francisco: HarperSanFrancisco, 1990]). These organizations admit men and do not define themselves as spiritual feminist undertakings, but they are responsible for introducing many women to the basic concepts of feminist spirituality and to each other.

11. New York Open Center catalog, New York, Spring 1991. These sessions were led by Starhawk, Jennifer Barker Woolger, Nancy Qualls Corbett, Layne Redmond, Nancy Qualls Corbett, and Elinor Gadon, respectively.

12. Women's Alliance flyer, Nevada City, Calif.; Re-formed Congregation of the Goddess flyer, Madison, Wis.; Womongathering flyer, Franklinville, N.J.; Wise Woman Center program schedule, Woodstock, N.Y.

13. Full Circle Workshops flyer, Amherst, Mass.; Sisterhood of the Lavender Dawn flyer, Baltimore. Full Moon Rising of Greenfield, Mass., offers a one-week training school called "Pilgrim Warrior Training."

14. Re-formed Congregation of the Goddess, ♀ *Thealogical Institute Cella Training Program* (Madison, Wis.: Triple Crescent Press, 9989 [1989]); Hygieia College flyer, Monroe,

Utah; Marah newsletter, Madison, N.J.; Shekhinah Mountainwater catalog, Santa Cruz, Calif.

15. Circles of Exchange flyers and newsletter, Seattle.

16. Laura; Frankel; Littlefield, Copeland; Schulman; Bjorkman; Veracruz; Logan; Boehnert; Robison; Gordon; Turcott.

Chapter 2: The Women of the Feminist Spirituality Movement

1. Courveline.

2. As noted before, this profile is not quantitatively tested but based on my perception of the movement via participation, observation, and interview data. Festival and ritual attendance, interviews, and discussions found in newsletters and magazines all work together to form this picture in my mind.

3. Luisah Teish, *Jambalaya: The Natural Woman's Book of Personal Charms and Practical Rituals* (San Francisco: Harper and Row, 1985), 47, 70–71.

4. Micol Seigel, "Womanspirit Magazine: (Re-)Incarnating the Goddess" (sr. essay, Yale University, 1990), 1:16 (from private communication with Ruth and Jean Mountaingrove, founders of *Womanspirit*); Diane Stein, *The Women's Spirituality Book* (St. Paul: Llewellyn Publications, 1987), xiii; Landau. At the FSC Retreat, June 1990, of about one hundred women present, there was one woman who appeared Asian-American, and the rest were white. Without any prompting from me, several of the women I spoke with apologized for this, saying the group was making efforts to include women of other races, and adding in their defense that they were a varied group in other ways (straight/lesbian, single/married, highly/poorly educated, upper/middle/lower class, etc.).

5. Littlefield; Landau; Robison; Schulman.

6. Price; Foster.

7. Chandler, *Understanding the New Age*, 122. Chandler is citing Rosemary Curb and Nancy Manahan, eds., *Lesbian Nuns: Breaking Silence* (Tallahassee, Fla.: Naiad Press, 1985), xxx–xxxi.

8. *Catholic Mind* 75 (May 1977): 52–64.

9. Margot Adler, *Drawing Down the Moon: Witches, Druids, Goddess-Worshippers, and Other Pagans in America Today* (Boston: Beacon Press, 1979), 14, 20.

10. Marion Zimmer Bradley, interview with Merlin Stone for radio show "Return of the Goddess," Canadian Broadcasting Corp., 1985; Starhawk, quoted in Michele Jamal, *Shape Shifters: Shaman Women in Contemporary Society* (New York and London: Arkana, 1988), 122; Miw; Washington; Susun Weed, interview with Stone, "Return of the Goddess." See also Starhawk, *The Spiral Dance: A Rebirth of the Ancient Religion of the Great Goddess*, 2d ed. (San Francisco: Harper and Row, 1989), 2; Whiting; Jennifer, letter to editor, *Of a Like Mind* (Summer 9989 [1989]): 2; Carol P. Christ, *Laughter of Aphrodite: Reflections on a Journey to the Goddess* (San Francisco: Harper and Row, 1987), 106.

11. Maddox. See also Antiga, interview with Stone, "Return of the Goddess"; also Hoffman, Sackner, McIntyre, Woods.

12. Keane; Turcott.

13. Larissa Vilenskaya, Lynn Andrews, and Petey Stevens, quoted in Jamal, *Shape Shifters*, 83, 21, and 97, respectively.

14. Frankel; Hoffman; Garawitz; Whiting.

15. Copeland.

16. Foster.

17. Teish, quoted in Jamal, *Shape Shifters*, 30.

18. Logan.

19. Sackner.

20. Turcott; Zsuzsanna E. Budapest, *The Grandmother of Time: A Women's Book of Celebrations, Spells, and Sacred Objects for Every Month of the Year* (San Francisco: Harper and Row, 1989), 209–217; Teish, *Jambalaya*, 7; Littlefield; Stevens, quoted in Jamal, *Shape Shifters*, 99.

21. Starhawk, quoted in Jamal, *Shape Shifters*, 121; Frankel. See also Christ, *Laughter of Aphrodite*, 209; also Whiting.

22. Miw; Jonnie Vance, quoted in Patrice Wynne, *The Womanspirit Sourcebook* (San Francisco: Harper and Row, 1988), 183.

23. Barbara G. Walker, *The Skeptical Feminist: Discovering the Virgin, Mother, and Crone* (San Francisco: Harper and Row, 1987), 79.

24. Ibid., 81.

25. Adler, *Drawing Down the Moon*; Whiting; Erica Jong, interview with Stone, "Return of the Goddess." Also Schulman, Miw, Keane, Sackner.

26. Veracruz. Also Robison, McIntyre.

27. Engler; Sackner; Robison. Also Frankel.

28. Mendel.

29. Teish, *Jambalaya*, 32; Logan; Schulman; Veracruz; Sharp; Robison; Christ, *Laughter of Aphrodite*, 106.

30. For example, Foster, Robison.

31. Laura; Frankel; Littlefield; Copeland; Schulman; Bjorkman; Veracruz; Logan; Hoffman; Katherine F. H. Heart, "Healing Through Solitary Practice," *Circle Network News* 11/1 (Spring 1989): 12; Robison; Gordon; Marion Zimmer Bradley, *The Mists of Avalon* (New York: Ballantine Books, 1982); Delores Cole, "Feminist Wicca Philosophy" (workshop presented at FSC Retreat, June 1990).

32. For information on the harmonic convergence, see Chandler, *Understanding the New Age*, 96–102.

33. Landau.

34. Robison; Engler; feminist spirituality group in New Haven, Conn.; Miw; Sackner; Price; participants at Womongathering: A Festival of Womyn's Spirituality, Oxford, Penn., May 1990 (hereinafter referred to as "Womongathering, May 1990).

35. Fleming. Also Mendel, Foster.

36. Jade, *To Know: A Guide to Women's Magic and Spirituality* (Oak Park, Ill.: Delphi Press, 1991), 135–36.

37. Ranck, *Cakes for the Queen;* Covenant of Unitarian Universalist Pagans newsletter, Cambridge, Mass.; Hart; Woods. See also Tsultrim Allione, quoted in Jamal, *Shape Shifters*, 44.

38. Schulman.

39. Otto.

40. Turcott.

41. Whiting.

Chapter 3: The Birth of a New Religion

1. Examples of this sentiment can be found in Sonia Johnson, interview with Stone, "Return of the Goddess"; Culpepper, "Contemporary Goddess Thealogy," 54; also Robison, Veracruz.

2. Joachim Wach, *Sociology of Religion* (Chicago: University of Chicago Press, 1944), 17–33.

3. Robert S. Ellwood, Jr., *Alternative Altars: Unconventional and Eastern Spirituality in America*, Chicago History of American Religion Series, ed. Martin E. Marty (Chicago: University of Chicago Press, 1979), 19.

4. Ibid., 16, 21.

5. Emily Culpepper, "The Spiritual Movement of Radical Feminist Consciousness,"

in *Understanding the New Religions*, ed. Jacob Needleman and G. Baker (New York: Seabury, 1978), 233, 221; Billie Potts, "Toward the Year 12,000: Lesbian Specialism," *Medusan Update* 2/1 (Summer 1991): 2; Seigel, "(Re-)Incarnating the Goddess," 1:16; Christ, *Laughter of Aphrodite*, 49. See also Char McKee, quoted in Wynne, *Womanspirit Sourcebook*, 127; Starhawk, *The Spiral Dance: A Rebirth of the Ancient Religion of the Great Goddess*, 1st ed. (San Francisco: Harper and Row, 1979), 196.

6. Jean Mountaingrove, quoted in Adler, *Drawing Down the Moon*, 178.

7. Veracruz. Also Washington, Courveline, Foster.

8. Anita Shreve, *Women Together, Women Alone: The Legacy of the Consciousness-Raising Movement* (New York: Fawcett Columbine, 1989), 5–6, 9–14. See also that book's appendix for a list of suggested topics for CR, distributed by the New York Radical Feminists and dating to the early 1970s.

9. Grace Shinell, "Women's Collective Spirit: Exemplified and Envisioned," in *The Politics of Women's Spirituality: Essays on the Rise of Spiritual Power Within the Feminist Movement*, ed. Charlene Spretnak (Garden City, N.Y.: Anchor Books, 1982), 510; Carol P. Christ, *Diving Deep and Surfacing: Women Writers on Spiritual Quest* (Boston: Beacon Press, 1980), 127; Jade, *To Know*, 11.

10. In fact, one woman I interviewed recounted experiences with two CR groups she participated in in the early 1970s that did not bring her even remotely close to feminist spirituality. She discovered feminist spirituality some fifteen years later, and refers to it as her "third wave of feminism" (Schulman).

11. For definitions and descriptions of cultural feminism, see Alice Echols, *Daring to Be Bad: Radical Feminism in America, 1967–1975* (Minneapolis: University of Minnesota Press, 1990); and Gayle Kimball, "Women's Culture: Themes and Images," in *Women's Culture: The Women's Renaissance of the Seventies*, ed. Gayle Kimball (Metuchen, N.J.: Scarecrow Press, 1980), 2–29.

12. Feminist Spiritual Community brochure, Portland, Maine.

13. Sackner.

14. Ibid.

15. Elizabeth Cady Stanton, *The Woman's Bible*, 2 vols. (New York: European Publishing Company, 1895, 1898); Matilda Joslyn Gage, *Woman, Church, and State* (1893; reprint, Watertown, Mass.: Persephone Press, 1980).

16. Mary Daly, "The Qualitative Leap Beyond Patriarchal Religion," *Quest* 1/4 (Spring 1975): 34; Phyllis Trible, *God and the Rhetoric of Sexuality* (Philadelphia: Fortress Press, 1978); Valerie Saiving, "The Human Situation: A Feminine View," *Journal of Religion* 40 (April 1960): 100–12; Elisabeth Schüssler-Fiorenza, *In Memory of Her: A Feminist Theological Reconstruction of Christian Origins* (New York: Crossroad, 1983); Judith Plaskow, *Sex, Sin, and Grace: Women's Experience and the Theologies of Reinhold Niebuhr and Paul Tillich* (Washington, D.C.: University Press of America, 1980). For a description of this progression in reformist and revolutionary feminism within established religions, see King, *Women and Spirituality*, 37.

17. A description of this exodus and the quote from Daly's sermon can be found in King, *Women and Spirituality*, 170; Mary Daly, "After the Death of God the Father: Women's Liberation and the Transformation of Christian Consciousness," in *Womanspirit Rising: A Feminist Reader in Religion*, ed. Carol P. Christ and Judith Plaskow (San Francisco: Harper and Row, 1979), 57.

18. Mary Daly, *Beyond God the Father: Toward a Philosophy of Women's Liberation* (Boston: Beacon Press, 1973), 13; Walker, *Skeptical Feminist*, 3; Charlene Spretnak, "The Politics of Women's Spirituality," in *Politics of Women's Spirituality*, ed. Spretnak, 394. See also Anne Kent Rush, "The Politics of Feminist Spirituality," in *Politics of Women's Spirituality*, ed. Spretnak, 384; Diane Mariechild, *Mother Wit: A Guide to Healing and Psychic Development*,

rev. ed. (Freedom, Calif.: Crossing Press, 1988), 176; Hallie Austen Iglehart, *Womanspirit: A Guide to Women's Wisdom* (San Francisco: Harper and Row, 1983), 7. (Iglehart's more recent works can be found under the name Hallie Iglehart Austen.)

19. Starhawk, *Dreaming the Dark: Magic, Sex, and Politics* (Boston: Beacon Press, 1982), 72; Merlin Stone, *When God Was a Woman* (New York: Harcourt, Brace, Jovanovich, 1976), xi.

20. Mary Daly, *Gyn/Ecology: The Metaethics of Radical Feminism* (Boston: Beacon Press, 1978), xi. See also Daly, *Beyond God the Father*, 17–18; Christ, *Laughter of Aphrodite*, 113; Carol P. Christ, "Why Women Need the Goddess: Phenomenological, Psychological, and Political Reflections," in *Womanspirit Rising*, ed. Christ and Plaskow, 274–75.

21. Ranck, *Cakes for the Queen*, 9.

22. Covenant of the Goddess, Berkeley. Information on the role of the Covenant of the Goddess in the neopagan movement can be found in Aidan Kelly, "An Update on Neopagan Witchcraft in America" (paper delivered at the annual meeting of the American Academy of Religion, Boston, Mass., Nov. 1987), along with Kelly's estimate of the movement's size.

23. Jesse Helms, quoted in Ann Forfreedom, *Feminist Wicce Works* (Berkeley: Ann Forfreedom, 9987 [1987]), 4; Starhawk, *Spiral Dance*, first ed., 5. See also Starhawk, interview with Stone, "Return of the Goddess"; Anne Marie Lux, "Witches nothing to be scared of, witch says" (interview with Selena Fox), *The Sunday Gazette* (Janesville, Wis.), Oct. 30, 1988; Miw. At a workshop on "Feminist Wicca Philosophy" (FSC Retreat, June 1990), Delores Cole gave a fairly typical disclaimer, saying that one cannot have Satanism without Christianity, that "Satanism is the death side of Christianity," and thus bears no relation to paganism.

24. Adler, *Drawing Down the Moon*, 60–66, 80–84. See also Marion Weinstein, *Positive Magic: Occult Self-Help*, rev. ed. (Custer, Wash.: Phoenix Publishing, 1981), 93.

25. See, for example, Starhawk, *Spiral Dance*, 2d ed., 229; also Miw.

26. Gwydion Pendderwen, quoted in Adler, *Drawing Down the Moon*, 88. See also Starhawk, *Spiral Dance*, first ed., 188.

27. Lux, "Witches nothing to be scared of." For other definitions of witchcraft or neopaganism, see Forfreedom, *Feminist Wicce Works*, 1; Starhawk, *Spiral Dance*, first ed., 2; Weinstein, *Positive Magic*, 68; Adler, *Drawing Down the Moon*, v.

28. Antiga, interview with Stone, "Return of the Goddess."

29. Robin Morgan, ed., *Sisterhood Is Powerful: An Anthology of Writings from the Women's Liberation Movement* (New York: Random House, 1970), 538–39; Robin Morgan, *Going Too Far: The Personal Chronicle of a Feminist* (New York: Random House, 1977), 77; Robin Morgan, "WITCH: Spooking the Patriarchy during the Late Sixties," in *Politics of Women's Spirituality*, ed. Spretnak, 428.

30. Morgan, "WITCH: Spooking the Patriarchy," 428–29.

31. Andrea Dworkin, *Woman Hating* (New York: E.P. Dutton, 1974), 118–50; Daly, *Beyond God the Father*, 62–64; and Daly, *Gyn/Ecology*, 178–222.

32. Gayle Kimball, "Goddess Worship in Wicce: Interview with Z Budapest," in *Women's Culture*, ed. Kimball, 238; Adler, *Drawing Down the Moon*, 76–77; Zsuzsanna Budapest, *The Holy Book of Women's Mysteries: Feminist Witchcraft, Goddess Rituals, Spellcasting, and other womanly arts . . .* , complete in one vol. (Berkeley: Wingbow Press, 1989), 258, 264–268; Budapest, *Grandmother of Time*, 84.

33. Kimball, "Goddess Worship in Wicce," 239; Adler, *Drawing Down the Moon*, 119; Z. Budapest, *The Holy Book of Women's Mysteries*, vol. 1 (Oakland: Susan B. Anthony Coven No. 1, 1979), 82; Rhiannon, interview with author, Los Angeles, Apr. 14, 1983.

34. Budapest, *Holy Book of Women's Mysteries* (1979), 9–10.

35. Jade, "Witchcraft Philosophy and Practice" (workshop at Womongathering, May 1990); Stone, *When God Was a Woman.*

36. Nikki Bado, "Stirring the Caldron: The Impact of the Women's Movement on the Old Religion" (paper delivered at the annual meeting of the American Academy of Religion, New Orleans, Nov. 1990); Jade, *To Know,* 66; Adler, *Drawing Down the Moon,* 22, 171–222.

37. Woods. Also Sackner.

38. Miw.

39. For a description of this encounter, see Budapest, *Holy Book of Women's Mysteries* (1989), xiv.

40. Adler, *Drawing Down the Moon,* 200; Starhawk, *Spiral Dance,* 2d ed., 220. Jade *(To Know,* 64) says that women are more numerous in mainstream neopaganism than are men. However, it seems that there are more mainstream neopagans than specifically feminist witches. Jade lists journals and newsletters of both feminist witchcraft and mainstream neopaganism, and the latter vastly outnumber the former. Information published by Circle Network (Mount Horeb, Wis.) gives the same impression. The term *Dianic witchcraft* is discussed by Jade in *To Know,* 60. Though usually reserved for lesbian or female-separatist witchcraft, the term *Dianic* is also used by a small group of mainstream pagans who worship both male and female deities and draw on the writings of Margaret Murray; they have no relation to feminist witchcraft.

41. Hoffman. The WITCH group with the name "Wild Independent-Thinking Crones and Hags" is located in Cambridge, Mass. I have not been able to discover the origin of the song "Who Are the Witches?" though I have heard it numerous times in different locations.

42. Garawitz; Bjorkman; Foster; Veracruz; Gordon; Washington; Frankel; Otto; Robison; Schulman; Copeland; Whiting; Sackner; Sharp; Teish, *Jambalaya,* 250; Mary Jo Neitz, "In Goddess We Trust," in *In Gods We Trust: New Patterns of Religious Pluralism in America,* ed. Thomas Robbins and Dick Anthony, 2d ed. (New Brunswick, N.J.: Transaction Publishers, 1990), 366; Anne Carson, *Feminist Spirituality and the Feminine Divine: An Annotated Bibliography* (Trumansburg, N.Y.: Crossing Press, 1986), 9; J. Gordon Melton, *Magic, Witchcraft, and Paganism in America: A Bibliography* (New York: Garland, 1982), 131. Emily Culpepper uses the phrase "Woman-Identified Culture" to refer to the broader feminist movement; see Culpepper, "Spiritual Movement of Radical Feminist Consciousness," 224.

Chapter 4: Affinities and Appropriations

1. Ellwood, *Alternative Altars,* 40. See also Mary Farrell Bednarowski, "Women in Occult America," in *The Occult in America: New Historical Perspectives,* ed. Howard Kerr and C. L. Crow (Urbana: University of Illinois Press, 1983), 178.

2. Susan Rennie and Kirsten Grimstad, "Spiritual Explorations Cross-Country," *Quest* 1/4 (Spring 1975): 49–50.

3. Chandler, *Understanding the New Age,* 17–18, 48.

4. Logan; Hoffman. For example, the New Age journal *Creation,* the brainchild of Matthew Fox, includes articles by Charlene Spretnak and Deena Metzger, both of whom are writers in the feminist spirituality movement.

5. Stein, *Women's Spirituality Book,* 154–55; Mariechild, *Mother Wit,* 45–52; Teish, *Jambalaya,* 217. Also Littlefield; Landau.

6. Marion Garbo Todd, "Bodywork for Adult Children of Alcoholics" (workshop at Womongathering, May 1990); Hoffman. See also Christina Robb, "In Goddess They Trust: Feminists Eschew Tradition in Pursuit of 'Deeper' Worship," *Boston Globe,* July 9, 1990, Living/Arts section.

7. Vicki Noble, "The Shakti Woman," *Snake Power* (Hallowmas 1989): 27.

8. Stone, "Return of the Goddess"; Littlefield; Veracruz; Bjorkman; *Of a Like Mind* 6/1 (May Day/Summer Solstice 9989 [1989]): 1.

9. Christ, *Laughter of Aphrodite*, 154.

10. Ellwood, *Alternative Altars*, 105–106.

11. Garawitz; Littlefield; Sharp; Logan; Keane; Mendel; Foster; Veracruz; Copeland; Landau; Washington; Charlene Spretnak, "Introduction," in *Politics of Women's Spirituality,* ed. Spretnak, xvi.

12. Logan. See also Monica Sjöö and Barbara Mor, *The Great Cosmic Mother: Rediscovering the Religion of the Earth* (San Francisco: Harper and Row, 1987), 219; Teish, *Jambalaya,* 150; also Woods.

13. Sjöö and Mor, *Great Cosmic Mother,* 221; Sackner; Keane. See also Starhawk, *Spiral Dance,* first ed., 193; also Robison, Gordon, Veracruz.

14. Logan; Engler; Mendel; Sandy Boucher, "Daughters of the Theris: American Women's Transformation of Buddhism," *woman of power* 12 (Winter 1989): 35.

15. Lynn Andrews, *Medicine Woman* (San Francisco: Harper and Row, 1981); Lynn Andrews, *Flight of the Seventh Moon* (San Francisco: Harper and Row, 1984); Lynn Andrews, *Jaguar Woman* (San Francisco: Harper and Row, 1985); Lynn Andrews, *Star Woman* (New York: Warner Books, 1986); Lynn Andrews, *Crystal Woman* (New York: Warner Books, 1987).

16. Shirley Schnirel, "The Modern Medicine Woman" (flyer from Rising Signs, Summit Park, Utah).

17. Jamal, *Shape Shifters,* 159; Sunray Meditation Society, "The Peacekeeper Mission" (flyer, Bristol, Vermont); Melissa Moore, "One Road of Beauty: Dhyani Ywahoo Speaks on Native American and Buddhist Teachings," *The Vajradhatu Sun* 6/6 (Aug.-Sept. 1984): n.p.

18. Anne Cameron, *Daughters of Copper Woman* (Vancouver: Press Gang Publishers, 1981), 7; Amy Lee, workshop on "Sharing the Medicine Bundle: A Giveaway from the Grandmothers" (workshop at Womongathering, May 1990); Jeanette C. Armstrong, "Cultural Robbery: Imperialism, Voices of Native Women," *Trivia* 14 (Spring 1989): 23.

19. Paula Gunn Allen, "Grandmother of the Sun: The Power of Woman in Native America," in *Weaving the Visions: New Patterns in Feminist Spirituality,* ed. Judith Plaskow and Carol P. Christ (San Francisco: Harper and Row, 1989), 27.

20. Carol Lee Sanchez, "New World Tribal Communities: An Alternative Approach for Recreating Egalitarian Societies," in *Weaving the Visions,* ed. Plaskow and Christ, 346. See also Jade, *To Know,* 70; Christ, *Laughter of Aphrodite,* 110.

21. Seigel, "(Re-)Incarnating the Goddess," 1:8; Sabrina Sojourner, "From the House of Yemanja: The Goddess Heritage of Black Women," in *Politics of Women's Spirituality,* ed. Spretnak, 58; Teish, *Jambalaya,* xi, 171. Serious researchers and practitioners of African religions have been hindered somewhat by what they call "contemporary patriarchs of the Yoruban [West African] culture," who they say have twisted an originally female-oriented religion into a patriarchal one; it turns out that African religions too have had to be reclaimed. Black intellectuals of the 1960s sought out African religions, but it has been left to women of the 1980s and 1990s to rescue them for women. Sabrina Sojourner explains that these women believe "that half-truths and false taboos have been imposed on them [as women] and the Yoruban manifestations of the goddess, that undue power has been placed in the hands of men, and that it is their duty as the daughters of Yemanja, Oshun, and Oya to restore their mothers as the heads of the House and regain respect for women" (Sojourner, "From the House of Yemanja," 60).

22. Sjöö and Mor, *Great Cosmic Mother,* 210. See also Teish, *Jambalaya,* 33; also Sackner.

23. Maddox; Laura. Most feminist revisions of Jewish rituals take place in groups that

are dominantly or totally Jewish, and thus would, in my construction of feminist spirituality, be limited to the movement's margins where Jewish and Christian feminism meet feminist spirituality. For resources on Jewish feminist spirituality, see Penina Adelman, *Miriam's Well: Rituals for Jewish Women Around the Year* (Sunnyside, N.Y.: Biblio Press, 1986); E. M. Broner, "Honor and Ceremony in Women's Rituals," in *Politics of Women's Spirituality*, ed. Spretnak, 236; Maureen Murdock, "Changing Woman: Contemporary Faces of the Goddess," *woman of power* 12 (Winter 1989): 42 (description of Naomi Newman's performances with the Traveling Jewish Theater).

24. Otto. See also Rose Romano, "In Praise of Santa Lucia," *SageWoman* (Spring 9989 [1989]): 23; also Miw.

25. Littlefield. Also Whiting, Keane.

26. Otto; Woods; Budapest, *Grandmother of Time,* xv. See also Lynn Andrews, quoted in Jamal, *Shape Shifters,* 26; Garawitz, Hoffman.

27. FSC Retreat, June 1990.

28. Andrea Smith, "Indian Spiritual Abuse" (handout at the annual meeting of the National Women's Studies Association, 1990).

29. Andrews, *Medicine Woman,* 5, 14, 29, 30, 35, 77.

30. Andrews, *Crystal Woman,* xv, 3; Andrews, *Medicine Woman,* ix, 37, 50; Elinor W. Gadon, *The Once and Future Goddess: A Sweeping Visual Chronicle of the Sacred Female and Her Reemergence in the Cultural Mythology of Our Time* (San Francisco: Harper and Row, 1989), 352; Sjöö and Mor, *Great Cosmic Mother,* 43, 210; Brian Swimme, "How to Heal a Lobotomy," in *Reweaving the World: The Emergence of Ecofeminism,* ed. Irene Diamond and Gloria Feman Orenstein (San Francisco: Sierra Club Books, 1990), 17; Budapest, *Grandmother of Time,* 58.

31. Seigel, "(Re-)Incarnating the Goddess," 1:3. For differing opinions on the existence or lack thereof of a pan-Indian spirituality, see Sam D. Gill, *Mother Earth: An American Story* (Chicago: University of Chicago Press, 1987) and Åke Hultkrantz, "The Religion of the Goddess in America," in *The Book of the Goddess, Past and Present,* ed. Carl Olson (New York: Crossroad, 1983).

32. Lorraine Bethel, "What Chou Mean *We,* White Girl," in *Conditions: Five—The Black Women's Issue,* ed. Lorraine Bethel and Barbara Smith (New York: Conditions, 1979), 88. See also Blanche Jackson, "Sakti-Root" (workshop at Womongathering, May 1990).

33. Monica Sjöö, "New Age or Armageddon?" *woman of power* 16 (Spring 1990): 65.

34. Renato Rosaldo, *Culture and Truth: The Remaking of Social Analysis* (Boston: Beacon Press, 1989), 68–87.

35. Veracruz; Whiting.

36. Keane; Sharp.

37. Price. See also Shuli Goodman and Diane Mariechild, "Keepers of the Flame" (workshop at Womongathering, May 1990); also Mendel.

38. Portia Cornell, quoted in Wynne, *Womanspirit Sourcebook,* 187.

39. Landau; Logan; Robison.

40. Frankel; Weinstein, *Positive Magic,* xxiv; Budapest, *Holy Book of Women's Mysteries* (1989), 239. See also Cole, "Feminist Wicca Philosophy"; Budapest, *Grandmother of Time,* 58–59.

41. Price.

42. Garawitz; Engler; Washington; Littlefield; Andrews, *Crystal Woman,* xv–xvi.

43. Sackner.

44. Hallie Iglehart Austen, *The Heart of the Goddess: Art, Myth, and Meditations of the World's Sacred Feminine* (Berkeley: Wingbow Press, 1990), xxiii. (Austen's earlier works can be found under the name Hallie Austen Iglehart.) See also Starhawk, *Truth or Dare: Power, Authority, and Magic* (San Francisco: Harper and Row, 1987), 136.

45. Seigel, "(Re-)Incarnating the Goddess," 1:14.

46. Morgan Grey and Julia Penelope, *Found Goddesses: Asphalta to Viscera* (Norwich, Vt.: New Victoria Publishers, 1988), 1, 18–19.

Chapter 5: Encountering the Sacred

1. Iglehart, *Womanspirit*, 33.

2. Gloria Feman Orenstein, *The Reflowering of the Goddess* (New York: Pergamon Press, 1990), 79. See also Starhawk, *Dreaming the Dark*, 26; Mariechild, *Mother Wit*, 170; Corinne Foster, "A Statement on Ritual" (unpublished, privately held); Adler, *Drawing Down the Moon*, 159; Alice Pratt, "We Gather to Affirm, Value and Shape," *Feminist Spiritual Community News Journal* 6/7 (Summer 1990): 2; Brigit McCallum, advertisement for services as "ritualer, liturgist, retreats, workshops, individual spiritual companioning," Cambridge, Mass.

3. Stein, *Women's Spirituality Book*, 16–17. See also Teish, *Jambalaya*, 249.

4. Budapest, *The Holy Book of Women's Mysteries* (1989), 75–90.

5. Women Spirit Rising of Costa Mesa, "Women Who Bleed for Life Ceremony" (flyer, Costa Mesa, Calif.); Allione, quoted in Jamal, *Shape Shifters*, 49; Sjöö and Mor, *Great Cosmic Mother*, 186, 189; Iglehart, *Womanspirit*, 162; Pia M. Godavitarne, "Shamanic Witchcraft," *woman of power* 8 (Winter 1988): 43; Stein, *Women's Spirituality Book*, 108–109; Demetra George, "Mysteries of the Dark Moon Lilith," *Snake Power* (Hallowmas 1989): 20.

6. Susana Valadez, "The Eye of the Cobra," *Snake Power* (Hallowmas 1989): 25. See also Christ, *Laughter of Aphrodite*, 193; Budapest, *Grandmother of Time*, 50; Betsy Bayley, Amy Chirman, Grace Darcy, and Elaine Gill, *Celebrating Women's Spirituality* (Freedom, Calif.: Crossing Press, 1989), n.p.

7. Cameron, *Daughters of Copper Woman*, 103.

8. Brooke Medicine Eagle, "Moon Lodge Teachings" (audiotape). See also Valadez, "Eye of the Cobra," 25; Kisma Stepanich, "Seasonal Musings from Kisma," *Women Spirit Rising of Costa Mesa* (Summer 9990 [1990]): n.p.; Susun Weed, "Blood of the Ancients" (3-day workshop described in Wise Woman Center catalog, Woodstock, N.Y., 1989).

9. Sackner.

10. Gadon, *Once and Future Goddess*, 2; Medicine Eagle, "Moon Lodge Teachings"; Starhawk, *Spiral Dance*, first ed., 99. See also Judy Grahn, "From Sacred Blood to the Curse and Beyond," in *Politics of Women's Spirituality*, ed. Spretnak, 268; Sunray Meditation Society, "Dance of the Holy Mother: A Women's Medicine Circle" (workshop described in The Peace Village and Summer Program at Hope Mountain catalog, Bristol, Vt.); Faith Queman, "Theater of the Spirit" (workshop at Womongathering, May 1990); Nancy Passmore, *1989 Lunar Calendar* (Boston: Luna Press, 1989), n.p.

11. Bloodroot Collective, *The Political Palate* (Bridgeport, Conn.: Sanguinaria, 1980), xii–xiii; Sarah Scholfield, "The Four Directions," *Snake Power* (Hallowmas 1989): 9; Hoffman; Stone, "Return of the Goddess"; Otto; anonymous spiritual feminist, "Dyke Separatist Unioning," anonymous spiritual feminist publication; Keane.

12. Marah, "Marah's Almanac Full Flowering," Summer 1990, No. 7; Budapest, *Grandmother of Time*. See also Budapest, *Holy Book of Women's Mysteries* (1989).

13. See, for example, Jade, *To Know*, 82; Budapest, *Holy Book of Women's Mysteries* (1989), 115.

14. Keane; Otto.

15. See, for example, Starhawk, *Spiral Dance*, first ed., 14; Pratt, "We Gather to Affirm," 2.

16. Starhawk, *Dreaming the Dark*, 19. Also Foster, Schulman.

17. For example, Sackner.

18. Budapest, *Grandmother of Time,* 248. See also Re-formed Congregation of the Goddess flyer.

19. Woods; Schulman; Copeland; Starhawk, *Spiral Dance,* 2d ed., 10; Garawitz; Cole, "Feminist Wicca Philosophy"; Stein, *Women's Spirituality Book,* 60.

20. Keane; Z. Budapest, "The Vows, Wows, and Joys of the High Priestess or What Do You People Do Anyway?" in *Politics of Women's Spirituality,* ed. Spretnak, 539; Budapest, *Grandmother of Time,* 13, 37, 244. See also Budapest, *Holy Book of Women's Mysteries* (1989), xv, 213, 217; also Miw.

21. Forfreedom, *Feminist Wicce Works,* 13.

22. Schulman. Also Garawitz.

23. Garawitz. See also Susun Weed, "Green Witch Week" (week-long workshop described in Wise Woman Center catalog, Woodstock, N.Y., 1989); Antiga, interview with Stone, "Return of the Goddess"; also Mendel, Robison, Copeland, Schulman.

24. The distinction between "distance senses" (hearing and sight) and "proximity senses" (taste, touch, and smell) is the work of psychoanalyst Ernest G. Schachtel. For a discussion of his theory and its significance to religious ritual, see Ellwood, *Alternative Altars,* 59–61.

25. Schulman; Jade, *To Know,* 80, 96; Forfreedom, *Feminist Wicce Works,* 1; Budapest, *Holy Book of Women's Mysteries* (1989), 21.

26. Budapest, *Holy Book of Women's Mysteries* (1989), 17; Keane; Washington; Frankel; Foster; Woods; Margot Adler, "Demystifying Ritual" (workshop at Womongathering, May 1990); FSC Retreat, June 1990.

27. Budapest, *Grandmother of Time,* 40; Starhawk, *Truth or Dare,* 103. Also Hoffman.

28. Forfreedom, *Feminist Wicce Works,* 4; Courveline; Keane. A number of enterprising women sell reproductions of ancient goddess figurines for use as jewelry or altar symbols (for example, Star River Productions, North Brunswick, N.J.).

29. Mariechild, *Mother Wit,* 149; Stein, *Women's Spirituality Book,* 62–63; Forfreedom, *Feminist Wicce Works;* Budapest, *Holy Book of Women's Mysteries* (1979), 26–27.

30. Stein, *Women's Spirituality Book,* 71. See also Reba Rose, "Hallowmas," *Snake Power* (Hallowmas 1989): 49. For general reflections on sacred space and time, see Mircea Eliade, *The Myth of the Eternal Return,* trans. Willard R. Trask (Princeton: Princeton University Press, 1971), 20.

31. Stein, *Women's Spirituality Book,* 70; Mariechild, *Mother Wit,* 152; Starhawk, *Spiral Dance,* first ed., 201–204.

32. Starhawk, *Spiral Dance,* first ed., 55–56.

33. Stein, *Women's Spirituality Book,* 66.

34. Adriana Diaz, quoted in Teish, *Jambalaya,* 243.

35. Budapest, *Holy Book of Women's Mysteries* (1979), 27.

36. Stein, *Women's Spirituality Book,* 72; Garawitz. See also Budapest, *Grandmother of Time,* 245–46.

37. These chants are attributed to Starhawk, Shekhinah Mountainwater, Deena Metzger, and Native American tradition, respectively.

38. Foster; Layne Redmond, "Woman, Rhythm, and the Frame Drum" (workshop described in New York Open Center catalog, New York, Spring 1990).

39. Ayla Heartsong, "Spiral Dance" (xeroxed sheet distributed at Womongathering, May 1990). See also Medicine Eagle, "Moon Lodge Teachings"; also Veracruz, Garawitz. All of the elements of raising energy—chanting, drumming, dancing—are seen as devices to promote alternative states of consciousness, to bring the divine into sharp (if regrettably temporary) focus. When pushed to its logical conclusion, raising energy becomes trance or divine possession. Such extremes are not common in feminist spirituality. They are

generally regarded as desirable, but they are also feared, and most women are content to do a little boisterous singing and shouting and leave it at that. The majority of spiritual feminists are fond of feeling in control, at least to a degree. Many associate loss of control with vulnerability, and a prime attraction of feminism for them has been its promise of lessening their culturally prescribed vulnerability as women and increasing their sense of power and control. Also, most spiritual feminists are white and nominally middle-class, coming from a subculture where loss of control is normally avoided rather than aggressively sought out. Still, there are some spiritual feminists who welcome the feeling of losing their ordinary selves in the rapture of the divine or in a journey to other worlds, and some who can imagine no greater joy than being possessed by the goddess: to speak in her voice, to move with her body, to think her thoughts, to well up with her emotions. I have not witnessed actual possession. The accounts I have heard of it have come from women who regard themselves as witches, recovering what they believe to be the practices of an ancient religion, or from women deeply involved in voodoo, Santeria, or Native American traditions. For comments on possession, see Starhawk, *Truth or Dare*, 96; also Schulman, Courveline, Sackner, Engler.

40. Starhawk, *Spiral Dance*, 2d ed., 223; Friday night full moon ritual, FSC Retreat, June 1990.

41. Starhawk, *Truth or Dare*, 111–12. See also Stein, *Women's Spirituality Book*, 73.

42. Budapest, *Grandmother of Time*, 247. See also Iglehart, *Womanspirit*, 141; Starhawk, *Spiral Dance*, first ed., 157; Eisler and Loye, *Partnership Way*, 49.

43. Copeland. Also Landau. Talking circles are not always this intimate, and rarely this protracted. Sometimes they are used as a vehicle for group discussion of topics of concern to participants. The Feminist Spiritual Community (FSC) in Maine, for example, uses the talking circle (which it calls a "listening") to work toward consensus on divisive issues. Crediting the Quaker tradition for the inspiration, the FSC regularly schedules listenings to encourage each member to speak and to listen to others in a nonjudgmental frame of mind.

44. Austen, *Heart of the Goddess*, 42. See also Mariechild, *Mother Wit*, 94–95, 126–27; Stein, *Women's Spirituality Book*, 139; Penelope Pureheart, "Creating a Feminist Future" (workshop at Womongathering, May 1990); also Landau.

45. Copeland; Austen, *Heart of the Goddess*, 24; Mariechild, *Mother Wit*, 124–25, 173; Christ, *Laughter of Aphrodite*, 202–203. See also Jean Mountaingrove, "Menstruation: Our Link to Ancient Wisdom," *woman of power* 8 (Winter 1988): 64–67; Garawitz.

46. Budapest, *Holy Book of Women's Mysteries* (1979), 48; Garawitz; Sackner. See also Sonia Nazario, "Is Goddess Worship Finally Going to Put Men in Their Place?" *Wall Street Journal* 115/11 (June 7, 1990); Stein, *Women's Spirituality Book*, 98.

Chapter 6: *Magic and Other Spiritual Practices*

1. Foster, "A Statement on Ritual"; Naomi Kronlokken, "Psychosynthesis: Identity and Choice" (workshop at FSC Retreat, June 1990); Whiting; Starhawk, *Dreaming the Dark*, 45–46.

2. Budapest, *Holy Book of Women's Mysteries* (1989), 11.

3. Budapest, *Holy Book of Women's Mysteries* (1979), 5. See also Mariechild, *Mother Wit*, 171.

4. Teish, *Jambalaya*, 94–95.

5. Felicity Artemis Flowers, *The P.M.S. Conspiracy* (Marina del Rey, Calif.: Circle of Aradia Productions, 1986), 12.

6. Budapest, *Holy Book of Women's Mysteries* (1989), 62–63; Stein, *Women's Spirituality Book*, 113; Austen, *Heart of the Goddess*, xxii.

7. Turcott.

8. Price; Woods; Sharp; Sackner; Otto.

9. Rose, "Hallowmas," 49; Patrice Wynne, "An Interview with Luisah Teish," *Sage-Woman* (Spring 9989 [1989]), 16; Budapest, *Holy Book of Women's Mysteries* (1979), 19; Mendel; Landau; Washington.

10. Foster; Garawitz; Littlefield; Gordon; Bjorkman; Robison; Veracruz; Hoffman; Copeland; Schulman; Price; Woods; Sharp; Sackner; Otto.

11. Wynne, "Interview with Luisah Teish," 16; Whiting. Also Frankel, Garawitz, Logan.

12. Keane; Copeland. Also Courveline, Landau, Gordon, Sharp.

13. Veracruz; Stein, *Women's Spirituality Book*, 182; Iglehart, *Womanspirit*, 67, 71.

14. Wynne, "Interview with Luisah Teish," 16. Also Fleming, Sharp.

15. Catherine L. Albanese, *Nature Religion in America: From the Algonkian Indians to the New Age* (Chicago: University of Chicago Press, 1990), 117–52.

16. Chandler, *Understanding the New Age*, 163–67; Jade, *To Know*, 151, 153; Mariechild, *Mother Wit*, 72–73. For a historical perspective on this mind-set, see Albanese, *Nature Religion in America*, 126; for a nuanced discussion of the implications of regarding disease this way, see Mariechild, *Mother Wit*, 66–72.

17. Stein, *Women's Spirituality Book*, 154–61; Teish, *Jambalaya*, 217; Mariechild, *Mother Wit*, 77; Laurel Moran, "Toning and Balancing the Chakras through Sound" (workshop at FSC Retreat, June 1990); Hart.

18. Advertisements for "The Marketplace," Womongathering, May 1990; Marie Summerwood, "Simple Touch the Wise Woman Way" (workshop described in Wise Woman Center catalog, Woodstock, N.Y., 1990); Stein, *Women's Spirituality Book*, 74, 153, 164; Vicki Noble, quoted in Jamal, *Shape Shifters*, 111; Sisterhood of the Lavender Dawn, "Way of the Mother" (workshop described in flyer, Baltimore); Morgana Davis and Jane Cassidy, "Introduction to Homeopathy—The Energy Medicine" (workshop at Womongathering, May 1990); Mariechild, *Mother Wit*, 78.

19. Littlefield; Mendel; Hoffman.

20. Chellis Glendinning, "The Healing Powers of Women," in *Politics of Women's Spirituality*, ed. Spretnak, 291.

21. Budapest, *Holy Book of Women's Mysteries* (1979), 77–82; Jeannine Parvati Baker, advertisement for Hygieia College, Monroe, Utah; Deborah Maia, "Releasing Spirit Life Within the Womb" (workshop described in Wise Woman Center catalog, Woodstock, N.Y., 1989). See also Jeanne Achterberg, *Woman as Healer* (Boston: Shambala, 1991); Billie Potts, *Witches Heal*, 2d. ed. (Ann Arbor: DuRêve Publishers, 1988); Diane Stein, *All Women are Healers: A Comprehensive Guide to Natural Healing* (Freedom, Calif.: Crossing Press, 1990).

22. Jade, *To Know*, 108–131; Godavitarne, "Shamanic Witchcraft," 43; Medicine Eagle, "Moon Lodge Teachings"; Marion Weinstein, *Earth Magic: A Dianic Book of Shadows* (Custer, Wash.: Phoenix Publishing, 1986); Stein, *Women's Spirituality Book*, 249.

23. In a perusal of bookstore and catalog titles, I have seen four astrology handbooks marketed exclusively to women, three spiritual feminist versions of the *I Ching*, and no less than seventeen feminist tarot decks and/or handbooks for their interpretation. Some tarot decks are peopled exclusively with women; others limit "male" cards to one or a few out of seventy-eight cards; others rely on standard tarot decks but offer feminist interpretations. A further innovation is that some of the decks are composed of round rather than rectangular cards, the circle being understood as a "female" symbol. Spiritual feminist guides to astrology include: Lindsay River and Sally Gillespie, *The Knot of Time: Astrology and the Female Experience* (New York: Harper and Row, 1987); Geraldine Thorsten, *The Goddess in Your Stars* (1980; reprint, New York: Simon and Schuster, 1989); Sheila

Farrant, *Symbols for Women: A Matrilineal Zodiac* (London: Mandala, 1989); Geraldine Hatch Hanon, *Sacred Space: A Feminist Vision of Astrology* (Ithaca, N.Y.: Firebrand Books, 1990). Spiritual feminist revisions of the *I Ching* include: Rowena Pattee, *Moving With Change: A Woman's Re-Integration of the I Ching* (London and New York: Arkana, 1986); Diane Stein, *The Kwan Yin Book of Changes* (St. Paul: Llewellyn Publishers, 1987); Barbara G. Walker, *The I Ching of the Goddess* (San Francisco: Harper and Row, 1986). Spiritual feminist tarot decks and/or guides to interpretation include: Sally Gearhart and Susan Rennie, *A Feminist Tarot* (Venice, Calif.: Pandora's Box, 1976); Jesse Cougar, "A Poet's Tarot" (Little River, Calif.: Tough Dove Books, 1986); Billie Potts, Susun Weed, and River Lightwoman, "Amazon Tarot" and "New Amazon Tarot" (Albany, N.Y.: Hecuba's Daughters Press); Billie Potts, *A New Women's Tarot* (Woodstock, N.Y.: Elf and Dragons Press, 1978); Gail Fairfield, *Choice Centered Tarot* (Seattle: Choices, 1984); Vicki Noble and Karen Vogel, "Motherpeace Tarot" (St. Paul: Llewellyn Publishers); Vicki Noble, *Motherpeace: A Way to the Goddess Through Myth, Art and Tarot* (San Francisco: Harper and Row, 1983); Ruth West, "Thea's Tarot" (Leverett, Mass.: Medusa Graphics, 1984); Jean Van Slyke, "Book of Aradia Tarot"; Shekhinah Mountainwater, "Shekhinah's Tarot"; Ffiona Morgan, "Daughters of the Moon Tarot"; Mary Greer, *Tarot for Yourself: A Workbook for Personal Transformation* (Van Nuys, Calif.: Newcastle Publishing Company, 1987); Barbara G. Walker, *The Secrets of the Tarot: Origins, History, and Symbolism* (San Francisco: Harper and Row, 1984); Stein, *Women's Spirituality Book*, 198–211; Jean Freer, *The New Feminist Tarot* (Northamptonshire, England: Aquarian Press, 1987); Carol Herzer Abram, "Cosmo Deck" and "AstroTarot"; Budapest, *Holy Book of Women's Mysteries* (1979), 90–100; Carol Bridges, *Medicine Woman Tarot* (Nashville, Ind.: Earth Nation). Examples of other forms of spiritual feminist divination include: Shekhinah Mountainwater, "Womanrunes" catalog, Santa Cruz, Calif.; Lynnie Levy, "Sacred Symbols: The Language of the Runes" (workshop at Womongathering, May 1990); Shirley Schnirel, "Goddess Channeling Cards" (Summit Park, Utah: Rising Signs).

24. Budapest, *Holy Book of Women's Mysteries* (1989), 191; Jade, *To Know*, 112, 117; Stein, *Women's Spirituality Book*, 195.

25. Budapest, *Holy Book of Women's Mysteries* (1989), 182–83. See also Noble, *Motherpeace*, 18–19; Noble, quoted in Jamal, *Shape Shifters*, 114. For another example of divinatory practices borrowed from "ancient Goddess cultures," see Merlin Stone, "A Letter from Merlin" (self-published newsletter, New York, Summer 9990 [1990]).

26. Stein, *Women's Spirituality Book*, 198; Weinstein, *Positive Magic*, 150; Jade, *To Know*, 103, 104; Erica Langley and Shirley Schnirel, advertisement for Goddess Channeling Cards (Summit Park, Utah: Rising Signs).

27. Woods; Turcott; Schulman; Otto.

28. Jane Iris Designs, Inc., flyer, Graton, Calif.; Star River Productions, North Brunswick, N.J.; Rowena Pattee, quoted in Jamal, *Shape Shifters*, 63; Mimi Lobell, interview with Stone, "Return of the Goddess." See also Judith Bell, "The Art of Healing" (article on artist Nancy Azara), *Taxi* (April 1990): 18; Tina Stack, "Luna," in Passmore, *1989 Lunar Calendar*; also Hoffman.

29. *Ladyslipper Catalog*, "the world's most comprenhensive Catalog and Resource Guide of Records and Tapes by Women," is published annually by Ladyslipper, Inc., Durham, N.C.; Lisa Thiel, "Faerie Songs and Goddess Chants" (workshop described in Wise Woman Center catalog, Woodstock, N.Y., 1990); Budapest, *Holy Book of Women's Mysteries* (1989), xiv.

30. Nancy Brooks and Jane Winslow, WomanShine Theatre flyer, Bloomington, Ind.; Orenstein, *Reflowering of the Goddess*, 104; Mary Beth Edelson, interview with Stone, "Return of the Goddess"; Mary Daly, et al., "Patriarchy on Trial" (public performance at Harvard University, Cambridge, Mass., May 14, 1989). See also Mary Beth Edelson, "See

for Yourself: Women's Spirituality in Holistic Art," in *Politics of Women's Spirituality*, ed. Spretnak, 325.

31. A. L. Rawe, "Planetary Acupuncture," *Common Ground of Puget Sound* 6/2 (Fall 1991): 8; Christ, *Laughter of Aphrodite*, 201–202; Christine Downing, *The Goddess: Mythological Images of the Feminine* (New York: Crossroad, 1981), 143. See also Ellwood, *Alternative Altars*, 38; also Keane.

32. Patricia Reis, quoted in Wynne, *Womanspirit Sourcebook*, 179.

33. Miriam Sidell, interview with Stone, "Return of the Goddess."

34. Orenstein, *Reflowering of the Goddess*, 101; Feminist Spiritual Community, *News Journal* 6/7 (Summer 1990); Anneli S. Rufus and Kristan Lawson, *Goddess Sites: Europe* (San Francisco: HarperSanFrancisco, 1991).

35. Budapest, *Holy Book of Women's Mysteries* (1989), 8–9; Washington; Bjorkman; Schulman.

36. Those women who stick solely to a theory of subconscious motivation tend not to practice magic. But by holding to this theory, they are able to feel at home within a spiritual movement that talks incessantly of magic. This understanding of magic, that it works on practitioners' minds, but not on "reality" per se, has been proposed and elaborated by anthropologist Bronislaw Malinowski. See Stanley Jeyaraja Tambiah, *Magic, Science, Religion, and the Scope of Rationality* (New York: Cambridge University Press, 1990), 65–81.

37. Miw. See also Stein, *Women's Spirituality Book*, 137; Budapest, *Holy Book of Women's Mysteries* (1989), 110; Teish, *Jambalaya*, 213.

38. Starhawk, *Spiral Dance*, first ed., 18; Albanese, *Nature Religion in America*, 108–109. See also Starhawk, *Dreaming the Dark*, 13; Barbara Mor and Monica Sjöö, "Respell the World," *woman of power* 12 (Winter 1989): 19.

39. Mariechild, *Mother Wit*, 32. See also Starhawk, *Spiral Dance*, first ed., 13–14.

40. Starhawk, *Spiral Dance*, first ed., 112. See also Mariechild, *Mother Wit*, 53; also Robison, Courveline.

41. Starhawk, *Dreaming the Dark*, 53.

42. Teish, *Jambalaya*, 251.

43. Shekhinah Mountainwater catalog, Santa Cruz, Calif.; Weinstein, *Positive Magic*, 9; Weinstein, *Earth Magic*, 2, 18, 87; Jade, "Witchcraft Philosophy and Practice"; Vicki Noble, quoted in Cathleen Rountree, "Female Shamans: Technicians of the Sacred," *woman of power* 12 (Winter 1989): 60; Iglehart, *Womanspirit*, 124; Teish, *Jambalaya*, 207.

44. Sackner. See also Weinstein, *Earth Magic*, 5, 18.

45. Budapest, *Holy Book of Women's Mysteries* (1989), 8.

46. Walker, *Skeptical Feminist*, 251–52; Teish, *Jambalaya*, 225. For a scholary discussion of the theory that magic is lawlike, see Tambiah, *Magic, Science, Religion*, 7.

47. Starhawk, *Truth or Dare*, 24.

48. Courveline; Logan; McIntyre; Stein, *Women's Spirituality Book*, 116; Price; Schulman. See also Grey and Penelope, *Found Goddesses*, 4; also Gordon, Garawitz.

49. Hoffman; Teish, *Jambalaya*, 244; Starhawk, *Spiral Dance*, 109. See also Budapest, *Holy Book of Women's Mysteries* (1979), 55; also Frankel, Woods.

50. Jade, *To Know*, 26; Courveline. See also Weinstein, *Positive Magic*, 10; Shekhinah Mountainwater catalog.

51. Budapest, *Holy Book of Women's Mysteries* (1979), 56–69; Budapest, *Grandmother of Time*, 99–101, 120; Budapest, *Holy Book of Women's Mysteries* (1989), 23–49. Other spiritual feminist books that include magical recipes include: Mariechild, *Mother Wit*; Diane Mariechild, *Crystal Visions: Nine Meditations for Personal and Planetary Peace* (Freedom, Calif.: Crossing Press, 1985); Stein, *Women's Spirituality Book*; Diane Stein, *Stroking the Python: Women's Psychic Lives* (St. Paul: Llewellyn Publishers, 1988); Weinstein, *Earth Magic*;

Weinstein, *Positive Magic*; Starhawk, *Spiral Dance*, first ed.; Teish, *Jambalaya*; Ann Forfreedom and Julie Ann, comps., *The Book of the Goddess* (Sacramento: Temple of the Goddess Within, 1980).

52. Price; Courveline.

53. Mariechild, *Mother Wit*, 6–7. See also Woods; Starhawk, *Spiral Dance*, first ed.,74.

54. Starhawk, *Spiral Dance*, first ed., 124; Teish, *Jambalaya*, 21–22.

55. Stein, *Women's Spirituality Book*, 144; Garawitz. See also Teish, *Jambalaya*, 133; Budapest, *Holy Book of Women's Mysteries* (1979), 58.

56. Kay Turner, "Contemporary Feminist Rituals," *Heresies* 2/1 (1982): 21 (special issue, "The Great Goddess," rev. ed.).

57. Otto. Also Garawitz, Mendel, Sharp, Schulman, Frankel.

58. Jade, *To Know*, 45–48. Delores Cole ("Feminist Wicca Philosophy") reports that disagreements over whether to hex or limit oneself to positive magic are the biggest conflicts to surface at Dianic (womyn's) conferences.

59. Mariechild, *Mother Wit*, 32, 51; Schulman; Gordon.

60. Starhawk, *Spiral Dance*, 2d ed., 26–27; Weinstein, *Earth Magic*, 1; Jade, *To Know*, 47; Kira Ma'at-ka-re, "Everything Has Its Price," *The Beltane Papers* (North 87/88): 7; Starhawk, *Spiral Dance*, first ed., 67; Starhawk, *Dreaming the Dark*, 34–35; Jade, "Witchcraft Philosophy and Practice"; Miw; Courveline; Copeland; Mendel; Washington; Frankel; Teish, *Jambalaya*, 203.

61. Sackner. Also Price.

62. Forfreedom, *Feminist Wicce Works*, 2; Budapest, *Holy Book of Women's Mysteries* (1979), 55; Jade, *To Know*, 46.

63. Stein, *Women's Spirituality Book*, 142–43; Schulman; Washington. See also Starhawk, *Spiral Dance*, 2d ed., 237; Weinstein, *Positive Magic*, 54–55; Pagan Spirit Alliance, "A Pledge to Pagan Spirituality" flyer, Mount Horeb, Wis.; Mariechild, *Mother Wit*, xx–xxi; also Logan, Sackner.

64. Mariechild, *Mother Wit*, xx–xxi.

65. Teish, *Jambalaya*, 200. See also Budapest, *Grandmother of Time*, 63–64; Zsuzsanna Budapest, "Political Witchcraft," *woman of power* 8 (Winter 1988): 38.

66. Teish, *Jambalaya*, 200; Zsuzsanna Budapest, quoted in Kimball, "Goddess Worship in Wicce," 245; Budapest, *Holy Book of Women's Mysteries* (1979), 63–64, 75. See also Budapest, *Holy Book of Women's Mysteries* (1989), 17; also Turcott.

67. Budapest, *Grandmother of Time*, 61.

Chapter 7: Not Just God in a Skirt

1. Shoshana Hathaway, letter to editor, *SageWoman* (Spring 9989 [1989]): 32.

2. Christ, *Laughter of Aphrodite*, 110.

3. Keane.

4. Sackner; Foster.

5. Whiting. Also Gordon, Frankel.

6. Titles in the singular: Melanie Lofland Gendron and Shawn Evans, *The Goddess Remembered* (Freedom, Calif.: Crossing Press, 1990); Adele Getty, *Goddess: Mother of Living Nature* (London: Thames and Hudson, 1990); Marija Gimbutas, *The Language of the Goddess: Unearthing the Hidden Symbols of Western Civilization* (San Francisco: Harper and Row, 1989); Janine Canan, ed., *She Rises Like the Sun: Invocations of the Goddess by Contemporary American Women Poets* (Freedom, Calif.: Crossing Press, 1989); Buffie Johnson, *Lady of the Beasts: Ancient Images of the Great Goddess and her Sacred Animals* (San Francisco: Harper and Row, 1988); Mary Condren, *The Serpent and the Goddess: Women, Religion, and Power in Celtic Ireland* (San Francisco: Harper and Row, 1989); Nor Hall, *The Moon and the Virgin:*

Reflections on the Archetypal Feminine (San Francisco: Harper and Row, 1980); Mariam Baker, *Woman as Divine: Tales of the Goddess* (Eugene, Ore.: Crescent Heart Press, 1982); Meinrad Craighead, *The Mother's Songs: Images of God the Mother* (New York: Paulist Press, 1986); Judith Laura, *She Lives! The Return of Our Great Mother* (Freedom, Calif.: Crossing Press, 1989); Shirley Nicholson, ed., *The Goddess Re-Awakening: The Feminine Principle Today* (Wheaton, Ill.: Quest Books, 1989); Olson, ed., *Book of the Goddess*; Austen, *Heart of the Goddess*; Budapest, *Grandmother of Time*; Carson, *Feminist Spirituality and Feminine Divine*; Christ, *Laughter of Aphrodite*; Downing, *The Goddess*; Gadon, *Once and Future Goddess*; "The Great Goddess," special issue of *Heresies* (Spring 1978, rev. ed. 1982); Susan Lee/Susanah Libana, *You Said, What Is This for, This Interest in Goddess, Prehistoric Religions?* (Austin, Tex.: Plain View Press, 1985); Noble, *Motherpeace*; Ranck, *Cakes for the Queen*; Sjöö and Mor, *Great Cosmic Mother*; Starhawk, *The Spiral Dance: A Rebirth of the Ancient Religion of the Great Goddess*; Stone, "The Return of the Goddess." Titles in the plural: Marija Gimbutas, *The Goddesses and Gods of Old Europe: Myths and Cult Images* (Berkeley: University of California Press, 1982); Patricia Monaghan, *The Book of Goddesses and Heroines* (St. Paul: Llewellyn Publishers, 1990); Mayumi Oda, *Goddesses* (Volcano, Calif.: Volcano Press/Kazan Books, 1988); Susanne Heine, *Matriarchs, Goddesses, and Images of God* (Philadelphia: Fortress Press, 1989); Grey and Penelope, *Found Goddesses*; Charlene Spretnak, *Lost Goddesses of Early Greece: A Collection of Pre-Hellenic Myths* (Boston: Beacon Press, 1981); Walker, *The Skeptical Feminist: Discovering the Virgin, Mother, and Crone.*

7. Frankel; Price; Woods.

8. Spretnak, "Politics of Women's Spirituality," 394. For another example of a litany using multiple goddess names, see Starhawk, *Spiral Dance*, first ed., 86.

9. Price; Mendel; Teish, *Jambalaya*, 40.

10. Ellwood, *Alternative Altars*, 37. See also Albanese, *Nature Religion in America*, 64. For examples of this ultimate monism / intermediate polytheism among spiritual feminists, see Teish, *Jambalaya*, 60; Rachel V., quoted in Wynne, *Womanspirit Sourcebook*, 163; also Logan, Schulman, Mendel, Woods.

11. Woods; Sharp; Schulman. See also Teish, *Jambalaya*; Budapest, *The Holy Book of Women's Mysteries* (1989), 161–162; also Copeland, Sackner, Gordon, Courveline.

12. Elizabeth Dodson Gray, "Women's Experience and Naming the Sacred," *woman of power* 12 (Winter 1989): 11.

13. Doreen Valiente, quoted in Starhawk, *The Spiral Dance*, 2d ed., 90–91.

14. Starhawk, *Dreaming the Dark*, 9; Starhawk, *Truth or Dare*, 7. See also Heide Göttner-Abendroth, *Matriarchal Mythology in Former Times and Today* (Freedom, Calif.: Crossing Press, 1987), 12. See also Starhawk, *Spiral Dance*, 2d ed., 10.

15. Hoffman.

16. Mariechild, *Mother Wit*, 157; Noble, *Motherpeace*, 246.

17. Austen, *Heart of the Goddess*, 30. Also Keane.

18. Sharp; Copeland; Robison; Price; Keane.

19. Garawitz; Littlefield. See also Dhyani Ywahoo, "Renewing the Sacred Hoop," *woman of power* 2 (1985); Stone, "Return of the Goddess"; also Engler, Otto, Hoffman, Foster, Gordon, Schulman.

20. James E. Lovelock and Sidney Epton, "The Quest for Gaia," *New Scientist* 65 (1975): 304; J. E. Lovelock, *Gaia: A New Look at Life on Earth* (New York: Oxford University Press, 1979). The Gaia theory is a recent version of the very old "geocosm theory," which held sway from the classical era to the Middle Ages, according to Carolyn Merchant. In her book *The Death of Nature* (San Francisco: Harper and Row, 1989) Merchant explains that geocosm theorists "compared the earth to the living human body, with breath, blood, sweat, and elimination systems" (23).

21. M. Lynn Schiavi, "Only Goddess Can Make a Tree," (illustration) *Cornucopia* (May

1991): n.p. See also Marjorie P. Graybeal, "Into the Realm of the Goddess," *Pagan Nuus* 4/1 (Beltane 1990): 3; also Courveline, Washington, Frankel, Miw, Bjorkman.

22. This is consistent with the pattern in other alternative religions in America; see Ellwood, *Alternative Altars*, 37.

23. Birdwoman, "My Creation Story," *SageWoman* (Spring 9989 [1989]): 21. See also Noble, *Motherpeace*, 23.

24. Culpepper, "Contemporary Goddess Thealogy," 56. See also Noble, *Motherpeace*, 23; Starhawk, *Spiral Dance*, first ed., 24–25.

25. Luisah Teish and Uzuri Amini, "Eye of the Vulture," *woman of power* 8 (Winter 1988): 54; Austen, *Heart of the Goddess*, 52.

26. Gloria Orenstein, interview with Stone, "Return of the Goddess"; Sjöö and Mor, *Great Cosmic Mother*, 407; Downing, *The Goddess*, 154; Bjorkman; Gordon.

27. Whiting.

28. Starhawk, *Spiral Dance*, first ed., 77–78.

29. Sharp; Copeland. See also Neitz, "In Goddess We Trust," 356; Adler, *Drawing Down the Moon*, 170; also Whiting.

30. Hart.

31. Whiting. See also Sjöö and Mor, *Great Cosmic Mother*, 335; also Courveline, Keane, Price, Schulman, Gordon.

32. Walker, *Skeptical Feminist*, 15; Sackner; Littlefield.

33. Eleanor H. Haney, *Vision and Struggle: Meditations on Feminist Spirituality and Politics* (Portland, Maine: Astarte Shell Press, 1989), 8.

34. Budapest, *Holy Book of Women's Mysteries* (1989), 283.

35. *SageWoman* 3/9 (Spring 9989 [1989]); Seigel, "(Re-)Incarnating the Goddess," 2:2; Hoffman; FSC Retreat, June 1990.

36. Lynn Andrews, quoted in Jamal, *Shape Shifters*, 23; Sonia Johnson, interview with Stone, "Return of the Goddess"; Iglehart, *Womanspirit*, 97.

37. Chandler, *Understanding the New Age*, 20.

38. Turcott; Petey Stevens, quoted in Jamal, *Shape Shifters*, 106. See also Weinstein, *Earth Magic*, 80; also Logan, Otto.

39. Maddox; Gordon.

40. Kim Chernin, in *Reinventing Eve: Modern Woman in Search of Herself* (San Francisco: Harper and Row, 1987), and Kathie Carlson, in *In Her Image: The Unhealed Daughter's Search for Her Mother* (Boston: Shambala, 1989), both argue that the human mother/daughter relationship is overburdened with disappointment and unfulfilled expectation, and they suggest that the rediscovery or invention of a mother goddess can help to heal this relationship by rerouting certain aspects of motherhood to this female deity.

41. Logan; Lunaea Weatherstone, "The Princess, the Goddess, and the Dune," *SageWoman* 3/9 (Spring 9989 [1989]): 7–8.

42. Stein, *Women's Spirituality Book*, 40–41.

43. Lynn Andrews, in her narratives of spiritual adventure, fills this sort of daughterly role in relation to her spiritual mentors. Where her Native American guides are wise and competent, she is confused and uncertain. They are her mothers, she is their little girl; they encourage, protect, and discipline her; she frets and rebels but ultimately sees the wisdom of their choices for her as she emerges the spiritual victor over male forces. Though she is an adult in these adventures, it is poignant to note how often her mentors feed her, wake her up, put her to bed at night, and sit watching over her while she sleeps (*Medicine Woman; Flight of the Seventh Moon; Jaguar Woman; Star Woman; Crystal Woman*).

44. Womongathering, May 1990.

45. Jennifer Paine Welwood, "Hymn to Kali," *Snake Power* (Hallowmas 1989): 51.

46. Susan Griffin, "This Earth Is My Sister," in *Weaving the Visions*, ed. Plaskow and Christ, 105.

47. Janet R. Price, "Liturgy Circa 1976," *Heresies* 2/1 (1982): 84.

48. Weinstein, *Earth Magic*, 46; Jade, *To Know*, 38.

49. Jade, *To Know*, 122; Iglehart, *Womanspirit*, 43; Mariechild, *Mother Wit*, xvii; Petey Stevens, quoted in Jamal, *Shape Shifters*, 101. Also Price.

50. Teish, *Jambalaya*, xi–xii, 80, 82; Foster; Engler; Judyth Reichenberg-Ullman, "Healing Your Unborn Child," *Spiritual Women's Times* (Summer 1989): 12.

51. Weinstein, *Earth Magic*, 43.

52. Cara, "The New Witch Hunts," *Medusan Update* 2/1 (Summer 1991): 2, 7; Sjöö and Mor, *Great Cosmic Mother*, 314; Noble, *Motherpeace*, 113. See also Jade, *To Know*, 12; also Miw, Frankel.

53. Teish, *Jambalaya*, 188–91; Weinstein, *Earth Magic*, 55–62; Budapest, *Holy Book of Women's Mysteries* (1989), 232–35.

54. Weinstein, *Earth Magic*, 56.

55. Courveline; Grey and Penelope, *Found Goddesses*, 107.

56. Budapest, *Holy Book of Women's Mysteries* (1979), 30. Starhawk, in recent writings, presents herself as an exception to this tendency to view the universe as entirely ordered, even determined. She writes: "In the Craft the Goddess is not omnipotent. The cosmos is interesting rather than perfect, and everything is not part of some greater plan, nor is all necessarily under control" (*Spiral Dance*, 2d ed., 231).

Chapter 8: The Rise and Fall of Women's Power

1. Budapest, *Holy Book of Women's Mysteries* (1979), 36.

2. Flowers, *P.M.S. Conspiracy*, 2–3.

3. Eliade, *Myth of Eternal Return*, xiv.

4. Frederich Engels, quoted in Sharon Tiffany, "The Power of Matriarchal Ideas," *International Journal of Women's Studies* 5/2 (1982): 142; Frederick Engels, *The Origin of the Family, Private Property, and the State* (1891; reprint New York: Pathfinder Press, 1972); J. J. Bachofen, *Myth, Religion, and Mother Right*, trans. Ralph Manheim (1861; reprint Princeton: Princeton University Press, 1967); Sir Edward Burnett Tylor, *Primitive Culture: Research into the Development of Mythology, Philosophy, Religion, Language, Art, and Custom* (London: John Murray, 1871); Lewis Henry Morgan, *Ancient Society* (New York: World Publishing, 1877).

5. Sir James Frazer, *The Golden Bough* (London: Macmillan, 1911); Robert Briffault, *The Mothers: The Matriarchal Theory of Social Origins*, abridged by Gordon Rottray Taylor (1927; reprint New York: Atheneum, 1977); Robert Graves, *The White Goddess: A Historical Grammar of Poetic Myth* (New York: Farrar, Straus, and Giroux, 1973); Margaret Murray, *The Witch-Cult in Western Europe* (Oxford: Oxford University Press, 1921); Margaret Murray, *The God of the Witches* (London: Sampson Low, Marston, and Co., Ltd., 1933); Erich Neumann, *The Great Mother* (1955; reprint Princeton: Princeton University Press, 1963). For recent archaeological findings, see James Mellaart, *Çatal Hüyük: A Neolithic Town in Anatolia* (New York: McGraw Hill, 1967).

6. P. M. Pederson, "Non sumus qualis erasmus," *Heresies* 2/1 (1982): 6.

7. Robb, "In Goddess They Trust," 32, 36; Ranck, *Cakes for the Queen*; Eisler and Loye, *Partnership Way*; Noble, *Motherpeace*, 244; Hallie Iglehart Austen and Karen Vogel, "Visions of the Sacred Feminine: Goddesses of Birth, Death and Sexuality" (slide show described in Women in Spiritual Education [WISE] flyer, Point Reyes, Calif.); Zsuzsanna Budapest, *The Rise of the Fates: A Mystical Comedy in Eight Acts* (Los Angeles: Susan B. Anthony Coven No. 1, 1976), 91.

8. Stone, "Return of the Goddess."

9. Christ, *Laughter of Aphrodite*, 192. For an example of how feminist spirituality's sacred history has been expressed through performance art, see Orenstein, *Reflowering of the Goddess*, 104.

10. Riane Eisler, *The Chalice and the Blade: Our History, Our Future* (San Francisco: Harper and Row, 1987); publication statistics from HarperSanFrancisco: from May 1987 to Sept. 1990 for hardcover, from Sept. 1988 to Jan. 1993 for softcover.

11. Eisler and Loye, *Partnership Way*, 1, 5. Academic feminists attracted to feminist spirituality often make the same split Eisler does, favoring sacred history over ritual. Gerda Lerner, for example, also turns her attention to feminist spirituality's sacred history in *The Creation of Patriarchy* (Oxford: Oxford University Press, 1986). Although she is precise and scholarly in her work, she ends up endorsing most points of feminist spirituality's sacred history: (1) patriarchy did not always exist; (2) unless we understand that, we cannot fight it effectively; (3) patriarchy is ending now as we are in the midst of a planetary crisis; (4) there is no way to know if the future will go for us or against us; (5) women's involvement is crucial for ensuring that the future will go for us. See also Orenstein, *Reflowering of the Goddess*; and Gimbutas, *Goddesses and Gods of Old Europe*.

12. Helen Farias, "The College of Hera," *The Beltane Papers* (North 87/88): 8; Austen, *Heart of the Goddess*, xvii; Noble, "Shakti Woman," 26; "Statement of Purpose," *Snake Power* (Hallowmas 1989): 2.

13. My critique of feminist spirituality's sacred history will be included in my forthcoming book, *Gender Politics and Feminist Religion*. Criticism of feminist spirituality's sacred history is not yet collected in any one place, but relevant pieces of criticism can be found in Joan B. Townsend, "The Goddess: Fact, Fallacy, and Revitalization Movement," in *Goddesses in Religion and Modern Debate*, ed. Larry W. Hurtado, University of Manitoba Studies in Religion (Atlanta: Scholars Press, 1990), 179–203; Sally R. Binford, "Myths and Matriarchies," in *Politics of Women's Spirituality*, ed. Spretnak, 544–47; Sherry B. Ortner, "Is Female to Male as Nature Is to Culture?" *Feminist Studies* 1/2 (Fall 1972): 8; King, *Women and Spirituality*, 147; Lerner, *Creation of Patriarchy*, 29; Jo Ann Hackett, "Can a Sexist Model Liberate Us?" *Journal of Feminist Studies in Religion* 5/1 (Spring 1989): 66, 75; Mary Jo Weaver, "Who Is the Goddess and Where Does She Get Us?" *Journal of Feminist Studies in Religion* 5/1 (Spring 1989): 57. Of these, Townsend offers the most thorough critique; Binford's is also illuminating.

14. Stone, *When God Was a Woman*, xii; Stone, "Letter From Merlin"; Miw; Morgan McFarland, "Witchcraft: The Art of Remembering," *Quest* 1/4 (Spring 1975): 42. See also Charlene Spretnak, "The Spiritual Experience of the Female Psyche/Soma" (lecture, April 24, 1982, Los Angeles).

15. Elizabeth Gould Davis, *The First Sex* (New York: Penguin Books, 1971), 33; Austen, *Heart of the Goddess*, xvii. See also Stein, *Women's Spirituality Book*, 4. Critiques of the European ethnocentrism of feminist spirituality's sacred history can be found in Starhawk, *Spiral Dance*, 2d ed., 214; Culpepper, "Contemporary Goddess Thealogy," 52–53; Ranck, *Cakes for the Queen*, 12–13. Examples of efforts to extend the geographical scope of ancient goddess-worship/matriarchy can be found in Robert S. Ellwood, "The Sujin Religious Revolution," *Japanese Journal of Religious Studies* 17/2–3 (June-Sept. 1990): 207; Amoja Three Rivers, "Spirituality of the Matriarchs: The African Connections" (workshop at Womongathering, May 1990); Sjöö and Mor, *Great Cosmic Mother*, 21–22; Allen, "Grandmother of the Sun," 23; Gloria Anzaldúa, "Entering into the Serpent," in *Weaving the Visions*, ed. Plaskow and Christ, 81.

16. Veracruz; Sjöö and Mor, *Great Cosmic Mother*, 47; Iglehart, *Womanspirit*, 10–11; Rosemary J. Dudley, "She Who Bleeds, Yet Does Not Die," *Heresies* 2/1 (1982): 112–13. See also Buffie Johnson, "Lady of the Beasts," *woman of power* 16 (Spring 1990): 70; Sophie Drinker,

"The Origins of Music: Women's Goddess Worship," in *Politics of Women's Spirituality*, ed. Spretnak, 43; Stein, *Women's Spirituality Book*, 5, 25; Jong, interview with Stone, "Return of the Goddess"; Riane Eisler, "The Chalice and the Blade" (paper presented at the annual meeting of the American Academy of Religion, Anaheim, Calif., Nov. 1989).

17. Judy Chicago, "Our Heritage Is Our Power," in *Politics of Women's Spirituality*, ed. Spretnak, 152; Davis, *First Sex*, 34–35, 87, 133; Sjöö and Mor, *Great Cosmic Mother*, 26; Stein, *Women's Spirituality Book*, 5; Gadon, *Once and Future Goddess*, 36; Budapest, *Holy Book of Women's Mysteries* (1989), 55; participants from workshop with Amoja Three Rivers, titled "Spirituality of the Matriarchs: The African Connections" (Womongathering, May 1990). See also Stone, *When God Was A Woman*, 25; also Littlefield, Washington.

18. Starhawk, *Truth or Dare*, 346 n. 4; Marija Gimbutas, "Women and Culture in Goddess-Oriented Old Europe," in *Weaving the Visions*, ed. Plaskow and Christ, 70; Gadon, *Once and Future Goddess*, 37.

19. Vicki Noble, "Marija Gimbutas: Reclaiming the Great Goddess," *Snake Power* (Hallowmas 1989): 5; Gimbutas, "Women and Culture," 64. See also Gimbutas, *Goddesses and Gods of Old Europe*; Gimbutas, *Language of the Goddess*; Marija Gimbutas, *The Civilization of the Goddess: The World of Old Europe* (San Francisco: HarperSanFrancisco, 1991).

20. Stone, *When God Was a Woman*, 22; Gadon, *Once and Future Goddess*, 8, 14, 43, 46, 50; Austen, *Heart of the Goddess*, 8, 12; Eisler, *Chalice and the Blade*, 6, 18.

21. Davis, *First Sex*, 39; Drinker, "Origins of Music," 42; Ria Stavrides, quoted in minutes of Columbia University Seminar on Studies in Religion, Dec. 2, 1991. See also Ranck, *Cakes for the Queen*, 28–29; Mariechild, *Mother Wit*, 180; Chicago, "Our Heritage is Our Power," 152; also Veracruz.

22. Marija Gimbutas, quoted in Eisler, *Chalice and the Blade*, 14.

23. Gadon, *Once and Future Goddess*, 27–28; Lerner, *Creation of Patriarchy*, 32–35; Eisler, *Chalice and the Blade*, 25.

24. Lerner, *Creation of Patriarchy*, 29; Stone, *When God Was a Woman*, 32, 58; Christ, *Laughter of Aphrodite*, 167.

25. The contention that ancient societies were peaceful is supported by archaeological evidence showing a lack of fortifications or pictorial representations of warfare. Critics maintain that the archaeological evidence is inconclusive, that even nonfortified cities like Çatal Hüyük had other means of defense, and that if these societies were peaceful, it may have been because they had no neighbors close enough to provoke conflict. Townsend ("Goddess: Fact, Fallacy, and Revitalization Movement") notes (following James Mellaart, the principal researcher at Çatal Hüyük) that "the solid pueblo-style houses with entry only by ladder from the roof" characteristic of Çatal Hüyük "were excellent for defense." She further notes that "mace heads and other weapons" were found in some male graves in Çatal Hüyük, and that "head wounds were common on skulls" retrieved from this site (193–94).

26. Göttner-Abendroth, *Matriarchal Mythology*, 13. See also anonymous spiritual feminist, "Journey Through Time," anonymous spiritual feminist publication; Marija Gimbutas, "The World View of the Culture of the Goddess," *Snake Power* (Hallowmas 1989): 46; Mendel; Flowers, *P.M.S. Conspiracy*, 2; Mor and Sjöö, "Respell the World," 18; Adler, *Drawing Down the Moon*, 188; Starhawk, *Dreaming the Dark*; Iglehart, *Womanspirit*, 87; Gadon, *Once and Future Goddess*, 24, 138; Davis, *First Sex*, 65, 116; Eisler, *Chalice and the Blade*, 17–18, 32; Shekhinah Mountainwater, "In Search of the Mother Goddess," *The Beltane Papers* (West 1987): 7; Nancy Qualls Corbett, "The Sacred Prostitute: Eternal Aspects of the Feminine" (course described in New York Open Center catalog, New York, Spring 1990); Budapest, *Holy Book of Women's Mysteries* (1979), 123–24; Stone, *When God Was A Woman*, 131, 154–55, 157; Jamal, *Shape Shifters*, 175; Shinell, "Women's Collective Spirit," 515–16, 522–23; also Miw, Courveline, Gordon, Woods, Frankel.

27. Eisler, *Chalice and the Blade*, xvi, 66–73; Morgan McFarland, "Womyn's Lost Herstory," anonymous spiritual feminist publication; Orenstein, *Reflowering of the Goddess*, 13; Stone, *When God Was a Woman*, xxiv; Sjöö and Mor, *Great Cosmic Mother*, 33, 39, 146; Spretnak, "Spiritual Experience of Female Psyche/Soma."

28. Orenstein, *Reflowering of the Goddess*, 185; Göttner-Abendroth, *Matriarchal Mythology*, 2; Flowers, *P.M.S. Conspiracy*, 2; Eisler, *Chalice and the Blade*, xvi–xvii, 27–28. See also Sjöö and Mor, *Great Cosmic Mother*, 241, 248; Noble, *Motherpeace*, 8; Eisler and Loye, *Partnership Way*, 55; Gadon, *Once and Future Goddess*, 303; Daly, "Qualitative Leap," 35; Johnson, "Lady of the Beasts," 69; also Gordon, Bjorkman.

29. The earliest dates for the patriarchal revolution are given by Potts, "Toward the Year 12,000," 1; Sally Gearhart, "Womanpower: Energy Re-sourcement," in *Politics of Women's Spirituality*, ed. Spretnak, 196. The most recent dates are given by Davis, *First Sex*, 241; Sackner; Susan Cady, Marian Ronan, and Hal Taussig, *Wisdom's Feast: Sophia in Study and Celebration* (San Francisco: Harper and Row, 1989); Robert Corin Morris, "Mother Spirit, Sister Guide" (study group, Short Hills, N.J., June 12, 1991); Walker, *Skeptical Feminist*, 5. More typical dates are offered by Miw; Hoffman; Keane; Otto; Gordon; Logan; Spretnak, "Introduction," xi; Jamal, *Shape Shifters*, 5.

30. See Carson, *Feminist Spirituality and Feminine Divine*, 6; Lerner, *Creation of Patriarchy*, 11. Some effort has been made to document the patriarchal revolution in other places, particularly India, where archaeological evidence similar to that for the ancient Near East exists (see, for example, Spretnak, *Lost Goddesses of Early Greece*; Tsultrim Allione, quoted in Jamal, *Shape Shifters*, 45–46; Gadon, *Once and Future Goddess*, xiii). Descriptions of the patriarchal revolution in other geographical areas include China (Stein, *Women's Spirituality Book*, 235), Japan (Robert Ellwood, "Patriarchal Revolution in Ancient Japan: Episodes from the *Nihonshiki* Sujin Chronicle," *Journal of Feminist Studies in Religion* 2/2 [Fall 1986]: 23–37; Ellwood, "Sujin Religious Revolution"; Rita Nakashima Brock, "On Mirrors, Mists, and Murmurs: Toward an Asian American Thealogy," in *Weaving the Visions*, ed. Plaskow and Christ, 241–42), Africa (Sojourner, "From the House of Yemanja," 62–63), and Mexico (Anzaldúa, "Entering into the Serpent," 77, 80–81).

31. Veracruz; Washington; Mendel; Hart. See also Spretnak, "Introduction," xii; Gadon, *Once and Future Goddess*, 213; Austen, *Heart of the Goddess*, xviii; McFarland, "Womyn's Lost Herstory"; Ranck, *Cakes for the Queen*, 35.

32. Lerner, *Creation of Patriarchy*, 46, 81; Schulman; Stein, *Women's Spirituality Book*, 6–7; Eisler, *Chalice and the Blade*, 43, 57; Robison; Logan; Christ, *Laughter of Aphrodite*, 87–88.

33. Hart; Austen, *Heart of the Goddess*, 153; Otto; Elizabeth Fisher, *Woman's Creation* (Garden City, N.Y.: Anchor-Doubleday, 1980); Sjöö and Mor, *Great Cosmic Mother*, 201; Hargreaves; Price; Frankel; Stone, *When God Was a Woman*, 161; Walker, *Skeptical Feminist*, 128; Lerner, *Creation of Patriarchy*, 8–9.

34. Davis, *First Sex*, 16–17, 89, 96, 131, 148, 158–59, 335.

35. Budapest, *Holy Book of Women's Mysteries* (1989), 294–95; Gordon; Copeland. Also Sackner, Whiting, Frankel, Woods, Miw.

36. Demetra George, "Mysteries of the Dark Moon," *woman of power* 8 (Winter 1988): 31; Weinstein, *Positive Magic*, 20; Hart; participants from workshop with Amoja Three Rivers, "Spirituality of the Matriarchs: The African Connection" (Womongathering, May 1990).

37. Sjöö and Mor, *Great Cosmic Mother*, 258; Gimbutas, "Women and Culture," 69; Eisler, *Chalice and the Blade*, 44; Eisler, "Chalice and the Blade." See also Lerner, *Creation of Patriarchy*, 8; Christ, *Laughter of Aphrodite*, 75, 171; Davis, *First Sex*, 177–78; Stone, "Return of the Goddess"; Orenstein, *Reflowering of the Goddess*, 5; Chernin, *Reinventing Eve*, 29; Starhawk, *The Spiral Dance*, 1st ed., 4; also Keane, Whiting, Hoffman. Archaeologists appear, by and large, to agree that these migrations from north to south took place

during these times, that they can be tracked archaeologically and linguistically. But not all agree that the migrations were accompanied by violence. For a dissenting opinion, see Townsend, "Goddess: Fact, Fallacy, and Revitalization Movement," 194, 196.

38. Davis, *First Sex*, 141, 200–202, 230. See also Eisler, *Chalice and the Blade*, 44, 93.

39. It is ironic that only a few years after seeing their people formally cleared by the Roman Catholic church of the charge of deicide—killing god in the form of Jesus Christ—Jews are back on the same hook once more, this time charged with killing the goddess. Most spiritual feminists, not wishing to alienate their Jewish sisters, invite them to see themselves as the first victims of a patriarchal revolution instigated either by Jewish men or by bands of invading patriarchs who corrupted Hebrew societies. Jewish women, say spiritual feminists, were merely the first to be crushed by the patriarchs, certainly not the last. Most Jewish feminists do not seem to find this reassuring. See Susannah Heschel, quoted in King, *Women and Spirituality*, 195; Annette Daum, "Blaming Jews for the Death of the Goddess," *Lilith* 7 (1980): 12–13; Judith Plaskow, "Blaming Jews for Inventing Patriarchy," *Lilith* 7 (1980): 12–14; Sjöö and Mor, *Great Cosmic Mother*, 273; Stone, *When God Was a Woman*, 104; Frankel.

40. Courveline; Lerner, *Creation of Patriarchy*, 9; Whiting; Miw; Woods; Jade, *To Know*, 8; Budapest, *Holy Book of Women's Mysteries* (1989), 182; Sjöö and Mor, *Great Cosmic Mother*, 25.

41. Christ, *Laughter of Aphrodite*, 13; Budapest, *Holy Book of Women's Mysteries* (1989), 111. See also Walker, *Skeptical Feminist*, 147; Stone, *When God Was a Woman*, xiii.

42. Sjöö and Mor, *Great Cosmic Mother*, 247. See also Bella Debrida, "Drawing from Mythology in Women's Quest for Selfhood," in *Politics of Women's Spirituality*, ed. Spretnak, 142; Starhawk, *Truth or Dare*, 40; Downing, *The Goddess*, 63; Daly, *Gyn/Ecology*, 84–85.

43. Ranck, *Cakes for the Queen*, 34; Daly, *Gyn/Ecology*, 76; Göttner-Abendroth, *Matriarchal Mythology*, 4–10; Austen, *Heart of the Goddess*, 84, 128; Budapest, *Holy Book of Women's Mysteries* (1979), 88; Gadon, *Once and Future Goddess*, xii; Walker, *Skeptical Feminist*, 9; Eisler, *Chalice and the Blade*, 53, 87; Starhawk, *Truth or Dare*, 63; Noble, *Motherpeace*, 49; Downing, *The Goddess*, 14, 20; Vicki Noble, "Shakti Woman," 26; Sjöö and Mor, *Great Cosmic Mother*, 171, 255–56; Vicki Noble, quoted in Jamal, *Shape Shifters*, 114; Stone, *When God Was a Woman*, 228; Vicki Noble, "The Dark Goddess: Remembering the Sacred," *woman of power* 12 (Winter 1989): 58; Patricia Reis, "The Dark Goddess," *woman of power* 8 (Winter 1988): 24–25; Christ, *Laughter of Aphrodite*, 172.

44. Ranck, *Cakes for the Queen*, 42–43; Sjöö and Mor, *Great Cosmic Mother*, 264–65; Noble, *Motherpeace*, 55; Veracruz; Stone, *When God Was a Woman*, 166, 198; Davis, *First Sex*, 67, 238; Chicago, "Our Heritage Is Our Power," 167; Sjöö and Mor, *Great Cosmic Mother*, 277; Otto.

45. Lerner, *Creation of Patriarchy*, 89, 114, 202.

46. Miw; Fleming; Barbara Starrett, "The Metaphors of Power," in *Politics of Women's Spirituality*, ed. Spretnak, 187–88; Grace Shinell, "Woman's Primacy in the Coming Reformation," *Heresies* 2/1 (1982): 49; Audre Lorde, "Uses of the Erotic: The Erotic as Power," in *Weaving the Visions*, ed. Plaskow and Christ, 208. See also Sjöö and Mor, *Great Cosmic Mother*, 261, 270; Daly, *Beyond God the Father*, 193–94; also Engler, Robison, Keane.

47. Farias, "College of Hera," 9; Frankel; Spretnak, "Spiritual Experience of Female Psyche/Soma"; Stein, *Women's Spirituality Book*, 119. See also Flowers, *P.M.S. Conspiracy*, 5–9; Walker, *Skeptical Feminist*, 122; Iglehart, *Womanspirit*, 156, 162; Sjöö and Mor, *Great Cosmic Mother*, 193; Judith Antonelli, "Feminist Spirituality: The Politics of the Psyche," in *Politics of Women's Spirituality*, ed. Spretnak, 401–402; also Miw.

48. Eisler, "Chalice and the Blade." See also Eisler, *Chalice and the Blade*, xvii, 17–18; Sjöö and Mor, *Great Cosmic Mother*, 430; Starhawk, *Truth or Dare*, 54; Starhawk, *Dreaming the Dark*, 3–4; also Hargreaves.

49. Copeland; Gordon; Sackner; Walker, *Skeptical Feminist*, 123, 188–89. See also Starrett, "Metaphors of Power," 186–87; Rosemary Radford Ruether, "Motherearth and the Megamachine: A Theology of Liberation in a Feminine, Somatic, and Ecological Perspective," in *Womanspirit Rising*, ed. Christ and Plaskow, 44, 46; Stone, *When God Was a Woman*, 66; "Statement of Purpose," *Snake Power*; Antonelli, "Politics of the Psyche"; Sheila D. Collins, "The Personal Is Political," in *Politics of Women's Spirituality*, ed. Spretnak, 363–64; Charlene Spretnak, quoted in Wynne, *Womanspirit Sourcebook*, 90; Eisler, *Chalice and the Blade*, xvi–xvii, 104; Starhawk, *Dreaming the Dark*, xii–xiii; Starhawk, *Truth or Dare*, 16; also Otto, Courveline, Whiting, Schulman, Woods, Frankel, Washington.

50. Not all spiritual feminists make an exception for a feminist Jesus. Zsuzsanna Budapest puts these words in the mouth of Jesus in her play "The Rise of the Fates": "I have come to destroy the work of the female. Do not think I came to put peace upon the earth; I came to put not peace but the sword. . . . guilt, flagellation, martyrdom, death, and the ever-popular war. . . . The work of the female was difficult to get rid of, but I think we cleansed the world of her" (*Rise of the Fates*, 62).

51. Veracruz; Landau; Miw. See also Eisler, *Chalice and the Blade*, 102, 119, 129; Sjöö and Mor, *Great Cosmic Mother*, 286–87.

52. There are dissenting opinions about Mary just as there are about Jesus. Monica Sjöö and Barbara Mor (*Great Cosmic Mother*, 350) describe Mary not as the great mother goddess reborn, but as "a mere, lowly, mortal woman, 'lifted up' by Yahweh's divinely disembodied attention . . . to produce a son for the heavenly Father." She "has nothing of the primal creatrix about her."

53. Davis, *First Sex*, 243, 246; Gadon, *Once and Future Goddess*, 189, 199; Stein, *Women's Spirituality Book*, 11; Judy Chicago, quoted in Gayle Kimball, "A Female Form Language: Interview with Judy Chicago," in *Women's Culture*, ed. Kimball, 63; Eisler and Loye, *Partnership Way*, 106–107; Otto; Eisler, *Chalice and the Blade*, 76.

54. Stone, "Return of the Goddess"; Sjöö and Mor, *Great Cosmic Mother*, 321; Gadon, *Once and Future Goddess*, 40, 233.

55. Weinstein, *Positive Magic*, 81.

56. H. R. Trevor-Roper, *The European Witch-Craze of the Sixteenth and Seventeenth Centuries and Other Essays* (New York: Harper Torchbooks, 1969), 94–95.

57. Ibid., 92, 97, 101–104; Sjöö and Mor, *Great Cosmic Mother*, 299.

58. Trevor-Roper, *European Witch-Craze*, 116–18; Mircea Eliade, *Occultism, Witchcraft, and Cultural Fashions* (Chicago: University of Chicago Press, 1976), 71, 84–85, 91–92. A helpful discussion of the range of scholarly opinion about the existence of medieval witchcraft can be found in Adler, *Drawing Down the Moon*, 45–56. Those who take the position that witchcraft was created by its persecutors include Norman Cohn, *Europe's Inner Demons: An Enquiry Inspired by the Great Witch-Hunt* (New York: Basic Books, 1975); Trevor-Roper, *European Witch-Craze*; Henry Charles Lea, *History of the Inquisition in the Middle Ages*, 3 vols. (New York: Harper and Brothers, 1883); and Arthur Howland, ed., *Materials Toward a History of Witchcraft*, 3 vols. (Philadelphia: University of Pennsylvania, 1939). Those who make greater allowance for the existence of some alternative religious practices persecuted as witchcraft include Eliade, *Occultism, Witchcraft, and Cultural Fashions*; Jakob Grimm, *Deutsche Mythologie* (Göttingen, 1835); W. G. Soldan, *Geschichte der Hexenprozesse* (Stuttgart, 1843); Jules Michelet, *Satanism and Witchcraft* (1862; reprint New York: Citadel Press, 1939); Murray, *Witch-Cult in Western Europe* and *God of the Witches*.

59. Shinell, "Woman's Primacy," 49. See also McFarland, "Womyn's Lost Herstory"; Mary Beth Edelson, interview with Stone, "Return of the Goddess"; Ranck, *Cakes for the Queen*, 69; Jade, *To Know*, 10; Spretnak, *Lost Goddesses of Early Greece*, 28; also Price, Miw.

60. Chicago WITCH statement, quoted in Morgan, ed., *Sisterhood Is Powerful*; Davis, *First Sex*, 229; Stein, *Women's Spirituality Book*, 11–12; Austen, *Heart of the Goddess*, 40;

Merchant, *Death of Nature*, 15, 136. A few spiritual feminists allow for the possibility that some devil worship or "negative" magic was part of medieval witchcraft, and argue that this stemmed from women's social and economic disempowerment and their hope of exercising at least some limited power through magical means. See Weinstein, *Positive Magic*, 37, 45; Merchant, *Death of Nature*, 140.

61. McFarland, "Witchcraft: Art of Remembering," 44; Miw; Starhawk, *Spiral Dance*, first ed., 6; Carson, *Feminist Spirituality and Feminine Divine*, 3; Lois Holub, "Who Were the Witches?" *woman of power* 16 (Spring 1990): 56; Daly, *Gyn/Ecology*, 182–84; Judy Chicago, quoted in Kimball, "Female Form Language," 65; Stein, *Women's Spirituality Book*, 12; Starhawk, *Dreaming the Dark*, 188; Jade, *To Know*, 11; Gadon, *Once and Future Goddess*, 113. Once the witch craze was in full swing, there were economic incentives for accusing others of witchcraft: the successful accuser received one-tenth of the dead witch's worldly posessions (Budapest, *Holy Book of Women's Mysteries* [1989], 274). Krämer and Sprenger, authors of the *Malleus* and the two most prominent witch hunters, were finally reprimanded by the church for "fabricating evidence of 'witchery.'" Monica Sjöö and Barbara Mor (*Great Cosmic Mother*, 300–301) report that Krämer once paid an "old drunk woman to hide in ovens and make weird noises, thus 'proving' to her neighbors that the woman of the house was 'possessed.'"

62. Starhawk, *Spiral Dance*, first ed., 6; Merchant, *Death of Nature*, 132–36, 138; Noble, *Motherpeace*, 113; Budapest, *Holy Book of Women's Mysteries* (1989), xxiii, 271; Daly, *Gyn/Ecology*, 180; Anne Llewellyn Barstow, "On Studying Witchcraft as Women's History: A Historiography of the European Witch Persecutions," *Journal of Feminist Studies in Religion* 4/2 (Fall 1988): 8; Forfreedom, *Feminist Wicce Works*, 9; Starhawk, *Dreaming the Dark*, 189; Rosemary Radford Ruether, *Sexism and God-Talk* (Boston: Beacon Press, 1983), 82.

63. This is a tremendous number when compared to Europe's total population at the time. If nine million people were killed as witches, most of them women, this means that one-fifth to one-tenth of the total population was put to death on charges of witchcraft, and that as many as two out of five women died in this manner. (These percentages do not account for the fact that the deaths occurred over the span of at least two hundred years; the percentage of the population murdered at any one time would be smaller.) Rosemary Radford Ruether has suggested that the use of the nine million figure represents an effort on the part of spiritual feminists to "top" the six million figure for Jews killed in the Holocaust ("Goddesses and Witches: Liberation and Countercultural Feminism," *The Christian Century* 97 [10–17 Sept. 1980]: 844). Zsuzsanna Budapest has explicitly disavowed this motivation (letter to the editor, *The Christian Century* 97 [26 Nov. 1980]: 1162, 1164). Still, there is a peculiar relationship between spiritual feminists and the Holocaust, one deserving of further comment. Gloria Feman Orenstein, in *The Reflowering of the Goddess*, suggests that "matricide" is perhaps the underlying theme of the Holocaust, saying that "the most haunting image [of the Holocaust] is that of the ovens, the crematoria, literally wombs of death (rather than wombs of life) invented by 'wombless men'" (137). In *The Skeptical Feminist*, Barbara Walker makes a rapid segue from the nine million witches killed in medieval Europe to the Holocaust, seeing in it a further attempt at gynocide, the murder of women: "Even in our own century: women who went into the ovens at Auschwitz, Dachau, Buchenwald, Treblinka. Women dying in the fires of Hiroshima and Nagasaki, London and Essen and Cologne, not to mention the pitiful villages of Korea and Vietnam; innocent women and children killed by all the fires of men's wars." It is easy to detect misogyny in the European witch burnings, but it is harder to construe the massacres of the twentieth century as crimes directed primarily toward women. It seems to me, then, that the inflation of the figures for the European witch burnings may in fact be motivated by a desire to "top the Jews"; not out of any anti-Semitism, but out of desire to show that women have suffered more, and less justifiably, than any other

group on record. The nine million figure is found in Mary Beth Edelson, interview with Stone, "Return of the Goddess"; Ranck, *Cakes for the Queen*, 69; Miw; Stein, *Women's Spirituality Book*, 11–12; Judy Chicago, quoted in Kimball, "Female Form Language," 65; Gadon, *Once and Future Goddess*, 113; Starhawk, "Witchcraft and Women's Culture," in *Womanspirit Rising*, ed. Christ and Plaskow; Sjöö and Mor, *Great Cosmic Mother*, 192; Walker, *Skeptical Feminist*, 104–105, 215; Weinstein, *Positive Magic*; Starhawk, *Spiral Dance*, first ed., 5;

64. Scholarly estimates for the number of people murdered as witches during the European witch persecutions can be found in Felix Morrow, "Foreword," in Montague Summers, *The History of Witchcraft and Demonology* (Secaucus, N.J.: Citadel Press, 1971), viii; Rossell Hope Robbins, *The Encyclopedia of Witchcraft and Demonology* (New York: Crown, 1959), 180; Barstow, "Studying Witchcraft as Women's History," 7 n. 1; Merchant, *Death of Nature*, 132–33, 138; E. William Monter, ed., *European Witchcraft* (New York: Wiley, 1969), 73. Some spiritual feminists have responded to this scholarly conservatism and uncertainty and now give an estimated range, though nine million still stands as the upper end of the range. Spiritual feminists who express a range of possible figures for those killed as witches in the European witch persecutions include Starhawk, introduction to Teish, *Jambalaya*, xv–xvi; Starhawk, *Dreaming the Dark*, 187; Starhawk, *Spiral Dance*, 2d ed., 214–15; Daly, *Beyond God the Father*, 63; Sjöö and Mor, *Great Cosmic Mother*, 298; Chicago, "Our Heritage Is Our Power," 154–55. Only Zsuzsanna Budapest has ventured higher; she now numbers the witch deaths at eleven million (Budapest, *Holy Book of Women's Mysteries* [1989], xxiii, 295).

65. Davis, *First Sex*, 257; Jean Bodin, et al., cited in Merchant, *Death of Nature*, 138; Richard Kieckhefer, *European Witch Trials: Their Foundations in Popular and Learned Culture, 1300–1500* (Berkeley: University of California Press, 1976), 96. The following scholarly works on medieval witchcraft (among others) use female-gendered language to refer to witches: Monter, ed., *European Witchcraft*; Trevor-Roper, *European Witch-Craze*; Jeffrey B. Russell, *Witchcraft in the Middle Ages* (Ithaca, New York: Cornell University Press, 1972); Jeffrey B. Russell, *A History of Witchcraft: Sorcerers, Heretics, and Pagans* (London: Thames and Hudson, 1980); Kieckhefer, *European Witch Trials*; Pennethorne Hughes, *Witchcraft* (London: Longmans, Green, 1952). This predominance of women among the persecuted is a fact with which scholars of medieval witchcraft have little concerned themselves. Theories as to why the witch burnings began and so rapidly spread abound: some say they were the result of tensions between Protestants and Catholics or the lower and upper classes; some say they stemmed from psychological fantasies deeply rooted in the European psyche (scholars who offer nongendered theories of the witch persecutions include Trevor-Roper, *European Witch-Craze*, 165; Cohn, *Europe's Inner Demons*; Jules Michelet, *Satanism and Witchcraft*). But to my knowledge, before feminist scholars arrived on the scene, no one proposed that the witch burnings had anything to do with misogyny, or indeed with gender at all. As Anne Llewellyn Barstow remarks in her article "On Studying Witchcraft as Women's History": "Reading these [histories of the European witch trials] is like reading accounts of the Nazi holocaust in which everyone agrees that the majority of victims were Jewish, but no one mentions anti-Semitism or the history of violent persecution against Jews, implying that it was 'natural' for Jews to be victims" (7, 13). To spiritual feminists, the fact that most accused witches were women is a fact worth remarking upon.

66. Kathryn Theatana, "The Priestesses of Hecate," *woman of power* 8 (Winter 1988): 35; Walker, *Skeptical Feminist*, 104–105; Hoffman; Daly, *Gyn/Ecology*, 196. See also Starhawk, *Dreaming the Dark*, 187; Starhawk, *Spiral Dance*, 2d ed., 214–15; Shekhinah Mountainwater catalog; also Keane.

67. Catherine Madsen, "Allu Mari Mu Portate" (lyrics on song sheet enclosed in album

by Ruth Barrett and Cyntia Smith, *Deepening* [Marina del Rey, Calif.: Aeolus Music, 1984]). The Italian chorus is taken from Hecker, *Epidemics of the Middle Ages* (London, 1844), and accounts of these mass suicides can be found in W. E. H. Lecky, *History of European Morals*, 2d ed., 2 vols. (New York: D. Appleton, 1919), vol. 2: 54–55. See Daly, *Gyn/Ecology*, 210–11.

68. Miw.

69. Davis, *First Sex*, 297 ff.; Budapest, *Grandmother of Time*, 33, 143; Stein, *Women's Spirituality Book*, 13; Daly, *Gyn/Ecology*, xviii; Budapest, "Political Witchcraft," 40.

70. Weinstein, *Positive Magic*, 20, 24; Jade, *To Know*, 168–69; Noble, *Motherpeace*, 119; Hart; Cole, "Feminist Wicca Philosophy"; Price. See also Brooke Medicine Eagle, quoted in Wynne, *Womanspirit Sourcebook*, 234; also Landau, Engler.

71. Keane; Robison; Hoffman; Courveline; Laura; Maddox; Fleming. Also Schulman, Whiting, Gordon, Bjorkman.

72. Noble, *Motherpeace*, 248; Noble, "Shakti Woman," 27–28; Starhawk, *Spiral Dance*, 2d ed., 11; Miw; Otto; Hoffman. See also Haney, *Vision and Struggle*, 62; Eisler, *Chalice and the Blade*, xiv, xx; Austen, *Heart of the Goddess*, xviii, also Sackner, Veracruz.

73. Stone, "Return of the Goddess"; Sjöö and Mor, *Great Cosmic Mother*, 42; Miw; Price; Foster; Eisler, *Chalice and the Blade*, 153; Davis, *First Sex*, 339. See also Walker, *Skeptical Feminist*, 19–20; Göttner-Abendroth, "Hagia: Academy and Coven"; also Landau.

74. Dhyani Ywahoo, quoted in David McNamara, "Ancient Wisdom for a Re-awakening World," *One Earth* 2/6 (Sept. 1982). See also Vicki Noble, quoted in Rountree, "Female Shamans," 61.

75. Engler. See also Noble, "The Shakti Woman," 27; also Littlefield.

76. Eisler, *Chalice and the Blade*, 59, 170–71; Sonia Johnson, "Going Out of Our Minds," *woman of power* 8 (Winter 1988): 75; Gearhart, "Womanpower: Energy Re-sourcement," 206. See also Gadon, *Once and Future Goddess*, 230. In *The Myth of the Eternal Return*, historian of religion Mircea Eliade argues that this is a common pattern in religious thought, making an extremely negative assessment of the present moment while having oddly high hopes for the future. He explains: "The contemporary moment (whatever its chronological position) represents a decadence in relation to preceding historical moments. Not only is the contemporary aeon inferior to the other ages (gold, silver, and so on) but, even within the frame of the reigning age (that is, of the reigning cycle), the 'instant' in which man lives grows worse as time passes. This tendency toward devaluation of the contemporary moment should not be regarded as a sign of pessimism. On the contrary, it reveals an excess of optimism, for, in the deterioration of the contemporary situation, at least a portion of mankind saw signs fortelling the regeneration that must necessarily follow" (131–32).

77. Gearhart, "Womanpower: Energy Re-sourcement," 206; Miw; Charlene Spretnak, "Feminist Politics and the Nature of Mind," in *Politics of Women's Spirituality*, ed. Spretnak, 573. See also Jade, *To Know*, 169–70; Spretnak, "Spiritual Experience of Female Psyche/ Soma"; Budapest, "Political Witchcraft"; Lynn Aune, "Sacred Psychology and the Rise of the Feminine," *woman of power* 12 (Winter 1989): 24; Diane Mariechild, "Women's Voices, Women's Hearts" (workshop at Womongathering, May 1990); Budapest, *Grandmother of Time*, 19; Davis, *First Sex*, 18, 339; Jamal, *Shape Shifters*, 6; Schnirel, "Modern Medicine Woman"; Starrett, "Metaphors of Power," 188; Johnson, "Going Out of Our Minds," 74–75; Mariechild, *Mother Wit*, xiii; Sjöö and Mor, *Great Cosmic Mother*, 431; Andrews, *Crystal Woman*, xv; Mor and Sjöö, "Respell the World," 21; also Landau.

78. Miw; Price. Also Courveline, Bjorkman.

79. Stone, "Return of the Goddess"; Chernin, *Reinventing Eve*, 25. See also Zsuzsanna Budapest, quoted in Kimball, "Goddess Worship in Wicce," 247; Budapest, *Grandmother of Time*, 147; Noble, "Shakti Woman," 28; "Statement of Purpose," *Snake Power*; Orenstein,

Reflowering of the Goddess, 187. See also Budapest, *Rise of the Fates*, 85; also Gordon, Courveline.

80. Starhawk, *Truth or Dare*, 310–311; Orenstein, *Reflowering of the Goddess*, 76–77. See also Stein, *Women's Spirituality Book*, 17; McFarland, "Womyn's Lost Herstory"; Shekhinah Mountainwater catalog; Starhawk, "Witchcraft and Women's Culture," 268; Kira Ma'at-ka-re, "A Saving Wombhold," *The Beltane Papers* (West 87): 9; also Woods, Whiting, Keane, Sackner, Frankel, Washington, Price, Copeland, Schulman, Foster. In *New Religions and the Theological Imagination in America* (Bloomington: Indiana University Press, 1989), Mary Farrell Bednarowski sees this as a pattern in other present-day alternative religions. Even Christian sects put responsibility for the state of the world and its future on human beings rather than divine ones. Bednarowski explains the nature of this Arminian or "works" theology: "What does what we do or think, we ask ourselves, have to do with what we eventually achieve, whether materially or psychically or spiritually? 'Almost everything,' say the new religions. And, on the other side, what responsibility do we bear for the evil that befalls both us as individuals and the world? 'Almost all,' is the answer" (136–37). Bednarowski argues that this "works" theology is not only present in alternative religions, but is part of a general cultural drift in American history.

81. Eisler, *Chalice and the Blade*, 198–203; Starhawk, *Truth or Dare*, 334–36.

82. Starhawk, *Truth or Dare*, 310–11.

83. Woods. See also Ranck, *Cakes for the Queen*, 11; Göttner-Abendroth, "Hagia: Academy and Coven"; Turner, "Contemporary Feminist Rituals"; Gadon, *Once and Future Goddess*, 377; Davis, *First Sex*, 338; also Garawitz.

84. Charlene Spretnak, "Introduction," xiii.

Chapter 9: Feminist Politics and Feminist Spirituality

1. Sally R. Binford, "Counter Response," in *Politics of Women's Spirituality*, ed. Spretnak, 559. See also Sjöö and Mor, *Great Cosmic Mother*, 416–17; Seigel, "(Re-)Incarnating the Goddess," 1:15; Hester Eisenstein, *Contemporary Feminist Thought* (Boston: G.K. Hall, 1983), 131–32; Budapest, *Holy Book of Women's Mysteries* (1989), 225; Ynestra King, "Healing the Wounds: Feminism, Ecology, and the Nature/Culture Dualism," in *Reweaving the World*, ed. Diamond and Orenstein, 117; Janet Biehl, paraphrased in Jennifer Sells and Helen Cordes, "New Goddess Worship Troubles Skeptics: Is There a Danger of a New Eco-orthodoxy?" *Utne Reader* (May/June 1991): 19; Gearhart, "Womanpower: Energy Resourcement," 201–202; Adler, *Drawing Down the Moon*, 209; also Mendel.

2. Carson, *Feminist Spirituality and Feminine Divine*, 4; Thomas Robbins, "The Monstrous Regiment of Women" (paper presented at the annual meeting of the Society for the Scientific Study of Religion, Oct. 1989, Salt Lake City; Binford, "Counter Response," 559.

3. Shreve, *Women Together, Women Alone*, 10–11.

4. Budapest, "Political Witchcraft," 38; Garawitz. See also Budapest, *Grandmother of Time*, 165–66; Spretnak, "Politics of Women's Spirituality," 393–98.

5. Bloodroot Collective, interview with author, August 6, 1989, Bridgeport, Conn.

6. Budapest, *Grandmother of Time*, 16, 108–109. See also Ann Forfreedom, "Inspirational Women of Our Time," *The Wise Woman* 9/4 (1988): 19; Iglehart, *Womanspirit*, 172–73.

7. Budapest, *Holy Book of Women's Mysteries* (1989), 299; Budapest, *Grandmother of Time*, 19; Jade, *To Know*, 13. See also Neitz, "In Goddess We Trust," 368; also Hart.

8. For example, Woods, Bjorkman, Keane, Copeland, Schulman, Otto, Washington, Courveline.

9. Charlene Spretnak, "Ecofeminism: Our Roots and Flowering," in *Reweaving the*

World, ed. Diamond and Orenstein, 8; Carolyn Merchant, "Ecofeminism and Feminist Theory," in *Reweaving the World,* ed. Diamond and Orenstein, 100.

10. Arisika Razak, "Toward a Womanist Analysis of Birth," in *Reweaving the World,* ed. Diamond and Orenstein, 165.

11. Sjöö and Mor, *Great Cosmic Mother,* 411. See also Ynestra King, "Eco-Feminism— Where the Spiritual and the Political Come Together," *Women for Life on Earth* (Winter 1984): 4–7; Women's Alliance, "Commitment in the 90s" (flyer for summer solstice camp, Nevada City, Calif.); Woods; Pam Conrad, "Connecting with Gaia: Ecology and Feminism" (workshop at Womongathering, May 1990); also Woods. For more on ecofeminism, see Judith Plant, ed., *Healing the Wounds: The Promise of Ecofeminism* (Philadelphia: New Society Publishers, 1989); Charlene Spretnak, *The Spiritual Dimension of Green Politics* (Santa Fe, N.M.: Bear and Company, 1986).

12. Woods; Stone, "Return of the Goddess"; Gadon, *Once and Future Goddess,* 341; Orenstein, *Reflowering of the Goddess,* 15, 26; Starhawk, *Dreaming the Dark,* 143; Miw; Portia Cornell, quoted in Wynne, *Womanspirit Sourcebook,* 187. For a critique of using Mother Earth or other female images in the ecology movement, see Catherine Roach, "Looking at Woman Looking at Nature: Feminist and Ecological Perspectives on Woman-Nature/ Man-Culture" (paper presented at the annual meeting of the American Academy of Religion, Nov. 1989, Anaheim).

13. Spretnak, "Ecofeminism: Our Roots and Flowering," 5; Ruether, *Sexism and God-Talk,* 72–73; Woods; Frankel. Also Foster, Courveline, Washington, Otto.

14. Budapest, *Grandmother of Time,* 127; Sackner.

15. Shamanic Convergence bookstore, bookmark, Seattle.

16. Women's Spirituality Forum, spring 1990 calendar, Oakland; Women's Spirituality Forum, *Callisto* (Fall 1990): 1; Mendel.

17. Price; Starhawk, *Spiral Dance,* first ed., 7. See also Deirdre Pulgràm Arthen, quoted in Godavitarne, "Shamanic Witchcraft," 41; Amber K, "Ask Amber," *Of a Like Mind* (Summer 9989 [1989]): 3; Judith Barr, "Healing the Witch Within" (workshop described in Wise Woman Center catalog, Woodstock, N.Y., 1990); Neitz, "In Goddess We Trust," 362; Daly, *Gyn/Ecology,* 221; Budapest, *Holy Book of Women's Mysteries* (1989), xvii, xxiv; Daly, "Qualitative Leap," 28–29; Merchant, *Death of Nature,* 155; Howard Eilberg-Schwartz, "Witches of the West," *Journal of Feminist Studies in Religion* 5/1 (Spring 1989): 84–85; Hart; Kay Sunstein Hymowitz, "Rumplestiltskin Gets Bumped from the Schoolyard," *Globe and Mail* (August 1991); Weinstein, *Earth Magic,* 6–7; Adler, *Drawing Down the Moon,* 42–43; Starhawk, *Truth or Dare,* 345 n. 2; also Keane, Hoffman, Woods, Courveline, Hart.

18. Starhawk, *Spiral Dance,* 2d ed., 250. See also Ellen Sue Spivak, "Eating With the Earth in Mind" (workshop at Womongathering, May 1990); "Statement of Philosophy," *woman of power* 16 (Spring 1990), 1; Bloodroot Collective, *Political Palate,* xi; Budapest, *Holy Book of Women's Mysteries* (1979), 32; Foster, "Statement on Ritual"; also Mendel, Gordon, Washington, Schulman, Foster, Otto.

19. Song sheet, Womongathering, May 1990; Medicine Eagle, "Moon Lodge Teachings."

20. Otto.

21. Veracruz; Stein, *Women's Spirituality Book,* 195, 249; Rennie and Grimstad, "Spiritual Explorations Cross-Country," 51; Sharp; Sherry Mostelle, interview with Stone, "Return of the Goddess"; Budapest, *Grandmother of Time,* 19; Womancenter at Plainville (Mass.) 1988–89 calendar; Christ, *Diving Deep ,* 131; Karen Iris Bogen, "Seizing Eternity: Meeting the Spiritual Challenge of Rape," *Spiritual Women's Times* (Summer 1989): 15; Garawitz; Hart; Schulman; Women's Alliance, "Enactment" (camp flyer, Nevada City, Calif., 1989).

22. Foster; Otto. See also Austen, *Heart of the Goddess,* 122; also Mendel, McIntyre, Frankel, Whiting, Keane, Engler..

23. Logan; "Witches Against Animal Abuse" (flyer, New York); Heart, "Healing Through Solitary Practice," 12; Ann Forfreedom, *The Wise Woman* 9/4 (1988): 1–32; Schulman; Gina Foglia and Dorit Wolffberg, "Spiritual Dimensions of Feminist Anti-Nuclear Activism," in *Politics of Women's Spirituality*, ed. Spretnak, 458–59; Foster; Otto. See also Spretnak, "Spiritual Experience of Female Psyche/Soma"; Gadon, *Once and Future Goddess*, 360; also Price.

24. Starhawk, *Truth or Dare*, 17, 336–38; Starhawk, *Dreaming the Dark*, xv–xvi, 41, 93; Starhawk, *Spiral Dance*, first ed., 189; Starhawk, interview with Stone, "Return of the Goddess"; Starhawk, "Power, Authority, and Mystery: Ecofeminism and Earth-Based Spirituality," in *Reweaving the World*, ed. Diamond and Orenstein, 74; Woods; Whiting. See also Mariechild, *Mother Wit*, 69; also Garawitz, Sackner.

25. Price; Johnson, "Going Out of Our Minds," 8–9, 11; Sackner. See also Gearhart, "Womanpower: Energy Re-sourcement," 194–95, 200; Mariechild, *Mother Wit*, 178; Antonelli, "Politics of the Psyche," 400; also Keane, Hart.

26. On the falseness of the split between spirituality and politics, see Adler, *Drawing Down the Moon*, 175, 180; Judith Todd, "Opposing the Rape of Mother Earth," *Heresies* 2/1 (1982): 49; Budapest, "Political Witchcraft," 38; Göttner-Abendroth, "Hagia: Academy and Coven"; Sjöö and Mor, *Great Cosmic Mother*, 417; Mariechild, *Mother Wit*; "Statement of Philosophy," *woman of power*.

27. Daly, "Qualitative Leap," 21; Judy Davis and Juanita Weaver, "Dimensions of Spirituality," *Quest* 1/4 (Spring 1975): 5; "Statement of Philosophy," *woman of power*; Sisterhood of the Lavender Dawn, "The Way of the Mother"; Gadon, *Once and Future Goddess*, 339; Starhawk, *Truth or Dare*, 6; Starhawk, *Spiral Dance*, 2d ed., 11; Budapest, *Grandmother of Time*, 60, 245; Stein, *Women's Spirituality Book*, n.p.; Luisah Teish, quoted in Jamal, *Shape Shifters*, 30; Forfreedom, *Feminist Wicce Works*; Mendel; Hoffman; Starhawk, *Spiral Dance*, first ed., 132; Jade, *To Know*, 44–45; Sisterhood of the Lavender Dawn, "Freeing the Heroine Within" (workshop described in flyer, Baltimore).

28. Budapest, *Holy Book of Women's Mysteries* (1989), 127–28. See also Kira Ma'at-ka-re, "Everything Has Its Price," 7.

29. Anonymous lesbian separatist, letter to editor, anonymous spiritual feminist publication.

30. Budapest, *Holy Book of Women's Mysteries* (1989): 35–36; Woods; Washington; Wynne, *Womanspirit Sourcebook*, 232; Schulman; Gordon; Full Circle Workshops, "Keepers of the Flame 90/91" (advertisement, Amherst, Mass.); "Witches Against Animal Abuse"; Medicine Eagle, "Moon Lodge Teachings"; Weed, "Blood of the Ancients"; Allione, quoted in Jamal, *Shape Shifters*, 54–55.

31. Miw.

32. Zsuzsanna Budapest, quoted in Kimball, "Goddess Worship in Wicce," 243; Engler. Also Miw.

33. Jade, *To Know*, 39, 171; Mariechild, *Mother Wit*, 84; Starhawk, "Power, Authority, and Mystery," 76. See also Starhawk, *Dreaming the Dark*, 13; Budapest, *Holy Book of Women's Mysteries* (1989), 297; also Bjorkman, Price.

34. Johnson, "Going Out of Our Minds," 72; Iglehart, *Womanspirit*, 49; Hallie Iglehart Austen, quoted in Wynne, *Womanspirit Sourcebook*, 108; Austen, *Heart of the Goddess*, 30. See also "Statement of Purpose," *Snake Power*; Noble, "The Shakti Woman," 28; also Hoffman.

35. Dale Lewis and Robyn Posin, "Woman Is Medicine," *Venus Rising* 3/1 (1989): n.p.; Starrett, "Metaphors of Power," 190; Daly, *Gyn/Ecology*, 379; Medicine Eagle, "Moon Lodge Teachings." Also Landau.

36. Frankel; Zsuzsanna Budapest, quoted in Adler, *Drawing Down the Moon*, 183. See also Budapest, *Holy Book of Women's Mysteries* (1979), 10, 86–87, 89; Z. Budapest, "Witch

Is to Womon as Womb Is to Birth," *Quest* 2/1 (Summer 1975): 51; Budapest, *Holy Book of Women's Mysteries* (1989), 7; Vicki Noble, quoted in Jamal, *Shape Shifters*, 115; Mor and Sjöö, "Respell the World," 18; Layne Redmond, "Rhythm and the Frame Drum," *woman of power* 15: 22; Gadon, *Once and Future Goddess*, 376; Gloria Feman Orenstein, "Artists as Healers: Envisioning Life-Giving Culture," in *Reweaving the World*, ed. Diamond and Orenstein, 286.

37. Maddox; Gearhart, "Womanpower: Energy Re-sourcement," 203; Ruth-Inge Heinze, quoted in Jamal, *Shape Shifters*, 72–73. See also Adler, *Drawing Down the Moon*, 181; also Laura.

38. Rush, "Politics of Feminist Spirituality," 384; Göttner-Abendroth, "Hagia: Academy and Coven"; Price. See also Jean Mountaingrove, quoted in Wynne, *Womanspirit Sourcebook*, 130; Lewis and Posin, "Woman Is Medicine," n.p.; Pureheart, "Creating a Feminist Future"; also Maddox, Sackner, Woods.

39. Miw; Starhawk, *Spiral Dance*, 2d ed., 7.

40. Boucher, "Daughters of the Theris," 34. See also Starhawk, "Power, Authority, and Mystery," 78; Starhawk, quoted in Jamal, *Shape Shifters*, 125.

41. Gloria Orenstein, interview with Stone, "Return of the Goddess"; Charlotte Kelly, "Director's Report" (flyer on "Woman's Alliance Summer Solstice Camp: Her Voice, Our Voices," Nevada City, Calif., Spring 1990); Jean Houston, "The Rise of the Feminine," *woman of power* 12 (Winter 1989): 25; Engler; Medicine Eagle, "Moon Lodge Teachings."

42. Friday night full moon ritual, FSC Retreat, June 1990. See also Rowena Pattee, quoted in Jamal, *Shape Shifters*, 63; Jade, *To Know*, 171; Weinstein, *Earth Magic*, 69; Bednarowski, *New Religions and Theological Imagination*, 123; Iglehart, *Womanspirit*, 11, 14–15; Jamal, *Shape Shifters*, 171–92; Eisler, *Chalice and the Blade*, 198–203; Spretnak, "Ecofeminism: Our Roots and Flowering," 9; Eisenstein, *Contemporary Feminist Thought*, 136; Noble, *Motherpeace*, 13–14; WomenCircles flyer, Rowe Camp, Conn.; Graybeal, "Into the Realm of the Goddess," 3; Mariechild, *Mother Wit*, xii; Stone, "Return of the Goddess"; Lynn Andrews, quoted in Wynne, *Womanspirit Sourcebook*, 58.

43. Gearhart, "Womanpower: Energy Re-sourcement," 205. See also Culpepper, "Contemporary Goddess Thealogy," 69.

44. Anonymous spiritual feminist, "The Circle Complete," anonymous spiritual feminist publication; Hallie Iglehart, "The Unnatural Divorce of Spirituality and Politics," in *Politics of Women's Spirituality*, ed. Spretnak, 413; Gordon; Iglehart, *Womanspirit*, xiii, 81; Haney, *Vision and Struggle*, 20; Otto; Ywahoo, "Renewing the Sacred Hoop," 277–78.

Chapter 10: Why Feminist Spirituality?

1. David Aberle, "A Note on Relative Deprivation Theory as Applied to Millenarian and Other Cult Movements," in *Reader in Comparative Religion: An Anthropological Approach*, ed. W. A. Lessa and E. Z. Vogt, 3d ed. (New York: Harper and Row, 1972), 527–31; Robert N. Bellah, "New Religious Consciousness and the Crisis in Modernity," in *The New Religious Consciousness*, ed. Charles Y. Glock and Robert N. Bellah (Berkeley: University of California Press, 1976), 333–52; Allan W. Eister, "Culture Crises and New Religious Movements: A Paradigmatic Statement of a Theory of Cults," in *Religious Movements in Contemporary America*, ed. Irving I. Zaretsky and Mark P. Leone (Princeton: Princeton University Press, 1974), 612–27; Charles Y. Glock, "The Role of Deprivation in the Origin and Evolution of Religious Groups," in *Religion and Social Conflict*, ed. Robert Lee and Martin E. Marty (New York: Oxford University Press, 1964), 24–36; Virginia H. Hine, "The Deprivation and Disorganization Theories of Social Movements," in *Religious Movements in Contemporary America*, ed. Zaretsky and Leone, 646–61.

2. Aberle, "Note on Relative Deprivation Theory," 528.

3. Glock, "Role of Deprivation," 29.

4. Robbins, "Monstrous Regiment of Women." See also Eisenstein, *Contemporary Feminist Thought*, 137; Forfreedom, *Feminist Wicce Works*, 16–17; Juanita Weaver, "Images and Models—In Process," in *Politics of Women's Spirituality*, ed. Spretnak, 251; Cole, "Feminist Wicca Philosophy"; also Frankel, Engler, Price.

5. R. Laurence Moore, *Religious Outsiders and the Making of Americans* (New York: Oxford University Press, 1986), 119.

6. In a study of the Pentecostal Movement in Christianity conducted in the late 1960s and early 1970s ("The Deprivation and Disorganization Theories of Social Movements"), Virginia H. Hine tested the deprivation thesis, and concluded that the only type of deprivation that correlated with participation in the movement was status deprivation (which she then reinterpreted as power deprivation). I have no quantitative measures of this in the case of feminist spirituality, but all the qualitative data suggest that as for Pentecostals two decades ago, spiritual feminists are responding to their perception of their own powerlessness as measured against their putatively realistic ambitions for personal power (658–61).

7. Katherine LeMaster, quoted in Bayley, et al., *Celebrating Women's Spirituality*, n.p.

8. Song sheet, FSC Retreat, June 1990.

9. Anon., "Circle Complete." See also Christ, "Why Women Need the Goddess," 284; Jean Mountaingrove, quoted in Wynne, *Womanspirit Sourcebook*, 129; Opening ritual, FSC Retreat, June 1990; anonymous spiritual feminist, "Path of the Warrior," anonymous spiritual feminist publication; Foster. In *Understanding the New Age*, Russell Chandler suggests that all New Age religions offer their adherents "omnipotence and indestructibility" (25).

10. Antiga, interview with Stone, "Return of the Goddess"; Christ, *Laughter of Aphrodite*, 202–203; Stepanich, "Seasonal Musings," n.p.; Christ, *Diving Deep*, 24.

11. Gadon, *Once and Future Goddess*, 255; Christ, "Why Women Need the Goddess," 278; anonymous spiritual feminist, quoted in Adler, *Drawing Down the Moon*, 198; Frankel. See also Luisah Teish, interview with Stone, "Return of the Goddess"; Sonia Ganz, "The Magic of Your Word," *Women Spirit Rising of Costa Mesa* 2/5 (Spring 1990): 4; Jennifer Barker Woolger, "The Goddess Within: Discovering the Qualities of the Inner Feminine" (course described in New York Open Center catalog, New York, Spring 1990); Budapest, "Political Witchcraft," 38; Tsultrim Allione, "Dakini Wisdom," *Snake Power* (Hallowmas 1989): 33; Carol Christ, "Rituals for Daily Life," quoted in Budapest, *Holy Book of Women's Mysteries* (1989), 72; Austen, *Heart of the Goddess*, xxii, 98; Chernin, *Reinventing Eve*, xx, 29; also Schulman.

12. Sackner. See also Naomi Goldenberg, interview with Stone, "Return of the Goddess"; also Whiting, Hoffman.

13. Jean Shinoda Bolen, interview with Stone, "Return of the Goddess."

14. Downing, *The Goddess*, 105. See also Patricia Reis, quoted in Wynne, *Womanspirit Sourcebook*, 177; Forfreedom, *Feminist Wicce Works*, 7; also Whiting..

15. Chernin, *Reinventing Eve*, xv, 123–124.

16. Claire Jones, "The Goddess of the Dune," *SageWoman* (Spring 9989[1989]): 5.

17. Lynn Andrews, quoted in Jamal, *Shape Shifters*, 22.

18. Schulman; Hoffman; Garawitz. For somewhat different personal conflicts that are similarly resolved by emphasizing femaleness, see Orenstein, *Reflowering of the Goddess*, 39; Patricia Reis, quoted in Wynne, *Womanspirit Sourcebook*, 179; Chernin, *Reinventing Eve*, 68.

19. Copeland.

20. Ibid.

21. Ellwood, *Alternative Altars*, 44.

22. Teish, *Jambalaya*, 40.

23. Frankel; Woods; Keane; Littlefield; Bjorkman.
24. Budapest, "Vows, Wows, and Joys."
25. Gearhart, "Womanpower: Energy Re-Sourcement," 205.
26. Chris Carol, "The Witches' Warning," quoted in Budapest, *Holy Book of Women's Mysteries* (1989), 133.
27. Moore, *Religious Outsiders*, 35.
28. Robison; Miw; Sharp; Sackner; Veracruz; Hoffman; Copeland; Otto; Mendel; Washington; Hoffman.
29. Price.
30. Logan.
31. Jade, *To Know*, 89–91.
32. Cole, "Feminist Wicca Philosophy."
33. Kimball, "Goddess Worship in Wicce," 241. See also Helen Farias and Julie Falanga, "Our House Is the Earth, Our Circle Is Everywhere: The Voice of Experience, Part 2," *The Beltane Papers* (North 87/88): 4–5; Budapest, *Holy Book of Women's Mysteries* (1989), 239; Robin Morgan, "Metaphysical Feminism," in *Politics of Women's Spirituality*, ed. Spretnak, 388; Daly, *Gyn/Ecology*, 17–18; Sjöö and Mor, *Great Cosmic Mother*, 288, 347; also Laura, Fleming.
34. Woods; Foster; Engler; Robison; Gordon; Hoffman; Copeland; Landau; Miw; Adler, *Drawing Down the Moon*, 101.
35. Price; Logan; Schulman; Sharp; Veracruz; Sackner. It may be that women I interviewed were inclined to say supportive things about Christian feminists working in the church because I appeared at interviews with informational sheets and release forms on divinity school letterhead, and they may have been trying not to offend against my presumed Christian sympathies. However, if this was a factor, I believe it was not a large one, as similar sentiments surface in feminist spirituality literature.
36. Christ, *Laughter of Aphrodite*, 59; Weaver, "Who Is the Goddess?" 60–61; Hoffman; Whiting; Susan Ackley, "A Meditation on Diapers," *woman of power* 12 (Winter 1989):13.
37. Gordon; Schulman; Foster. See also Brigit McCallum, advertisement for services as "ritualer, liturgist, retreats, workshops, individual spiritual companioning," Cambridge, Mass.; Barr, "Healing the Witch Within"; Beverly Little Thunder, "Talking Circle" (workshop at Womongathering, May 1990); also Hoffman, Mendel, Garawitz, Copeland, Price.
38. Noble, *Motherpeace*, 235; Forfreedom, *Feminist Wicce Works*, 5; Mariechild, *Mother Wit*, 92. See also Marcia Germaine Hutchinson, quoted in Bayley, et al., *Celebrating Women's Spirituality*, n.p.; Jade, *To Know*, 104; Medicine Eagle, "Moon Lodge Teachings"; Ellen Chambers, quoted in Sharon Kaylen, "An Interview with Ellen Chambers," *Spiritual Women's Times* (Summer 1989): 8.
39. Weinstein, *Earth Magic*, 17; Stein, *Women's Spirituality Book*, 176–78, 200.
40. Georgette Psaris and Marlena Lyons, "Dreaming by the Light of the Full Moon," in Women's Alliance, "Commitment in the 90's" (camp flyer, Nevada City, Calif.).
41. Veracruz. Also Garawitz, Littlefield, Hoffman.
42. Price. See also Jean Callahan, quoted in Chandler, *Understanding the New Age*, 100; also Frankel, Bjorkman, Woods, Sharp, Foster, Garawitz.
43. Price; Landau; Littlefield; Otto. See also Cedar Spring, "Delphos Wilderness Sanctuary," Minneapolis; Donna Reed, interview with Stone, "Return of the Goddess"; Stone, "Letter From Merlin"; Weinstein, *Earth Magic*, 68; also Woods, Logan, Schulman, Veracruz.
44. Woods; Keane; Turcott; Miw; Luisah Teish, quoted in Jamal, *Shape Shifters*, 35. Also Mendel, Robison, Courveline.
45. Woods. Also Littlefield, Otto, Bjorkman.

Index